Sexual Assault

Sexual Assault:
The Victims, the Perpetrators, and the Criminal Justice System

EDITED BY:

Frances P. Reddington

AND

Betsy Wright Kreisel

Carolina Academic Press
Durham, North Carolina

Library of Congress Cataloging-in-Publication Data

Sexual assault: the victims, the perpetrators, and the criminal justice system /
    edited by Frances P. Reddington and Betsy Wright Kreisel.
        p. cm.
    Includes bibliographical references and index.
    ISBN 0-89089-334-9
    1. Sex crimes—United States. 2. Rape—United States. 3. Rape
victims—United States. 4. Sex offenders—United States. 5. Criminal justice, Administration of—United States. I. Reddington, Frances P. II.
Kreisel, Betsy Wright, 1970–

HV6561.S475 2003
364.15'32'0973—dc22   2003060583

Carolina Academic Press
700 Kent Street
Durham, North Carolina 27701
Telephone: (919) 489-7486
Fax: (919) 493-5668
Email: cap@cap-press.com
www.cap-press.com

Printed in the United States of America.

To the memory of my parents—
Francis and Pauline. FPR

To the Men in my Life—
Lyle and Jarrett.
Your support makes everything possible. BWK

Contents

Part II
The Victims

Part III
The Often Unacknowledged Victims

Part VI
Public Fear and the Legislative Response

Preface

All it takes is to listen to the news and hear the recent stories of sexual abuse in the clergy or to hear people both praising and vilifying the alleged victim, such as in the Kobe Bryant alleged rape case to know that sexual assault and the debatable issues it raises, such as should the alleged victim of rape be named in the media, are not uncommon in our society. In fact, it is frequently pushed to the front of our thoughts when something rocks our consciousness. But, in the world of sexual assault, the high profile cases are the rarest, and the daily business of those sex crimes that come to the attention of the criminal justice system are usually left to be done outside of much of the general public's notice.

This book attempts to fill a gap in our academic literature regarding rape, sexual assault, and in specific, the response of the criminal justice system to sex crimes. However, as the criminal justice system does not exist outside of our society, we felt it imperative to broaden the scope of this reader as well, and to include information designed to educate about the widely misunderstood crime of rape. That is why we included information about rape myths, the history of rape reform and an examination of sexual assault definitions.

Before we begin discussion of an overview of the reader we would like to make a couple of points. First, the words rape and sexual assault are used almost interchangeably by the authors in the following chapters. That is how it is in our society as well. Rape is still a crime in several states, though other states have changed the language in their criminal codes to something broader, such as sexual assault or sexual battery.

Secondly, most victims of sex crimes are women, and many authors chose to use the feminine pronoun in their articles when referring to victims, and the masculine pronoun when referring to offenders. Again, this was done to reflect the statistical findings that most known sex offenders are men. However, we believe that it was imperative to address the issue of male rape victims in this reader. There are several chapters, which will be discussed below, which address specifically male victims. Thus, we are not overlooking either male rape victims or female offenders, we are making sure that we represent a statistical reality.

And finally, we wanted to address the issue of the terms "victims" and "survivors." As you will no doubt note, they are used interchangeably as well throughout and within the various chapters. We did not ask the authors to follow any guidelines in their word selection, though some addressed the issue in their writings. The reason we did this, is because this work is designed to bring the reader into the criminal justice arena. In that arena, police, prosecutors and other employees of the criminal justice system, deal with victims of crime and those who victimize others. Victimology, and the study of crime victims, is a relatively new academic component of criminal justice. We did not think it would be right to change the system phraseology. Yet, those same employees of the criminal justice system deal with the survivors of a sexual assault as well. Though some of the literature suggests that survival is a state of recovery to be achieved, we do subscribe to the belief that if you live through a sexual assault—you are a survivor.

Part I

The Crime

In part one, the reader is acquainted with the crime of rape and sexual assault. The first chapter, *An Overview of Sexual Assault and Sexual Assault Myths*, presents a look at the definitions, contradictions and statistics regarding sexual assault. The incidence and prevalence of rape are examined, and are followed with a discussion of the problems associated with an examination of rape statistics. The chapter also includes a brief history of sexual victimization, which sets the stage for much that follows in the reader. The chapter concludes with a comprehensive look at rape myths.

The second chapter *Sexual Assault Definitions* provides a general definition of rape, and offers a discussion of the parameters associated with trying to define rape. The chapter also narrows to a thorough discussion of stranger rape, intimate (date) rape, spousal rape, and group and gang rape. The third chapter *Drug Facilitated Sexual Assault in Private and Professional Relationships: A Legal Perspective* examines the timely issue of the use of drugs as a facilitator in sexual assaults and professional sexual misconduct.

Part II

The Victims

In part two, the reader becomes acquainted with rape victimology. Chapter four, *Victim Response to Sexual Assault* is a thorough examination of the variety of responses and coping mechanisms that survivors often experience. In addition, the chapter discusses recovery from sexual assault, seeking help and crisis intervention. Chapter five, *The Impact of HIV/AIDS on Rape Survivors,* discusses the risk of infection, the choice of post-exposure prophylaxis and the decision to be tested. Chapter six, *The Ripple Effect: Secondary Sexual Assault Survivors,* presents an overview of the others who are impacted by a sexual assault: partners, family, and friends of the survivor. Chapter seven, *Sexual Abuse of Males,* examines male rape victims and discusses the research which suggests that male victimology can be alike, and yet quite different from female victimology. The differing circumstances of male rape are also presented.

Part III

The Often Unacknowledged Victims

In part III, the reader is brought deeper into the examination of sexual assault victimology and those victim groups where we tend to see even greater underreporting and less scientific research. Chapter eight, *Sexual Abuse of Men in Prison,* examines the prevalence of inmate-on-inmate rape in institutions housing males. While presenting the statistics available, this chapter also includes narrative accounts from actual victims. Chapter nine, *Labeling Theory as Etiological Paradigm for Prison Rape,* suggests that an integrated labeling theory–cognitive dissonance paradigm might explain the complex developments that lead from an inmate's first victimization to the eventual acceptance of their new label. This new social label is rooted in an ascribed social status that ultimately leads to the internalization of their new sex role as part of a newly adopted self identity. Chapter ten, *A Violation of Trust and Professional Ethics: Sexual Abuse of Women Prisoners by Correctional Staff,* examines the issues of female inmates who are victimized by institutional employees. Chapter eleven presents an overview of *Child Sexual Abuse.* Chapter twelve presents a moving account of one survivor's journey from victimization as a child to resolution in *Reading Incest: Interpreting Signs of Victimization and Family Dysfunction in One Survivor's Account.*

Part IV

The Offenders

Part four offers a comprehensive discussion of sex crime offenders. Chapter thirteen, *Rapists,* offers a thorough discussion of many aspects of those who rape. The chapter begins with a discussion of human behavior and motivation. The chapter continues with a discussion of sex offender typologies– the attempt to classify sex offenders into different groups based on their motivations, choice of victims and actions during the attack. This chapter also discusses classifications of child molesters.

Part V

The Criminal Justice System

Part five overviews the various components of the criminal justice system as they address the issues of sexual assault. Chapter fourteen presents *A Brief History of Rape Law and Rape Law Reform in the United States*. This chapter offers a discussion of the roots of American rape law and the major changes in rape law that were initiated in the 1970s. This discussion will lead the reader into the chapters regarding police investigation, prosecutorial duties, and correctional treatment. Chapter fifteen addresses issues regarding *The Police and Victims of Sexual Assault*. Chapter sixteen examines why rape has historically been the most under prosecuted crime in *Prosecution of Sex Crimes*. Chapter seventeen, *Sex Offender Treatment: An Overview* offers a thorough discussion of the last twenty years, more or less, with an emphasis on the last ten years of programs and treatments designed to deal with those who sexually offend.

Part VI

Public Fear and Legislative Response

Part six addresses the legislative response to sexual assault. With public sentiment suggesting that the criminal justice system was failing in rehabilitating or incapacitating sex offenders, the legislature stepped in and created new laws that would address this issue. Chapter eighteen, *Sex Offender Laws: Some Legislative Responses*, presents an examination of the creation of registration, notification, sexual predator and chemical castration laws. This chapter also addresses concerns expressed regarding the constitutionality of these laws.

Acknowledgments

Many people did a lot of work to make this book happen. We must start with acknowledging the contributions of the authors. The collection of authors in this book is, in a word, diverse. Our contributors include academicians, university students from Master's to Ph.D. level, practitioners in the field, and survivors of sexual assault. We did this because we believe that the collective voice needed to be heard. We especially wanted to give graduate students who have studied sexual assault a chance to speak to other students through this work. The common theme of all our contributors is that they believed that this work was important and that it needed to be done. They devoted their time, talent and energies to make this happen. The result is a reader that is exhaustive in its study of the topic of sexual assault. There are a wide variety of voices to be heard here—from survivors to those who work in the field everyday, to those who study the field. The collective product is truly a reflection of their dedication.

We would like to acknowledge Carolina Academic Press for their support, and specifically Catherine O'Connor, our editor, who kept us on task and offered us her support. From day one, they also believed this was a work that needed to be done.

We would like to thank Central Missouri State University for the support we receive. We must especially thank Cynthia Adams, our graduate assistant, whose assistance on this project proved invaluable.

And finally, we need to recognize the survivors of sexual assault and the people who work everyday in any one of numerous capacities to seek justice, healing and hope with them. We only hope that this work serves to enlighten about sexual assault and the people that it has touched.

Sexual Assault

PART I

THE CRIME

Chapter 1

An Overview of Sexual Assault and Sexual Assault Myths

Tammy Garland

Upon the release of *The Accused* (1988), once again, the New Bedford Case that rocked a small town community during the early 1980s was brought to the forefront of public attention. This reconceptualized version of the rape of a young Portuguese woman, Cheryl Araujo, portrayed the heinous crime in a very different light than the original media coverage. The movie depicted the victim, played by Jodi Foster, as just that, a victim. However, the movie failed to illustrate the backlash created by the trial and the incessant media scrutiny. In contrast to the storybook ending in which the victim is vindicated, the initial news coverage of the trial generated a media frenzy leading the Portuguese community to eventually vilify the victim for her own victimization and in essence treat the perpetrators as if they were heroes (Chancer 1998).

The significance of this case is paramount due to its nature and attitudes toward sexual assault. Even though the victim was without a doubt raped in a public place, surrounded by witnesses, and brutalized mercilessly, the victim was still blamed for her own assault. "Victim blaming" in rape cases is a common phenomenon especially in cases in which the accuser has a questionable background. For instance, Henry Wigmore (1942) in the highly respected *Evidence in Trials at Common Law* asserted that "no judge should ever let a sex offense charge go to jury unless the female complainant's social history and mental makeup have been examined and testified by a qualified physician" (Cuklanz 1996, 737). Thus, rather than trying the perpetrator in a court of law, the character of the victim goes on trial. This thought process of victim blaming is a throw-back to the historical and mythological misperceptions of sexual assault. Hence, this chapter will focus on the development and belief of rape myths. Prior to addressing these issues, this chapter must first define what constitutes sexual assault and its prevalence in society.

What Is Sexual Assault?

The literature has demonstrated that methodological problems exist in defining the term, sexual assault. Typically, sexual assault has been used to characterize the word, rape, in a less offensive and unthreatening manner. The term ignores other forms of sexual victimization such as child sexual abuse and sexual harassment, and in addition fails to recognize attempted rape and threat. For the purposes of this chapter, sexual assault will be used interchangeably to define the phenomenon of rape, attempted rape, rape by threat of force, and coercion. In addition, the historical and mythical misperceptions regarding rape will concentrate mainly on the plight of women in society; however, since rape is not limited to women alone, the chapter will also look at nontraditional myths regarding rape including male sexual assaults and interspecies victimization.

The word rape stems from the Latin word rapere, which is defined as "to take by force." Even though this word in itself seems to clearly establish a foundation for rape, historically, the legal definitions of rape has been limited in scope. Under English Common Law, rape was defined as penetration of the vagina by the penis where ejaculation had taken place (Clark 1987, 8 — cited in Belknap 2001). In addition, common law held that rape only occurs when a man engages "in intercourse with a woman not his wife; by force or threat of force; against her will and without her consent" (Estrich 1987, 8 — cited in Belknap 2001). Although these aforementioned definitions have been expanded to incorporate other factors into the meaning of rape, many of the definitions used today still reflect this archaic ideology. Some states refuse to expand the definition of rape to crimes against males. For instance, rape other than vaginal sexual intercourse in North Carolina is not considered a crime; therefore, the North Carolina State Law on sexual assault does not apply to men (North Carolina State Law §14-27.2). Moreover, many federal government agencies still define rape as penile — vaginal intercourse. The Uniform Crime Reports define forcible rape as "the carnal knowledge of a female, forcibly and against her will" (Federal Bureau of Investigation 1997, 395). Under this limited classification of sexual assault at both the state and federal levels, males are excluded from obtaining justice against their perpetrator under the law. In an attempt to remedy this problem, the National Crime Victimization Survey expanded the definition of rape as "forced sexual intercourse in which the victim may be either male or female and the offender may be of a different or the same sex as the victim" (BJS 1997, 31). However, this definition fails to take into consideration a number of other factors involved in rape such as sodomy, oral intercourse, attempted rape, threat of rape, and coercion. Even though, a number of governmental agencies have expanded their definition of rape (see Table 1), their definitions still remain limited in scope.

Table 1: Summary of definitional elements of rape and other sex offenses
as used in U.S. Department of Justice statistical series

| Statistical series | Victims | | | Includes | |
	Age	Sex	Attempts?	Forcible rape?	Other sexual assault?
NCVS	Excludes under 12	Both	Yes	Yes	Yes, attacks involving unwanted sexual contact.
UCR	All	Females only	Yes	Yes	Limited to arrests only. Includes statutory rape and offenses against chastity, common decency, and morals
NIBRS	All	Both	Yes	Yes	Yes, includes sodomy, fondling, incest, statutory rape, and sexual assault with an object.
NPRP	No victim data	No victim data	Yes	Yes	No
NJRP	No victim data	No victim data	Yes	Yes	No
SISCF	Limited to offenses against children	No victim data	Yes	Yes	Yes, includes forcible sodomy, statutory rape, and lewd acts with children
NCRP	Limited to offenses against children	No victim data	Yes	Yes	Yes, includes forcible sodomy, statutory rape, and lewd acts with. children
SHR	All	Both	Yes, but excludes murder	Yes	Yes, includes statutory rape, attempted sodomy, and incest.

Bureau of Justice Statistics. 1997. Sex offenses and offenders: An analysis of data on rape and sexual assault. Washington, D.C.: U.S. Dept. of Justice, 33.

Even in the academic literature, the majority of the literature focuses solely on the sexual victimization of women. Thus, this work will attempt to address the changing perceptions and definitions of rape within our society.

Sexual Assault Statistics

With the women's movement of the early 1970s, rape became a major concern in both the United States and the world. By 1989, the Worldwatch Institute had declared that violence against women was the most common crime worldwide (Lonsway and Fitzgerald 1994; Wolf 1991). Estimates vary on the number of women who will be sexually victimized every year. The World Health Organization (2000) approximates that between 12 and 25 percent of women around the world have been victims of sexual assault. Since obtaining data on rape is difficult to determine, this section will focus on prevalence and incidence rates in the United States.

Incidence and Prevalence among Sexual Assault Victims

Incidence rates are based on measurements collected annually to determine changes in victimization from year to year. UCR and NCVS statistics measure incidence rates (Belknap 2001). According to the Bureau of Justice Statistics (1997), an estimated 260,300 persons, ages 12 or older, reported attempted or completed rapes and approximately 95,000 additional cases were threatened or completed sexual assaults other than rape in 1995. Out of a total of 335,300 victimizations reported in the United States, only 32 percent were reported to law enforcement officials (BJS 1997). Based on the data, the number of rates reported in 1995 significantly decreased from 1993. Between 1993 and 1995, the number of sexual assaults reported decreased from 1 in 435 to 1 in 625. Of these victims, the statistical analysis revealed that those facing the highest risk of sexual victimization are females who are young, unmarried, lower-income, unemployed, and living in a large city (Karmen 2001). As evidenced, rapes/sexual assaults were found to be highest among residents age 16–19, low income residents, and urban residents (BJS 1997). Females are more likely to be victims of sexual assault than men; an estimated 91 percent of the victims of rape/sexual assault were female (BJS 1997). Although reports often argue that minorities, in particular black females, appear to be at a higher risk of rape than their female counterparts (Amir 1971; Russell 1984), BJS (1995) reported that no significant differences in victimization were found based on race of the victim. This inconsistency may be attributable to Russell's analysis (1984) which found that black females are more at risk of stranger rape, while white females were more at risk of acquaintance rapes (Belknap 2001). Even though the data has some discrepancies, the characteristics of those sexually assaulted seldom change.

In contrast to incidence rates, prevalence rates measure the victimization or chance of becoming victimized over a persons' lifetime. Estimations of sexual violence against the female population within the United States range anywhere from 12 to 50 percent (see Edward and Macleod 1999). The UCR indicated that 1 in 4 women may become a victim of rape during her lifetime (FBI 1997). Consistent with this assessment, Koss and Cook (1998) estimated that 1 in 4 college-aged women might have experienced an attempted or completed rape since the age of 14 years old. Moreover, Kilpatrick, Edmunds, and Seymour (1992) asserted that approximately 1.3 forcible rapes occur every minute in this country and that 12.1 million women will be raped during their lifetime (Edward and Macleod 1999). Further data collected using the National Violence Against Women Survey indicated that approximately 18 percent of women and 3 percent of men experienced sexual victimization (Tjaden and Thoennes 1998)—1 in 6 women and 1 in 33 men (Belknap 2001).

Offender Characteristics

What kind of a person commits a rape? Most of the research conducted on rape focuses on the victim; however, there is some research that examines the characteristics of the offender. The literature has consistently found that most rapists tend to be young, white males. As noted by BJS (1997), 99 in 100 rapists are male, 6 in 10 rapists are white, and the average age of a rapist is in their early twenties. Even though statistics have shown that white men are more likely to rape than black males, black men still remain overrepresented in rape cases. This phenomenon is attributable to the fact that black males are more likely to be prosecuted by the criminal justice system and that rapes by white males are typically not reported since the majority of these offenders are known to the victim (Belknap 2001).

Since we know who rapes, we must question why men rape. Nicholas Groth (1979) concluded in his analysis of 500 convicted rapists that men rape for three reasons: power, anger, and sadism. Groth determined that 55 percent of rapes were those of power characterized by a need to possess and control the victim. Although Groth's study allows for insight into the reasons for sexual assault, they do not clearly explain the reasons for rape since the majority of rapists are never convicted (Belknap 2001). Approximately half of those arrested for rape are never convicted (BJS 1997). Interestingly, as social class increases, the likelihood for conviction decreases. "When professional people are accused in the United States, their numbers drop precipitously when the rape charge gets to the prosecutor's office, while the other occupational groups remain about the same (Bartol 1999, 280). In summation, what we know is that most offenders are never reported or caught. Moreover, if those who are caught do not fit the "myth" of a rapist, they are often released.

Problems with Rape Statistics

Although these statistics are extraordinary estimations of the number of sexual victimizations occurring, criminologists must realize that survey figures only represent reported crimes (Allison and Kollenbroich-Shea 2001). As previous research has noted, the majority of rapes/sexual assaults go underreported. Simply put, rape is the most underreported crime in the United States (Allison and Kollenbroich-Shea 2001; Lonsway and Fitzgerald 1994; Ullman 1997).

The problem with determining accurate sexual assault rates is multi-faceted due to the nature of the crime. Until 1973, statistics on sexual victimization were not even collected; however, with the creation of the National Crime Victimization Survey[1] and the Uniform Crime Reports, data has become obtainable allowing for estimations of sexual assault to be retrieved. The problem remains that most people fail to admit to sexual assault, and when they do, they fall short of reporting it to the police. This can be attributed to the dehumanizing effect that rape has on its victims. Most victims have no desire to tell anyone of their victimization including researchers and law enforcement officials; therefore, sexual victimization rates are inordinately underrepresented (Belknap 2001; Karmen 2001).

Another explanation for the invalidation of sexual assault statistics is due to the definition of the crime. The majority of the definitions of rape/sexual assault, as noted above, have historically been vague in their description as to what constitutes this particular type of crime. Not only have many of the definitions failed to acknowledge men as victims, oral and anal intercourse, the sex of the offender, and many other mitigating factors, the definition of rape has been construed as one of force. The problem with this conceptualization

---

1. In actuality, the National Crime Victimization Survey was not created until 1992 when it replaced the National Crime Survey. The survey was redesigned in an attempt to ask questions regarding rape in a more forthright manner. After the survey was redesigned, the number of estimated rapes jumped 157 percent (Kindermann and Lynch 1997 cited in Karmen 2001).

of rape constructs an image of victims who have been brutally beaten by a minority stranger. This perception of rape by society has been coined "real" rapes, thus anything other than this has not historically been considered rape by the criminal justice system. Society has failed to acknowledge that victims of rape are more likely to be sexually assaulted by someone they know than by a stranger. Even the Bureau of Justice Statistics (1997) noted that, "three out of four rape/sexual assault victimizations involved offenders with whom the victim had a prior relationship as a family member, intimate, or acquaintance" (p. 4). However, since neither society nor the criminal justice system has defined rapes under these guidelines, many victims fail to realize that they have even been raped (Belknap 2001; Schwartz and Leggett 1999; Sudderth 1998). For instance, Sudderth (1998) found younger women who were raped by men to be the least likely to define the assaults as rape (Belknap 2001). When rape victims do realize that they have been sexually violated, they are often too embarrassed or afraid that they will not be believed by their friends, their family, and even the community, thus creating a situation that will never be reported.

The History of Sexual Victimization

The fear and shame experienced by rape victims stems from a long cultural and legal precedent that has enabled men to subjugate women without any concern for retribution. Even though the women's movement of the late 1960s/early 1970s helped to change the laws so women could receive equal protection under the legal system, women continue to be indoctrinated with beliefs that keep them fearful of rape. Women remain afraid of being assaulted in the streets; therefore, many do not dare to venture out at night or "to leave their well-guarded fortresses" (Eigenberg 2001, 1). "They learn that their vulnerability restricts their options: where and how they live, and where and when they work and go out" (Belknap 2001, 228). Ironically, as this chapter will address in depth in the myth section, women should not be afraid of those lurking in the streets but those whom they view everyday. Women are far more likely to be victimized by men they know than by a stranger; however, through socialization, those in control of women's behaviors, fathers, husbands, brothers, etc., reiterate this myth to maintain dominance over their "weaker" counterparts. Even though women today have more power than ever before to resist the terror that maintains their seemingly powerless position, centuries of subjugation through violence is a difficult phenomenon to overcome.

The Law and Rape

Prior to second wave feminism, the criminal justice system approached rape cases with disregard. Since the American judicial system was based upon that of English Common Law, many of the ideas that prevailed in the old country were incorporated into the new world. As noted by Maschke (1997), most state laws only recognized a rape if the man forced a woman to have sex under the threat of injury, when she had resisted strenuously, and when there was outside corroboration (Van Wormer and Bartollas 2000). Not only were these criterion necessary but proving the "honorable nature" of the victim was also needed to obtain a rape conviction. "The belief that a woman's sexual past is relevant to her complaint of rape reflects, as does the resistance requirement, the law's punitive celebration of female chastity and its unwillingness to protect women who lack its version of virtue" (Estrich 1987, 48). Thus, a woman whose chastity was in question was often forced to prove that she was a legitimate victim of rape. This tradition of discounting rape was neither endemic to the United States nor the time period.

Throughout history, the rape of women has not only been overlooked but has in essence been encouraged by the patriarchal order. Brownmiller (1975) found that the earliest form of mating relationships was characterized by a man raping his intended "bride" to stake his claim. As man evolved, women began to be viewed as property. This newfound perception of women gave men a means to "protect" his chattel under the law against anyone who would dare taint his possession. For instance, under the system of lex talionis (an eye for an eye), men were permitted to rape the assailant's wife if his daughter had been raped (Brownmiller 1975). In addition, a rapist could be put to death for the rape of a virgin; however, this means of protection did not apply to married women. If a married woman was raped, she was considered blameworthy and was to be executed along with her attacker unless her husband intervened on her behalf (Karmen 2001).

Throughout the middle-ages, men used rape as a means of obtaining economic power. By raping the daughter of a wealthy man, the aggressor would ensure his position within the family. This caused considerable problems within the social structure since "a common person might bring perpetual disgrace upon a woman of nobility and good family by a single act of defilement and take her to wife to the disgrace of her family" (Brownmiller 1975, 27). As time evolved, only the rape of a woman from nobility carried any form of punishment. Forcing a peasant woman or others not deemed propertied (matrons, nuns, widows, concubines, and prostitutes) rarely received any punishment since loss of wealth was not in question. Even if punishment would have been sought by a victim of non-noble status, the nobleman would not take responsibility but instead blame the crime on his men (Brownmiller 1975). Noblemen were protected from any action for their transgressions and given free reign to victimize as desired. This same approach carried over into the home where rape was justifiable since wives were merely property, and their sole purpose was to please their "master."

Slavery and Rape

Sexual victimization during the United States during the 16th and 17th centuries was common practice. During this period, African-American women were vulnerable to sexual assault due to the implementation of slavery within society. Unlike their white female counterparts, who were protected from sexual victimization by any man other than their husband, female slaves had no such rights (Brownmiller 1975). Slaves were forbidden to marry; therefore, the rape of black women was not sanctioned by the law. In contrast to "white rapes" no reparations could be obtained for the defilement of a female slave. Since the female slave belonged entirely to her white master, she had no legal right to refuse his advances (Brownmiller 1975) even though many states had laws against sexual encounters between the differing races. However, these laws were not applied to white men but only white females to ensure they were not "mixing." Thus, it was acceptable for white men to sleep with black women; however, the rape of female slaves was not limited to that of the master. Often, female slaves were also raped by their black brothers (Van Wormer and Bartollas 2000). Rape of female slaves was not punishable but encouraged since a union might produce another "piece of property," a child.

War and Rape

The taking of women at will evolved from the same lines as the long held belief that women were simply the spoils of war; they, too, were to be conquered. History is laden with references of the capture and defilement of women dating back to Antiquity with stories such as *The Iliad* and the rape of the Sabine Women. This trend persisted throughout history. Rape has been used as a weapon of both terror and revenge in which one final blow could be dealt to the enemy. Even though Article 120 of the American Uniform Code of Military Justice has declared that rape during times of war is to be punishable by death or imprisonment, rape continues to be a common occurrence during wartime (Brownmiller 1975). Recently, the world has watched as the conflicts in Rwanda and the former Yugoslavia have resulted in an outright war against women.

> War provides men with the perfect psychologic backdrop to give vent to their contempt for women. The very maleness of the military—the brute power of weaponry exclusive to their hands, the spiritual bonding of men at arms, the manly discipline of orders given and orders obeyed, the simple logic of the hierarchal command—confirms for men what they long suspect, that women are peripheral, irrelevant to the world that counts, passive spectators to the action in the center ring (Brownmiller 1975, 32).

Thus, the shear nature of war allows men to transform themselves into a power in which the enemy, women, are at their mercy.

Rape Myths

Rape is pervasive within our society cutting though all cultural, racial, and class lines (Grana 2002). Although the ubiquitous nature of rape has been acknowledged within the last thirty years, many acts of sexual aggression are still not considered rape. This stems from the historical treatment of this traditionally ignored phenomenon. The problem in addressing rape is due to "conventional sex-role socialization in a gender-stratified society, and traditional sex-role attitudes that serve as the basis for stereotypic beliefs about sexual aggression—"rape myths" (Schwendinger and Schwendinger 1974 cited in Orcutt and Figaro 1988). Simply put, the patriarchal order has socialized women to believe that sexual acts not deemed inappropriate by the traditional, stringent definition of rape does not equate to sexual victimization.

The term, "rape myths," was initially defined by Burt (1980) as "prejudicial, stereotyped, or false beliefs about rape, rape victims, and rapists" (p. 217). Although this definition established a foundation for others to base their work, this definition is limited due to its failure to clearly establish what is meant by the term "myth." In an attempt to rectify the problems in defining rape myths, Lonsway and Fitzgerald (1994) combined the perspectives of various fields to define rape myths as "attitudes and beliefs that are generally false but are widely and persistently held, and that serve to deny and justify male sexual aggression against women" (p. 134). This definition applies to the traditional myths regarding rape; however, when non-traditional myths are taken into consideration, this definition of rape myths also remains limited in scope. Thus, Lonsway and Fitzgerald's definition must be expanded and made generalizeable to include "all sexual aggression against any living creature."

Since Burt's (1980) research on rape myths, a plethora of research has emerged. The diversity of this enormous literature base covers areas ranging from the rape myth acceptance (RMA) (see Lonsway and Fitzgerald 1994, for a review of the literature) to the link between rape myths and religiosity (Freymeyer 1997). Thus, the question must be asked, "What do we know about rape myths?" Even though the majority of the rape myth literature is contradictory, we do know certain things. The one consistent finding in the majority of the research has determined that men are more likely to adhere to rape myths than are women. Other demographic relationships that have been measured in the RMA literature are race/ethnicity, age, and educational/occupational variables have produced incongruous results as have many of the non-demographic variables associated with RMA: responsibility, adversarial sexual beliefs, sex roles, attitudes toward rape, self-esteem, violence acceptance, conviction of rapists, and exposure to sexual and/or violent media (see Lonsway and Fitzgerald 1994). For instance, several studies have noted significant relationships between RMA and sexually aggressive behaviors (Field 1978; Koss, Leonard, Beezley and Oros 1985; Malamuth, et al. 1991; Muehlenhard and Linton 1987; Murphy, et al. 1986; Reilly, et al. 1992) while others have not found such relationships (Epps, Haworth and Swaffer 1993; Forbes and Adams-Curtis 2001; Greendlinger and Byrne 1987; Overholser and Beck 1986). Inconsistencies in the rape myth literature have been attributed to differing instruments used to measure rape myth acceptance.

Even though the literature is often contradictory in its conclusions on rape myths, we must realize that "many Americans indeed believe rape myths," (Burt 1980, 229) and "these views about rape are strongly connected to other, deeply held attitudes such as sex-role stereotyping, distrust of the opposite sex, and acceptance of interpersonal violence" (Orcutt and Faison 1988, 590). The real problem in these societal beliefs about rape is in the fact that they have no basis in reality but produce damaging biases towards the victims of sexual assault (Edward and Macleod 1999). This is especially problematic when the acceptance of rape myths carries over into the criminal justice system. As documented by the historical evidence, the criminal justice system has been less than supportive of rape victims due to their acceptance of rape myths. Police, prosecutors, and jurors often treat the victims as criminals leading them to conclude that there is no basis for their claims.

These stereotypical attitudes held by members of society and the criminal justice system has created an atmosphere in which women are the targets of their own victimization. Therefore, in order to understand these labels, we will look at many of the traditional myths surrounding rape. Since there are a vast number of myths that affect the way rape is perceived, this chapter will look at the most popular myths regarding the rape of women. Many of these myths will be linked to one another; therefore, the history and perceptions of why they exist may be linked to the same tradition. In addition to looking at the traditional myths that have affected women throughout history, the chapter will also address some of the non-traditional myths that apply to rape today. These myths are based on the same principles as those that have been used to target and discriminate against women.

Traditional Rape Myths

The Majority of Rape Claims Are False

The assumption that the majority of rape claims are false is one of the most widely accepted rape myths held within our society. Proponents of this rape myth often argue that women engage in such behavior for two major reasons: guilt and/or vengeance. Proponents of rape myths have construed rape as simply a woman's attempt to redefine an intimate situation in which she feels guilty about after the fact. This myth can be traced back to the idea that women are to remain chaste until marriage; therefore, any sexual transgressions that occur prior to marriage are deemed inappropriate. In theory, any self-respecting woman would want to deny her indiscretion. Advocates of this myth maintain that by crying rape, blame is deflected from the victim (Freymeyer 1997), and the reputation of the female remains intact in most cultures. However, this myth contradicts the reality of rape since any woman who brought forth a claim of rape lost her credibility and value as a prospective wife (Belknap 2001). Thus, a woman would not attempt to regain her innocence through revealing her indiscretions.

In addition to the belief that women cry rape because of guilt, antagonists have argued that women will often cry rape in an attempt to seek vengeance against an individual for not reciprocating her advances. This notion originated and became extremely prevalent in ancient Antiquity; however, the most notable version of this account lies in the Biblical story of Joseph. Joseph, a Hebrew slave of Potiphar, is tempted by Potiphar's wife to engage in sexual acts. Upon her order, the legend holds that the honorable man fled to avoid sinning but was accused by the vengeful woman of rape. Even though Joseph was "innocent" of this accusation, he was thrown in jail until divine intervention won his freedom. According to Brownmiller (1975), the moral of this story "is that a woman scorned can get a good man into a hell of a lot of trouble by crying rape" (p. 22).

This invalidation of women's testimony has occurred throughout history and has remained prevalent even in the last century. As late as the 1960s, legal journals went as far as to argue that rape victims were untrustworthy. A monograph in the Columbia Law Review addressed the untrustworthiness of women by reasoning that

> false accusations of sex crimes in general, and rape in particular, are generally believed to be much more frequent than untrue charges of other crimes. A woman may accuse an innocent man of raping her because she is mentally sick or given to delusions; or because, having consented to intercourse, she is ashamed of herself and bitter at her partner; or because she is pregnant, and prefers a false explanation to the true one; or simply because she hates the man whom she accuses. Since stories of rape are frequently lies or fantasies…such a story, in itself, should not be enough to convict a man of the crime. (Corroborating Charges of Rape 1967, 1138 cited in Cuklanz 1996).

In an attempt to remedy any false accusations of rape, many state laws required corroboration if rape cases were to go to trial.

Even though it has been established that rapes are severely underreported, this myth has been perpetuated by criminal justice agencies "confirmation" that women lie about rape. In 1991, the FBI using UCR data suggested that 8 percent of forcible rape complaints were "unfounded" (Lonsway and Fitzgerald 1994, 135). By painting the picture that rapes are more likely to be unfounded than other felonies, law enforcement statistics have reinforced this myth. Ironically, Bourque (1989) found that these unfounded cases were simply a measure of the percentage of cases that were not successfully brought to trial due to reasons such as sending victim reports to the wrong police jurisdiction, failure of victims to appear in court, and inadequately gathered evidence by both police and medical personnel (cited in Cuklanz 1996). In essence, data collected by law enforcement agencies have only established bias in dealing with rape cases since those deemed unfounded were caused by their own error rather than any wrongdoing of the victim.

Rape Only Happens to "Bad" Women

The belief that we live in a "just world" where bad things happen to bad people and good things happen to good people remains prevalent within our society (Lerner 1980). Hence, there is often a need for society to believe that people get what they deserve, karma. Simply put, victims warrant their own fate. This ideology has led the population to believe that the only women who are victims of rape are those whom society has deemed deviant. Thus, women and girls who fail to adhere to "society's unwritten rules" are blamed when they are raped (Belknap 2001, 215).

Traditionally, there have been two types of women within society, the Madonna or the whore. The Madonna/Whore Duality arises from Judeo-Christian theology where women were viewed as either the traditional wife and/or mother, or characterized as lustful creatures who often prompted men to lose control leading to unseemly behavior (Feinman 1994). This custom of placing women and girls into these mutually exclusive categories has led society to categorize women who do not fit the model of "the Madonna" to be viewed as promiscuous, thus deserving of rape. Women who dress provocatively, have prior sexual experience, drink alcohol, or engage in activities at inappropriate places and/or times are labeled as deviant even though their actions have no connection with the true motivation for rape: power. Nevertheless, the just world approach of blaming the victim values all of these insignificant factors as reasons for rape. According to Lonsway and Fitzgerald (1994), "The belief that only certain types of women are raped functions to obscure and deny the personal vulnerability of all women by suggesting that only 'other' women are raped" (p. 136). This rationalization enables society to believe that only certain types of people will be victimized while those who adhere to the rules of society remain protected from rape (Belknap 2001).

Perceiving victims as "other" not only allows society to place the blame on "bad girls," but it also labels individuals who do not fall into the category of white, middle-class as "other," therefore labeling socially marginal or minority groups deviant. DeFour (1990) argues that women of color are never portrayed as the "good girl," but are depicted as highly sexual, exotic, and/or hot-blooded. For instance, research has indicated that harsher sentences have been handed down when the victim is white than when the victim is black (White, Strube, and Fisher 1998). The reasons behind these discrepancies in sentencing are linked to vestiges of imperialism, colonialism, and slavery. These colonialistic attitudes equate women of color with those who are considered "bad." Thus, their race becomes another means for simply blaming the victim.

The Majority of Rapes are Committed by a Stranger

From childhood, girls are taught to be weary of strangers. This fear of the unknown does not subside in adulthood but instead is reaffirmed by the myth that women are in constant danger of being raped. Women are inundated with stories and images from childhood (i.e. Little Red Riding Hood) that lead them to believe that out there in the bushes lurks a black man waiting to prey upon them. The idea that African-American men were looking to rape white women originated in the south during the Reconstruction Era. In response, our legal system took hold of the idea and began to incorporate harsher sentences based on this belief. Even though this myth has been proven invalid time and time using statistical evidence, much of the population still maintains that stranger rape, especially those committed by African-Americans, is widespread throughout the nation.

In reality, rape rarely occurs in this manner. Contrary to the popular myth, the majority of rapes are perpetrated by someone the victim knows: family, friends, ex-lovers, and other acquaintances. As noted in the literature, increasing evidence has determined that there is a high incidence of date and marital rape in which the perpetrator was the same race as the victim (Cuklanz 1996). For instance, the Bureau of Justice Statistics (1997) found that 2 in 3 rapes were committed by an acquaintance and 9 in 10 rapes by a family member. Ironically, victims of sexual assault are less likely to report rapes when they have been victimized by someone they know. The nature of this myth creates problems for the victim since many individuals do not consider date, marital, and acquaintance rape as "real rape" (Estrich 1987). Thus, the victims experience all of the negative effects of rape but rarely are able to seek justice.

Rape Is a Black-On-White Crime

This myth stems from the same stereotypical ideology that has perpetuated the belief that all rapists are black even though research has indicated that white males are more likely to be perpetrators of this violent crime. This narrow focus on the rape of white women by black men originated during slavery and continues to prevail throughout society. Despite the literature which has evinced that the majority of rapes occur among victims and perpetrators of the same race, the myth that rape is a black-on-white crime remains imbedded within our culture (Koss and Harvey 1991; White, Strube, and Fisher 1998; Wriggins 1983). This mentality not only "unfairly targets black men as rapists but obscures the significance of the rape of black women" (White, Strube, and Fisher 1998). In addition, Wriggins (1983) maintains that this stereotype also denies the sexual victimizations of white women since the majority of these crimes are perpetrated by white men. Thus, both black and white women are denied vindication within our society.

Women Secretly Wish to Be Raped

This myth stems from the belief that women find satisfaction in being forced to engage in sexual behavior. Hence, proponents of this myth believe that women fantasize about being raped (Allison and Kollenbroich-Shea 2000). Historically our legal system has fortified this myth by creating an image of the female "victim" as lustful. One summation in the Yale Law Journal found that "[A] woman's need for sexual satisfaction may lead to unconscious desire for forceful penetration, the coercion serving neatly to avoid the guilt feeling which might arise after willing participation" (Estrich 1987, 39). This perception not only exists within our criminal justice system but is reified by the media. In the popular film, *Gone with the Wind*, the rape of Scarlet O'Hara by her husband, Rhett Butler, reinforces the idea that women want to be raped. With this assault, the heroine wakes to a new and improved attitude after her "night of passion." Ironically, this portrayal of rape is tame compared to current-day scenes of sexual encounters in which movie goers are immersed. For instance, the movie, *Sliver*, has an unsuspecting Sharon Stone walking though a door only to be thrown against a wall by William Baldwin. Even though the act is construed as "rough sex," the true nature of the scene is that of forced sexual intercourse. These depictions reinforce the traditional belief that women are passive and men are aggressive allowing the myth that women need to be "taken" to remain alive.

When a Woman Says "No" to Sex, She Really Means "Yes"

The widely held myth that "no" means "yes" can be traced back to the aforementioned myth in which women want to be raped. Women are not supposed to be sexual—any contact delineating from the traditional roles assigned to them are viewed as abnormal; therefore, women will protest in an attempt to stay true to that stereotype. As many of the other myths regarding rape, the "no means yes" myth had been reinforced by the legal system. An article in the Stanford Law Review (1966) asserted:

> Although a woman may desire sexual intercourse, it is customary for her to say, "no, no, no" (although meaning "yes, yes, yes") and to expect the male to be the aggressor...It is always difficult in rape cases to determine whether the female really meant "no"...The problem of determining what the female "really meant" is compounded when, in fact, the female had no clearly determined attitude—that is, her attitude was one of ambivalence (Estrich 1987, 38).

In essence, the myth holds that in order to fit the assigned role as a passive participant and not be labeled as deviant, women say "no" and allow their male counterparts to be seen as the aggressor.

Rapists are Mentally Ill

The myth that rapists are mentally ill has prevailed in our society. The typical rapist has been portrayed as mentally insane, crazy, or psychotic. However, the psychoanalytic response to sexual offenders has failed to prove that rapists are any more likely to be mentally ill than non-rapists (Belknap 2001). Rapists do not adhere to the stereotype which society has created. Rapists are typically considered the "average Joe" who fits into any group within our society—students, professionals, and of course, even family members.

Non-Traditional Rape Myths

Men Cannot Be Victims of Rape

The myth that men cannot be victims of rape stems from the traditional idea that women are passive and men are aggressive, thus, women are always the victims and men are always the perpetrators. Admittedly, this is partially true. Men are almost always the perpetrators of sexual assault; however, our society fails to realize that men may also be the victims as well. Male rape first came to the public's attention during the 1970s when men began to publicly acknowledge they had been sexually assaulted while incarcerated. The rape of men in prison was seen as an anomaly that took place due to fact that this "closed society" was without women. What society has failed to realize is that rape is prison is not about sex nor is male-on-male rape about homosexuality. Male sexual assault is perpetrated for the same reason as female sexual assault, an attempt to gain power over another. Although it has long been recognized that men are raped in prison (see Brownmiller 1975), most individuals, especially men, do not believe that rape happens in the real world. Even more shocking is that our criminal justice system has ignored this trend until recently. This is due to the taboo nature of the crime. Reports have indicated that nearly 8 percent of all reported rapes were male victimizations. In addition, rape crisis center record indicated that approximately 1 of every 10 callers were males (Karmen 2001).

Male victims are subject to the same kind of disbelief in which women have been subjected for centuries. Like women, they too are blamed for their own "indiscretions." However, men face a new problem, being labeled homosexual. Men are disparaged for not being "real men" since they were unable to thwart their attackers (Karmen 2001). Thus, in order to prevent this stereotyping from occurring, most men, as do most women, fail to report their victimization.

Rape is Strictly Limited to Interactions between Humans

Although many would find this myth to be harmless within our society, one must realize that this myth helps to perpetuate the same mentality as those myths applied to female sexual assault. The idea that animals are forced into intercourse does not typically register in the human mind as sexual assault or rape. However, if one looks at sexism and speciesism, there is a solid like between the two ideologies. According to Piers Beirne (1997), "interspecies sexual assault is the product of a masculinity that sees women, animals, and nature as objects that can be controlled, manipulated, and exploited" (p. 327). We fail to realize that when women are verbally degraded, they are described in animalistic references: bitches, cows, chicks, beavers, pussies, etc. This derogatory language allows the aggressor to dehumanize his "prey" and establish women as "less than" (Bierne 1997).

Today, the system attempts to protect women from sexual victimization; however, few laws exist within our society to protect animals. There are no federal laws to prosecute the sexual victimization of animals and only 27 of 50 states have any statutes that protect against bestiality (see Posner and Silbaugh 1996 cited in Bierne 1997). In addition, when the majority of cases in which interspecies sexual assault occurs, the perpetrator is only charged with a misdemeanor. Even though animals suffer great pain often resulting in death due to human-animal sexual relations, the law fails to seek retribution in any real form. Thus, the tradition of victimization continues within our society.

Conclusion

The acceptance of rape myths within our society is based on the history of the subjugation of women. Traditionally, women were discredited when they brought their victimization to the attention of the criminal justice system. Not only did the system fail to define sexual victimization, they established laws which ensured that sexual offenders would remain unpunished. By establishing criterion such as corroboration, resistance, and no prior relationship with the offender, the legal system maintained the status quo. It was not until the late 1960s/early 1970s that the criminal justice system began to approach rape cases without automatically condemning the victim. For instance, in 1976, Nebraska became the first state to criminalize marital rape (Eigenberg 2001).

Even though laws have been established to protect victims of sexual assault from being victimized twice (the initial assault and the assault by the criminal justice system), police officers, prosecutors, judges, and even members of the jury still look to the victim to prove her/her own victimization. This is attributed to the fact that rape myths are still widely accepted within our society. Although a plethora of research has shed light on many of these myths, as noted, society cannot seem to rid itself of these traditionally held beliefs. This creates an environment in which rape victims are afraid to come forward for fear of being humiliated by the legal system.

In order to rid society of the misperceptions of rape created by those who wish to maintain the patriarchal order, the criminal justice system must seek new methods in approaching sexual assault cases. First and foremost, law enforcement officials must be reeducated in their response to rape. Rather than approaching the case from the perspective that the victim must prove their own victimization, police must approach sexual assault cases as they approach other felonious crimes. In addition, departments must ensure that "evidence" collected during the investigation gets catalogued and appropriately stored for use if the crime goes to trial. Second, police officers, prosecutors, and judges must be educated about the realities of sexual assault (Belknap 2001). Although date, marital, and acquaintance rapes make up the vast majority of sexual assaults against women, prosecutors still hold on to the myth of the "stranger" rape. Since acquaintance rapes are typically in private and seldom leave "tale-tale signs" of brutalization, prosecutors will often fail to try a case in court. Thus, rapists are often released before they ever go to trial. Finally, the public must also be educated and sensitized to the reality of sexual assault. These individuals are the ones serving on juries and ensuring that justice is obtained. By ensuring that all those involved in the trial process in a sexual assault case are informed, society will be able to eliminate the traditional rape myths that have prevailed throughout history. Thus, this will bring society one step closer to eliminating the need to control and dominate another being.

References

Allison, J. and I. Kollenbroich-Shea. "Sexual Assault." In *Women, Crime, and Criminal Justice*, eds. C. Renzetti and L. Goodstein, 154–175. Los Angeles, CA: Roxbury, 2001.

Amir, M. *Patterns in Forcible Rape*. Chicago: University of Chicago Press, 1971.

Bartol, C. *Criminal Behavior: A Psychosocial Approach*. New Jersey: Prentice Hall, 1999.

Belknap, J. *The Invisible Woman*, 2nd ed. Boulder, CO: Wadsworth, 2001.

Bierne, P. "Rethinking Bestiality: Towards a Concept of Interspecies Sexual Assault." *Theoretical Criminology 1*, (1997): 317–340.

Brownmiller, S. *Against Our Will: Men, Women, and Rape.* New York: Bantham, 1975.

Bureau of Justice Statistics. *Sex offenses and Offenders: An Analysis of Date Rape and Sexual Assault.* Washington, D.C.: U.S. Department of Justice, 1997.

Burt, M.R. "Cultural Myths and Supports for Rape." *Personality and Social Psychology 38*, (1980): 217–230.

Chancer, L. S. "Gender, Class, and Race in Three High Profile Crimes: The Cases of New Bedford, Central Park, and Bensonhurst." In *Crime Control and Women*, ed. S. L. Miller, 72–94. Thousand Oaks, CA: Sage Publications, 1998.

Clark, A. *Women's Silence, Men's Violence: Sexual Assault in England, 1770–1845.* London: Pandora Press, 1987.

Cuklanz, L.M. *Rape On Trial: How the Mass Media Construct Legal Reform and Social Change.* Philadelphia: University of Pennsylvania Press, 1996.

DeFour, D.C. "The Interface of Racism and Sexism on College Campuses." In *Ivory Power: Sexual Harassment on Campus,* ed. M. A. Paludi. Albany, NY: State University Press of New York, 1990.

Edward, K.E. and M. D. Macleod. "The Reality and Myth of Rape: Implications for the Criminal Justice System." *Expert Evidence 7*, (1999): 37–58.

Eigenberg, H.M. *Woman Battering in The United States: Till Death Do Us Part.* Prospect Heights, IL: Waveland Press, 2001.

Epps, K.J., R. Haworth, and T. Swaffer. "Attitudes Toward Women and Rape Among Male Adolescents Convicted of Sexual Versus Nonsexual Crimes." *Journal of Psychology 127*, (1993): 501–506.

Estrich, S. *Real Rape.* Cambridge, MA: Harvard University Press, 1987.

Federal Bureau of Investigation. *Uniform Crime Reports.* Washington, DC: Department of Justice, 1997.

Feinman. *Women in the Criminal Justice System.* Westport, CT: Praeger, 1994.

Field, H.S. "Attitudes Toward Rape: A Comparative Analysis of Police, Rapists, Crisis Counselors, and Citizens." *Journal of Personality and Social Psychology 36*, (1978): 156–179.

Forbes, G.B. and L. E. Adams-Curtis. "Experiences With Sexual Coercion in College Males and Females: Role of Family Conflict, Sexist Attitudes, Acceptance of Rape Myths, Self-Esteem, and the Big-Five Personality Factors." *Journal of Interpersonal Violence 16*, (2001): 865–889.

Freymeyer, R. H. "Rape Myths and Religiosity." *Sociological Spectrum 17*, (1997): 473–491.

Grana, S. J. *Women and (In)Justice: The criminal and Civil Effects of the Common Law on Women's Lives*. Boston, MA: Allyn and Bacon, 2002.

Greendlinger, V. and D. Byrne. "Coercive Sexual Fantasies of College Men as Predictors of Self-Reported Likelihood To Rape and Overt Sexual Aggression." *Journal of Sex Research 23*, (1987): 1–11.

Groth, N.A. *Men Who Rape: The Psychology of the Offender*. New York: Plenum Press, 1979.

Karmen, A. *Crime Victims: An Introduction to Victimology*. Belmont, CA: Wadsworth, 2001.

Kilpatrick, D.G., C. N. Edmunds, and A. Seymour. *Rape in America: A Report to the Nation*. Arlington, VA: National Victim Center, 1992.

Koss, M. and S. Cook. "Facing the Facts: Data and Acquaintance Rape are Significant Problems for Women." In *Issues in Intimate Violence*, ed. R. Bergen, 147–156. Thousand Oaks, CA: Sage, 1998.

Koss, M.P. and M. R. Harvey. *The Rape Victim: Clinical and Community Interventions* (2nd ed.). Newbury Park, CA: Sage, 1991.

Koss, M.P., K.E. Leonard, D. A. Beezley, and C. J. Oros. "Nonstranger Sexual Aggression: A Discriminant Analysis of the Psychological Characteristics of Undetected Offenders." *Sex Roles 12*, (1985): 981–992.

Lerner, M.J. *The Belief in a Just World. A Fundamental Delusion*. New York: Plenum, 1980.

Lonsway, K.A. and L. F. Fitzgerald. "Rape Myths: In Review." *Psychology of Women Quarterly* 18, (1994): 133–164.

Malamuth, N.M., R. J. Sockloskie, M. P. Joss, and J. S. Tanaka. "Characteristics of Aggressor Against Women: Testing a Model Using a National Sample of College Students." *Journal of Consultating and Clinical Psychology* 59 (1991): 670–681.

Maschke, K. (ed.). *The Legal Response to Violence Against Women*. New York: Garland Publishing, 1997.

Miller, S. L. (ed.). *Crime Control and Women: Feminist Implications of Criminal Justice Policy*. Thousand Oaks, CA: Sage Publications, 1998.

Muehlenhard, C.L. and M. A. Linton. "Date Rape and Sexual Aggression in Dating Situations: Incidence and Risk Factors." *Journal of Counseling Psychology 34*, (1987)186–196.

Murphy, W.D., E. M. Coleman, and M. R. Hayes. "Factors Related to Coercive Sexual Behavior in a Nonclinical Sample of Males." *Violence and Victims* 1, (1986): 255–278.

North Carolina State Law §14-27.2

Orcutt, J.D. and R. Faison. "Sex-Role Attitude Change and Reporting of Rape Victimization, 1973–1985." *The Sociological Quarterly* 29, (1988): 589–604.

Overholser, J.C. and S. Beck. "Multimethod Assessment of Rapists, Child Molesters, and Three Control Groups on Behavioral and Psychological Measures." *Journal of Consulting and Clinical Psychology* 56, (1986): 682–687.

Posner, R.A. and K. B. Silbaugh. *A Guide to America's Sex Laws.* Chicago: University of Chicago Press, 1996.

Reilly, M.E., B. Lott, D. Caldwell, and L. DeLuca. "Tolerance for Sexual Harassment Related to Self-Reported Sexual Victimization." *Gender and Society* 6, (1992): 122–138.

Renzetti, C.M. and L. Goodstein. *Women, Crime, and Criminal Justice: Original Feminist Readings.* Los Angeles, CA: Roxbury, 2001.

Russell, D.E.H. *Sexual Exploitation: Rape, Child Sexual Abuse, and Workplace Harassment.* Beverly Hills, CA: Sage, 1984.

Schwartz, M.D. and M. S. Leggett. "Bad Dates or Emotional Trauma? The Aftermath of Campus Sexual Assault." *Violence Against Women* 5, (1999): 251–271.

Sudderth, L.K. "'It'll Come Right Back at Me': The Interactional Context of Discussing Rape With Others." *Violence Against Women* 4, (1998): 559–571.

Ullman, S. "Review and Critique of Empirical Studies of Rape Avoidance." *Criminal Justice Behavior* 24, (1997): 177–204.

Tjaden, P. and N. Thoennes. *Stalking in America: Findings from the National Violence Against Women Survey.* Washington, D.C.: National Institute of Justice, 1998.

Van Wormer, K.S. and C. Bartollas, eds. *Women and the Criminal Justice System.* Needham Heights, MA: Allyn and Bacon, 2000.

White, A.M., M. J. Strube, and S. Fisher. "A Black Feminist Model of Rape Myth Acceptance: Implications for Research and Antirape Advocacy in Black Communities." *Psychology of Women Quarterly* 22, (1998): 157–175.

Wolf, N. *The Beauty Myth*. New York: William Morrow, 1991.

World Health Organization. "Violence Against Women," 2000. http://www.who.int/inf-fs/en/fact239.html

Wriggins, J. "Rape, Racism, and the Law." *Harvard Women's Law Journal* 6, (1983): 103–41.

Chapter 2

Sexual Assault Definitions

Robert Hanser, Ph.D.

A General Definition of Female Rape

As implied, this section addresses the issue of sexual assault definitions. However, the reader should understand that the term "sexual assault" is used as a blanket term that refers to a number of sexually related forms of victimization. This term includes all types of sexual offenses that involve touching or penetration of an intimate part of a person's body without consent (LeBeau and Mozayani 2001). Thus, sexual assault includes rape, forced sodomy, forced oral copulation, and any form of undesired sexually related touching (LeBeau and Mozayani 2001). However, society tends to refer to such forms of crime as simply rape. Further, many legal sources continue to use the term rape, particularly in specialized situations such as date rape and/or marital rape. Thus, this discussion will use the term rape most frequently to describe definitions of specific categories of sexual assault.

Also, it should be pointed out that the terms "victim" and "survivor" are used interchangeably throughout this discussion. The particular selection of terms was made, in each case, according to what seemed most appropriate to the particular context in which the issue of rape was being addressed. Likewise, it is important to note that this chapter will focus on definitions of rape that involve female victims. It is fully understood and acknowledged that victims of rape may be male as well as female. But the issue of male victims will not be covered due to the fact that the majority of victims (survivors) are female. Rape of male victims, whether by male or female perpetrators, is covered in other sections of this reader and is so specialized as to not be integral to the broad nature of this chapter. Further, child sexual assault/molestation will not be specifically covered (outside of statutory rape which is not an identical phenomenon) because this is an entire issue unto itself. Though the dynamics have similarities, there are significant distinctions from adult rape. With these points in mind, it is important to provide a rudimentary definition of the rape phenomenon as a baseline for the more in-depth definitions of rape that follow.

For purposes of this chapter, rape is the act of forced penetration of any bodily orifice (vaginally, anally, or orally), or forced cunnilingus or felatio, involving violation of the survivor's body and psychological well being. The assault is accomplished by the use of force, the threat of force, or without force when the survivor is unable to physically or mentally give their consent. Rape is an experience of violation, degradation, and humiliation that has serious negative impact on the survivor. The survivor's reactions can, and often do, vary according to the person, the event, and a number of other multiple variables. Further, the survivor's perception of the experience is affected by many factors such as prior socialization, reactions from people that are told about the incident, and the reactions of criminal justice agencies. It is important to realize that there are numerous types and definitions of rape. It should be understood that there are personal, social, political, and clinical implications that affect the rape phenomenon. Because of this, it is important to not only examine the physical and psychological well-being of the survivor, but to examine the larger societal constructs attributed to the rape phenomenon as well.

General Rape

Numerous Ways to Define Rape

One main point of this chapter is to illustrate the numerous definitions of rape. These definitions are more varied than may be generally acknowledged. Further, Bourque (1989) notes that this diversity has important ramifications for how rape is reported, prevented, treated, and even researched. In fact, definitions of rape can vary with the defining person's social standing, education, perceptions of, and attitudes towards violence and sexuality (Bourque 1989).

Definitions of rape also vary greatly from state to state, and in many states the term "sexual assault" has replaced the term of rape in their criminal statutes (Bartol 1999). The U.S. Department of Justice defines rape as the "unlawful sexual intercourse with a female, by force or without legal or factual consent" (U. S. Department of Justice, 1988). But other jurisdictions vary widely in their definitions of rape often disagreeing with the Department of Justice's definition. Such disagreement has hampered the effective classification and study of rape offenses (Bartol, 1999).

Bartol (1999) points out that in defining rape, prosecutors require exacting and stringent evidence before even considering an incident as probable rape. From survey data, it has been found that prosecutors often look for four minimal criteria for filling out a complaint for forcible rape: (1) evidence of penetration; (2) a lack of victim consent; (3) threat of force; and (4) and usually the victim must be female (Bartol 1999; Chappell 1977). More contemporary prosecutors may differ on some of these points, particularly with respect to the victim being female, depending on jurisdiction and the crime alleged. However, these differences, combined with the differences among state legislatures, law enforcement agencies, and researchers, demonstrate a need for a clear and distinct definition of rape.

The act of rape should be viewed as but one of many violent and sexual behaviors that humans may engage in. This is because the tendency to separate rape from other human behavior has had two unfortunate consequences (Bourque 1989). First, it has allowed members of society to ignore the wide variety of behaviors that technically meet the definition of rape (Bourque 1989). Second, it ignores the fact that rape only differs in the degree of severity from other violent interactions (Bourque 1989). If we are to lower our tolerance for rape and develop consistent sanctions for dealing with perpetrators, we must understand the wide range of behaviors that rape encompasses.

Sadly enough, many people continue to view "real" rape as some unforeseen attack by some stranger in an isolated area (Bourque 1989). Such a limited definition, allows most people to distance themselves from the reality of rape. This limited definition can also minimize the trauma for survivors of various types of rape. The irony is that this denial of the actual occurrence of rape works not only in the minds of people who are not involved with a rape incident, but also works to mitigate the perceptions of perpetrators, and even those of the victims as well. Thus, some perpetrators may genuinely not perceive their actions as rape. More disturbing is that many victims often do not, themselves, realize that they have been raped (Brownmiller 1975; Buchwald, Fletcher, and Roth 1993).

One useful theory for explaining perceptions of rape is attribution theory (Bourque 1989). In the case of sexual assault, it is assumed that both the perpetrator and survivor of the incident, as well as other observers such as family, friends, and police will evaluate the situation to determine if a rape occurred. It is also assumed that conclusions reached will affect future behavior, future feelings that the victim will have about themselves, and future judgments of other similar situations. Bourque (1989) states that if the woman concludes that a rape did occur and that she was responsible for it, this theory predicts that her behavior will change in ways that are likely to prevent future rapes. It is also assumed that she will feel that other women who are raped under similar circumstances are similarly responsible for assaults made upon them (Bourque 1989). What is alarming about this is that some women may in fact blame themselves for rape to the point that the perpetrator's behavior is normalized or excused.

Conversely, if she concludes that she was not responsible for the rape, her behavior may be less likely to change and her judgments of other rapes will tend to absolve women of responsibility (Bourque 1989). While it is preferred that a victim does not blame themselves for a rape that has been committed against them, it is hoped that victims will see themselves as survivors capable of affecting the outcome of future rape for themselves and others. This of course does happen with many rape survivors. But the example demonstrates that some women may learn a state of helplessness that places them at a greater likelihood for repeat victimization. Thus, the manner in which blame, guilt, and responsibility is attributed is important because when people decide that a rape has occurred, their perception of the rape often considers issues of victim and offender self-responsibility in making this determination. In other words, most observers of rape at least topically consider if the victim and offender acted responsibly or negligently. Many people may consider the possibility that the victim deliberately placed themselves in the precarious position that led to the rape (Bourque 1989). This is despite the fact that it is the perpetrator who is guilty of the rape, not the survivor.

Outlooks such as those previously described often revolve around the particular locus of control that an observer might possess (Rotter 1966). Locus of control differentiates between beliefs about internal and external control events. Locus of control has often been used to describe "states" and "traits." In other words, it can refer to an individual's perception of his or her ability to control events in a single instance, or it can be used to describe the person's general personality profile (Bourque 1989). This concept is important to rape perceptions and definitions because evidence exists that locus of control varies with sex-role attitudes and that it influences both people's perceptions of rape and the victims' sense of self-responsibility (Bourque, 1989). Women who score high on internal control also score high on nontraditional feminism, thus viewing women to be more capable of aggressive behaviors. On the other hand, women scoring high on the external control measure tend to accept socially defined, normative roles of passivity for women. This has also been found to correlate with attitudes on how rape is perceived by some women (Bourque 1989; Krulewitz and Payne 1978).

This has obvious implications for how women may develop self-definitions of rape. Naturally then, this would equally affect rates of reporting rape. Further, men likewise form attributions toward women in rape situations based on an internal/external locus of control schema (Bourque 1989; Rotter 1966). Men, who tend to score higher than women on internal loci of control, tend to hold women as partially or even entirely responsible for the rape acts committed against them. Those scoring lower on internal loci of control may blame environmental factors as well as the perpetrator. Thus, attributions that people make toward the rapist and the survivor affect how they will define rape (Bourque 1989).

Another similar theory that explains how people develop perceptions, and by proxy definitions of rape is the "just world hypothesis" (Bartol 1999; Lerner 1980).This is the simplistic belief that a person gets what they deserve in life. Often people who subscribe to this viewpoint claim that poor life choices and/or deliberately counterproductive decisions serve to place the victim in a position where the consequence is a natural and foreseeable product. This theory contends that victims of misfortune or crime deserve their fate (Bartol 1999). Naturally, those people who subscribe to this theory hold this to be true for survivors of rape as well. According to Bartol (1999), these people will use any number of rationalizations to explain their viewpoints (i.e. she should not be at a bar alone, she should have worn a bra, she should not dance with someone she just met, etc...) and, as will later be seen, are touted so widely that some of the rationalizations have become rape myths believed by a number of people in society.

In addition to individual perceptions, much of the process of defining rape is likewise dependent on cultural and social factors (Sanday 1981). Naturally, these factors affect individual perceptions, including those held by perpetrators and survivors of rape. Even local community views on rape may greatly affect the likelihood of reporting, the likelihood of apprehension for the offender, and the treatment of the victim (Bourque 1989; Sanday 1981). Therefore, Bourque (1989) contends that community surveys provide the best information about what most community members think about rape. With respect to social indicators, social status and life-style of the persons involved in rape can all have important effects on the perceptions and definitions of rape. Particularly, age, sex, income, education, and religion have been found to affect perceptions of rape (Williams and Holmes 1981).

This is important, because many researchers contend that rape is not about sex, but is about the perpetrator's need to express and exert power (Buchwald,

Fletcher, Roth 1993; Steinem 1993). This is often coupled with the idea that our culture in general, and men in particular, hold women as lower status citizens when compared to men (Buchwald, Fletcher, Roth 1993; Dworkin 1993). Such attitudes are often what lead many researchers to conclude that rape has more to do with a desire to express power and domination than to gratify sexual urges (Brownmiller 1975; Groth 1979; Steinem 1993). These attitudes toward women, and the attitudes that women hold about themselves, are held to be products of socialization stemming from both the family and the broader society. But it is society that generates numerous messages that bombard the family with perceptions that dictate the place of women and their role with the rape experience.

One frequently cited medium that affects rape perceptions and definitions comes in the form of erotica and pornography (Steinem 1993). In fact, Steinem states bluntly that "pornography is not about sex, it's about an imbalance of power that allows and even requires sex to be used as some form of aggression" (1993, 31). Perceptions and informal definitions of rape for many people may be greatly affected by visual media, with pornography being a foremost contributor to the confusing manner by which sex and violence are intertwined in much of American culture. The contention is that sex is confused with violence and aggression in all forms of popular culture. The idea that aggression is a normal part of male sexuality, and that passivity is a normal part of female sexuality, are part of the male-dominant culture (Steinem, 1993). Because of the deep-seated differential social value placed upon men and women, and because the issue of power and dominance is interwoven into this differential social value, it becomes clear that untangling sex from aggression would be a very difficult task indeed (Steinem 1993). This point is important, because it is the underlying dynamic that affects the perceptions of men and women toward rape, and by the same token, affects any formal or informal definitions of rape.

But it should also be made clear that social and cultural messages affecting definitions of rape are not limited to direct media processes like pornography. Rather, the linguistics in the general media can affect our definitions of rape as well. Benedict (1993) contends that in the media, the English language itself is a language of rape. Through vocabulary and profiles on television, women are portrayed as sexual or childlike temptresses (Benedict 1993). Such portrayals perpetuate the idea that women are legitimate sexual prey. The scenarios presented in movies often portray rape as an act of unintended pleasure, or of comedy, rather than violence (Benedict 1993). Benedict (1993) even maintains that newspapers and newscasts use words that describe the victim in terms of their beauty; these news media likewise describe the incident so that it diminishes the criminality of the act committed. The language chosen by journalists and news reporters can make rape seem either sexy or not so traumatic (Benedict 1993).

These are all significant observations, because such depictions serve to normalize the occurrence of rape and serve to desensitize the public to its effects. This failure to accurately report the damage to the victim likewise allows viewers to ignore the stark reality of rape. And of course, the news media, just like individuals in the general population, can itself be responsible for inaccurate attributions made by the reporter who makes the scene. This process tends to reinforce many of the informal social norms and mores that maintain a tolerance of rape. Thus, those seeking to change the manner by which rape is addressed would claim that definitions of rape are biased due to personal perceptions and social factors that affect those perceptions. To ignore this is to ignore the very groundwork upon which all definitions of rape are based.

Rape by Criminal Law v. Civil Law

As has been previously mentioned, creating definitions of rape can be somewhat elusive when one is asked to concretely operationalize the term. From the discussion of perceptions and their effects on definitions, it can be seen that there is likely to be a diversity of viewpoints. More to the point, this seems to have translated into a number of methods by which rape is defined. For example, rape has varying criminal definitions among the fifty states, though most state definitions of rape have their earliest origins in the English common law. Thus this section will provide a general examination of early common law explanations of rape definitions and statutes to provide backdrop knowledge of the earliest definitions of rape. Further, rape has differing definitions based on the type of law being utilized; criminal law vis-à-vis civil law definitions. Lastly, this section will present a variety of criminal law definitions and will conclude with a civil law definition of rape. The diverging origin (crime against the people v. crime against the individual) from which these two forms of law operate provide the background in determining exactly how a rape is processed.

Analyzing statutes as sources of law requires a brief look at common law, which is mainly law that has emanated from long traditions and customs, or from various decisions throughout passed down case law. This is in direct contrast to codified laws that are passed by state legislatures or other governing and law making bodies. According to Reid (1992), the term "common law" generally refers to England's ancient laws that developed from judicial decisions which were decided on a case-by-case basis. The decisions from these cases were passed down to lower courts or were used by other courts and became "precedent" or "case law" upon which future cases were decided (Reid 1992). Early American case law developed from this English tradition which were based on English customs and norms (common law). As American case law developed, it was codified and is now what we know as statutory criminal law.

Under common law, rape was defined as the unlawful carnal knowledge of a female without her consent. For centuries this definition was interpreted to exclude a husband's forced sexual intercourse with his wife (Reid 1992). The carnal knowledge component of the definition referred to sexual intercourse and was strictly limited to acts of penile penetration of the vagina (Reid 1992). Common law rape applied only to female victims and forcing a male to engage in sex was not considered a rape (Reid 1992). Lastly, the issue of consent was a paramount yet difficult component to prove. Proving a lack of consent became a burden that the rape survivor's defense would have to bear.

Similarly, Paquin (1995) defines common law rape as an act of sexual intercourse by a man with a woman, who is not his wife, by force and against her will. Again, the consent issue is particularly problematic; but in situations where the woman is not able to consent, intercourse was generally held to be against her will (Paquin 1995). Situations where the woman could not consent would include those where she is incompetent, drugged, or underage (often referred to as statutory rape and defined later in this section). Paquin (1995) also adds that consent is the primary issue of fact that a court must agree upon. This is especially true in cases where the perpetrator and victim may know each other as cohorts, friends, or even romantic partners who are not married (Paquin 1995). The consent issue then was of critical importance in early rape history and, as will be discovered throughout this discussion of rape definitions, has continued to be the pivotal point in defining an act as rape.

According to Paquin (1995), many feminist scholars claim that the common law intent against rape was to protect her "virtue" or chastity rather than her freedom to choose sexual partners. This is because in centuries past, women were considered to be the property of their fathers or husbands. In several ways, it is the victim's character that is at issue as much as the actions of the rapist under the common law system.

As stated previously, the distinctions between common law and criminal law mostly have to do with the codification of the law. However, MacDonald (1995) provides a clear definition of criminal rape. As one can tell, this definition sounds very familiar to the earlier common law definition. MacDonald (1995) defines rape under criminal law "as the unlawful sexual intercourse with a female without her consent, or when consent is obtained by threats of violence; by deception, for example, by impersonating the woman's husband; or by the administration of intoxicating substances. Women of unsound mind may be incapable of giving legal consent. Penetration of the vagina need not be complete, the slightest penetration is sufficient, and ejaculation need not occur" (p. 4). As can be seen, the issue of consent is the primary concern in determining if a rape has occurred. Factors that mitigate or aggravate the likelihood of truly informed consent likewise become material in defining the occurrence of rape. Thus, consent has historically remained the major snafu in most all instances of rape between adults.

Two other categories of rape that are commonly employed in criminal statutes include statutory rape and rape by fraud. Statutory rape, defined by MacDonald (1995) is unlawful sexual intercourse with a willing female child under the age of consent. At present, the age of consent in American jurisdictions ranges from eleven to seventeen years (MacDonald 1995). In analyzing statutory rape provisions, MacDonald (1995) contends that the age should not be so young that little protection is provided for a child, nor so late that a man can be held for statutory rape when the "victim" is fully capable of informed consent and readily acquiesced to a proposal or even invited a sexual relationship. Boumil, Friedman, and Taylor (1992) explain that unlike other types of rape, statutory rape usually refers to consensual sexual activity, including intercourse between a male and a girl who is under a certain prescribed age that is necessary for legal consent. If the girl is under the statutory age of consent, and even if she willingly participated, the male engaging in sexual activity with her is guilty of statutory rape (Boumil, Friedman, and Taylor 1992). It is also not considered a defense if the man was not aware of the victim's age (Boumil, Friedman, and Taylor 1992). This is of course a controversial concept among many people affected by rape.

The term "statutory" in statutory rape means that the law will call the act rape regardless of whether or not the victim was willing because that victim is considered legally incapable of giving true consent due their diminished ability to fully understand the consequences of their decisions (Boumil, Friedman, and Taylor 1992). This is of course held to be a product of their youth (Boumil, Friedman, and Taylor 1992). Every state has a law that sets a minimum age at which this consent can be given. The minimum age of consent is not necessarily the point of reaching adulthood (i.e. eighteen) and can be much younger than eighteen, depending on the particular state and the particular circumstances (Boumil, Friedman, and Taylor 1992; MacDonald, 1995). The main purpose of these laws is to protect underage children rather than to morally restrict sex from a given population group (Boumil, Friedman, and Taylor 1992; MacDonald 1995). Thus the intent of statutory rape laws is to deter those who would take advantage of a potential victim's youth. All of these laws, regardless of the state in which they are enacted, share the common holding that it does not matter if the victim was willing (Boumil, Friedman, and Taylor 1992). If the child is below the state's minimum age of consent, then it is statutory rape. Further, if the victim was both below the minimum age and not willing, the crime is not only statutory rape, but can likewise be classified as child molestation or child sexual abuse (Boumil, Friedman, and Taylor 1992).

The category of rape by fraud occurs when the perpetrator employs actual, deliberate misrepresentation or concealment to gain access to sexual activity with the victim. Essentially, rape by fraud is having sexual relations with a consenting adult female, but the consent is given under fraudulent conditions (Bartol 1999). Examples of this type of rape might be where the man presents himself as some other identity (such as in the dark impersonating the husband or boyfriend of the victim). Other types of rape by fraud include when the court finds such to exist after examining the nature of a contract or from the relationship of the parties involved. An example of this might be where the man, through acts of deception, tricks the victim into thinking they have been legally married and the two consummate their new marriage, only for the victim to later find that the marriage was a hoax. Another example is when a psychotherapist or a clergy member has sexual intercourse with a patient under the guise of providing treatment or spiritual guidance. Rape by fraud can also occur among women who typically are not considered worthy of such legal protections, though such fraudulent forms of sexual manipulation can and do occur. For example, consider a female prostitute who has sex with a male customer who upon completion of the act, does not pay as agreed. This in fact, can consist of a legal definition for rape by fraud in areas where prostitution is legal or at least decriminalized. Because it is often consensual (even though the causes for consent were given under false pretenses), rape by fraud is very difficult to prove in many cases. Despite this, it is important to remember that this is not "informed consent" in the true sense of the word, and regardless of the woman's position in society, this type of manipulation is considered rape nonetheless because true consent is in fact lacking.

Rape in the Civil Law Context

According to Paquin (1995), rape is not only a crime, but it is also a personal injury against the victim. In addition to criminal systems of recourse, victims may pursue civil systems of redress to obtain financial compensation for the damages they have suffered. There are two primary benefits for rape victims who decide to pursue redress under civil law conditions of rape (Paquin 1995). First, the victim needs a much lower standard of proof than in criminal courts. The standard of proof needed for a civil case is a simple preponderance of the evidence. Thus, at least hypothetically, a case that did not meet the criminal law definition could still meet the level of proof for the civil law definition for liability (Paquin 1995). Second, damages incurred will be compensated directly to the victim. This is because the act of violence is a personal injury to the plaintiff (in this case, the victim of the rape) and as such, liability is strictly maintained from the perpetrator to the victim as a personal injury (Paquin 1999). Thus, civil law tends to "desexualize" the rape and instead treats the act as any form of deliberate personal injury inflicted by a liable party. The result is that the victim has increased odds of obtaining redress under this definition due to lower evidentiary standards when compared to criminal charges of rape.

Stranger Rape—A Stereotypical Definition

For the purposes of this discussion, stranger rape is defined as nonconsensual, or forced sex, on a person who does not know their attacker. According to Boumil (1992), this type of rape is what people usually think of when they think of rape. Most people envision a rapist as an unknown man who ambushes his victim at night armed with some type of weapon that they use to force compliance from their victim (Boumil 1992). The victim is caught by surprise and may or may not resist the attack, depending upon how terrified she is and whether she perceives that it may save her from further attack and/or injury (Boumil 1992). This type of stranger rape can occur in any place where a potential victim can be found, including the victim's home, car, or anywhere outside (Boumil 1992).

This is the stereotypical rape that common law definitions originally recognized. As such, most people have no problems defining this type of rape and empathy for victims of this type of rape is usually readily extended. Because this definition of rape is so well accepted and so straightforward in nature, there is little need for extensive discussion in explaining its definition. The actual rate of frequency of stranger rape as compared to other types of rape has varied depending on the researchers (Bartol 1999; Parrot and Bechhofer 1991; Wiehe and Richards 1995). It must be made clear that the point of this discussion is not to provide exact rates of occurrence for each type of rape, but is to instead demonstrate the various methods for defining rape.

The occurrence of stranger rape, in this society, is more widely accepted than acquaintance rape. This acceptance that stranger rape receives does not limit the shame attached to rape or the trauma felt by the survivor. However, stranger rape is usually seen as "real rape". The purpose of this discussion is not to devalue and belittle the experience of stranger rape. Rather, it should be made clear that other forms of rape do indeed exist. It is the hope that survivors of all types of rape will encounter understanding and awareness and that people close to survivors of rape will recognize the possible differences in the experience of stranger and acquaintance rape. With this is mind, we now move forward to another category of rape that is perhaps less well understood by the general public.

Intimate (Date) Rape

Acquaintance rape is treated with ambivalence by society and the legal system partly because it is difficult to identify situations that clearly constitute acquaintance rape. Therefore, a basic and pragmatic definition of the term must be provided. This definition is borrowed from Parrot and Bechhofer (1991) who describe acquaintance rape as nonconsensual sex between adults who know each other. The word acquaintance is sometimes used to describe a person that is known but who is not close to the person. The word can also be used to describe any person who is known to the victim, this would include any and everyone who is not a stranger (Parrot and Bechhofer 1991). Date rape is a narrower term referring to nonconsensual sex between people who are dating or on a date. Although the two terms "acquaintance rape" and "date rape" are used interchangeably, they do not have the same meaning (Parrot and Bechhofer 1991). Date rape is only one form of acquaintance rape (Parrot and Bechhofer 1991).

In distinguishing between types of rape, one should understand that rape definitions held by individuals in this culture may be broad and inclusive or narrow and restrictive (Parrot and Bechhofer 1991). People whose definitions are at the inclusive extreme believe that all coerced sex is rape, whether the coercion used is physical, psychological, or economic (Parrot and Bechhofer 1991). Those whose definitions lie at the restrictive extreme believe that there is no such thing as rape, or if there is any, it will fit the classic perception of typical stranger rape. According to Parrot and Bechhofer (1991), most people's definition of rape falls somewhere between these two extremes. This includes some acts of coerced sex but also excludes many on the basis of belief in rape myths. People have in their heads an idea of a "real" rape (Boumil

1992). Usually their idea is much narrower than the legal definition and excludes many types of rape that happen more frequently than the classic rape (Parrot and Bechhofer 1991).

The classic "real" rape for many people, is a rape similar to that earlier described as stranger rape. The rapist is commonly thought to be a stranger, attack at night, use a weapon, and the victim resists but is overpowered. But a high number of rapes do not actually fit these criteria (Parrot and Bechhofer 1991). Thus the classic rape scenario does not leave room for acquaintance rape or date rape. Most date or acquaintance rapes and most group rapes, as will be discussed later, do not use a weapon in committing the assault. Further, the victim often has engaged in some type of voluntary communication with the perpetrator, which can be as brief as a few leisure conversations to fully intimate discussions among dating or married couples. The problem here is in determining exactly when the voluntary interaction between the two ended and the coercion and/or force began (Parrot and Bechhofer 1991). Since many people have a difficult time explaining these disparities between their definition of rape and the actual circumstances that surround a rape, they create mechanisms that help to justify their ability to disqualify a rape incident from their idea of real rape (Parrot and Bechhofer 1991). These rationalizations are called rape myths (Parrot and Bechhofer 1991).

These common rape myths, as described by Burt (1991), warrant a bit of attention because they serve to "explain away" the significance of acquaintance rape. One myth that is sometimes utilized is that nothing in fact happened (Burt 1991). This myth is based on the notion that a large number of women falsely accuse men of rape to fulfill other ulterior agendas. A second commonly used myth is that no actual harm was done to the victim (Burt 1991; Sanday 1990; Wiehe and Richards 1995). Sexual intercourse is admitted, but the coercion and harm inflicted is denied (Burt 1991). Beliefs that rape is "just sex" fall within this category as well (Burt 1991; Sanday 1990). Further, remarks like "relax and enjoy it" or "at least you were not a virgin" reflect this belief (Burt 1991). Another common myth is the notion that the survivor really wanted the sexual incident to take place (Burt 1991). Essentially, this myth would contend that the woman invited the rape through victim precipitated behavior or that she enjoyed it (Burt, 1991). An example of this exists among fraternities that claim that women who get drunk at their functions do so because they actually desire to have sex with the fraternity members (Burt 1991; Sanday 1990).

Wiehe and Richards (1995) likewise point toward the effects of rape myths, particularly with respect to acquaintance rape. Among these myths is the idea that the victim is responsible for the rape (Wiehe and Richards 1995). Attributions to how the victim was dressed, if she drank alcohol, etc. fall within this line of thinking. What is interesting is that the victim may actually blame themselves for drinking or choosing certain attire, and thus may begin to feel responsible for the rape itself, just as was earlier presented in the discussion of attribution theory (Bourque, 1989; Wiehe and Richards 1995). Yet another myth discussed by Wiehe and Richards (1995) is that women say "no" but really mean "yes." Thinking along this line contends that the woman wants to have sex but has to go through some charade so that it does not appear as if she is promiscuous. Men are aggressive and women are passive, according to this myth, in their sexual encounters (Wiehe and Richards 1995). Thus, women must say no by this gender-based stereotype. One last myth that is commonly purported is that once men are sexually aroused, sex is inevitable (Wiehe and Richards 1995). Essentially, this contends that men have no control over their behavior once their arousal state reaches a certain point. This is of course preposterous and simply serves as an excuse to justify rape.

Rape myths allow rapists to rape without fear of retribution. These myths teach women to blame themselves for their own victimization (Bourque 1989; Burt 1991; Wiehe and Richards 1995). These myths also transform an acquaintance rape into a simple sex act between two people who knew each other, and thus makes it as if there were no rape at all (Burt 1991; Wiehe and Richards 1995). What is more, these myths completely deny the possibility that someone can be raped by someone they know (Burt 1991; Wiehe and Richards 1995). Further, rape myths serve to keep the victim quiet. This is especially true with acquaintance rape where the woman's credibility is at stake, again calling into question any claims of a lack of consent. This is compounded by the fact that lack of consent is perceived to have been less likely if she previously knew her attacker. Thus rape myths, while negatively affecting public perceptions in all types of rape, are especially damaging in acquaintance rape situations.

With stranger rape, it is presumed that as long as the woman resisted, and did not conduct herself in a provocative fashion, then she is not necessarily to blame. But with acquaintance rape, there is a need to explain what may seem perplexing (Bartol 1999; Burt 1991; Wiehe and Richards 1995). The easiest solution is to blame the victim, as this provides some basis for overcoming the need to resolve questions of consent (Burt 1991; Wiehe and Richards 1995). Thus acquaintance rape is about rape and the question of consent. Acquaintance rape does not, and often is not, about force during the act but nonetheless is an act of exploitation rather than sex between two people who know each other. The exploitation comes in the form of robbing the person of the power to give or deny consent to the initiator of the sexual encounter. It is at this point, whether through force, coercion, or sense of obligation, that true consent is questionable and the issue of possible rape arises. In acquaintance rape situations, this is the most difficult area to clearly prove and creates a "grey zone" for those trying to determine if rape in fact exists.

Acquaintance rape is a fairly new notion that has received mixed public support. But the laws are changing as well as social attitudes. Rape myths provide resistance to these positive changes and also reflect cultural attitudes toward the rights of women, the self-control of men, and societal connections attributed to sex, violence, and exploitation (Bourque 1989; Burt 1991; Wiehe and Richards 1995). Acquaintance rape subjects the victim to all of the traumatic experiences encountered in stranger rape. In fact, it could easily be argued that the trauma is greater because the victim must often times face their perpetrator on future occasions. Likewise, in acquaintance rape there is the betrayal of trust between the two who had previously known each other. This is especially true in loving relationships where care and mutual respect are thought to be the basis of the union. It is with this in mind that we now move to our next category of acquaintance rape…marital rape, which presumes that more personal as opposed to casual knowledge exists between the victim and perpetrator.

Spousal Rape

Wiehe and Richards (1995) define marital rape as any sexual activity by a legal spouse that is performed or caused to be performed without the consent of the other spouse. These activities, as with acquaintance rape, include fondling, oral sex, anal sex, intercourse, or any other unwanted sexual activity. Husband is defined as the male spouse who is legally bound to his wife in marriage (Wiehe and Richards 1995). Wife is defined as the female spouse who is legally bound to her husband in marriage (Wiehe and Richards 1995). Marriage is defined as the legal union of a man and a woman (Wiehe and Richards 1995). With these definitions in mind, it is necessary to at least briefly discuss the history of rape in western civilization to understand why marital rape has traditionally been excluded. With this understanding it will become clearer why marital rape is a necessary category deserving attention of its own.

The basis of the legal history of the marital rape exemption is found in early English common law (Paquin 1995; Reid 1992; Wiehe and Richards 1995). According to this legal framework, the point when the wife consented to marriage expressly implied that she consented to all activities associated with marriage and that therefore there can be no rape in marriage. From the moment of marriage forward, the wife had "given herself" to her husband and could not refuse him sex throughout the term of the marriage (Wiehe and Richards 1995). Another point to understand with rape in general, and with marital rape specifically, is that women were considered chattel of their fathers or their husbands (Brownmiller 1975; Paquin 1995; Wiehe and Richards 1995). Thus traditional rape was viewed as a crime against the economic concerns of the father, if the woman was unmarried, or the economic concerns of the husband, if the woman was the man's wife. Since this economic logic for rape was the framework of the definition, and since the wife was the husband's property, the husband was not thought to be able to rape his own property. Even if this was imaginable, if she is his property, then it was thought that the husband has the right to utilize his property in any manner that seems fitting. After all, it was his to own, have, and hold.

But social concern, social awareness, and societal demand for action have resulted in important changes in the marital rape exemption in laws within the United States. In 1977, Oregon became the first state to repeal the marital rape exemption (Pagelow 1992; Wiehe and Richards 1995). Since then, many states have examined their laws to assess the marital rape exemption (Pagelow 1992; Wiehe and Richards 1995. Currently, all states hold that a husband can be held guilty of raping his wife.

The lack of public awareness of marital rape can be attributed to the secrecy that surrounds the problem (Finkelhor and Yllo 1995). This secrecy is maintained by most parties familiar with the situation, such as the victim, the rapist, and even extended family members who wish to protect the rapist or who believe that marriage problems should be handled between the two involved (Finkelhor and Yllo 1995). In this case, the marital rapist is nothing less than a marital abuser since in fact rape is an assault (Finkelhor and Yllo 1995). These abusers may keep the victim quiet through intimidation, threats, emotional blackmail, and even manipulative forms of "turning the tables," so to speak, making it seem as if the incident(s) were somehow the victim's fault. In discussing these similarities between standard marital violence and marital rape, Finkelhor and Yllo (1995) have created some distinctions with marital rape. Two of these categories, the battering marital rapist and the force-only marital rapist will be presented to demonstrate the differences in force and rationales presented to explain that use of force.

The battering marital rape is a phenomenon in which marital rape victims experience all the typical trauma from abuse, assault, entrapment, and terror as part of being a battered wife (Finkelhor and Yllo 1995). In these types of marital rape occurrences, the sexual violence is just one aspect of the general abuse that the victim must suffer. Thus, just as other researchers contend, rape in this case is more an assault to exploit, humiliate, and degrade, rather than to just gratify sexual needs. The force-only marital rape, according to Finkelhor and Yllo (1995), is when marital rape also occurs in relationships where rape is mainly the only type of violence utilized. In these cases, the amount of force used is usually the minimum amount necessary for the rapist to accomplish their goal (Finkelhor and Yllo 1995). Though these assaults are just as humiliating and create a sense of powerlessness, the use of other types of force in these cases is limited to just enough to accomplish the sex act.

What is important with respect to the rape act is to understand that in both instances the rape is a humiliating, terrorizing, and degrading experience. This act, whether with excessive or minimal force, employs force and lacks consent. Thus, it is an attack upon the person in either case. Further, the fact that both are married tends to minimize the consent issue in the eyes of much of the public, particularly when minimal force is employed. This rationale allows people to then describe such a scenario as little more than a typical "disagreement" about sex in the marriage. However, this is not the case and the completion of the rape simply provides an avenue for the male rapist to demonstrate his power over his spousal victim. Lastly, it should be noted that the traumatic effects of marital rape are the same for the victim as they are in any other rape situation, showing all the more that rape is an assault, and therefore, an act of violence.

The solution to the problem of marital rape starts with breaking the silence that is attributed to rape. It is commonly accepted that reported rapes represent only a small segment of those that actually occur (Wiehe and Richards 1995). Many wives do not seriously consider their right to say no to sexual advances to apply to their marital relationship. It is important to understand that consent is paramount regardless of the relationship, and that consent must be fully informed. This understanding is the key to preventing marital rape. This right to decline sexual activity is nothing less than an indicator of gender equality within the relationship (Wiehe and Richards 1995). Therefore, it is imperative that social perceptions of marital rape entail both a broader understanding of rape definitions and an increased concern for gender equality in and outside of the marital relationship (Wiehe and Richards 1995). Such factors are necessary precursors if wives are to truly be elevated to an equal status with their husbands.

Group Rape and Gang Rape: Rape Defined by Number of Perpetrators

Brownmiller (1975) defines group rape as any situation in which two or more men sexually assault one female victim. In many cases, victims of rape have suffered at the hands of two or more assailants (Brownmiller 1975; Mac-Donald 1995; Schwartz and DeKeseredy 1997). This definition may seem objectionable since some researchers (MacDonald 1995) make a distinction between pair rape and group rape. For the purposes of this chapter, such a distinction will be avoided since the dynamics of both types of rape are essentially the same. With both types, there is a sought after advantage through sheer numbers. The increased numerical odds of multiple assailants acting in methodical unison is proof of brutal intention and the desire to humiliate the victim beyond the act of general rape through a process of mass assault (Brownmiller 1975). The act of group rape forges an alliance among the perpetrators against the victim (Brownmiller 1975). This sense of alliance is seen among group rape perpetrators of both male (such as in prisons) and female victims. For female rape however, the group rape is much more common in the broader society and creates a sense of group anonymity among men. This anonymity exists whether the rape occurs among a group by chance such as at a nightclub, or is the product of a group acting with deliberation such as a violent youth gang.

MacDonald (1995) discusses group rape that occurs among men by chance, giving scenarios that have been commonly experienced by victims. An example might be a young woman at a drinking party who remains after the other women have left. The woman may find that the men take advantage of the situation encouraging and even coercing her to drink while "gently" convincing the woman to have sex with one or even all of them (MacDonald 1995). Though the exact point in which consent can be truly given may vary, the amount of "coercion" and the deliberation to drug the victim can result in nothing less than overt sexual assault.

Further, group rape can often be perpetrated against a victim that is already involved or associated with the group. MacDonald (1995) describes one such pattern among group rapists in which a man who has had prior sexual relations with a woman may deliberately place her in a social situation to get raped. The supposed "boyfriend" will invite the woman to a party and upon arriving, the woman may notice that no other women are present. If concern is expressed, the men will explain that other women are on the way. After some drinking and idle conversation, the woman is forcibly raped by all present except her supposed boyfriend. The other men go through the motions of threatening the boyfriend with some sort of weapon to prevent intervention on behalf of the victim, who often has no idea that that her boyfriend was part of the scheme to begin with. This example clearly demonstrates the level of duplicity that may go into group schemes to commit an act of rape (Mac-Donald 1995). Through the use of previously discussed rape myths, the use of group thought and rationalizations, the group may find justifications for such an action that only serves as further cement in the sense of alliance held among these perpetrators. Such rationalizations often exist as group subcultural norms that encourage and reward such actions.

To expound on this sense of alliance, is should be noted that group rapes can and often do occur with perpetrators who share an initial bond that leads to their acting together in a sexual assault. While this is widely recognized as a behavior among gang members, there are other socially accepted and supported groups that, perhaps unbeknownst to the supportive public, also have a propensity toward rape (Boumil, Friedman, and Taylor 1993; MacDonald 1995; O'Sullivan 1993; Sanday 1990; Schwartz and DeKeseredy 1997). One type of group, the college fraternity, has developed a notorious reputation for engaging in acts that demean women, including sexual assault (Martin and Hummer 1995; O'Sullivan 1993; Sanday 1990). Some researchers demonstrate that group think and notions of in-group superiority, coupled with group reinforcement of masculine behavior are the base elements that encourage group rape among fraternity members (Boumil, Friedman, and Taylor 1993; MacDonald 1995; O'Sullivan 1993; Sanday 1990; Schwartz and DeKeseredy 1997).

According to Martin and Hummer (1995), valued members of fraternities subscribe to narrow conceptions of masculinity that stress competition, athleticism, dominance, winning, conflict, materialism, ability to drink, and sexual prowess with women. Beyond the basic belief-systems inherent to many fraternities, there are some specific practices that fraternities utilize in their method of committing rape. Two are highly relevant and are hallmarks of fraternity rape; the excessive and manipulative use of alcohol, and the commodification of women (LeBeau and Mozayani 2001; Martin and Hummer 1995; Sanday 1990; Schwartz and DeKeseredy 1997). Both of these components need some illustration.

The use of alcohol by fraternity men is considered part of the group's social norm (Martin and Hummer 1995; Schwartz and DeKeseredy 1997). The use of alcohol to obtain sex from women is a common practice that is used to overcome reluctance among female victims (Martin and Hummer 1995; Sanday 1990). Several researchers have found, through firsthand interviews that alcohol is a major tool used to gain sexual mastery over women (Adams and Abarbanel 1988; Ehrhart and Sandler 1985; Martin and Hummer 1995; Sanday 1990; Schwartz and DeKeseredy 1997). In fraternity gang rape scenarios, many fraternity members make a point to target women who are especially vulnerable to alcohol or who have a drinking problem (LeBeau and Mozayani 2001; Sanday 1990; Schwartz and DeKeseredy 1997). Further, in many fraternity subcultures, such strategies for sex are not considered grounds for a lack of consent and therefore are not seen as rape (Martin and Hummer 1995; Sanday 1990). In fact, many fraternities contend that women who drink with fraternities actually desire such sexual activity but do not wish to be viewed as promiscuous, using the drunken incident as a cover to their deep seated desire to have sex with multiple partners (Sanday 1990).

The commodification of women refers to the practice of knowingly and intentionally using women as bait for new members, as servers of fraternity member's needs, and as sexual prey (Martin and Hummer 1995). Through the use of women as bait, the fraternity entices new members by "showing off" women friendly to the fraternity. The message is clear; join the fraternity and we can provide you access to beautiful women (Martin and Hummer 1995). Using women to serve the fraternity usually comes in the form of the "little sister" program, where such women are expected to attend and hostess fraternity parties and to stay around the fraternity house to make it more appealing (Martin and Hummer 1995). Fraternity men are referred to as "big brothers" and assist "little sisters" with such functions as the sorority rush, but the very names big brother and little sister serve to denote the status and rank of each of these persons within the fraternity/sorority power structure (Martin and Hummer 1995). This is important because it reinforces the masculine sub-cultural norms of many fraternities (Martin and Hummer 1995).

Lastly, little sisters are utilized as a sexual tool (Martin and Hummer 1995; Sanday 1990). Many of these women do not belong to sororities and thus have no peer support to refrain from sex if they should decide, for whatever reason, that they do not wish to engage in sex with a fraternity member (Martin and Hummer 1995; Sanday 1990). The access to women that the little sister system provides and absence of support to refuse sexual advances place these women in a particularly vulnerable position during potential sexual encounters with fraternity men (Martin and Hummer 1995; Sanday 1990).

Thus, fraternity norms and practices can heavily influence members to view the sexual coercion of women as a sport, contest, or a game (Martin and Hummer 1995). Further, some fraternity values serve to reinforce specific practices. Values that include a narrow definition of masculinity, an emphasis on competition, athleticism, dominance, and winning, coupled with the emphasis on sexual prowess with women, can reinforce the likelihood of rape among little sisters or other women desiring affiliation with the fraternity. The use of alcohol to commit rape is likewise reinforced by these value systems (Martin and Hummer 1995; Schwartz and DeKeseredy 1997; Sanday 1990). Given all of these coalescing variables, it should not be surprising that group rape is a potentially common occurrence among some fraternities (Martin and Hummer 1995; Sanday 1990).

Another group that is likely to be implicated in group rape is a sports team (Schwartz and DeKeseredy 1997). When looking at the wider question of rapes and sexual assaults of all types, various researchers agree on the basic notion that there is a social problem with male athletes sexually victimizing women (Schwartz and DeKeseredy 1997). Many of the same factors that affect fraternities are important with athletes as well (MacDonald 1995; Schwartz and DeKeseredy 1997). Much of the heightened propensity toward rape among athletic groups is centered on values of hypermasculinity that devalue men who are weak, equating them with being women (Schwartz and DeKeseredy 1997). In this case, women are essentially spurned and toughness is idealized as the prime concern for being a winner. The use of degrading language describing women, whether from coaches or among athletes in the locker rooms, are thought to create an environment that is charged with rape overtones (Schwartz and DeKeseredy 1997).

The effects of this sub-cultural climate are clearly illustrated by MacDonald (1995) in his description of the Spur Posse, a group of high school athletes in Lakewood, California who attracted national attention in 1991. This group consisted of eight members who were arrested for the rape of at least seven girls, ages ten to sixteen (Kimmel 1993; MacDonald 1995). The members of this group scored a point each time they had sex with a different girl. The top scorer had 66 points (MacDonald 1995). Some girls complained that they agreed to have sex with one member of the posse and were then intimidated into having sex with other members of the group (MacDonald 1995). What is interesting is that some of the parents of these boys defended their acts by blaming the victims. There were even reports that some posse members were congratulated when they returned to their classes (MacDonald 1995).

This example is interesting because it demonstrates how group rape among athletes is directly equated to a point scoring athletic event. This shows how subcultural norms among some athletic groups can pervade the sexual realm as well, construing sex as an "event" based on aggressive competition to win. This of course dehumanizes the victim of such conquest. What is even more tragic is that public support for athletes can then be translated as tacit approval for rape by athletes. This disturbing possibility shows how some group subcultural norms may be nothing more than extreme microcosms of values that are also held, albeit to a less grand scale, by the broader society as a whole.

It is also interesting to note that most incidents of group rape occur at the college level (Schwartz and Keseredy 1997). Thus, the vision of group rape being one committed by unsophisticated gangsters in the urban jungle is overly simplistic and serves to ignore a significant source of danger for many victims. Further, incidents are also known to occur among professional athletes (see *Victoria C. v. The Cincinnati Bengals*, a case involving the group rape of a female by numerous members of this professional football team) and other fraternal organizations such as the U. S. Navy (i.e. Tailhook Scandal involving college educated officers who are expected to demonstrate leadership qualities), demonstrating the prevalence of group rape among men belonging to organizations that emphasize athletic achievement, winning, and competition (Buchwald, Fletcher, and Roth 1993; Kimmel 1993; Schwartz and DeKeseredy 1997). Thus, group rape among athletes is a phenomenon that seems to occur throughout the spectrum of age and education levels, leaving room to speculate that it is perhaps the climate of athletic organizations that can encourage such activity.

The last type of rape to be discussed within this category is the phenomenon of gang rape. MacDonald (1995) points out that informal rituals of adolescent gangs are somewhat similar to puberty rites in primitive societies. In many primitive societies, puberty rites may require the male youth to commit rape to prove his manhood (MacDonald 1995). This idea of gender identification through rape has been cited in various public incidents of gang rape. "Gang bangs" or "trains" are a part of the social life of street gangs and serve as initiation rites and confirmation of loyalty and bonding to the gang (Chancer 1994; MacDonald 1995; Ullman 1999). The attack and gang rape of a young female jogger in New York City's Central Park in April 1989 is discussed by Chancer (1994) and demonstrates the manner in which such gangs may execute such rapes. It is important to note that gang rapes have been found to be characterized by fewer weapons, more night attacks, less victim resistance, and more severe sexual assault outcomes when compared with rapes committed by individuals (Ullman 1999). The distinction between gang rape and group rape may in fact be a bit blurred, but the term gang rape is typically reserved for rapes committed by street gangs who are criminally oriented rather than formal or professional groups who are typically created for purposes outside of the criminal enterprise.

Rape Defined as a War Crime

Rape as a war crime has been well documented throughout history (Allen 1996; Brownmiller 1975; Kadic 1995; Schwendinger and Schwendinger 1983). Some researchers have likened rape during warfare as an economic or political policy, reflecting the general value held of women during warfare (Allen 1996; Brownmiller 1975; Kadic 1995; Schwendinger and Schwendinger 1983).

The rape of women is not only a sexual act, but is again an act that is designed to demoralize, humiliate, and degrade its victim and those who care about the victim (Brownmiller 1975; Schwendinger and Schwendinger 1983). Rape when used in war becomes an instrument for terrorizing a conquered population, dominating a racial group, defiling an enemy, and seeking vengeance (Schwendinger and Schwendinger 1983).

Recorded accounts have exposed systematic rape by soldiers throughout history. Brownmiller (1975) provides an excellent historical overview of rape throughout ancient and modern warfare up until the 1970's. Within the work of a number of authors there are numerous written accounts and verbal narratives on rape during any number of wars (Allen 1996; Kadic 1995; Schwendinger and Schwendinger 1983). These reports tell of women who have been humiliated, raped, and murdered in front of their families and communities by invading armies (Allen 1996; Kadic 1995; Schwendinger and Schwendinger 1983).

With rape during warfare, the distinction is the manner in which the act is committed. For instance, when committed in public, there is an obvious motive of fear that is implicated. When done in seclusion, the multiple rapes by numerous soldiers demonstrate a savagery that injures the victim much more tragically than a given incident where a woman has sex with multiple sex partners. This is important, because the manner in which the act is committed exceeds the level of injury and force necessary for these male assaulters to simply gratify their sexual urges. Instead, the act is again designed to accomplish violent purposes of intimidation and humiliation (Allen 1996; Brownmiller 1975).

One of the most atrocious acts of warfare consists of the systematic raping of enemy women known as genocidal rape. Allen (1996) refers to incidents in Bosnia-Herzegovina and Croatia in describing these acts as a military policy of rape for the purpose of genocide. One manner in which this is executed is when Serb forces enter a Bosnian-Herzegovinian or Croatian village, take several women from their homes, rape them in public view, and then depart (Allen 1996; Kadic 1995). Another method of conducting genocidal rape that has been experienced during this war is when Bosnian-Herzegovinian and Croatian women held in Serb concentration camps are chosen at random to be raped, often as a prelude to ultimate death (Allen 1996; Kadic 1995). Yet another manner by which this gruesome act is perpetrated is through the use of rape/death camps (Allen 1996; Kadic 1995). Within these camps, the Serbs raped enemy women systematically for extended periods of time (Allen 1996; Kadic 1995). Such rapes were either part of torture preceding death or part of torture leading to forced pregnancy. Pregnant victims were then raped consistently until their pregnancies had advanced beyond the possibility of a safe abortion and were then released (Allen 1996). Thus, either through death of the victim or the forced pregnancy of a Serb child, the Serbian goal of genocide was perpetrated (Allen 1996). This Serbian war policy considers the child to be Serb and thus an accomplishment toward the genocidal goals of the Serbs (Allen 1996).

One must understand that the ultimate goal of this systematic rape was not sexual in nature, at least not exclusively. The underlying dynamic that motivated these rapes was one of violence and aggression to the enemy. Such violence was a methodical and systematically executed attempt to ultimately displace Serbian enemies. The fact that sexual gratification is included was of course valued by the perpetrators, but the long-term goal of this ghastly form of mass rape was to ultimately exterminate certain races of people. This then demonstrates how genocidal rape is in essence an assault against an entire people.

As was stated earlier in this discussion, rape is one of many acts of violence that humans may engage in. As such, the main distinguishing factor comes in the means of the severity of physical and psychological damage done to the victim (Bourque 1989). In the case of genocidal rape, the ulterior intention is to inflict physical and psychological damage to the specific victim, and to that victim's entire ethnic group. The sexual gratification, while instrumental in partly explaining the rape act, cannot explain such acts of genocidal rape in full. The level of violence and forethought go well beyond that necessary to meet sexual gratification needs. This point is important as this demonstrates the truly violent nature of the rape act itself, rather than emphasizing the sexualized nature of this crime as many rape myths tend to do. Recognition of rape as a form of assault is thus the first step in recognizing the crime against the victim and the actual criminal behavior of the perpetrator.

Conclusion

Sexual assault is a more contemporary term for the crime of rape. Social definitions of rape have been shown to be historically limited and narrow. Public understanding of rape has been affected by a variety of perceptions that demonstrate various biases affected by individual and group social beliefs. The tendency to explain incidents of rape that do not fall within such narrow definitions have become manifest through the form of rape myths. These myths are perpetuated throughout society and fail to acknowledge the varied forms of rape that exist. Further, these myths and their accompanying narrow definitions of rape serve to trivialize the experiences of those who have survived such traumatic and tragic injuries.

Lastly, it is through the clarification of the numerous definitions and distinctions of rape that a true understanding of the blanket term "sexual assault" will occur. This very term serves to denote the assaultive, and thus violent and aggressive nature of rape; being of course, coupled with a sexual component. But it is important for the public to understand that rape is not about simple sexual gratification, but is about the desire to dominate, exploit, and humiliate another person. Failure to acknowledge this is a failure to acknowledge the damage to the survivor that occurs during such trauma inducing experiences. Failure to acknowledge this is nothing less than a failure to acknowledge the victim.

References

Adams, A., and G. Abarbanel. *Sexual Assault on Campus: What Colleges Can Do*. Santa Monica, CA: Rape Treatment Center, 1988.

Allen, B. *Rape Warfare: The Hidden Genocide in Bosnia-Herzegovina and Croatia*. Minneapolis, MN: University of Minnesota Press, 1996.

Bartol, C. R. *Criminal Behavior: Psychosocial Approach* (5th ed.). Upper Saddle River, NJ: Prentice Hall, 1999.

Benedict, H. "The Language of Rape." In *Transforming a Rape Culture*, eds. E. Buchwald, P. R. Fletcher, and M. Roth. Minneapolis, MN: Milkweed Editions, 1993.

Boumil, M. M., J. Friedman, and B. E. Taylor. *Date Rape: What it is, What it Isn't, What it Does to You, What You Can Do About It*. Deerfield Beach, FL: Health Communications, Inc, 1992.

Bourque, L. B. *Defining Rape*. Duke University Press, 1989.

Brownmiller, S. *Against Our Will: Men, Women and Rape*. New York: Simon and Schuster, 1975.

Buchwald, E., P. R. Fletcher, and M. Roth. *Transforming a Rape Culture*. Minneapolis, MN: Milkweed Editions, 1993.

Burt, M. R. "Rape Myths and Acquaintance Rape." *In Acquaintance Rape: The Hidden Crime*, eds. A. Parrot and L. Bechhofer. New York: Wiley-Interscience Publication, 1991.

Chancer, L. "Gender, Class and Race in Three High Profile Crimes: The Cases of New Bedford, Central Park, and Bensonhurst." *Journal of Crime and Justice 17* no. 2 (1994): 167–187

Chappell, D. *Forcible Rape: A National Survey of the Response by Police (LEAA)*. Washington, DC: USPGO, 1977.

Dworkin, A. "I Want a Twenty-Four-Hour Truce During Which There is No Rape." In *Transforming a Rape Culture*, eds. E. Buchwald, P. R. Fletcher, and M. Roth. Minneapolis, MN: Milkweed Editions, 1993.

Ehrhart, J., and B. Sandler. *Campus Gang Rape: Party Games?* Washington, DC: Association of American Colleges, 1985.

Finkelhor, D., and K. Yllo. "Types of Marital Rape." In *Rape and Society: Readings On the Problem of Sexual Assault*, eds. P. Searles and R. J. Berger. Boulder, CO: Westview Press, Inc, 1995.

Groth, A. N. *Men Who Rape: The Psychology of the Offender*. New York: Plenum Press, 1979.

Kadic, Nina. "Dispatch from Bosnia-Herzegovina: A Seventeen-Year-Old Survivor Testifies to Systematic Rape." In *Rape and Society: Readings on the Problems of Sexual Assault*, eds. P. Searles and R. J. Berger. Boulder, CO: Westview Press, Inc, 1995.

Kimmel, M. S. "Clarence, William, Iron Mike, Tailhook, Senator Packwood, Spur Posse, Magic....and Us." In *Transforming a Rape Culture*, eds. E. Buchwald, P. R. Fletcher, and M. Roth. Minneapolis, MN: Milkweed Editions, 1993.

Krulewitz, J. E., and E. J. Payne. "Attributions About Rape: Effects of Rapist Force, Observer Sex and Sex Role Attitudes." *Journal of Applied Social Psychology 8*, (1978): 291–305.

LeBeau, M. A., and A. Mozayani. *Drug Facilitated Sexual Assault: A Forensic Handbook*. New York: Academic Press, 2001.

Lerner, M. J. *The Belief in a Just World: A Fundamental Delusion*. New York: Plenum Press, 1980.

MacDonald. *Rape: Controversial Issues*. Springfield, IL: Charles C. Thomas Publisher, 1995.

Martin, P. Y., and R. A. Hummer. "Fraternities and Rape on Campus." In *Rape and Society: Readings on the Problem of Sexual Assault*, eds. P. Searles and R. J. Berger. Boulder, CO: Westview Press, Inc, 1995.

O'Sullivan, C. "Fraternities and the Rape Culture." In *Transforming a Rape Culture*, eds. E. Buchwald, P. R. Fletcher, and M. Roth. Minneapolis, MN: Milkweed Editions, 1993.

Pagelow, M. D. Adult Victims of Domestic Violence: Battered Women. *Journal of Interpersonal Violence 7*, (1992): 87–120.

Paquin, G. W. "The Legal Aspects of Acquaintance Rape." *In Intimate Betrayal: Understanding and Responding to the Trauma of Acquaintance Rape*, eds. V. R. Wiehe, and A. L. Richards. Thousand Oaks, CA: SAGE Publications, 1995.

Parrot, A. and L. Bechhofer. *Acquaintance Rape: The Hidden Crime*. New York: Wiley-Interscience Publication, 1991.

Reid, S. T. *Criminal Law* (2nd ed.). New York: MacMillan Publishing Company, 1992.

Rotter, J. B. "Generalized Expectancies for Internal and External Control of Reinforcement." *Psychological Monographs: General and Applied, 80* no 1, 1966.

Sanday, P. R. "The Socio-Cultural Context of Rape: A Cross-Cultural Study." *Journal of Social* Issues 37, (1981*): 5–27.

Sanday, P. R. *Fraternity Gang Rape: Sex, Brotherhood, and Privilege on Campus*. New York: New York University Press, 1990.

Schwartz, M. D., and W. S. DeKeseredy. *Sexual Assault on the College Campus: The Role of Male Peer Support*. Thousand Oaks, CA: SAGE Publications, 1997.

Schwendinger, J. R., and H. Schwendinger. *Rape and Inequality*. Beverly Hills, CA: SAGE Publications, Inc, 1983.

Searles P. and R. J. Berger. *Rape and Society: Readings on the Problem of Sexual Assault*. Boulder, CO: Westview Press, Inc, 1995.

Steinem, G. "Erotica vs. Pornography." In *Transforming a Rape Culture*, eds. E. Buchwald, P. R. Fletcher, and M. Roth. Minneapolis, MN: Milkweed Editions, 1993.

Ullman, S. E. "A Comparison of Gang and Individual Rape Incidents." *Violence and Victims 14* no 2, (1999): 123–133.

U. S. Department of Justice. *Report to the Nation on Crime and Justice: The Data* (2nd ed.). Washington, DC: USGPO, 1988.

Victoria C. v. The Cincinnati Bengals, Inc., et al., Order No. C92-658 (Feb. 24, 1993).

Wiehe, V. R., and A. L. Richards. *Intimate Betrayal: Understanding and Responding to the* Trauma of Acquaintance Rape. Thousand Oaks, CA: SAGE Publications, 1995.

Williams, J. E., and K. A. Holmes. *The Second Assault: Rape and Public Attitudes*. Westport, CT: Greenwood Press, 1981.

Scoring with the Spur Posse

All is not well in Lakewood, Calif. True, it looks like the kind of place where there's a Brady Bunch in every split-level. But Lakewood is also the home of a group called the Spur Posse, 20 to 30 local boys who award themselves points for having carnal knowledge of young girls. The champion claims 66.

Lakewood suffers the usual problems of its time: shaky families, shaky employment rates. But there's nothing new about the Spur Posse. They're another chapter in the same old story: Young girl eager to be liked—or noticed, anyway—services young jock eager to prove his masculinity in the easiest, most obvious way. She gets a reputation as a "slut"; he gets a reputation as a "stud".

And if he's Kris Belman, he also gets a father who's busting with excuses. "Nothing my boy did was anything that any red-blooded American boy wouldn't do at his age.... Those girls around my son are giving it away." Bill Shehan's pretty defensive about his son, too. "I don't see these kids acting much different from professional athletes, like when Wilt Chamberlain came out in his book and said he had 20,000 women." By Mr. Shehan's book, that seems to make his son's behavior acceptable.

Nine members of the Spur Posse spent a few days in jail last week, accused of molesting and raping girls as young as 10. They say all the girls were willing; a few of the girls say they weren't. The one said to have had a 10-year-old partner is still inside, but the others are strutting their stuff through Lakewood High again.

"They're not the prettiest, you know," a recent graduate said of the girls who got the guys in trouble. "So they take whatever they can get," sniffed his girlfriend. So much for sisterhood.

"They pass out condoms, teach sex education and pregnancy-this and pregnancy-that," one high-scoring Posse member said of the Lakewood schools. "But they don't teach us any rules." More importantly, their parents don't appear to, either.

Before the rape charges, several of the boys were being investigated for theft, burglary and assault. But only seven parents arrived when the sheriff's department invited 22 families with kids in the Spur Posse to come in and discuss what their sons were up to. Now they know.

The New York Times (March 30, 1993). Section A; Page 22; Column 1.

Chapter 3

Drug-Facilitated Sexual Assault in Private and Professional Relationships: A Legal Perspective

Elizabeth Quinn DeValve

Introduction

Sexual assault by any means is a crime that legislatures and courts are addressing with a greater amount of seriousness in large part due to activism by feminist groups in the 1960s and 1970s. This is evident when looking at state statutes and relatively recent case law. Though this was not always the case for all types of sexual assault, particularly spousal sexual assault, it is evident that the trend is toward harsh punishment for those convicted of this crime. The crime of sexual assault, though definitions vary from state to state, can usually be described as a forceful act of sexual conduct when the assaulted has not given, or is not able to give, consent because of age, intoxicated status, being drugged, or mental capacity. Two phenomena that have come to the attention of legal scholars and academia alike are date rape (also known as acquaintance rape) and professional/therapist–client (professional–client) sexual misconduct. Legislation and litigation address the issues of date rape and professional–client sexual misconduct, but an area of extreme violation less examined involves sexual assaults through the use of drugs to incapacitate the victim for least resistance. As with sexual assault cases in general, obstacles remain that limit the ability of the prosecutor to successfully litigate a case. As will be explained, drug-facilitated sexual assault cases can be both easier and at the same time more difficult to prosecute.

It is the purpose of this chapter to offer a legal perspective of drug-facilitated sexual assault and sexual misconduct by either a private or professional individual through examining state statutes, case law and law reviews.

This chapter is traced along two separate lines to illustrate the direction of court holdings for cases involving drug-facilitated sexual assault. Because there are only a limited amount cases that illustrate criminal case decisions in regard to drug-facilitated sexual assault by professionals it is necessary to explore similar types of cases to determine where rulings may come on these issues. Legislation for sexual assault by private individuals exists for every state and guidelines against sexual misconduct for professionals exist within the major health-care and mental health professional associations. Both drug-facilitated date rape cases and cases in which therapists and other professional personnel were sued by patients alleging sexual assault while conscious are found in previous legal research and the holdings reflect the same disdain for inappropriate sexual contact. However, little exists on sexual misconduct/assault by professionals aside from the issue of malpractice insurance coverage. It is thought that together the two areas of date rape by private individuals through drug facilitation and sexual misconduct/assault cases filed by clients who were conscious during the assault against professionals will guide our understanding of drug-facilitated sexual assault by a professional in a patient-client relationship.

A brief review of private individual date rape will be discussed followed by a more extensive discussion of professional sexual misconduct or assault through drug facilitation.

Sexual Assault/Rape Statutes, Case Law and Law Review

State Statutes

Every state has in its criminal or penal codes something that identifies either sexual assault or rape as a felony offense. Additionally, alcohol and drug related issues intermixed with sexual assault are well represented in legislation as the following quote illustrates:

> The Model Penal Code (MPC) and most state penal codes directly address alcohol-related sexual assaults. Most codes contain sexual assault provisions that define rape to include situations in which the defendant has sexual intercourse with an unconscious person and

situations in which the complainant's ability to resist is substantially impaired by alcohol or drugs.

Section 213 of the MPC, for example, defines rape as a male having sexual intercourse with "a female not his wife" if:

(b) he has substantially impaired her power to appraise or control her conduct by administering or employing without her knowledge drugs, intoxicants or other means for the purpose of preventing resistance; or (c) the female is unconscious.

To determine how states outline their sexual assault statutes and to see where drug facilitation and professional misconduct are represented in those statutes a content analysis was completed on rape/sexual assault statutes for all 50 states and the District of Columbia. The analysis revealed that five categorizations were found: 1) common definition of rape along with specific mention of drugs as a means to incapacitate the victim and physician/therapist-client sexual misconduct (12 states); 2) common definition of rape along with specific mention of drugs and broad mention of professionals in government fields performing sexual misconduct (9 states); 3) common definition of rape as well as noted prohibition of the use of intoxicants to mentally incapacitate the victim (21 states); 4) common definition of rape only (6 states); and 5) common definition of rape and prohibition of professional sexual misconduct (3 states). It is obvious from this analysis that the states are taking the issue of incapacitation of a victim by use of intoxicants seriously and addressing it in their sexual assault/rape statutes.

Aside from alcohol, there are two drugs that are commonly associated as date rape drugs: Rohypnol and gamma-hydroxybutyrate (GHB). Rohypnol, or roofies, is the most common drug used to incapacitate an individual (in an acquaintance type relationship), for the purpose of engaging in sexual behavior. According to the Drug Enforcement Administration, Rohypnol is a benzodiazepine "used in the short-term treatment of insomnia and as a sedative hypnotic and preanesthetic medication". It is considered a Schedule IV drug, along with Valium, but is 10 times more potent. Some states have placed Rohypnol on a higher Schedule assignment to further indicate its potential for abuse and dangerousness. The cost on the black market is usually under $5.00 a tablet. Though it is not manufactured in the United States, or approved for prescription by medical professionals, it is smuggled in through Mexico and Latin American countries. Florida and Texas are the most affected states, probably because of their proximity to the smuggling countries. Perhaps this is why, at least in Texas, there are very explicit and strict guidelines in the Penal Codes in terms of sexual assault in conjunction with the use of this drug. The drug is now produced on the street as well as by Hoffman-La Rouche; therefore, those drugs produced on the street will not have the safety components added to Rohypnol as implemented by Hoffman-La Rouche, Inc. For the most part, the copycat drugs are brownish in color and odorless and dissolve quickly in liquids. GHB is just as potent of a drug and operates in a similar manner, however it can be used in liquid form.

Probably one of the most powerful pieces of federal legislation that exists to combat date rape through drug-facilitation is the "Drug-Induced Rape Prevention and Punishment Act", an amendment to the Controlled Substances Act. The Drug-Induced Rape...Act states, "a person who intends to commit a crime of violence and administers a controlled substance to a victim without the victim's knowledge shall be imprisoned for up to twenty years". This act specifically identifies Flunitrazepam, or Rohypnol, and GHB as the "date rape" drugs and suggests further study for proper classification of the drugs. Currently, the pharmaceutical company, Hoffman-La Rouche, Inc., who manufacture Rohypnol, are fighting against the DEA's proposal to list Rohypnol as a Schedule I drug, thereby criminalizing its existence in the United States.

Case Law on Rape/Sexual Assault Through Drug Facilitation by Private Individuals

Though case law on drug-facilitated sexual assault by private individuals is somewhat sparse, the combination of harsh sentences for the few cases examined and strict nature of state sexual assault/rape codes (previously mentioned) specifically criminalizing that behavior indicate intolerance for sexual assault through drug-facilitated means. The following example of acquaintance rape with the use of drugs illustrates this point.

In *Ortiz v. State* (1992), an individual was charged and convicted of aggravated sexual assault and sentenced to 65 years in prison because he and some "other men kidnapped two women at knifepoint, took them to a nearby house, locked the exits, forced them to take drugs and sexually assaulted them orally, vaginally and anally." It is evident from this case alone, that the actions of the defendant were perceived as morally reprehensible and deserving of extreme punishment. It is no doubt that the kidnapping and demand to ingest drugs worked together to secure such a severe sentence. This case demonstrates intolerance for drug-facilitated sexual assault.

A more recent case examines the issue of victim precipitation and subsequent standing to sue the seller of illegally purchased alcohol. In *K.R. v. Sanford* (2000) the female victim was the purchaser of alcohol in an illegal manner and after drinking with a former co-worker/friend and two acquaintances she was given a "roofie" to help her fall asleep. After taking the pill (in addition to previously drinking alcohol and snorting one line of cocaine) she woke periodically to find the three individuals mentioned sexually assaulting her. The court found that K.R. did in fact have standing to sue the establishment from which she illegally purchased the alcohol as an aggrieved/injured party.

These two cases illustrate that the court is sympathetic to the victim of drug-facilitated sexual assault when the assault is committed by an acquaintance. This demonstrates that the use of a drug to incapacitate a victim may place the seriousness level of sexual assault by an acquaintance at the same seriousness level as sexual assault committed by a stranger.

Case Law Indicating the Criminalization of Professional–Client Sexual Misconduct

The issue of professional–client sexual misconduct has been studied by individual attorneys, as well as, addressed by professional organizations. Pamela K. Sutherland, J.D., has established a very informative website on the topic of therapist-patient sexual misconduct (http://members.tripod.com/~PKSutherland/). She specifically investigates the relationship between sexual misconduct and insurance coverage for victims of sexual assaults committed by professionals in a therapeutic or advising relationship. Both the American Psychological Association and the American Psychiatric Association have guidelines that prohibit therapist-client sexual relations (Jorgenson and Sutherland 2000). Similarly, in 1991 the American Medical Association declared "it unethical for physicians to engage in sexual relations with patients during the course of the professional relationship" (Jorgenson and Sutherland 2000). Likewise, the American Bar Association discourages sexual relations between the lawyer and client (Silver 1999). Not until the latter half of the 20th century did there become more allegations of sexual misconduct by patients/clients. Most interesting, however, is the amount of case law that exists on this topic. Two issues stand out in case law on this topic. First, most cases deal with the topic of professional–client transference and counter-transference in the therapist-client relationship. Second, the majority of the cases are not submitted to determine the guilt of the abusive party, but instead to determine the liability of the abuser's malpractice insurance company. For the most part, these two issues intermix and are difficult to discuss separately. Within the therapist-client relationship transference is referred to as falling within the realm of the therapist's professional services, because it is a required part of the healing process. "Professional services" play a large part in determining insurance carriers' liability for professionals who chose to perform or participate in sexual misconduct with their patients, both in the psychiatric/psychological, other medical fields and non-medical type professions (Sutherland 2000; Silver 1999).

In *Cotton v. Kambly* (1980), the court stated that there is no need to distinguish between a therapist's mishandling of transference and other improper actions, such as the misadministration of drugs or a defective operation (Sutherland 2000). In therapist-client relationships where transference is the method employed by the psychotherapist to "cure" the client, that act is seen as identical to drug administration and such, as described above. "Many experts believe that it is not the sexual contact per se that harms the patient, but, rather, the erosion of boundaries and the consequent loss of the therapeutic help the patient needed when he or she sought treatment" (Sutherland 2000, 1).

In cases where it was determined that the sexual misconduct fell within the professional's "professional services" insurance carriers have been liable. More recently, however, some insurance carriers have "modified their policies to either limit or exclude coverage for damages caused by 'actual or alleged erotic contact'" (Sutherland 2000, 2).

Accordingly, "professional services" has limited the degree of insurance companies in other professional–client areas. In *Roe v. Federal Insurance Co.* (1992) the Massachusetts Supreme Judicial Court ruled that a dentist's sexual relations with a patient did not constitute professional services because it did not fall within the realm of his responsibilities to that patient. For that reason, his insurance company would not be held liable and the victim's only remedial course of action would be in a private tort lawsuit.

Further, when the act of sexual misconduct on the part of the professional falls both within and without the context of professional services, coverage by insurance is appropriate for the plaintiff's injuries. This theory was first applied in *Cranford Insurance Company v. Allwest* Insurance Company (1986), in which it was alleged that the victim's psychotherapist both abused the transference process and abandoned the client after the sexual misconduct, one action that fell within professional services and one that did not.

The very first case that addressed therapist sexual misconduct was *Zipkin v. Freeman* (1968), in which a psychotherapist mishandled a patient's transference by encouraging her to fall in love with him, taking her to "social outings, overnight trips and nude swimming parties"…engaging in "sexual relations with Mrs. Zipkin and convinc(ing) her to purchase a farm for him to work on…as a manual laborer, leave her husband, and then steal her husband's suits" for him to wear (Jorgenson and Sutherland 2000, 2). The court stated that it was clear that even had the nude swimming parties and sexual relations not taken place, Dr. Freeman negligently mishandled Mrs. Zipkin's transference, which could be seen as professional services, thus incurring restitution from Dr. Freeman's malpractice insurance. There are six more areas under which a professional can be held liable for his/her infliction of sexual assault as described by Jorgenson and Sutherland (2000): negligent infliction of emotional distress, intentional torts, breach of contract/breach of implied warranty, spousal claims, and employer liability. Also relevant is the time allowed for "discoverance" of the sexual misconduct and filing a claim against the professional for the inappropriate acts. A number of jurisdictions have adopted a "discovery rule" indicating that the patient may not be aware of the abuse while it is occurring, thus allowing for time after the discovery that the behavior was inappropriate for a victim to file (*Greenberg v. McCabe* (1978), *Coopersmith v. Gold* (1996)) (Jorgenson and Sutherland 2000). In a similar vein, some states and professional associations have outlawed professional–client relationships after the termination of services (Wisconsin, Colorado, California, Minnesota; American Psychological Association, American Psychiatric Association). One case on point for the logic of this argument is *Noto v. St. Vincent Hospital and Medical Center* (1990). In this case, the patient came to the hospital seeking to treat her drug abuse and "seductive behavior" (Jorgenson and Sutherland 2000, 9). Upon discharge, her therapist began sexual relations with her and turned her back on to drug use.

In addition to common law actions, criminal and civil laws exist in some states that address the issue of professional–client sexual misconduct. Studies indicate that between nine and fourteen states criminalize professional–client sexual misconduct and four states have adopted legislation that makes the behavior sanctionable in civil court (Rokosz 1999).

In terms of non-therapist professional sexual misconduct, in the last three to four decades there have been more and more allegations of physician misconduct. In *Hirst v. St. Paul Fire and Marine Insurance Co* (1984) the parents of a victimized teenage male brought a claim against their son's physician for sexual misconduct perpetrated on their son with the aid of drugs on several occasions. The court ruled that the insurance company was not responsible for paying out on the sexual misconduct committed by Dr. Donahue. The Idaho State Board of Medicine, to which the Hirst's first brought claim against Dr. Donahue, argued that the high dosage of certain drugs were contra-indicated for the injury suffered by the minor and were prescribed at that level for the soul purpose of incapacitating the client enough for the sexual misconduct to occur. The Board indicated that if malpractice included immoral conduct and criminal acts then the complainant's claims might have had merit. Because of this finding, the Hirst's brought suit against Dr. Donahue and ultimately a settlement was reached out of court between the two parties on a civil level. A monetary settlement was reached and when the Hirst's attempted to claim the compensation from the insurance company the court indicated the insurance company was not responsible for payment. In stark contrast, eight years later that reasoning was reversed in another case involving the same insurance company. In *St. Paul Fire and Marine Insurance Co. v. Shernow* (1992) the court "found the malpractice insurer liable for damages caused when a dentist gave his patient excessive doses of nitrous oxide and then sexually assaulted her" (Jorgenson and Sutherland 2000, 11). The court ruled that the issuance of nitrous oxide was negligent and fit within the context of "professional services" of the dentist.

Sometimes, the qualification that the sexual misconduct act be within the realm of "professional services", though somewhat making sense, sends the message that the assault is not inappropriate. In *Atienza v. Taub* (1987), the court ruled that sexual relations engaged in by the physician and patient were not inappropriate unless initiated by the physician. In *Jennings v. Friedman* (1989), it was further stated by a different court that the patient failed to state a claim because the assault did not occur within the realm of "professional services" and the physician did not state that the relations were part of the medical treatment necessary for her ailment.

Legal Research/Law Review on the Topic of Acquaintance Rape with Drug Facilitation

Before the drug Rohypnol was made available in the United States, some individuals were known to actively encourage and facilitate the intoxication of a woman with alcohol in order to have sex with her without resistance (Kramer 1994). Research indicates that women often do not report these cases because the individual is usually known to the assaulted and there is a sense of guilt and shame the victim feels after the fact (Bechhofer and Parrot 1991;Warshaw 1988). The intoxicated state of the victim does little to enhance her statement of the facts in that her credibility is de-valued through the mere fact that she "allowed" herself to become "out of control". With the use of Rohypnol, the same type of circumstances seem to occur...the victim often does not report the incident and the same feelings of guilt and shame are experienced after the fact...if the victim remembers what happened.

The typical case of drug-facilitated sexual assault with the use of Rohypnol is illustrated by Douglas Herring in his 1996 article on illicit smuggling of Rohypnol into the United States. The typical case is one in which the offender slips Rohypnol, or "roofie," into the victim's drink and within 30 minutes the victim becomes dizzy and incomprehensible. The victim physically cannot fend off the offender because the drug limits the motor ability of her arms and legs. Oftentimes, the victim does not remember the assault itself because the drug has an amnesiac component to it as well (Drug Enforcement Administration 2002; Herring 1996). Previous research suggests that drug tests were not available to test for Rohypnol in the system, but according to Pamela Sutherland (2000) this is no longer the case. In fact, subsequent law review articles have indicated that the pharmaceutical company that manufactures Rohypnol has offered to provide police departments with testing kits for the drug (Herring 1996). In addition, Hoffman-La Rouche, Inc. has added a safety component to the drug. Now if the drug is placed into an individual's drink it will turn the drink blue and give off an odor, thereby warning an unknowing potential victim that his or her drink has been tampered with (http://www.goaskalice.columbia.edu/0884.html).

Legal Research/Law Review on the Topic of Professional–Client Sexual Misconduct

The intimacy and trust inherent in a professional relationship speaks to the importance of prohibiting sexual contact between professionals and clients. Research has indicated that patients who have suffered sexual assault by a physician/therapist/clergy member/professor leave the situation feeling depressed, anxious, anger, hatred, inability to trust, worthlessness and so on (Sutherland 2000). Legal remedies, as discussed earlier, include civil and criminal suits, and licensing board complaints (Rokosz 1999).

Sutherland (2000), Silver (1999), and Rokosz (1999) report that approximately 10 percent of professionals engage in sexual misconduct with their patients/clients. It was stated that this might be a gross under-representation of the incidence because in another study it was indicated that physicians and psychiatrists reported treating between 12–62 percent of their patients that reported sexual relations with their previous medical or mental health professional. Rokosz (1999) indicates that between 1976 and 1986 sexual misconduct was listed as the most frequent cause of lawsuits against psychologists and that insurance carriers associated with the American Psychological Association spent a total of $7,019,165.00, or 44.8 percent of its insurance payouts, to victims of sexual misconduct.

From this information it seems that professional associations and the criminal justice system take the issue of professional–client sexual misconduct seriously. One could purport that drug-facilitated sexual assaults by the hands of professionals might fall more squarely under criminal statutes, or conversely, might be more successful in civil courts filing against the individual professional and/or licensing boards to actively work towards the suspension of the professional's license, if applicable.

Obstacles to Successfully Litigating Professional–Client Sexual Assault by Use of Drug-Facilitation

There are a number of problems associated with litigating a drug-facilitated sexual assault that are similar to "regular" sexual assault cases. The credibility of the victim, the obstacle to proving the victim was drugged and drugged by that specific person, the lack of memory or cognizance of the act until much later and the use of criminal sanctioning not always being the line of best recourse.

As with most types of sexual assault, litigating and winning a case is difficult for a number of reasons. In my work at a Rape Crisis Center over a two-year period, the following issues surfaced numerous times. Oftentimes it is difficult for the victim to prove that she did not consent to the sexual relations. In the case of professional–client sexual misconduct, it may be easier to prove for the mere fact that most, if not all, states, as well as, professional organizations admit that such relations are only detrimental.

It may be more difficult to prove that the perpetrator of the sexual assault in both private and professional realms actually drugged the individual if he/she did not get a blood test immediately after the sexual assault occurred.

It appears through the literature that not many victims report the crime immediately after the occurrence and/or do not consider it to be a crime until after a significant amount of time has passed. This will work against any such test for drugs in a victim's system.

Because of the side effects of certain drugs, and Rohypnol in particular, the victim may not have a memory of the assault, or rather a clear memory of the assault, and thus may not be seen to have a credible claim.

In the same way, a patient's credibility itself may be judged, in that if an individual is seeking psychotherapeutic help in the first place, he or she may be perceived as having emotional or mental problems and perhaps contriving the incident or bringing it on him or her self.

Finally, because of the small number of states creating codes or statutes penalizing professional–client sexual misconduct, the criminal and civil courts may not be the most satisfactory places to resolve the incident. As it appeared in the discussion above, the cases that made it to courts tended to revolve around whether the insurance company was liable for the professional's behavior and whether the victim was owed any restitution thereby. Not many cases existed that examined on face whether the act was wrong or not and prosecuting the professional for his/her misconduct.

Conclusion: A Victim's Legal Recourse

Overall it appears that case law, professional membership regulations, and state statutes suggest that both date rape (with and without drug-facilitation) and professional–client sexual misconduct are deemed inappropriate, if not criminal, in most states. Rape cases that showed the use of drugs to incapacitate the victim by the perpetrator often found the perpetrator guilty and 42 states specifically address the use of intoxicants to incapacitate the victim as criminal. Similarly, case law in terms of therapist-client sexual misconduct and some physician-patient sexual misconduct have indicated that medical boards/professional boards will not tolerate that behavior and the courts have admonished the perpetrators for acting in that manner (though not holding the insurance carriers liable).

It is thought that legislation and case law in the area of drug-facilitated professional–client sexual misconduct will follow what is seen for drug-facilitated date rape and professional–client sexual misconduct case law. The acts will be seen as inappropriate and damaging and the perpetrators will be penalized, through any number of means. It is felt that the court system may even continue on the course that it has taken in terms of statute of limitations in this respect as well, seeing that side effects of the drugs may be loss of memory and/or black outs with incomplete memories. The civil court route seems promising for the victim of professional–client sexual misconduct through drug facilitation, but obstacles still remain. Perhaps greater focus on this area in the future, and continued guidelines by professional organizations will ameliorate these actions on the part of professionals.

References

Atienza v. Taub, 194 Cal. App. 3d 388 (1987).

Bechhofer, L. and A. Parrot. "What is Acquaintance Rape?" In *Acquaintance Rape: The Hidden Crime ed.* L. Bechhofer and A. Parrot. New York: Wiley, 1991.

Columbia University. *Rohypnol "Roofie" and Rape*, retrieved 14 July 2002, http://www.goaskalice.columbia.edu/0884.html (13 July 1998).

Coopersmith v. Gold, 223 A. D. 2d 572 (1996)

Cotton v. Kambly, 101 Mich. App. 537 (1980).

Cranford Insurance Company v. Allwest Insurance Company, 645 F. Supp. 1440 (1986).

Drug Enforcement Administration. Flunitrazepam (Rohypnol), retrieved 14 July 2002, http://www.usdoj.gov/dea/pubs/rohypnol/rohypnol.htm. Greenberg v. McCabe, 453 F. Supp. 765 (1978).

Herring, D. "Comment, Getting High from South of the Border: Illicit Smuggling of Rohypnol as an Example of the Need to Modify U.S. Response to International Drug Smuggling After NAFTA." *Loyola of Los Angeles Int'l and Comparative Law Journal 841* no. 18, (1996).

Hirst v. St. Paul Fire and Marine Insurance Co., 106 Idaho 792 (1984).

Jennings v. Friedman, 875 F.2d 864 (1989).

Jorgenson, L. and Sutherland, P.K. Liability of Physicians, Therapists and Other Health Professionals for Sexual Misconduct with Patients, 10 October 2000, http://www.cs.utk.edu/~bartley/pamela/overview/overview1. html.

K.R. v. Sanford, 605 N.W.2d 387 (2000)

Kramer, K.M. "Comment, Rule by Myth: The Social and Legal Dynamics Governing Alcohol-Related Acquaintance Rape." *47 Stanford Law Review 47* no. 115, (1994).

Model Penal Code and Commentaries. Official Draft and Revised Comments. (MPC) (1985).

Noto v. St. Vincent Hospital and Medical Center, 160 A.D. 2d 656 (1990)

Ortiz v. State, 825 S.W. 2d 537 (1992)

Roe v. Federal Insurance Co., 412 Mass. 43 (1992)

Rokosz, G.J. "Comment, Princeton Insurance Co. v. Chunmuang—Does the Court's Result Signal a Need for Legislative Reform Broadening Malpractice Insurance Coverage for the Benefit of Victims of Physician Sexual Abuse?" *30 Seton Hall L. Rev. 30* no. 133, (1999).

Silver, M.A. "Comment, Love, Hate, and Other Emotional Interference in the Lawyer/Client Relationship." *Clinical Law Review 6* no. 259, (1999).

St. Paul Fire and Marine Insurance Co. v. Shernow, 222 Conn. 823 (1992)

Sutherland, Pamela K. Insurance Coverage in Massachusetts for Therapist-Patient Sexual Misconduct retrieved 10 October 2000, http://www.cs. utk.edu/~bartley/pamela/mass_insurance/massinsu1.html, (December 1996).

Sutherland, Pamela K. Attorney at Law Home Page, retrieved 14 July 2002, http://members.tripod.com/~PKSutherland/, (December 1996).

U.S. Drug-Induced Rape Prevention and Punishment Act, Enacted October 12, 1996.

Warshaw, R. *I Never Called it Rape: The Ms. Report on Recognizing, Fighting, and Surviving* Date and Acquaintance Rape. New York: Harper and Row, 1988.

Zipkin v. Freeman, 436 S.W. 2d 753 (1968)

PART II

The Victims

In the Words of a Rape Survivor

"One thing I always think about being a victim, now a survivor, I live a life sentence. Once I was a victim the first time I was stripped of my freedom. I haven't gotten that back in my fifty years. **Freedom.** They walk the streets and I live a life sentence. I'll live it to the day I die—I can't shake it."

"When both rapes happened, I learned the impact of **fear**—there was a knife in the first one and the second was physically violent so...I'm always worrying 'what if' ...so I try to avoid it at all costs."

"**Knowledge**—the more I would try to learn and read, the more I learned about rape. I would pick up bits and pieces. I would learn I was normal. Knowledge is the one thing that saved me."

"When a rape is reported, someone has to step in who can be **strong** for that person, because that person's not strong."

"You're kind of like a **leper**, too, if you've been raped."

KC
50 years of age
Survivor of 2 rapes—one at 14, one in her thirties

Chapter 4

Victim Response to Sexual Assault

Diane M. Daane, J.D.

Introduction

How a victim responds to a sexual assault depends on many different factors. The reaction will be affected by her age, life situation, personality, the circumstances of the rape, the response from those with whom she comes in contact immediately after the assault, the response of her family and friends, the response of the criminal justice system, and her own attitudes about rape. Many survivors have adopted society's traditional attitudes about rape, including many of the myths. If she believes in these myths, she may have greater difficulty understanding and integrating the rape into her life experiences.

Males and females can be sexual assault victims. Since the majority of known rape victims are female, and the majority of research involves female victims, the victim in this paper will be referred to by pronouns normally used to indicate a female. This is not intended to either deny the existence of male survivors or to trivialize the trauma experienced by male rape victims. However, information specific to male survivors is included. Limited research indicates that the responses of male victims of sexual violence are similar to the responses of female victims (Frazier 1993). The rapist will also be referred to as male for the same reasons.

Coping Behaviors at the Time of the Assault

Victim response before and during the actual attack also varies. Burgess and Holmstrom (1976) identified basic coping strategies used by sexual assault victims before the attack. The first strategy is cognitive assessment, which is where the victim copes with the threatened sexual assault by assessing the situation and determining possible alternatives. This may include looking for a means of escape or a plan to fight back, but most often it involves planning to remain calm so that the attacker does not panic and injure or kill the victim in response to her actions. The second coping strategy used by sexual assault victims before the attack involves verbal tactics, such as stalling for time or trying to talk their way out of the assault. Many victims try to reason with their attackers attempting to change their minds. Some victims try to gain sympathy from their assailant by telling him that they are pregnant or sick. Other victims use flattery, joking, sarcasm, and verbal aggression to prevent the attack. Another verbal strategy is to tell the rapist that someone is coming soon, or that the victim's brother, father, or boyfriend will find him and kill or hurt him. The majority of coping behaviors are verbal. The last coping strategy used before the attack identified by Burgess and Holmstrom is physical action. Physical action includes both physical resistance as well as running away.

There has been much debate over physical resistance by rape victims. Common law rape required victims to resist with all of their strength throughout the assault. Modern law has made significant changes in rape law, but many states still require some resistance by the victim as a measure of force used by the perpetrator. Many rape victims do not fight back physically because they fear that it will escalate the violence and result in greater injury to them. Ullman (1998) found that the type of resistance used by the victim matches the type of force used by the assailant. Forceful verbal resistance is a more common response to verbal attack. Physical resistance is more likely to be used by victims who are threatened with weapons or where the offender uses physical force initially.

Research indicates that women who physically fight back in response to the perpetrator's physical attack may experience less severe sexual abuse without suffering any greater injury than women who do not physically resist (Ullman 1998). Offender violence during and after the attack is related to the initial force used by the perpetrator rather than the resistance by the victim. Victim resistance in response to verbal or physical attacks may not lead to increased offender violence after the rape (Ullman 1998). It is important to remember that a victim who survives sexual assault responded appropriately. No amount of second-guessing can replicate the circumstances of the assault.

Many rape victims experience tonic immobility during their contact with their attacker (Galliano, Noble, Travis, and Puechl 1993). Tonic immobility "is an unlearned state of profound motor inhibition typically elicited by a high-fear situation that involves threat and/or restraint" (Galliano, Noble, Travis, and Puechl 1993, 110). Responses during tonic immobility include a catatonic-like posture, cessation of vocalization, tremors, periods of eye closure, a decrease in heart-rate, and an increase in body temperature and respiration. Tonic immobility has rarely been studied in humans, but has been linked to the immobility response experienced by many victims during a rape (Galliano, Noble, Travis, and Puechl 1993).

Earlier research referred to a similar response known as traumatic psychological infantilism (Symonds 1976). Psychological infantilism is induced by terror and results in helplessness that makes the victim appear friendly and cooperative. The victim experiencing psychological infantilism, also known as frozen fright response, will submit to the attacker in order to avoid being killed. Unfortunately, the victim's partner, family, friends, the police, hospital staff, crisis interveners, and even the victim may misinterpret this response. The survivor who misunderstands her own response during the rape itself may blame herself for her victimization and have a more difficult time recovering from the experience.

Some victims feel anger as well as fright, but normally if there is any hope for survival, fright will override anger and the victim will engage in submitting behavior (Symonds 1976). Anger may be shown through active or passive resistance. When anger is repressed we see passive resistance patterns that appear in the form of crying, slowness to obey commands, and the appearance that they are unable to understand exactly what is demanded of them. Passive patterns of resistance also include verbal attempts to make the rapist feel guilty or to appeal to his conscience in order to coerce him to cease the attack (Symonds 1976).

Active patterns of resistance attempt to produce in the attacker a fear of being hurt or apprehended. Since active, physical aggression has traditionally been socially disapproved for women, the rape victim's active patterns of resistance may also be verbal, though this may vary with the age of the victim (Symonds 1976). The victim's response at the time of the rape may have a substantial impact upon her ability to cope with the experience and her ultimate ability to recover from the incident.

Burgess and Holmstrom (1976) also identify coping strategies used by sexual assault victims during the attack. One coping strategy is the cognitive strategy where a victim focuses on something else during the attack. This helps victims to avoid the reality of the event and to focus on their own survival.

This coping strategy helps them to remain calm and to prevent provoking additional violence. Many victims will concentrate on memorizing details, such as the assailant's face or general appearance; others concentrate on advice they have been given on how to cope with such an occurrence. Compliance is often used to survive the attack and to get through it.

Coping strategies during the attack also include verbal strategies and physical action similar to the strategies used before the attack, such as screaming for help, talking to the attacker to try and calm him, threatening him, running away, and struggling with the attacker. Victims who struggle often struggle up to the point of penetration, and then realize that it is hopeless, so they stop struggling to avoid any further injury (Burgess and Holmstrom 1976).

Not all coping behavior is voluntary (Burgess and Holmstrom 1976). Victims report physiological responses such as choking, gagging, nausea, vomiting, pain, urination, hyperventilating, and losing consciousness. It is interesting that some rape prevention theorists and self-defense enthusiasts advocate responses such as urinating, defecating, and vomiting if attacked by a rapist. It is the rare victim who can engage in these behaviors at will, especially under such adverse circumstances.

Victims of drug-facilitated rape are incapacitated by the drug and unable to sense danger or employ coping strategies (Fitzgerald and Riley 2000). They are disabled and overpowered by an invisible drug (usually Rohypnol or GHB) slipped into their drink that renders them unconscious. Some victims of drug-facilitated rape remember brief, intermittent periods of awakening during their assault. They were aware of their surroundings, but were unable to move or speak before they passed out again.

Response After the Assault

Coping behavior is also important immediately after the attack. The victim must seek safety by escaping from the rapist, freeing herself from where she has been left, or securing her location. Generally she also tells others of her need for help or safety. When victims of drug-facilitated rape regain consciousness, sometimes hours later and in a different location, some are unsure if they have been sexually assaulted, while others find signs of their rape, such as being undressed, semen stains on their bodies, and/or physical trauma (Fitzgerald and Riley 2000). The victims were not only unconscious during their assault, but Rohypnol causes amnesia for the time period when the drug is in effect. Many drug-facilitated rape victims do not seek assistance because they are still impaired by the drug even after they regain consciousness and they are unable to recall exactly what happened.

There is a lack of consensus in the literature regarding the precise nature of the victim's reaction to a rape experience. The more recent literature often ignores the issue completely. However, there is agreement on some issues to victim response to rape. There is agreement that rape is a highly traumatic crisis causing disruption for the victim physically, behaviorally, emotionally, and interpersonally. There is also agreement that the victim's immediate reaction to rape is indicative of extreme disruption, and that long-term effects of the assault are fairly significant (Gilmartin-Zena 1985). This is generally true for all victims, regardless of ethnicity (Arellano, Kuhn, and Chavez 1997).

Rape-Related Posttraumatic Stress Disorder

Rape is a horrible, unspeakable event in the lives of victims. Most survivors suffer from distress symptoms and psychological harm from the trauma of rape. Very little attention was given to rape and the impact of rape on the victims before the women's movement of the 1970s. It was at this time that it was first recognized that women in civilian life suffer from post-traumatic problems. Many did not view post-traumatic stress, in general, as a credible problem. It was not until 1980 that the American Psychiatric Association included Posttraumatic Stress Disorder in its official manual of mental disorders (Posttraumatic Stress 2001).

Posttraumatic Stress Disorder involves the development of specific symptoms after an event that threatened death or serious bodily injury, or threat to one's physical integrity (American Psychiatric Association 2000). To meet the diagnostic criteria, the victim's response to the assault must involve intense fear, helplessness, or horror. The symptoms must include persistent reexperiencing of the assault, persistent avoidance of reminders of the rape, numbing of general responsiveness, and persistent symptoms of increased arousal. These symptoms must be present for more than one month and they must cause significant distress or impairment in social, occupational, or other important areas of the victim's life. Since rape involves the intentional actions of another human being rather than a natural disaster or other less personal trauma, the trauma may be especially severe or long lasting. The greater the intensity of the assault, the greater the chances the victim will develop Posttraumatic Stress Disorder.

Under the diagnostic criteria, reexperiencing the assault can take several different forms. The survivor may have repeated thoughts of the assault, or distressing dreams that are related to her victimization. Occasionally, a victim has flashbacks and behaves as though she is experiencing the attack at the moment. These flashbacks are often associated with some cue related to the incident, anniversaries of the rape, or criminal justice proceedings. Cues related to the rape are things that trigger a reminder of assault. A rape victim who is attacked by a man wearing a dark blue shirt may recall or reexperience the rape whenever she sees a man in a dark blue shirt. Cues are often visual, but can be associated with any sense, such as a scent or sound. Perhaps the attacker was wearing cologne or she heard a train whistle in the distance. Now every time the victim smells that cologne or hears a train whistle, she recalls or relives the attack.

Survivors who experience Posttraumatic Stress Disorder also avoid thoughts, feelings, or conversations about the rape, and avoid activities, situations, or people who cause her to recall her attack. For example, a victim who is assaulted while leaving the library may avoid the library, or a victim who is raped while on a date may stop dating. She will avoid situations where cues that will trigger recollection of the event are present.

Shortly after the rape, victims often experience psychic numbing, where their responses to the outside world are reduced. They may no longer wish to participate in activities that they enjoyed before their sexual assault, and may feel emotions less intensely than before the assault. Emotions related to sexuality, intimacy, and closeness are the most common areas for rape victims to experience a diminished capacity. Many victims also feel a sense of detachment from other people, and the feeling of a shortened lifespan. They may feel that their family and friends just don't, or can't, understand. They may not see any future for themselves.

Sexual assault survivors with Posttraumatic Stress Disorder are more anxious than before the assault. They may have nightmares, irritability, outbursts of anger, difficulty concentrating, or trouble sleeping. They may be unable to complete tasks, be extremely cautious, or be startled easily.

Attribution

Self-Blame

Who a victim blames for her sexual assault is referred to as attribution. Many victims blame themselves for the rape. Self-blame includes behavioral self-blame, which is based on the victims' belief that their behavior in some way brought about their rape. They believe that if they had done something differently, they would not have been assaulted. Perhaps they should not have slept with the window open, worn a short skirt, or accepted a date with someone they did not know very well. They may believe that if they fought the attacker, or fought harder, they would not have been sexually assaulted. Self-blame also includes characterological self-blame. With characterological self-blame, the victim believes that she was victimized because of her character. Self-blame is reinforced by society's myths about rape. It is not unusual for the police, hospital personnel, the victim's family and friends, coworkers, and the public to blame the victim. Ullman (1996) found that victims who experience a negative reaction when they disclose their victimization to others were more likely to blame themselves for the incident. Disapproving attitudes of those with whom the victims confide contribute to the victims' feelings of self-blame, especially if they already believe in the myths.

Certain types of victims are more likely to engage in self-blaming following a sexual assault. Society tends to be more supportive of victims of stranger rape who lead conservative lifestyles. There also tends to be more support and less blame for sexual assault victims who experience high levels of additional violence during the attack. Less blame by society often results in less self-blame. Victims of acquaintance rape generally receive more societal blame and are more likely to blame themselves than victims of stranger rape (Katz and Butt 1988 as cited in Arata 1999). Victims of drug-facilitated rape often have feelings of guilt or self-blame because they were drinking when they were drugged (Fitzgerald and Riley 2000). A history of child sexual assault or incest is also associated with greater self-blame after rape (Frazier 1991).

Galliano, Noble, Travis, and Puechl (1993) found that victims who were immobile during their assault held significantly stronger beliefs that greater resistance on their part would have stopped the rape and would also have decreased disbelief by others that they were raped. Survivors' immobility at the time of their victimization may lead to greater self-blame as well as less supportive responses by those to whom they disclosed their rape. The responses of others often have a dramatic impact on the survivors' feelings of self-blame, adjustment, and recovery.

Self-blame also leads to devaluation of self (Morrow and Sorrel 1989). Incest and sexual assault victims often see themselves as cheap or sexually devalued. Reaction of others after victim disclosure has a significant impact on self-blame and devaluating one-self for sexual abuse and assault victims. For childhood incest victims, response to disclosure by the mother and the perpetrator have a dramatic impact on the survivors' perception of self (Morrow and Sorrel 1989). Victims blame themselves less when their mother is supportive and the perpetrator accepts responsibility for the abuse.

Some theorists believe that a victims' feelings of guilt and self-blame are in fact defense mechanisms that help them to cope with the rape (Evans 1978).

If the victim believes that the rape was her fault, especially if she is experiencing behavioral self-blame, then she believes that by changing her behavior, she can prevent this from ever happening to her again. The thought of experiencing another sexual assault is generally intolerable for a rape victim. By believing that they can prevent a future assault, they are able to restore some sense of control and reduce their feelings of vulnerability.

Recent studies dispute the theory that behavioral self-blame is helpful for a sexual assault survivor. Frazier (2000) found that behavioral self-blame is not associated with the belief that future rapes can be prevented or are less likely by changing behavior. Frazier further found that a victim's perception about whether she could have prevented her assault is unrelated to the opinion that future assaults can be controlled or prevented. Many experts believe that guilt and self-blame by the victim prevent recognition of the trauma they have experienced and that it interferes with her ability to cope with crisis. Frazier recommends that sexual assault survivors distinguish between the responsibility for being raped and control over the future. Victims should be encouraged to decrease vulnerability without blaming themselves for past incidents. Whether self-blame is behavioral or characterological, it is associated with greater stress immediately after the rape, increased symptoms, and poorer long-term recovery.

Both behavioral, sometimes referred to as situational, and characterological self-blame are common in sexual assault survivors. Both types of self-blame are associated with greater distress both immediately after the rape and over time. Both are also associated with greater use of self-destructive coping strategies, increased symptom levels, and higher rates of Posttraumatic Stress Disorder (Arata 1999). Survivors who blame the assault on their own character, or on society tend to feel that sexual assaults in the future are likely and less controllable (Frazier 2000). Victims who blame themselves for the rape are often perceived by others as less adjusted and as more responsible for the rape, which can compound how they already feel about themselves and can negatively affect recovery (Thornton, et al. 1988).

External Blame

When a sexual assault survivor attributes her victimization to external factors, such as society, it is referred to as external attribution. Research indicates that rape victims blame external factors the most for their rape, followed by behavioral self-blame, then characterological self-blame (Frazier 2000). While most treatment programs for rape victims encourage blaming external factors for the assault, external blame is not always conducive to recovery. Blaming external factors often leads a victim to believe that bad things happen and that there is nothing that can be done to prevent it. Higher levels of hostility are often found in survivors who blame society. External attribution is also associated with high levels of anxiety and depression. Both behavioral self-blame and blaming society are strongly associated with depressive symptoms (Frazier 2000).

Coping Strategies After the Assault

Coping strategies used by sexual assault survivors often have a significant impact on their ultimate recovery. Research has tried to identify which coping strategies are the most effective in aiding victim recovery. Some coping strategies are actually associated with greater symptom levels in the survivor and a longer recovery period. The type of coping strategy used and its effectiveness are influenced by many factors. Several coping behaviors have been identified, but we still know very little about the coping process used by sexual assault victims.

Minimization

One coping strategy involves minimizing the seriousness of the assault and downplaying the violence and horrifying aspects of it (Burgess and Holmstrom 1979, Adaptive). Victims using this method of coping are less likely to seek help or support from others because they want to reduce the focus on the assault and act as though the incident was not as traumatizing as it was. The research is mixed on the effectiveness of minimization as a coping strategy.

There may be a greater tendency for African American women to minimize their assault because they believe that their inner strength to survive economic, racial, and gender oppression will get them through the aftermath of their assault (Neville and Pugh 1997). Staying strong and minimizing their trauma may be an adaptive coping strategy, but it places added stress on the survivor who must cope with their assault without assistance.

Cognitive Coping

Some victims cope by trying to make sense of the assault and explaining why it happened and why it happened to them (Arata 1999). Many victims will dwell on the incident going over every detail or reliving the event over and over. Cognitive coping that involves attributing blame is sometimes referred to as a cognitive appraisal rather than cognitive coping.

Avoidance

Other survivors try to forget about the rape. They try not to think about the assault and avoid any cues that would remind them about it. These survivors often sleep excessively or stay very busy. Avoidance is associated with greater levels of psychological distress and with social adjustment problems (Frazier and Burnett 1994). Avoidance is more likely to be used by sexual assault survivors who experienced negative reactions from others when they disclosed information about their assault (Arata 1999). There may also be greater use of avoidant coping by rape victims who are also survivors of childhood sexual abuse (Arata 1999).

Nervous/Anxious Coping

Being irritable, nervous and anxious is another coping mechanism. Survivors who engage in nervous/anxious coping are more likely to experience greater feelings of fear and negative mood states (Burr and Katz 1987 as cited in Frazier and Burnett 1994). They often experience more physical symptoms. Victims who have also experienced childhood sexual abuse are more likely to cope using nervous/anxious methods than victims who do not have a history of sexual abuse (Arata 1999).

Withdrawal

Some victims withdraw and stay at home with very little social contact. Withdrawal is associated with greater symptom levels, including fear, depression, and sexual dissatisfaction. Research indicates that fewer sexual assault survivors choose withdrawal as a means of coping with their attacks over other coping mechanisms (Frazier and Burnett 1994).

Taking Precautions

Taking precautions is one of the most common coping strategies used by rape survivors. This includes locking doors, not opening the door to a stranger, putting bars on the windows and moving to a safer location. Making lifestyle changes such as quitting drinking or being careful about where they go is also a form of taking precaution. While taking precaution is reported to be helpful by many survivors and is associated with lower symptom levels, it is not the most effective coping strategy associated with recovery (Frazier and Burnett 1994).

Expressive Strategies

Other survivors cry or express their feelings openly to trusted family members, friends, and counselors. Expressive coping is significantly associated with fewer trauma symptoms (Arata 1999), and is commonly mentioned by rape victims as helpful in their recovery process (Frazier and Burnett 1994). Expressive coping is also more likely to facilitate social support, which is identified by rape victims as very helpful and is clearly identified with better adjustment (Frazier and Burnett 1994). Social support is particularly important for rape victims because it helps to alleviate self-blame and because society in general may not be supportive due to the rape myths. It is important to recognize that social support is helpful for all sexual assault survivors, not just the survivors who choose to talk about the incident.

A survivor who chooses to talk about their assault within the first few days is most likely to tell her boyfriend, mother, female friends, or sister. Victims rate the sexual assault nurse examiners and their sisters as the most supportive (Frazier and Burnett 1994). Frazier and Burnett found husbands and male relatives to be the least frequently confided in by survivors, but other males were confided in as often as females, with males being rated as supportive, but less supportive than women.

Stress Reduction Techniques

Meditation, listening to music, long hot baths, drawing, and other stress reduction techniques are associated with fewer symptoms and better adjustment than staying at home and withdrawing (Frazier and Burnett 1994).

Self-Destructive Strategies

Some victims turned to self-destructive behaviors such as drug and alcohol abuse, smoking, and/or excessive eating. These coping behaviors are associated with longer recovery and more psychological symptoms such as depression, fear, and anxiety. Sexual assault is associated with suicide attempts by survivors, especially those who were subjected to oral and genital rape (Bridgeland, Duane, and Stewart 2001). Self-blame and guilt about the assault are also related to greater frequency of suicide attempts. Research on men who have been sexually assaulted reveals that they tend to have higher levels of depression than non-assaulted males and are also more likely to develop a dependence on alcohol after the assault (Larimer, Lydum, Anderson, and Turner 1999).

Age may be a factor related to the use of self-destructive strategies. Unwanted sexual activity during childhood or adolescence is associated with several psychological symptoms as well as with self-destructive behaviors such as suicide ideation, self-mutilation, binging or purging, increased voluntary sexual activity, and unsafe sexual practices (Morrow and Sorrel 1989). Saunders (1999) found increased substance abuse among child rape victims even into adulthood, and speculated that it may be a way of coping with abuse-related memories or the symptoms associated with depression and Posttraumatic Stress Disorder. Research comparing sexually active adolescent boys and girls who were forced into sexual activity found girls' responses included fighting, increased sexual activity, suicidal intent, and repeat pregnancies. Boys' responses included suicidal intent, increased sexual activity, and laxative abuse (Shrier, Pierce, Emans, and DuRant 1998). Type, severity, and duration of abuse are predictors of low self-esteem, depression, and negative behavior in incest victims (Morrow and Sorrel 1989). Negative behaviors included self-destructive coping behaviors such as attempted suicide, self-mutilation, drug and alcohol use, and promiscuousness.

Finding Positive Meaning

Finding positive meaning is another strategy that sexual assault survivors use to cope with their situation. Finding positive meaning includes appreciating life, being more assertive, reevaluating goals, strengthening relationships, being more cautious, taking better care of one's self, and growing spiritually in response to the rape. Finding positive meaning does not mean that the victims see their rape as a positive thing, only that they can continue to see the world in a positive light despite their assault. Individuals who are able to find positive meaning in tragic events are more likely to cope more successfully (Frazier 2000).

While feelings of guilt and many of the coping strategies used by sexual assault victims are not part of the diagnostic criteria for Posttraumatic Stress Disorder, they are associated with it, particularly in cases where rape is the traumatic event. Coping strategies and symptoms associated with Posttraumatic Stress Disorder are self-destructive and impulsive behavior, social withdrawal, hostility, and feeling constantly threatened.

Child Sexual Abuse or Prior Sexual Assault and Coping

Sexual abuse as a child or prior sexual assaults play a major role in the survivor's coping strategies and ultimate recovery from a recent sexual assault

(Arata 1999). Adult rape victims with a history of child sexual abuse generally have higher initial levels of distress and longer recovery times. Survivors with a history of sexual abuse are more likely to blame the assault on their character and to use negative coping strategies, such as avoidance, withdrawal, and self-destructive behaviors. They have higher symptom levels and longer recovery. Repeat victims who believe that they were victimized because of some character trait were more likely to adopt self-destructive coping behaviors, whereas, those who believed that external factors were to blame for their assault were more likely to use expressive coping and had fewer symptoms (Arata 1999).

The long range effects of child sexual abuse include diverse coping methods, lasting emotional problems, and high risk behaviors and suicide (Bridgeland, Duane, and Stewart 2001). Sexual abuse during childhood dramatically increases the risk for development of future psychological problems, adult depression, and Posttraumatic Stress Disorder (Saunders 1999).

Recovery from Sexual Assault

Several theorists labeled and identified stages or phases of recovery for rape survivors. These phases were originally identified as the acute phase and the long-term process by Burgess and Holmstrom (1974) in their classic article identifying Rape Trauma Syndrome. Some theorists divide recovery into three stages while others divide recovery into six or seven stages. This chapter will discuss only the commonalities of the literature on phases of recovery; it will not detail each author's interpretation. What is important to understand is that there is an acute and long-term recovery process as a result of an attempted or a completed sexual assault, and that the process lasts for months or years after the rape.

Acute/Impact Phase

The first phase of recovery is the Acute/Impact Phase that occurs during the period immediately following the rape. It may last for several days. During the initial phase the victim is generally experiencing an overwhelming sense of shock and is unable to believe what she has just gone through. She often has the feeling of total helplessness and powerlessness (Burgess and Holmstrom 1974). No one is ever prepared to experience such a traumatic event. The victim is also experiencing gross anxiety, feelings of total loss of control, confusion and a sense of unreality. She feels very vulnerable. Victims of drug-facilitated rape often suffer a more extreme sense of powerlessness due to their unconscious state during the attack and their lack of ability to recall what happened (Fitzgerald and Riley 2000). Guilt and shame are also fairly universal feelings immediately after a sexual assault. The experience itself will often bring on exhaustion, but she may not be able to sleep due to muscle tension or edginess.

One of the primary victim responses at this phase is extreme fear, sometimes bordering on panic. Many victims report that they believed that they would be killed. Their entire sense of safety has been shattered. Victims also fear retaliation by the rapist and that no one will believe them. Anger is not a primary emotion at this stage. Anger typically surfaces at later stages in the recovery process. When victims do feel anger, it is often aimed at themselves in a form of self-blame for putting themselves in a position to be raped or for not offering more resistance. Their anger may be repressed and be experienced as guilt or shame. Women traditionally have been expected to be passive and express less aggression, which often leads to anger being transformed into culturally supported self-blame (Notman and Nadelson 1976). While little research has been conducted on male survivors of sexual assault, studies that have been done find that males report similar responses as females, with one exception. Anger is a more common response to rape by male victims. Frazier (1993) found that males exhibit more depression and hostility than female victims, concluding that her results were consistent with the clinical data that males are more likely to react with anger.

Immediately after the assault, the victim is also faced with concerns about sexually transmitted diseases, the gynecological examination, and pregnancy as a result of the rape. If she plans to prosecute her attacker, she also has to undergo evidence collection for the rape kit and interviews while trying to understand the criminal justice process. She will endure many trying moments at a time when she is likely to be both physically and emotionally exhausted. Rape victims who do not report physical injury often experience soreness and bruising after the assault and often suffer from other symptoms such as nausea, stomach pains, loss of appetite, vaginal discharge, and an itchy, burning sensation upon urination. Survivors forced to perform oral sex may suffer oral irritation and throat infections, while victims of anal penetration often experience rectal bleeding and/or pain (Posttraumatic Stress 2001).

Outward Adjustment Phase

During the next phase of recovery through which a sexual assault survivor passes, she appears to have adjusted to the event. This phase is often referred to as the Outward Adjustment Phase, and may last for weeks or months (Posttraumatic Stress 2001). In reality, the victim rarely has adjusted well at all. She feels pressure from society to return to her previous lifestyle and appears to have adjusted. Returning to the normal routine as soon as possible denies the impact of the highly personal and violent nature of rape. The sexual assault victim is generally in psychological denial, with little insight into her situation. She tends to approach life very superficially and mechanically.

The victim continues to feel the same emotions that she felt immediately after the rape; however, these feelings generally will be less intense. In addition, victims often feel alienation, isolation, and depression. They may also experience nightmares, sleeplessness, flashbacks, and anxiety caused by some small cue that reminds them of the rape (Posttraumatic Stress 2001). These cues may be such things as being alone, darkness, a male whose appearance is similar to her attacker, or the make of a car in which the assault occurred. Many victims begin to avoid situations where those cues might be present. This aspect of the aftermath of sexual assault may be different for victims of drug-facilitated rape. Because they cannot remember what happened, they have to cope with a gap in their memory. "They experience the horror, powerlessness, and humiliation of not knowing what was done to them. They can only imagine what happened" (Fitzgerald and Riley 2000, 12).

The rape victim may also experience physical symptoms such as headaches, stomach or gastrointestinal problems, dizziness, unintentional weight loss, difficulty in breathing, and sexual dysfunction. Emotional responses include moodiness, decreased concentration, crying spells, tension, sadness, decreased self-confidence and self-esteem, and feelings of being out of control (Gilmartin 1985). She may also feel embarrassment and humiliation. She may want revenge, even though many victims blame themselves.

Depression Phase

The next phase, called the Depression Phase, for the sexual assault victim includes the same responses, but with some adjustment. She may suffer from obsessive memories, low self-esteem, and fear that she will not be able to bring her life back into control (Posttraumatic Stress 2001). It is at this time that the survivor tends to make lifestyle changes. She may move, change jobs, change phone numbers, refuse to go out alone or at night, and change patterns of work, studying or socializing. These are also often referred to as behavioral changes. It is at this time that victims begin to experience some interpersonal problems. She will often begin to experience difficulty in relationships with her husband or boyfriend, parents, children, employer, and/or friends. This phase may last for days or months.

Integration and Resolution Phase

Eventually the survivor reaches the phase where she feels anger, the Integration and Resolution Phase (Posttraumatic Stress 2001). Generally she has shifted the blame and anger from herself to the rapist. Her anger may also be directed toward the police, prosecutor, society, her counselor, or males in general. She is generally still anxious and depressed, and often lacks trust in men. She frequently wants someone to suffer for what has happened to her. However, the anger is rarely expressed in aggressive behavior. This phase may last months to years.

The victim who can successfully integrate the rape into her life experiences will also experience some sense of resolution (Forman 1980). She will finally be able to put the experience behind her, and will even be able to discuss it without intense feelings.

While several phases may be identifiable, it does not necessarily mean that each rape victim experiences each phase in sequence, or that each phase is experienced only once. It is common for a rape victim to have setbacks when she experiences another trauma, and especially when she again becomes involved in the criminal justice processing of her rape case. It is not unusual for a victim to experience extreme trauma during the trial.

Early theorists believed that most rape victims were able to accomplish resolution in a fairly short period of time. Unfortunately, recovery takes a substantial period of time, and for some victims, resolution where she returns to pre-rape levels of functioning never occurs. Kilpatrick, Resick, and Veronen (1981) found that victims continue to suffer from the effects of sexual assault for at least one year after the rape. Many problems experienced post rape are significant, but the primary problems are typically rape-related fear and anxiety. Kilpatrick, Resick, and Veronen further found that the bulk of improvement by rape victims occurs in the first three months following the rape. They found no significant difference in functioning between the three-month, six-month, and one-year time periods.

A sexual assault survivor's response to victimization and recovery depends on numerous factors, including age, life situation, prior abuse, and circumstances of the assault. It is suggested that life stage is a significant factor in adjusting to trauma. According to Notman and Nadelson (1976), younger victims, single victims, divorced or separated victims, and middle-aged victims experience more serious concern over their independence after a sexual assault. Research by Zweig, Crockett, Sayer, and Vicary (1999) suggests that greater levels of violence have more negative impact on sexual assault survivors' psychological and psychosocial adjustment.

Life situation may create a complex set of factors affecting the survivor's response. Homeless women often suffer a pattern of abuse beginning in their childhood. When a homeless woman is sexually assaulted, there is a strong possibility that it is not the first time she has been abused or suffered from sexual violence (Stermac and Paradis 2000). In addition, research shows that homeless women are more likely than housed women to be raped by a stranger, in a public place, and with greater levels of violence, all of which may impact her response to victimization and her recovery.

Seeking Help

Although sexual assault survivors generally experience many psychological problems as a result of their victimization, a majority of them do not seek mental health services. Sexual assault survivors are more likely to be seen by their primary care physician than they are by mental health professionals (Koss, Koss, and Woodruff 1991). Survivors often see themselves as being in poorer health than non-victims, and many report somatic symptoms that are commonly recognized as stress-related. Victims are more likely to see their doctor for the somatic symptoms of the stress of the assault than for injuries sustained during the rape. In addition to the perception of poorer health and the manifestation of stress in physical symptoms, sexual assault survivors may believe that there is less stigma involved in seeing a medical doctor than in seeing a mental health professional. One exception may be African American women, who cited inner strength as a factor in their decision not to seek any help after their assault (Neville and Pugh 1997).

Kimerling and Calhoun (1994) found that victims continued to have psychological symptoms throughout the year after their assault without seeking psychological services at no greater frequency than non-victims, but they did have an increased utilization of medical services. Their data also showed some evidence that sexual assault victims experience psychological distress as an illness and that victims often report symptoms such as pounding heartbeats, headaches, nausea, and unintentional weight changes, which are symptoms of depression and anxiety. It is also possible that rape victims report more somatic symptoms because psychological stress can result in weakening the immune system (Kiecolt-Glaser and Glaser 1992 as cited in Kimerling and Calhoun).

Support from friends and family members plays a major role in helping sexual assault survivors cope with the emotional distress and the somatic symptoms caused by the attack. A survivor who is supported by friends and family is more likely to see herself as healthy. Kimmerling and Calhoun (1994) found that "The victim's social network immediately after the assault seems particularly important. If the victim initially perceives positive social support, there is less evidence of increased medical service utilization 1 year post-assault" (p. 338).

Crisis Intervention

"Crisis intervention is obviously a humane effort to reduce the severity of a victim's crisis, to help the victim win as much mastery over the crisis experience as possible" (Understanding and Responding 2001, 2). Crisis intervention immediately after any type of sexual assault is critical to the victim's adjustment and recovery. Effective crisis intervention helps the victim get through the immediate crisis and helps her avoid severe adjustment problems and even psychological disorder as a result of the rape (Burgess and Holmstrom 1973). How a victim copes with rape depends for the most part on her experiences immediately following the rape. The short-term goal of crisis intervention is to help the victim cope with her immediate trauma and to restore her sense of security and control over her life (Woods 2000). The long-term goal is to provide the support necessary for the survivor to return to pre-rape levels of functioning.

Anyone who comes in contact with a victim immediately after her assault should be prepared to do crisis intervention. Victim advocates are not the only crisis interveners. A police officer is often the first person to respond to a victim, and therefore must be prepared to do intervention, in addition to assessing medical needs, collecting evidence, gathering information, notifying personnel that need to respond, and securing the crime scene. Interveners also include emergency medical personnel, investigators, hospital staff, and in many cases, volunteers. Friends are often the first person a victim calls, and must serve as crisis interveners. In a study of college freshmen, one third of the respondents reported that someone had disclosed a date/acquaintance rape experience to them, leading the authors to conclude that education about the aftermath of rape and helpful reactions to disclosures would be beneficial, particularly in a college environment (Dunn, Vail-Smith, and Knight 1999).

The circumstances and personality of the victim of each sexual assault vary. How the crisis intervener handles the situation will also vary according to the circumstances and the victim's needs. How the intervener approaches the victim will set the stage for any interaction the victim has with the crisis intervener (Woods 2000). The intervener should be calm, pleasant, and supportive. An intervener who is nervous, agitated, or shocked with the situation will not be helpful to the victim. The intervener must be able to put the victim at ease. The first thing that the crisis intervener needs to do is to introduce herself, using her title, and stating why she is present (Woods 2000). Sitting down to talk to the victim so that the victim and intervener are at the same level and can make eye contact can help to put the victim at ease with the intervener. It is important for the victim to understand that the crisis intervener is there to help her through the difficult period, and at times to be her advocate.

Believing the victim and being supportive is critical to effective crisis intervention (Dunn, et al. 1999). The intervener must learn to be patient with silence and allow the victim to share her experiences at a pace that is comfortable for her. The intervener should never be critical of the victim, no matter what the intervener personally believes. The intervener should not touch or hug the victim without asking the victim if she is comfortable with physical contact.

In rape cases, it is especially important for first responders to be prepared for any type of emotional reaction. Victims of sexual assault are deeply traumatized by the intensely personal nature of their assault, and by the fear that they will be killed or seriously injured during the attack. They may be crying uncontrollably, or present themselves in a very calm and subdued manner. Interveners must be nonjudgmental and supportive when faced with any type of reaction by the victim.

A rape victim's behavior may not be what people expect and may be misinterpreted. Crisis interveners and law enforcement officers must be careful not to misinterpret a victim's calm demeanor as evidence of a false report. Burgess and Holmstrom (1973) identified two different styles of behavior common among rape victims during the period immediately after the incident. This research is supported by Ruch, Gartrell, Ramelli, and Coyne (1991). One style is the expressed style where feelings of fear, anger, or anxiety are expressed verbally or shown through such behavior as crying, shaking, smiling, restlessness, and tenseness. Victims with the controlled style mask their feelings and appear calm, composed, and subdued.

Both behavioral styles are common. It is not unusual for one victim to have both responses during the course of one interview. While both responses are common and to be expected, Forman (1980) notes that the behavioral style most frequently displayed in metropolitan emergency rooms is the controlled style. The normal emotional style of the victim influences what behavioral style the victim of sexual assault will assume during the initial phase. Other factors such as exhaustion, the attitude of those in attendance, and her normal verbal style are also factors influencing her behavioral style.

If the intervener is called before the victim decides whether or not to report the rape to the police, the intervener must help the victim understand the issues involved and provide sufficient information to the victim so that she can make that decision. It is imperative that the intervener does not make that decision. The rape victim generally feels powerless, helpless, and a total loss of control (Understanding and Responding 2001). Allowing the victim to make the decision to report the crime will help the victim restore her sense of control. It is essential that the victim feels a sense of control return to her life as quickly as possible. The intervener faced with an emotionally devastated individual may think that they are making it easier for the victim by making this decision for her, but in reality, this prolongs her recovery process. Obviously if the victim is in immediate need of medical attention, the intervener cannot delay medical treatment.

Whether the victim chooses to report the rape to the police or not, she will need medical attention. She has suffered a physical trauma and should be examined for injury. If the intervener meets with the victim prior to her seeking medical treatment, the intervener must let the victim know how important it is to receive medical treatment, and encourage her to get medical attention, even if she thinks that she has not been injured (Woods 2000). The victim must not only consider treatment for injuries sustained in the assault, but also pregnancy and sexually transmitted diseases. Victims who seek medical attention tend to have a quicker emotional recovery than victims who do not seek treatment. Seeking medical attention helps the victim to recognize that she has undergone a serious physical trauma. The support she receives from medical personnel also serves as crisis intervention and helps her recovery process as well.

Many communities have specialized emergency medical technicians to respond to rape victims and to transport them to a hospital or medical center that also specializes in caring for sexual assault victims. If the victim's injuries are not life threatening or serious, she should be given the option to request such special assistance. These medical personnel are specially trained to treat not only the physical injuries of the victim, but also to attend to her emotional needs caused by the trauma. Perhaps one of the most important aspects of this specialized treatment is that most communities allow medical personnel to volunteer for the training and assignment, suggesting a commitment to help victims of sexual assault.

Victims' Basic Needs During Crisis Intervention

One of the first responsibilities of the intervener is to assess the needs of the victim. The three major needs of any crime victim are: the need to feel safe, the need to express their emotions, and the need for information about what will happen next (Woods 2000).

Victims' need to feel safe. One of the primary emotions felt by a rape victim is fear. The principal need for any rape victim, therefore, is the need to feel safe. Sexual assault survivors often feel vulnerable, fearful, and helpless (Understanding and Responding 2001). She typically experiences a sense of total loss of control. It is important to reassure the victim that she is safe now. The crisis intervener's mannerisms, tone of voice, and posture may do as much, or more, to reassure her as the words used. Using a sympathetic tone of voice, natural eye contact, and assuming the same level as the victim, rather than standing over her, can help a victim to feel safer (Woods 2000). A non-judgmental attitude and concerned approach is critical to good crisis intervention with a sexual assault victim.

Since a sexual assault survivor generally feels out of control, asking the survivor simple questions will allow her to make decisions and assert herself to regain some sense of control. Asking her how she would like to be addressed is an example. She may prefer to be called by her first name, or she may want to be addressed more formally. Offering to call friends or family not only can help her to regain control, but it may help her general sense of safety. Asking if the victim needs anything is helpful, but if she wants to prosecute the assault, she should not eat or drink anything if there was forced oral sex. She also should not use the bathroom or bathe. Small things concerning the victim's comfort, such as being cold, uncomfortable, or feeling exposed can have a significant impact on her feelings of safety and should be considered by the intervener (Understanding and Responding 2001). It is also helpful to keep the media away from the victim, or to help her respond to the media if she wishes to talk with them.

Many times the victim will express unrealistic or irrational concerns. The intervener can help to alleviate those concerns by discussing them with the victim and explaining why they may be unrealistic or irrational. This must be done in a supportive and non-condescending manner. The victim must feel free to express any feelings to the intervener without worrying about the intervener being judgmental (Understanding and Responding 2001). Anyone who has undergone a severe emotional and physical crisis like rape can be expected to have many concerns, some of which may be more realistic than others.

Fear and anxiety will continue to be the most predominate emotions for the victim to handle even months after the rape. No amount of support, crisis intervention, or counseling will completely eliminate her fear during the initial period after the assault. However, some amount of safety can be experienced if the proper emotional support is offered.

The victim's need to express their emotions. Victims need to allow their emotions to show and to be accepted by nonjudgmental listeners. Crisis interveners should be prepared to help a sexual assault survivor cope with her feelings. Typical emotional responses include fear, disbelief, self-blame, anger, shame, and sadness (Woods 2000). Emotional distress may be expressed in what the intervener sees as unusual ways. Victims may be calm, crying, or laughing, as found by Burgess and Holmstrom (1973) and Ruch, et al. (1991).

It is important for interveners to allow the victim to express their emotions in their own way. People are often uncomfortable when others show their emotions and sometimes tell them that their emotions are not legitimate or that they should not express them. This generally is not meant to be callous; it simply reflects discomfort with the expression of emotions. For example, someone might tell a victim not to cry, that everything will be all right. The truth is that it is beneficial for the victim to cry if that is how she is expressing her feelings, and everything is not going to be all right for quite some time. The victim who feels that her emotions are being discounted may withdraw, which may negatively impact her recovery. Crisis interveners should also be aware of a victim's body language, such as her posture, facial expressions, tone of voice, gestures, eye contact, and general appearance (Woods 2000). Reading a victim's body language helps the intervener to understand the victim's feelings and improves the ability to respond to her needs. The intervener must not force the victim to discuss or deal with her emotions before she is ready. A sense of trust must be developed between the intervener and the victim before any meaningful communication can begin.

While victims do not want to think that what has happened to them is common, it is helpful for them to know that their response to the traumatic event is not abnormal. "While most reactions are normal, most people have not experienced such intense feelings, so they think they are "going crazy." Survivors should be reassured that while the crisis has thrown their lives into chaos, they are not, as a consequence, crazy" (Understanding and Responding 2001, 7).

Since sexual assault victims often blame themselves for their assault, it is important for the crisis intervener to counter that self-blame (Woods 2000). Victims need to hear that they did not do anything wrong and that their assault was not their fault. It is also helpful for the victim to understand that self-blame is not uncommon for sexual assault survivors, but the responsibility for her victimization lies with her rapist, not with her. Helping the victim to understand that rape is a violent crime using sex as a means of power and violence may alleviate some of the survivor's feelings of guilt and self-blame.

An important technique in helping victims overcome feelings of guilt and self-blame is to explore the coping behavior that they used before and during the attack. They need to understand that their rapist used terrorization which, with most violent crime, leads to immediate compliance of the victim (Symonds 1976). Since many victims respond to the attack with frozen fright response, which appears to be cooperative behavior, they need to recognize that it is merely a means of reacting in order to preserve their life (Symonds 1976). Perhaps survivors who understand that their immobility was a reflexive response commonly experienced in high-fear situations will have better chances for adjustment and recovery.

Victims may respond to the sexual assault with a variety of coping behaviors. Helping the victim comprehend her coping behavior when faced with a traumatic event is an essential step in crisis intervention (Burgess and Holmstrom 1976). Listening to the sexual assault survivor tell their story of the rape, the intervener can identify coping behavior and help the victim understand her behavior. This support lets the victim know that her behavior helped her to survive and can help alleviate guilt and self-blame and enhance their recovery process. The intervener should remember that survivors who blame themselves tend to suffer from more symptoms and have a lengthier recovery process and, therefore, should encourage the victim to seek counseling soon after the event (Frazier 2000).

Victims need to tell their story after a crime (Woods 2000). Ventilation refers to the process of victims telling their story over and over again. "The repetitive process is a way of putting the pieces together and cognitively organizing the event so that it can be integrated into the survivor's life" (Understanding and Responding 2001, 5). This process takes place over a period of time. Crisis interveners should not force a victim to repeatedly tell their story, but should allow them to tell it if they choose to do so. It is normal for the victim's story to start very narrowly and become more complete over time (Understanding and Responding 2001). Interveners must allow victims a sense of permission to express their feelings and validation that those feelings are normal.

Victim's need for information. The rape victim will need information about what to do immediately after the rape as well as information about long-term issues. She will need information about medical and counseling services, the rights of victims, and the emotional and psychological consequences of rape. If she chooses to prosecute, she will also need information about what will be expected of her and what she can expect from the criminal justice system. Helping a victim to understand what to expect in the aftermath of the rape may relieve some of her anxiety (Woods 2000).

If the victim chooses to report the rape to the police, she should be advised not to wash, change clothes, or freshen-up in any way before going to the hospital. Bathing can wash away evidence that can help her to prosecute her case. Her appearance may also provide evidence that could be helpful for prosecution. Most victims feel dirty and want to bathe and change clothes before going anywhere. It is important for them to understand the importance of preserving evidence. Even if she does not wish to prosecute at this time, she may change her mind at a later date.

The victim should not be left alone in the emergency room. She will feel safer with someone with her, and she needs information about what is coming next. The crisis intervener can make the victim's hospital experience less traumatic by advising them what to expect and allowing her to regain some control over the procedures. Many times a rape victim with no life-threatening injuries will have a fairly long wait in a hospital emergency room before she is treated. It will help her if she knows that the hospital staff is taking her injuries seriously, but that those with life-threatening or serious injuries will be given priority. She may also need help completing forms and dealing with questions prior to her examination.

The crisis intervener can make her visit to the hospital less stressful by explaining to her what to expect and why the questions and procedures are important (Woods 2000). For example, she will be asked about her health, menstrual cycle, sexual practices, and details of her sexual assault. This information is important to diagnose and treat her appropriately. Her physical appearance and emotional state will be recorded for treatment and prosecution purposes.

A physical examination, including a pelvic exam, is generally performed on a sexual assault victim to evaluate injury and to collect evidence. It is critical that a rape victim be aware that these examinations will be performed before they begin. The victim often feels re-victimized by the process, but if she is informed about the process and the importance of it, she may find it easier to cope with the exam. Allowing the victim to indicate when she is ready to proceed with the examination helps her to reestablish some control in her life. This is where a crisis intervener may need to act as an advocate for the victim, making sure that the medical personnel know how important it is for the victim to have a sense of control.

It is also of utmost importance that the victim be examined in private. Privacy recognizes the trauma that the victim has already experienced as well as allowing her to regain some sense of control over the situation. If the medical staff does not automatically provide the victim with a private examining room, explain the medical process to her, and treat her with respect and empathy, the crisis intervener must be an advocate for the victim. Traditionally, medical staff did not see a rape victim as a legitimate consumer of medical services because her injuries often did not appear to be significant. Today, many hospitals and trauma centers have specially trained Sexual Assault Nurse Examiners to handle rape cases in an area of the hospital that is private and removed from the emergency room.

The sexual assault survivor should also be made aware that she will be asked to give blood samples for toxicology and serology testing to look for evidence of alcohol, drugs, and disease. If the victim has used any substance to try to cope with her assault, the hospital staff should be made aware of that fact. This may also help the victim's credibility if her sobriety at the time of the assault is an issue raised by the defense. The intervener helping a drug-facilitated rape victim should inform her that urine testing is necessary to detect traces of rape drugs in her system (Fitzgerald and Riley 2000). Since most jurisdictions use rape kits that do not routinely include obtaining a urine specimen, the drug-facilitated rape victim may have to request it.

Some of the more difficult parts of evidence collection, other than the pelvic exam, are head and pubic combings to collect hairs that may have been left by the rapist, head and pubic hair plucking, and using a Woods Lamp on the victims thighs and genital area to search for dried semen. The Woods Lamp will cause semen to fluoresce so that it can be swabbed and collected as evidence. Hair must be plucked to establish that the loose hairs found are not the victims. Fingernail scraping is less embarrassing, but also not a pleasant part of the procedure. Photographs of the victim may be taken to document injuries. If the victim is aware that these things will be done and why they are being done, she has a much better sense of control over the situation and is less likely to feel re-victimized. The victim should be made aware that she could request these photographs to be taken by a female police officer rather than a male.

In addition to treatment for immediate injuries and collecting evidence, the medical exam must also address issues of unwanted pregnancies and sexually transmitted diseases. The physician will discuss the victim's present birth control method and menstrual cycle with her, consider her present health, and determine what course of action to take. If she is given "the morning after pill," she should be advised of the side effects of the drug, including nausea and abdominal pains (Burgess and Holmstrom 1976). Since the crisis intervener may not have medical training, it would be more appropriate to act as an advocate asking the medical personnel to explain side effects to the victim. Routine treatment of rape victims usually includes antibiotics for the prevention of sexually transmitted diseases. The victim should be advised that six-week follow-up testing is advisable for both pregnancy and sexually transmitted diseases. The victim may also need assistance obtaining items after the exam, such as a glass of water, a warm washcloth, or fresh clothing. While it is not a good idea to go into too much detail on what to expect later in a criminal prosecution, the victim should be made aware of some of the general procedures and what will happen next. It may be helpful for her to know that she is likely to have more interviews with the police, that she may be asked to identify her attacker from a series of photographs, and that she may also have interviews with the prosecutor if her attacker is apprehended. The names and phone numbers of victim advocates with law enforcement agencies and the prosecutor's, as well as their role in helping the victim through the criminal justice process can help relieve some of the victim's anxieties about the system.

She may also need to prepare for how her friends, family, neighbors, and coworkers will react to her assault. Because a victim's mate, family, and friends may react to the rape based on their own beliefs in the myths about rape, the victim may choose not to tell them about the assault. Victims typically are selective in who they tell about their rape, often telling one person and asking them to tell others. Most victims tell persons whom they expect to be supportive (Frazier 1991; Frazier and Burnett 1994). Since support from others is important to the victim's adjustment and recovery, crisis interveners should assist the victim in determining who she can expect to be supportive and to whom she should not disclose her victimization (Burgess and Holmstrom 1979).

Since feeling safe is critical to a victim's adjustment and recovery, before the intervener leaves, she should make sure the victim's basic needs are cared for. If she wants friends and family present, they should be called. If she is in the hospital emergency room, transportation home, or wherever she wants to go, should be arranged. She should have adequate clothing if she is not at home. Many hospitals have a clothing closet for rape victims since their clothing is usually kept for evidence collection. The victim should be asked if she has any special concerns or needs (Woods 2000).

Crisis interveners should counsel victims that lapses of concentration, memory losses, depression, and physical complaints are normal reactions for sexual assault survivors and encourage them to seek counseling (Woods 2000). The crisis intervener should refer the victim to local agencies and programs that offer support and counseling services for sexual assault survivors. Ideally, the crisis intervener will follow-up with the victim through telephone calls 24 to 48 hours after the assault to check on her adjustment and to see if further assistance is necessary.

Conclusion

Sexual assault is a violent and traumatic event in the life of a victim. How the victim responds depends on a variety of factors, including the circumstances of the assault, the response of those to whom she discloses her rape, and her life situation. Coping strategies used before and during the assault may have a dramatic impact on her adjustment, recovery, and coping methods after the assault. Many victims suffer from Posttraumatic Stress Disorder, which may be complicated by feelings of self-blame.

Recovery from sexual assault is a long process that may take years. Some victims never integrate the rape into their lives and return to pre-rape levels of functioning. During the recovery process the victim will experience physical, psychological, behavioral, and social changes. A victim's chances of full recovery are greater if the victim has effective crisis intervention and a good support system.

References

American Psychiatric Association. *Diagnostic and Statistical Manual of Mental Disorders.* (4th ed. TR). Washington, DC: Author, 2000.

Arata, C. M. "Coping with Rape." *Journal of Interpersonal Violence* 14, (1999): 62–79.

Arellano, C. M., J. A. Kuhn, and E. L. Chavez. "Psychosocial Correlates of Sexual Assault Among Mexican American and White Non-Hispanic Adolescent Females." *Hispanic Journal of Behavioral Sciences* 19, (1997): 446–460.

Bridgeland, W. M., E. A. Duane, and C. S. Stewart. "Victimization and Attempted Suicide Among College Students." *College Student Journal 35*, (2001): 63–77.

Burgess, A. W., and L. L. Holmstrom. "The Rape Victim in the Emergency Ward." *American Journal of Nursing* 73, (1973): 1740–1745.

Burgess, A. W., and L. L. Holmstrom. "Rape Trauma Syndrome." *American Journal of Psychiatry* 131, (1974): 981–986.

Burgess, A. W., and L. L. Holmstrom. "Coping Behavior of the Rape Victim." *American Journal of Psychiatry* 133, (1976): 413–418.

Burgess, A. W., and L. L. Holmstrom. "Adaptive Strategies and Recovery from Rape." *American Journal of Psychiatry* 136, (1979): 1278–1282.

Burgess, A. W., and L.L. Holmstrom. "Rape: Disclosure to Parental Family Members." *Women and Health 4*, (1979): 255–268.

Dunn, P. C., K. Vail-Smith, and S. K. Knight. "What Date/Acquaintance Rape Victims Tell Others: A Study of College Student Recipients of Disclosure." *Journal of American College Health* 47, (1999): 213–220.

Evans, H. I. "Psychotherapy for the Rape Victim: Some Treatment Models." *Hospital and Community Psychiatry* 29, (1978): 309–312.

Fitzgerald, N. and K. J. Riley. "Drug-Facilitated Rape: Looking for the Missing Pieces." *National Institute of Justice Journal,* (April 2000): 9–15.

Forman, B. "Psychotherapy with Rape Victims." *Psychotherapy: Theory, Research, and Practice* 17, (1980): 304–311.

Frazier, P. A. "Self-Blame as a Mediator of Postrape Depressive Symptoms." *Journal of Social and Clinical Psychology* 10, (1991): 47–57.

Frazier, P. A. "A Comparative Study of Male and Female Rape Victims Seen at a Hospital-Based Rape Crisis Program." *Journal of Interpersonal Violence* 8, (1993): 64–76.

Frazier, P. A. "The Role of Attributions and Perceived Control in Recovery from Rape." *Journal of Personal and Interpersonal Loss* 5, (2000): 203–226.

Frazier, P. A. and J. W. Burnett. "Immediate Coping Strategies Among Rape Victims." *Journal* of Counseling and Development 72, (1994): 633–640.

Galliano, G., L. M. Noble, L. A. Travis, and C. Puechl. "Victim Reactions During Rape/Sexual Assault." *Journal of Interpersonal Violence* 8, (1993): 109–114.

Gilmartin-Zena, P. "Rape Impact: Immediately and Two Months Later." *Deviant Behavior,* 6, (1985): 347–361.

Kilpatrick, D. G., P. A. Resick, and L. J. Veronen. "Effects of a Rape Experience: A Longitudinal Study." *Journal of Social Issues 37,* (1981): 105–122.

Kimerling, R. and K. S. Calhoun. "Somatic Symptoms, Social Support, and Treatment Seeking Among Sexual Assault Victims." *Journal of Consulting and Clinical Psychology,* 62, (1994): 333–340.

Koss, M. P., P. G. Koss, and W. J. Woodruff. "Relation of Criminal Victimization to Health Perceptions among Women Medical Patients." *Journal of Consulting and Clinical Psychology* 58 no. 2, (1990): 147–152.

Larimer, M. E., A. R. Lydum, B. K. Anderson, and A. P. Turner. "Male and Female Recipients of Unwanted Sexual Contact in a College Student Sample: Prevalence Rates, Alcohol Use, and Depression Symptoms." *Sex Roles: A Journal of Research* 40, (1999): 295–308.

Morrow, K. B., and G. T. Sorrel. "Factors Affecting Self-Esteem, Depression, and Negative Behaviors in Sexually Abused Female Adolescents." *Journal of Marriage and the Family* 51, (1989): 677–686.

Neville, H. A. and A. O. Pugh. "General and Culture-Specific Factors Influencing African American Women's Reporting Patterns and Perceived Social Support Following Sexual Assault." *Violence Against Women* 3, (1997): 361–381.

Notman, M. T. and C. C. Nadelson. "The Rape Victim: Psychodynamic Considerations." *American Journal of Psychiatry* 133, (1976): 408–413.

Posttraumatic Stress Disorder, Rape Trauma Syndrome, and Battery. (April 19, 2001). In *Student Material: Victim Empowerment: Bridging the Systems Mental Health and Victim Service Providers* (chap. 3). Retrieved July 18, 2002 from http://www.ojp.usdoj.gov/ovc/publications/infores/student/welcome.html.

Ruch, L. O., J. W. Gartrell, A. Ramelli, and B. J. Coyne. "The Clinical Trauma Assessment: Evaluating Sexual Assault Victims in the Emergency Room." *Psychological Assessment* 3, (1991): 405–411.

Saunders, B. E. "Prevalence, Case Characteristics, and Long-Term Psychological Correlates of Child Rape Among Women: A National Survey." *Child Maltreatment* 4, (1999): 187–200.

Shrier, L. A., J. D. Pierce, S. J. Emans, and R. H. DuRant. "Gender Differences in Risk Behaviors Associated with Forced or Pressured Sex." *Archives of Pediatrics and Adolescent Medicine*, 152, (1998): 57–63.

Stermac, L. and E. K. Paradis. "Homeless Women and Victimization: Abuse and Mental Health History among Homeless Rape Survivors." *Resources for Feminist Research*, (Fall-Winter 2000): 65–81.

Symonds, M. "The Rape Victim: Psychological Patterns of Response." *The American Journal of Psychoanalysis* 36, (1976): 27–34.

Thornton, B., R. Ryckman, G. Kirchner, J. Jacobs, L. Kaczor, and R. Kuehnel. "Reaction to Self-Attributed Victim Responsibility: A Comparative Analysis of Rape Crisis Counselors and Lay Observers." *Journal of Applied Social Psychology* 18, (1988): 409–422.

Ullman, S. E. "Does Offender Violence Escalate When Rape Victims Fight Back?" *Journal of Interpersonal Violence* 13, (1998): 179–193.

Understanding and Responding to the Trauma of Victimization. In *Student Material: Victim Empowerment: Bridging the Systems Mental Health and Victim Service Providers* (chap. 2). (April 19, 2001). Retrieved July 18, 2002 from http://www.ojp.usdoj.gov/ovc/publications/infores/student/welcome.html.

Woods, T. O. *First Response to Victims of Crime*. Washington, DC: U. S. Department of Justice: Office for Victims of Crime, 2000.

Zweig, J. M., L. J. Crockett, A. Sayer, and J. R. Vicary. "A Longitudinal Examination of the Consequences of Sexual Victimization for Rural Young Adult Women." *The Journal of Sex Research* 36, (1999): 396–409.

Chapter 5

The Impact of HIV/AIDS on Rape Survivors

Mark Blumberg, Ph. D.

Introduction

Survivors of sexual assault have always had to confront psychological trauma and in many cases, physical injury. For the last two decades, these individuals have also been concerned that they had been infected with the Human Immunodeficiency Virus (HIV). Indeed, the National Women's Study found that 40 percent of rape survivors were fearful of contracting this virus as a result of being assaulted (Gostin, Lazzarini, Alexander, Brandt, Mayer, and Silverman 1994, 1437). How grave a threat is this disease and what steps should survivors take to minimize the risk?

Before addressing these questions, it is important to understand the nature of this epidemic. The first cases of Acquired Immunodeficiency Syndrome (AIDS) were identified among gay males in 1981. Soon cases were discovered among other groups including intravenous drug users (IVDU), recipients of blood transfusions, hemophiliacs and sex partners of persons in these risk groups. By 1985 we learned that the cause of AIDS is the Human Immunodeficiency Virus (HIV). Persons infected with this virus may show no symptoms of illness for many years. Eventually, their immune system becomes impaired and they become susceptible to a host of illnesses, funguses, and infections. Without treatment, this disease is almost always fatal. Fortunately, scientists have developed a number of anti-viral medications that can prolong the lives of persons with AIDS and improve their quality of life.

Risk of Infection

Intuitively, one would think that female victims of rape are at high-risk of becoming infected with HIV. After all, between 75 and 85 percent of the cases of HIV transmission through out the world are due to sexual activity (Royce, Sena, Cates, and Cohen 1997, 1072). How then does one explain the fact that relatively few cases have been reported in which rape survivors become infected as a result of being assaulted? The key reason is that rape is a one-time event and epidemiologists have noted that the risk of transmitting this virus during a single unprotected heterosexual encounter is quite low. Katz and Gerberding (1997, 1097) report that the probability of HIV transmission associated with unprotected anal intercourse is between 0.008 and 0.032. For vaginal intercourse, it is between 0.0005 and 0.0015. Utilizing the highest degree of risk and assuming that the offender is seropositive, the statistical probability of transmission for a survivor who has been vaginally raped would be approximately 1 in 666 and for those individuals who had been anally sodomized, around 1 in 31.

There are other reasons to be confident that HIV infection is unlikely to occur. For one thing, many rapists are impotent and unable to ejaculate. This would greatly lessen the chances for viral transmission. Second, the rate of HIV infection among heterosexual males who have no history of intravenous drugs is quite low. To date, 85 percent of AIDS cases in males have been reported among individuals who either had a history of sex with other men, the use of intravenous drugs, or both of these risk factors (Centers For Disease Control and Prevention 2001, 14). Fortunately, gay and bisexual men are unlikely to be involved in attacks on females. Intravenous drug users are also unlikely to commit rape. The drug of choice for most assailants is alcohol, not heroin or other illicit drugs that are injected.

Data collected among prison inmates also suggests that the overwhelming majority of rapists are not likely to be infected with HIV. According to a survey undertaken by the Bureau of Justice Statistics, 2.2 percent of state prisoners were seropositive as of December 31, 2000 (Maruschak 2002, 1). Unfortunately, infection rates were not calculated for various types of offenders and there are currently no data to determine if sex offenders have a higher rate HIV infection than other offenders (Gostin, et al. 1994). However, we know from previous research that the overwhelming majority of seropositive inmates have a history of intravenous drug use. As a consequence, it seems safe to assume that sex offenders have rates of HIV infection that are no higher than the national average and in fact, a far smaller percentage may be infected.

However, there are other factors associated with the crime of rape that may increase the risk of HIV transmission. For one thing, because of the violence that often accompanies this crime, tissue trauma is more likely to occur than in cases of consensual sex. This increases the risk of infection because the virus more easily enters the body when open wounds or bleeding are present. Second, many females who are the victims of sexual assault become infected with sexually transmitted diseases (STDs). Bamberger, Waldo, Gerberding, and Katz (1999) note that as many as 20 percent of penetrative rapes result in trichomoniasis or bacterial vaginosis (p. 324). STDs increase the individual's susceptibility to HIV infection.

Post-Exposure Prophylaxis

According to the National Crime Victimization Survey, there are approximately 131,950 completed rapes directed against females each year in the United States (Rennison 2002,1). Although several cases of HIV resulting from rape have been reported (Katz and Gerberding 1997), the risk of infection for any particular survivor is quite low given the number of sexual assaults that occur each year. Gostin, et al. (1994, 1437) estimate that viral transmission is likely to occur in approximately 1 out of 500 cases of sexual assault involving anal or vaginal penetration and exposure to the ejaculate from a seropositive assailant. It is very important that counselors and health workers try to reassure survivors that seroconversion is highly unlikely. However, because the virus is sexually transmitted, the risk is not zero. For this reason, survivors may wish to consider the use of anti-viral medication to prevent infection. Centers for Disease Control and Prevention guidelines recommend post-exposure treatment in cases of rape (Bamberger Waldo, Gerberding and Katz 1999). In an ideal world, physicians would carefully explain the risks and benefits to each woman who has been sexually assaulted. Unfortunately, many injured rape and sexual assault victims do not receive treatment for their injuries (Rennison 2002, 2).

For those survivors considering post-exposure prophylaxis, the decision on whether to pursue treatment would be much simpler if she could immediately be tested to determine whether she has been infected with HIV. Unfortunately, this is not possible because it usually takes at least 2 weeks until any detectable antibodies are discernable in the blood (Gostin, et al. 1994, 1438). Because it is recommended that treatment begin no later than 72 hours after exposure (Katz and Gerberding 1997, 1098), the survivor cannot wait to determine whether she has been infected before making the treatment decision. Even in those cases where the offender has already been arrested, it is quite improbable that the results of his HIV status will be known within the necessary time frame. Therefore, what should the survivor do under these circumstances?

Unfortunately, there are no research studies that have demonstrated this therapy is effective in preventing HIV infection as a result of sexual contact (Centers for Disease Control and Prevention 2002). However, Katz and Gerberding (1997, 1097) report that zidovudine reduced the probability of viral transmission by 79 percent in persons who had been exposed to the virus in an occupational setting (e.g., needle stick injuries). Proponents of post-exposure prophylaxis believe that there is a good chance the impact may be the same for persons who have been exposed to the virus through sexual contact whether it be consensual or coerced.

Survivors must consider a number of factors in deciding whether or not to commence therapy. The Centers For Disease Control and Prevention (2002, 2) note that "post-exposure antiviral therapy involves multiple drugs, taken several times a day, for at least 30 days. This is an extremely difficult and expensive regimen which can have severe side effects and costs between $600 and $1,000." Bamberger, Waldo, Gerberding, and Katz (1999, 324) report that approximately one-third of health care workers drop out of treatment because they are not able to tolerate the medication. Among a group of rape survivors in New York City, only 16 percent completed the regimen (Centers for Disease Control and Prevention 2002, 2). Furthermore, the benefit of anti-viral therapy in cases involving sexual transmission are unproven, insurance companies are likely to consider the treatment "experimental" and not eligible for reimbursement. Unless the medication is provided by a public health department, the survivor may be forced to pay out of pocket for this treatment. For many individuals, this could be a real financial burden.

HIV Testing

Finally, survivors of sexual assault have to decide whether or not to undergo a test to determine if they have been infected with HIV. Counseling and confidentiality testing should be offered to survivors but only after obtaining informed consent. Gostin, et al., (1994) note that HIV testing offers a numbers of benefits. For one thing, women do not have to wonder whether they have been infected. Second, individuals will be able to make appropriate decisions regarding their health needs, sexual and needle-sharing behavior, reproduction, breast-feeding and other aspects of their life that could be impacted by a positive test result.

Unfortunately, the survivor cannot determine from a post-assault test whether she has been infected. As previously noted, it usually takes two weeks after exposure before the body develops antibodies to this virus. In the vast majority of cases, detectable antibodies will be present within 3 to 6 months (Gostin, et al. 1994, 1438). For this reason, periodic testing should begin approximately six weeks after the assault. However, in cases where survivors hope to pursue a subsequent civil action to establish that they were infected with HIV by the assailant, an immediate baseline test will be necessary in order to demonstrate that the woman is not infected with the virus. Survivors who pursue this course of action should recognize that they will be surrendering a degree of privacy. Not only will the defense have access to their medical records, but other aspects of the woman's conduct may also be open to question as the defendant seeks to show that the seroconversion was not due to the assault but to other high-risk behaviors (Gostin, et al. 1994).

Conclusion

Despite the fact that HIV is a sexually transmitted virus, the threat of infection is quite low for rape survivors. This is the true for a couple of reasons. For one thing, the probability that the virus will be transmitted in a single heterosexual encounter is quite small. Second, relatively few offenders are likely to be infected with HIV. Nonetheless, these individuals should be offered the opportunity to receive antiviral medication designed to further reduce this danger. However, this decision to undergo treatment should always be made by the rape survivor. It is responsibility of medical personnel to explain all the potential benefits and risks associated with this treatment. Physicians must recognize that obtaining informed consent under these circumstances may be complicated because many survivors have been traumatized by the assault. Nonetheless, it is important to let victims know what risk they confront, what is known about the effectiveness of post-exposure therapy in cases involving sexual contact and any side effects they are likely to experience from the medication.

References

Bamberger, J.D., C.R. Waldo, J.L. Gerberding, and M.L. Katz. "Post-Exposure Prophylaxis for Human Immunodeficiency Virus (HIV) Infection Following Sexual Assault." *The American Journal of Medicine* 106, (1999): 323–326.

Centers for Disease Control and Prevention. *Preventive Therapy for Non-Occupational Exposures to HIV*. Division of HIV/AIDS Prevention, (February 4, 2002). http://www.cdc.gov/hiv/pubs/facts/petfact.htm.

Gostin, L.O., Z. Lazzarini, D. Alexander, A. M. Brandt, K. M. Mayer and D. C. Silverman. "HIV Testing, Counseling, and Prophylaxis After Sexual Assault." *JAMA* 271 no. 18 (1994): 1436–1444.

Katz, M.H. and J.L. Gerberding. "Post-exposure Treatment of People Exposed to the Human Immunodeficiency Virus through Sexual Contact or Injection Drug Use." *The New England Journal of Medicine* 336 no.15, (1997): 1097–1100.

Maruschak, L.M. *HIV in Prisons, 2000.* Bureau of Justice Statistics, October, 2002.

Rennison, Callie M. *Rape and Sexual Assault: Reporting to Police and Medical Attention, 1992–2000.* Bureau of Justice Statistics, August 2002.

Royce, R.A., A. Sena, W. Cates, and M.S. Cohen. "Sexual Transmission of HIV." *New England Journal of Medicine* 336 no. 15 (1997): 1072–1078.

Chapter 6

The Ripple Effect: Secondary Sexual Assault Survivors

Diane M. Daane, J.D.

Introduction

The family, partner, and friends of a sexual assault victim commonly experience emotional trauma as a result of the victimization of their loved one. Mental health professionals, victims' advocates, and volunteer crisis line workers suffer from secondary posttraumatic stress as well. The effect of sexual assault on the victim's personal or professional network has long been overlooked in the literature, in victim services agencies, and by the general public. Recognizing the impact of sexual assault on the people who care about sexual assault victims, and addressing their needs, not only helps them through the crisis, but also helps them to provide a better support network for the victim.

"Victimization has a ripple effect, spreading the damage in waves out from victims to all those with whom they have intimate contact" (Remer and Ferguson 1995, 407). Secondary posttraumatic stress is a natural response to learning about a traumatizing event experienced by a partner, friend, or family member, or the stress resulting from helping a traumatized crime victim (National Victim Assistance Academy 2002, chap. 6.1). Those who are affected by the sexual assault of the primary victim are secondary victims. The trauma suffered by secondary victims with a close relationship to the victim is similar to the trauma suffered by the primary victim (Schneider 2001). This includes feelings of powerlessness, guilt, vulnerability, and anger. In addition, they sometimes feel a sense of failure and self-blame for not protecting their loved one from harm (Schneider 2001).

Close family and friends are considered to be secondary victims because they did not directly experience the sexual assault. It is a common misperception that the feelings experienced by secondary victims are less intense than those experienced by the primary victim (Remer and Ferguson 1995). While there is no empirical data comparing levels of loss or suffering between primary and secondary rape victims, there is significant data and anecdotal evidence of significant trauma experienced by secondary victims. Little attention has been paid to the trauma experienced by secondary victims; what research has been done often examines the affect that secondary victims' responses have on the primary sexual assault victim, rather than concentrating on the impact of the assault on those close to the victim.

How a secondary victim responds to the sexual assault of a partner, family member, or friend depends on many different factors. Attitudes held before the rape, circumstances of the assault, and the closeness of the relationship held with the primary victim are critical issues in how a secondary victim responds to the sexual assault. Their own recovery and their ability to support the victim are also linked to these dynamics. While primary victims focus on their own healing first, secondary victims must provide support for the primary victim, then tend to their own healing process and the healing process for the relationship. While there is often a formal or informal support network for the primary victim, there is rarely any support network for the secondary victim.

Healing and Stages of Recovery

Several theorists have identified stages or phases of recovery for primary rape victims. Burgess and Holmstrom (1974) originally identified these phases as the acute phase and the long-term process. Very little research has been done on the phases of recovery for secondary victims, but limited study suggests that secondary victims heal in a very similar manner to primary victims. The process may last for months or years after the rape.

Trauma Awareness Phase

Secondary victims cope with rape and pass through stages of recovery in much the same way as the primary victim. One critical difference in the primary and secondary victims' experience is trauma awareness. The secondary victim is dependent upon the primary victim to provide information about the assault (Remer and Ferguson 1995). The primary victim sometimes has to experience some healing before she is able to discuss the rape, leaving the secondary victim in a position of crisis over the assault without knowing the facts about what occurred. It often takes days, weeks, or months before the primary victim is able to discuss the details of the assault with those closest to her. Some primary victims never arrive at this point and carry their trauma alone for life. Trauma awareness is generally an ongoing process because the primary victim may only reveal small bits and pieces of information about the assault at a time.

Crisis and Disorientation Phase

Once the secondary victim is aware of the trauma, a period of crisis and disorientation is generally experienced (Remer and Ferguson 1995). They will experience many of the same responses as the primary victim. This period of disorientation may include anger, sadness, self-blame, feelings of powerlessness, and disruption to routine activities. They may also suffer from rape-related Posttraumatic Stress Disorder. Secondary Posttraumatic Stress Disorder involves the transfer of trauma symptoms from those who are primary trauma victims to those who have close and extended contact with them (Motta, Kefer, Hertz, and Hafeez 1999). The American Psychiatric Association's (2000) diagnostic criteria for Posttraumatic Stress Disorder includes learning about unexpected serious harm or threat of death or injury experienced by a family member or someone with whom there is a close relationship. Posttraumatic Stress Disorder involves the development of specific symptoms after learning about the violence. To meet the diagnostic criteria, the secondary victim's response to learning of the assault must involve intense fear, helplessness, or horror. In addition, they must persistently reexperience the assault, avoid reminders of the rape, and repeatedly experience symptoms of increased arousal, such as difficulty sleeping, irritability, difficulty concentrating, or hypervigilance. These symptoms must be present for more than one month and they must cause significant distress or impairment in social, occupational, or other important areas of the secondary victim's life.

During the crisis and disorientation phase, attribution for the crime often manifests itself as self-blame, which is also similar to the response of primary victims. While primary victims blame themselves by believing that their behavior at the time of the assault caused their assault, or that they were attacked because of their character (Arata 1999), secondary victims often feel that it was their responsibility to protect the victim, and that they failed (Cwik 1996). This is especially true for husbands, boyfriends, fathers, and brothers, who may be seen by society as having the role of protector.

Outward Adjustment Phase

Like primary victims, secondary sexual assault victims use coping strategies to come to terms with the situation and to try to recover from the trauma (Remer and Ferguson 1995). These coping mechanisms often result in a period of apparent outward adjustment. During this phase, it appears that the lives of the primary and secondary victims have returned to a fairly normal routine. Others may actually believe that everything has returned to normal. But in reality, there may be little healing that has taken place.

The secondary victim's role is often seen as providing support for the primary victim without legitimately needing help or support of his or her own. This results in the secondary victim receiving very little support. They often feel pressured to act like nothing happened and to return to normal. This pressure from society to return to their previous lifestyle often makes it appear that the primary and secondary sexual assault victims have adjusted. Unfortunately, returning to the normal routine too soon may promote psychological denial, and may cause the primary and secondary victims to approach life very superficially and mechanically, with little insight into the situation.

There is also an outward adjustment phase for the relationship between primary and secondary victims. During this phase, previously established role patterns will prevail in these relationships (Remer and Ferguson 1995). The primary victim's relationship with her partner, family members, and friends appears to be the same as it has always been, even if they are just going through the motions out of routine or desire to return to a previously comfortable, or less stressful situation.

Reorganization Phase

Further healing by either the primary victim or the secondary victim will require a reevaluation and adjustment of the relationship. This phase, called the Reorganization Phase, will occur on both the personal and relationship levels (Remer and Ferguson 1995). During this phase, the primary victim tends to make lifestyle changes. These lifestyle changes often affect the secondary victim, particularly a partner, who is also going through a reorganization phase. The primary victim may want to move, change jobs, change phone numbers, or refuse to go out alone or at night. She may also change patterns of work, studying, or socializing. It is at this time that primary victims begin to experience more interpersonal problems, such as difficulty in relationships with their partner, parents, children, employer, and/or friends. During this phase, the relationship between the primary and secondary victim will evolve into new roles and new patterns of interaction will develop. These new roles and patterns may, or may not, be positive and healthy. Victims typically find themselves going through this phase several times. The trauma of rape is considerable, requiring significant healing that often takes place a little bit at a time.

Integration and Resolution Phase

Eventually the primary and secondary survivors reach the Integration and Resolution Phase, where they integrate the rape into life experiences and feel some sense of resolution (Forman 1980; Posttraumatic Stress 2001). Integration and resolution, in a sense, is no different for the secondary victim than for the primary one (Remer and Ferguson 1995). Early theorists believed that most rape victims were able to accomplish resolution and integration in a fairly short period of time. However, recovery takes a substantial amount of time, and for some primary and secondary victims, return to pre-rape levels of functioning never occurs.

While several phases may be identifiable, it does not necessarily mean that each victim experiences each phase in sequence, or that each phase is experienced only once. It is common for sexual assault victims to have setbacks, particularly as they are processed through the criminal justice system. The secondary victim's recovery is related to the primary victim's healing, and therefore, when the primary victim suffers a setback, the secondary victim also experiences it as well.

Partner Response

The research on partner reaction to the sexual assault of their mate is very limited, and often does not show males in a positive light. The vast majority of scholarship on partner reaction to rape focuses on males whose female partner is the primary victim. The literature also focuses greater attention on how the partner can help the primary victim rather than on what the partner experiences as a secondary victim.

Sexual assault victims often choose not to tell others about their assault because they are concerned about the reaction that they will receive. They generally choose whom they will tell based on the response they expect to receive from them. Persons whom the victim expects to be the most supportive and helpful are those most likely to be told of the assault (Frazier 1991; Frazier and Burnett 1994). This person is most commonly her husband, boyfriend, or lover (Feldman-Summers and Ashworth 1981).

Since males are most commonly the partners of sexual assault victims, it is relevant to look at male attitudes toward rape and rape victims. Research shows that males hold more negative attitudes toward rape victims (White, Robinson, and Sharon 1999). Young males often have the most negative attitudes toward rape victims and hold greater belief in the rape myths. "Men believed that a 'good girl' was less likely to be raped, and that if a woman was raped, she should blame herself because of her behaviors" (White, Robinson, and Sharon 1999, 993).

Some literature suggests that men are socialized to devalue women and to consider women as less moral and worthy of respect than men (Earl 1985). The objectification of women in the entertainment, advertisement, and pornography industries devalues women and encourages men to have negative beliefs towards women. These negative beliefs perpetuate the myths that rape victims are to blame for their victimization. "Many of these unstated beliefs or cultural experiences come to the surface in behaviors that are hostile to the victim of rape" (Earl 1985, 262).

Partner response and potential for secondary trauma, as well as possible support for the primary victim, depends on the partner's attitude about rape in general. Partners who believe in the myths about rape are generally less supportive of the primary victim and suffer a significantly different type of loss. One crucial element in the male mate's response to rape is whether he sees the rape as sex or violence. Primary victims generally see the sexual assault as violence, but their husbands or boyfriends may not be able to clearly distinguish between sex and violence (Cwik 1996). It is not unusual for a male partner to react to the sexual aspects of the crime rather than to the violent nature of the victimization (Silverman 1978). This is most likely to happen when the partner believes that nice women don't get raped or that if she really didn't want it to happen, she could have stopped it. This further results in anger, because they believe that the rape was somehow their mate's fault. These feelings of anger and resentment are often expressed indirectly rather than directly, in the form of doubting the truthfulness of the victim's story, suggesting that she was not as careful as she should have been, or that she enjoyed the sexual assault (Silverman 1978).

Another cultural myth is that a woman is the property of her father, boyfriend or spouse. If women are possessions to be admired by others, then a woman who has had sex, even forced sex, is devalued and tainted, decreasing the male's property interest in her (Earl 1985). Male mates may feel personally wronged by the rape because their exclusive right to their woman has been violated (Cwik 1996; Silverman 1978). While it is difficult to believe that many men have such opinions, it happens often enough that the concept cannot be ignored. Fortunately, the status of women has progressed sufficiently that rape is considered to be a violent personal crime, rather than a property crime against the proprietary rights of the male, as was true in ancient Rome and continues on in other cultures.

Another important issue in the reaction that male mates have to the rape of their partner is self-blame. Men who see themselves as the protector in the relationship often feel that they should have been there to protect their partner (Cwik 1996). These men often believe that the rape is their fault. They may feel guilty and believe that their masculinity has been challenged by their failure to protect their woman (Notman and Nadelson 1976). These feelings of guilt often lead to a desire for revenge or over protectiveness, neither of which is helpful toward healing or the relationship.

Feelings of powerlessness and loss of control are common reactions to rape for both primary and secondary victims. Revenge is often used as a means for the partner of a primary sexual assault victim to regain control. The partner's desire for revenge to regain control may lead to physical violence toward the perpetrator of the sexual assault (Cwik 1996), but more commonly these feelings remain at the fantasy level rather than leading to violence (Notman and Nadelson 1976). This desire for revenge by the secondary victim often puts the primary victim in the position of trying to comfort her partner, rather than focusing on her own well-being. It may also cause stress in the relationship because he may not be able to understand why she does not want to get back at her attacker. The secondary victim's wish for revenge may also make it difficult for him to understand the primary victim's reluctance to prosecute.

Feelings of responsibility for the assault because he did not protect her often lead to an effort to protect his partner at all times. After awhile, this may lead to resentment by the secondary victim that he has to spend so much time and effort protecting his partner (Cwik 1996). It also limits the primary victim's freedom, which may deny her the ability to regain control as soon as possible, and cause her to feel that her partner blames her for the rape or distrusts her or her judgment. This over-protectiveness may also cause stress in the relationship because both partners feel frustrated, out of control, and restricted by the other.

Belief in the rape myths and secondary trauma may make it extremely difficult for the male significant other to respond to the rape of his wife/girlfriend in an empathetic and supportive manner. Crisis Centers rarely provide adequate, if any, information to secondary victims, making it very difficult for even the most supportive partner to know what to expect or how to be supportive in this situation. Male socialization may also be a factor causing difficulty. "Since traditional male gender role socialization does not prepare a man to be emotionally expressive, the male significant other's ability to express his feelings about the rape and provide the needed emotional support is limited" (Cwik 1996, 102). Partners, even those with the best intentions, are often unaware that their attitudes and actions are not supportive or are detrimental to the primary victim's recovery.

While the research often focuses on the male partner's negative responses to rape, it is important to recognize that the partner is a legitimate secondary victim and that many males respond with genuine sympathy and support for the primary victim. Partners rarely receive the support they need to get through the crisis. Few sexual assault crisis agencies have counselors who work with the secondary victim at the time of initial disclosure or through the recovery process. The partner's feelings of crisis and the disruption in his life are overlooked both in the literature and in life, despite the fact that they are likely to be the primary victim's most important and constant source of support.

Research indicates that partner or spouse support is the most important support that a primary sexual assault victim can receive (Denkers 1999). Support from someone with whom the primary victim feels safe, secure, and close can most effectively support her after the assault. In fact, some research shows that primary victims not only need support from their partner the most, it also indicates that partners do, in fact, give the most support. Denkers (1999) found that primary victims received more support from their partners than they actually needed, and that only 6 percent of victims received less support from their mate than they needed. Denkers further found receiving sufficient support from their partner appeared to safeguard the primary victim's well-being.

Family Response

Families respond to the rape of one its members with shock, anger, and feelings of powerlessness and loss of control. They feel many of the same things that the primary victim feels. Family members also experience post-traumatic stress and go through phases of recovery. Their attitudes about rape before the incident will be a critical factor in their response to the assault. Attitudes that reflect societal myths about rape will make their reaction more challenging for the primary victim to cope with, and make everyone's recovery more difficult.

Family response to the rape of a family member can be very diverse, depending on a variety of factors. The family's ability to function and act as a support system prior to the assault will have a significant impact on the family's reaction to the rape and on their ability to cope with the situation. After a rape, family dynamics may change, interrupting routines and disrupting patterns of coping with everyday stresses. Family roles and attitudes must be adjusted in order to cope with the trauma of rape and to begin the healing process (Erickson 1989). The age, developmental stage, and maturity of the primary victim will also affect the family's response and ability to cope with the rape (Mitchell 1991).

Feelings of powerlessness and loss of control often lead to a loss of any sense of security and the desire for revenge on the part of family members in much the same way it does for partners. This wish for revenge is much more common among fathers and brothers of the primary victim than among other family members (Cwik 1996; Silverman 1978). Generally this desire for revenge does not lead to physical confrontation with the perpetrator; the response is limited to detailed descriptions of what the father or brother would do if they ever caught the rapist (Erickson 1989).

Like the primary victim's mate, family members often feel guilty for not protecting the victim. Mothers often face the realization that they could not protect their child the way they had hoped to do. This may lead to a sense of failure as a parent and a loss of identity as a mother (Mitchell 1991) and doubt about her maternal competence (Schneider 2001). Mothers are often seen as the rock in the family; they are the person who holds everything together during the tough times. The sexual assault of one of her children may cause significant grief, a sense of loss, and frustration at not being able to fix it. Her distress over the rape may be the first time the primary victim and other family members see their mother as vulnerable; they now have to face their mother as a human being with limits and shortcomings (Mitchell 1991).

Family members' feelings of guilt often result in patronization and overprotection of the primary victim (Silverman 1978). Families may move to a "safer" location or insist that someone goes with the primary victim everywhere she goes. The primary victim may be treated as if she is fragile and incompetent (Mitchell 1991). These attempts may serve to reinforce the victim's already existing feelings of helplessness and prevent her from using her own coping mechanisms (Mio and Foster 1991). The primary victim may lose any remaining sense of independence and self-confidence. Over-protection also makes it more difficult for the primary victim to regain control of her own life, which is one of the most important steps for her recovery.

Distraction is another coping mechanism often used by families (Silverman 1978). Distraction is where family members attempt to keep the primary victim busy, hoping that she will forget about the rape. This may make the primary victim feel that her family is trivializing the seriousness of her experience and trauma. She may be denied the opportunity to progress through the phases of recovery and to have genuine support. Families may also try to keep the primary victim busy because they are uncomfortable with the fact that she was raped. They may not know what to say or do, so they overcompensate by keeping her busy and avoiding the topic.

Other families may feel shame and humiliation because of the primary victim's rape. They may try to keep the incident a secret to prevent others from knowing about their failures or shame (Silverman 1978). Secondary victims may also want to keep the incident a secret because discussing it is too painful. Whatever the reason, treating the rape as a secret reinforces the primary victim's feelings of shame, guilt, and humiliation, and prevents her from validating her own perceptions (Mize, Bentley, Helms, Ledbetter, and Neblett 1995). It also denies her the support of her family. This refusal to discuss their feelings and fears also becomes destructive to the relationships in the family (Feinauer 1982). The family that refuses to deal openly with the situation will destroy any sense of family security and trust. When this loss of family support occurs, the trauma of the assault is worsened.

Children

Children in the family pose special problems for a family coping with rape. "Being part of a family system, children are affected by the changing boundaries that occur after the incident of rape" (Mio and Foster 1991, 147). Families often feel the need to protect children from the distressing news that their mother or older sister was raped, especially when the family views the rape as sexual rather than violent. Children are likely to know something is wrong. They may not know or understand what has happened, but they are aware that something has changed the family dynamics. If they are excluded from family discussions it is likely to have a significant negative impact on the children and prevent the child from being part of the healing process. Even minimal awareness of traumatic events can have a mild to profound effect on a child (Mio and Foster, 1991). The parents and older family members may be so involved in their own trauma that they do not notice the child's feelings of exclusion and inability to deal with the changing boundaries within the family.

We still know very little about children's responses to traumatic events and the factors that make some children more vulnerable to developing posttraumatic stress reaction than others. However, research does indicate that the child's degree of exposure to the traumatic event seems to be a critical variable (Udwin 1993). Children's posttraumatic stress is also directly related to the parents' reaction to the event. The more posttraumatic stress experienced by the parent, the greater the posttraumatic stress experienced by the child

(Udwin 1993). Children of emotionally distressed mothers have been found to demonstrate higher levels of anxiety and depression than other children (Newberger, Gremy, Waternaux, and Newberger 1993). The level of adjustment in the parent is a significant factor in a child's experience of trauma and ability to adjust (Leibowitz, Mendelsohn, and Michelson 1999). Research suggests that trauma in childhood may impact many aspects of the child's developmental process. The extent to which a child is able to resolve trauma is influenced by the manner in which other members of the family deal with it. The parents' inability to provide emotional support for the child is also an important factor in the child's posttraumatic stress.

The literature consistently suggests that children should be made aware of the traumatic event and involved in the healing process. However, it is not necessary for the child to be given all of the details of the incident, nor is it necessary for the child to be involved in all family discussions of the rape. Including children in the recovery process helps the child integrate the trauma of rape into the family system and learn how to cope with trauma in life.

Response of Friends

Friends are often the first people to whom a primary victim discloses her sexual assault, and as such, often provide invaluable social support (Mize, et al. 1995). Despite the fact that friends are often the first to know of a sexual assault, little is known about the disclosure or about the impact of the disclosure. Family therapists often work with the families of rape victims, but outside college campuses, there are few, if any, programs or groups designed to help people deal with a sexual assault disclosure by a friend. Even college campuses offer very little for secondary sexual assault victims.

The friends who are told about a rape by the primary victim are often friends with whom there is some degree of social intimacy or trust already existing in the relationship (Dunn, Vail-Smith, and Knight 1999). Friends' responses are generally supportive of the primary victim. These responses include offering comfort to the victim by listening, offering reassurance, believing the victim, and offering to go with the victim if she chooses to report the sexual assault to the police. Friends also offer advice to the primary victim. Advice generally includes the suggestion that the primary victim seek medical treatment and testing for sexually transmitted diseases, report the incident to the police, and speak with a professional counselor (Dunn, Vail-Smith, and Knight 1999).

Not all responses by friends of primary sexual assault victims are positive or supportive of the victim. Less than constructive responses from friends were similar to the negative responses by partners and family members. These responses include doubting the victim's story, blaming the victim, and seeking revenge on the perpetrator (Dunn, Vail-Smith, and Knight 1999). Friends, like family members and partners, who respond to disclosure in a counterproductive manner often do so because they are surprised and don't know what to do or say.

Dakof and Taylor (1990) found that friends, acquaintances, and co-workers are more likely to withdraw from the victim than are family members. Friends who are uncomfortable with what to say or how to act around the victim sometimes physically avoid the victim and decrease their communication with her. While Dakof and Taylor worked with victims of cancer, their work is applicable to sexual assault victims. The strain that victimization puts on a relationship varies with the nature of the relationship. Withdrawal leads to a lack of social support, which can worsen the trauma experienced by a primary sexual assault victim (Mitchell 1991) and lead to poorer functioning and negative changes in the relationship (Ahrens and Campbell 2000). Negative responses by family members are more likely to be overprotectiveness and hovering, while friends are more likely to withdraw. Dakof and Taylor (1990) report that victims find avoidance of social contact by friends to be the most unhelpful action exhibited by friends. Emotional support is the most helpful support from either friends or family.

Ahrens and Campbell (2000) found that most friends to whom the primary victim disclosed their sexual assault felt positive about the experience of helping their friend. They often felt needed and that the survivor was appreciative of the support provided. Many of these secondary victims reported that their friendship grew closer (Ahrens and Campbell 2000). They also found few incidents of friends avoiding the primary victim or friendships ending. Friends who reported a positive experience also exhibited more empathy, greater understanding of the life-threatening nature and devastating impact of sexual assault. They were also less likely to blame the primary victim for the assault.

Not all secondary victims in the study by Ahrens and Campbell (2000) reported a positive experience helping a friend through the trauma of sexual assault. Those who described their experience as neutral and having no positive or negative changes in the friendship also reported greater feelings of confusion, distress, and ineffectiveness in their help. Those who reported a negative experience indicated stronger feelings of ineffectiveness, more emotional distress, and did not feel good about the relationship. These friends also reported negative behavioral changes in the friendship.

The literature suggests that men may react more negatively to rape victims than women (Davis and Brickman 1991). "Compared with women, men

blamed the survivor more, were less empathetic, more confused, felt more ineffective, experienced fewer positive and more negative changes in the friendship" (Ahrens and Campbell 2000, 966). Despite the fact that Ahrens and
Campbell (2000) found men significantly less supportive than women, unsupportive behavior, even by male friends, is fairly rare.

Secondary victims who are friends of the primary victim also report experiencing trauma as a result of the disclosure (Dunn, Vail-Smith, and Knight
1999). The level of trauma in secondary victims is related to the closeness of
the relationship to the primary victim. Close friends report more trauma than
casual friends and acquaintances. Type of assault, level of violence, personal
assault history, length of friendship, and gender influence the level of secondary trauma and long-term consequences (Ahrens and Campbell 2000).
Ahrens and Campbell (2000) further found that friends of rape survivors
might be less traumatized than family members. Friends are likely to experience strong feelings of anger and revenge, but are less likely to feel depression
and shame than family members and partners.

Support for Secondary Victims

Most crime victims do not report the crime to the police; they usually seek
help from family and friends (Kaukinen 2002). Since sexual assault victims
are more likely to ask for help from family and friends than from the police
or the criminal justice system, there needs to be a means of providing support
to these informal help sources. Secondary victims need to be given the skills,
resources, and information they need to appropriately support the primary
victim and to cope with their own stress (Kaukinen 2002). While friends feel
positive about the support that they can provide for a primary sexual assault
survivor, they still need support and guidance during the process (Ahrens and
Campbell 2000).

Early intervention is critical to prevent psychological and psychosomatic
problems resulting from the sexual assault for both the primary and secondary sexual assault victim. Intervention should include education about rape
and its aftermath. This education should include the myths and facts about
rape, the coping strategies used by rape victims during and after the attack,
the phases of healing that the primary and secondary victims are likely to experience, the possibility of suffering from Posttraumatic Stress Disorder, the
best ways to support the primary victim, how to support other secondary victims, and where to go for help (Mio and Foster 1991). Helping secondary victims understand that the primary victim has suffered a life-threatening expe-

rience helps them to understand the primary victim's reactions and helps them to focus less on the sexual aspects of the crime (Silverman 1978). Educating secondary victims allows them to better understand what the primary victim is experiencing and helps them to anticipate some of the reactions and phases the primary victim will experience (Feinauer and Hippolite 1987).

Education also gives the secondary victim the confidence and skills to help the primary victim and to feel good about his or her role as a help provider. Secondary victims can learn how to allow a victim to express their feelings openly and freely and to provide the emotional support that can help the primary victim recover more quickly. The more prepared the secondary victim is to handle a rape disclosure, the better he or she will handle the situation. Less secondary trauma will also result when the secondary victim is prepared to handle the situation and feel positive about how it was handled.

In addition to education, support services should be made available to secondary sexual assault victims. Like the primary victim, the secondary victims must begin a process of healing to deal with the effects of the trauma. Secondary victims may need to adjust to their own roles, attitudes, and behaviors before they can heal. Relationships that have the ability to shift roles, such as the caregiver role, are more likely to have resolution than relationships that are less flexible (Cwik 1996). Without learning about victim response to rape and without adequate support, it is very difficult for secondary victims to heal.

Support services provided for secondary victims need to include friends as well as family (Mitchell 1991). Dunn, Vail-Smith, and Knight (1999) suggest that there is a need to alert both male and female college students about the possibility that they may be the recipients of rape-related disclosures, and that education about the aftermath of rape may help the secondary victim provide support for the primary victim and handle their own stress from the disclosure. Dunn, Vail-Smith, and Knight (1999) also recommend support services for friends and family who accompany a primary sexual assault victim to a health service provider.

Victim Advocate and Counselor Trauma

Secondary victimization is not limited to partners, family, and friends of the primary victim. Victim service providers such as sexual assault counselors, police officers, and crisis line volunteers are prime candidates for vicarious trauma. "Their acute and chronic exposure to the trauma, grief, and other reactions that are common to many crime victims can have a cumulative, and often devastating, effect on their view of the world and, sometimes, on their choice of careers" (National Victim Assistance Academy 2002, chap.6.2, p. 2). The personal and devastating nature of sexual victimization may intensify the vicarious trauma experienced by counselors and advocates working with sexual violence survivors.

Long-term exposure to the trauma experienced by sexual assault victims may effect the counselor's beliefs about the world, safety, and the trustworthiness of people (McCann and Pearlman 1990). The research indicates that the number of traumatized clients in a therapist's caseload may be related to secondary traumatic stress (Arvay 2001). While Baird and Jenkins (2003) indicate that counselors seeing more clients report less vicarious trauma, Schauben and Frazier (1995) report that counselors who have a large percentage of patients who are sexual violence survivors report more disrupted beliefs about themselves and others, more posttraumatic stress-related symptoms, and more vicarious trauma than counselors who see fewer sexual assault victims. Schauben and Frazier further found that the beliefs most likely to be altered by counselors working with sexual assault survivors are beliefs involving the goodness or trustworthiness of other people. Depression, anxiety, and hostility were not found to be related to working with victims. Like friends, many victim advocates and counselors feel positive about helping primary victims become survivors.

Conclusion

Anyone who is exposed to the trauma experienced by a sexual assault victim may experience secondary victimization. Family, friends, first responders, and sexual assault counselors are all at risk for suffering secondary trauma through their efforts to help a rape victim. The closeness of the relationship and the duration of the contact with the primary victim are factors in developing this secondary trauma. Other factors that have an impact on the development of secondary victimization are the attitudes held before the assault, the circumstances of the assault, and the availability of a support network.

Secondary victims often experience the same healing process and stages of recovery as the primary victim. One major difference in recovery is that the secondary victim is dependent upon the primary victim for information about the assault. This may be a lengthy process since the primary victim often has to experience some healing before they are able to share the details of their attack.

Partner response to a sexual assault is often not conducive to healing for the victim. Male partners who believe in the myths about rape may blame the victim for their rape or see the attack as a sexual encounter rather than as an act of violence. Partners often blame themselves for the sexual assault; they believe that it was their job to protect the victim, and that they failed in their responsibility. Partners may seek revenge on the perpetrator, often placing the victim in a position of calming her husband or boyfriend rather than focusing on her own recovery. Despite negative responses by males who believe in the myths about rape, many partners are supportive and help the sexual assault victim heal and become a sexual assault survivor.

Family members of sexual assault victims also experience secondary posttraumatic stress. Family members often become overprotective of the victim, depriving her of support and the opportunity to regain control over her own life. Family members may also try to distract the victim in the mistaken belief that keeping the victim busy and not allowing her to think about the assault will help her recovery. This also denies her support. Some families feel shame and humiliation at the rape of a family member and may try to keep the assault a secret. The family may feel that they are protecting the victim by keeping things quiet, but in reality they may be reinforcing the victim's feelings of guilt, shame and self-blame.

Friends are generally supportive of sexual assault victims, offering them reassurance, support, and advice. Friends often offer to accompany the victim to the police station or to the hospital. However, not all responses from friends are positive. Friends may doubt the victim's story, seek revenge, or withdraw from the victim because of their own discomfort with the situation. Friends are often less traumatized than family members or partners because there may be less closeness in the relationship.

Secondary sexual assault victims rarely receive the support and intervention that will help them heal and become secondary sexual assault survivors. Lack of knowledge of the truth about sexual assault and the recovery process may make secondary victimization more difficult to handle. Lack of knowledge may also impair their ability to be supportive and helpful to the primary victim's healing process. Lack of support for secondary victims generally impedes their own healing and recovery process.

In addition to partners, family, and friends of primary sexual assault victims, service providers for victims also suffer from the trauma of secondary victimization. Factors related to secondary trauma for counselors, volunteers, and first responders include the number of trauma victims they encounter and the support they receive. Many victim service providers are able to counter their trauma by feeling positive about the help and support they offer primary victims.

Secondary victimization is a fairly new concept in the literature as well as in victim services organizations. Additional research needs to be done to further explore the causes and consequences of secondary trauma on partners, family, friends, and service providers. Educational and support services for secondary sexual assault victims need to be implemented in law enforcement agencies, victim service groups, hospitals, and mental health care providers. Recognizing the plight of secondary sexual assault survivors is the first step in efforts to improve services for them.

References

Ahrens, C.E., and R. Cambell. "Assisting Rape Victims as They Recover From Rape: The Impact on Friends." *Journal of Interpersonal Violence* 15, (2000): 959–986.

American Psychiatric Association. *Diagnostic and Statistical Manual of Mental Disorders* (4th ed. TR). Washington, DC: Author, 2000.

Arata, C.M. "Coping With Rape." *Journal of Interpersonal Violence* 14, (1999): 62–79.

Arvay, M.J. "Secondary Trauma Stress Among Trauma Counselors: What Does the Research Say?" *International Journal for the Advancement of Counseling* 23, (2001): 283–293.

Baird, S. and S.R. Jenkins. "Vicarious Traumatization, Secondary Traumatic Stress, and Burnout in Sexual Assault and Domestic Violence Agency Staff." *Violence and Victims* 18, (2003): 71–86.

Burgess, A.W., and L.L. Holmstrom. "Rape Trauma Syndrome." *American Journal of Psychiatry* 131, (1974): 981–986.

Cwik, M.S. "The Many Effects of Rape: The Victim, Her Family, and Suggestions for Family Therapy." *Family Therapy* 23, (1996): 95–115.

Dakof, G.A., and S.E. Taylor. "Victims' Perceptions of Social Support: What is Helpful from Whom?" *Journal of Personality and Social Psychology* 58, (1990): 80–89.

Davis, R.C., E. Brickman, and T. Baker. "Supportive and Unsupportive Responses of Others to Rape Victims: Effects of Concurrent Victim Adjustment." *American Journal of Community Policing* 19, (1991): 443–451.

Denkers, A. "Factors Affecting Support After Criminal Victimization: Needed and Received Support from the Partner, the Social Network, and Distant Support Providers." *The Journal of Social Psychology* 139, (1999): 191–201.

Dunn, P.C., K. Vail-Smith, and S. M. Knight. "What Date/Acquaintance Rape Victims Tell Others: A Study of College Student Recipients of Disclosure." *Journal of American College Health* 47, (1999): 213–219.

Earl, W. "Rape as a Variable in Marital Therapy: Context and Treatment." *Family Therapy XII*, (1985): 259–272.

Erickson, C.A. "Rape and the Family." *In Treating Stress in Families*, ed. Figley, C.R, 257–289. New York: Brunner/Mazel, 1989.

Feinauer, L.L. "Rape: A Family Crisis." *The American Journal of Family Therapy* 10, (1982): 35–39.

Feinauer, L.L. and D.L. Hippolite. "Once a Princess, Always a Princess: A Strategy for Therapy with Families of Rape Victims." *Contemporary Family Therapy 9*, (1987): 252–262.

Feldman-Summers, S., and C. Ashworth. "Factors Related to Intentions to Report Rape." *Journal of Social Issues* 37, (1981): 53–70.

Forman, B. "Psychotherapy with Rape Victims." *Psychotherapy: Theory, Research and Practice* 17, (1980): 304–311.

Frazer, P.A. "Self-Blame as a Mediator of Postrape Depressive Symptoms." *Journal of Social and Clinical Psychology* 10, (1991): 47–57.

Frazier, P.A. and J.W. Burnett. "Immediate Coping Strategies Among Rape Victims." *Journal of Counseling and Development* 72, (1994): 633–640.

Kaukinen, C. "The Help-Seeking Decisions of Violent Crime Victims." *Journal of Interpersonal Violence* 17, (2002): 432–456.

Leibowitz, S., M. Mendelsohn, and C. Michelson. "Child Rape: Extending the Therapeutic Intervention to Include the Mother-Child Dyad." *South African Journal of Psychology* 29, (1999): 103–109.

McCann, I.L., and L.A. Pearlman. "Vicarious Traumatization: A Framework for Understanding the Psychological Effects of Working with Victims." *Journal of Traumatic Stress* 3, (1990): 131–149.

Mio, J.S. and J.D. Foster. "The Effects of Rape Upon Victims and Families: Implications for a Comprehensive Family Therapy." *The American Journal of Family Therapy* 19, (1991): 147–159.

Mitchell, M.E. "A Family Approach and Network Implications of Therapy for Victims of Violence as Applied in a Case of Rape." *Journal of Family Psychotherapy* 2, (1991): 1–13.

Mize, L.K., B. Bentley, S. Helms, J. Ledbetter, and K. Neblett. "Surviving Voices: Incest Survivors' Narratives of Their Process of Disclosure." *Journal of Family Psychotherapy* 4, (1995): 43–59.

Motta, R.W., J.M. Kefer, M.D. Hertz, and S. Hafeez. "Initial Evaluation of the Secondary Trauma Questionnaire." *Psychological Reports, 85*, (1999): 997–1002.

National Victim Assistance Academy (2002, June). "Mental Health Needs: Trauma and Assessment Intervention." In *National Victim Assistance Academy Textbook* (chap. 6.1) Retrieved May 25, 2003, from http://www.ojp.usdoj.gov/ovc/assist/nvaa2002/chapter6_1.html#1

National Victim Assistance Academy (2002, June). "Mental Health Needs: Stress Management." In *National Victim Assistance Academy Textbook* (chap. 6.2) Retrieved May 25, 2003, from http://www.ojp.usdoj.gov/ovc/assist/nvaa2002/chapter6_2.html#1

Newberger, C.M., I.M. Gremy, C.M. Waternaux, and E.H. Newberger. "Mothers of Sexually Abused Children: Trauma and Repair in Longitudinal Perspective." *American Journal of Orthopsychiatry* 63, (1993): 92–102.

Notman, M.T. and C.C. Nadelson. "The Rape Victim: Psychodynamic Considerations." *American Journal of Psychiatry* 133, (1976): 408–413.

Posttraumatic Stress Disorder, Rape Trauma Syndrome, and Battery. (April 19, 2001). In *Student* Material: Victim Empowerment: Bridging the Systems Mental Health and Victim Service Providers (chap. 3). Retrieved July 18, 2002 from http://www.ojp.usdoj.gov/ovc/publications/infores/student/welcome.html.

Remer, R. and R.A. Ferguson. "Becoming a Secondary Survivor of Sexual Assault." *Journal of Counseling and Development* 73, (1995): 407–412.

Schauben, L.J., and P.A. Frazier. "Vicarious Trauma: The Effects on Female Counselors of Working with Sexual Assault Survivors." *Psychology of Women Quarterly* 19, (1995): 49–64.

Schneider, H.J. "Victimological Developments in the World During the Past Three Decades: A Study of Comparative Victimology." *International Journal of Offender Therapy and Comparative Criminology* 45, (2001): 539–555.

Silverman, D.C. "Sharing the Crisis of Rape: Counseling the Mates and Families of Victims." *American Journal of Orthopsychiatry* 48, (1978): 166–173.

Udwin, O. "Children's Reactions to Traumatic Events." *Journal of Child Psychology and Psychiatry* 34, (1993): 115–127.

White, B.H., K. Robinson, and E. Sharon. "Attitudes Toward Rape Victims: Effect of Gender and Professional Status." *Journal of Interpersonal Violence* 14, (1999): 989–996.

Chapter 7

Sexual Abuse of Males

Elycia Daniel

Traditionally, when one thinks of rape, they think of a female as the victim. However, the face of the rape victim is ever changing to that of a male victim. While societal concern has focused on the female victims of rape, and the vast majority of literature on rape refers to the female victim, there has been some interest in male rape victims. Kaufman, et al. (1980), notes that male rape was believed to occur in one of three circumstances: an aberration of prison life, a form of vicarious rape against women and as a violent outgrowth of the homosexual culture. He also suggests that many people assume that the male victims of sexual assault are usually children and the prey of child molesters.

Sexual assault is the most rapidly growing violent crime in America (Dupre, Hampton, Morrison, and Meeks 1993). It is estimated that fewer than 50 percent of rapes are reported each year and male victims represent only 5 percent of these reported sexual assaults (American Academy of Pediatrics 1994). According to the U.S. Department of Justice Statistics, 1999, only 25,000 men are victims of rape or attempted rape compared to over 343,000 female rapes or attempted rapes. Rape crisis centers have reported that 10 to 20 percent of rape victims were men (Forman 1982; Kaufman, et al. 1980).

In a survey done by Sorenson (1987) of Los Angeles citizens, of 1480 men interviewed, 7.2 percent reported that as adults they had been pressured or forced to have sexual contact. They also further reported that the incidence rate rose to 16 percent for white, college educated men ages 18 to 39 years old. Most of the cases were by female acquaintances, usually by verbal pressure.

Not only are fewer male rapes reported, but, the legal consequences for the rapes appear to be different as well. A study conducted by Hill (2000) found that homosexual males accused of sexually assaulting non-homosexual males were most often found guilty than heterosexual males who assault heterosexual females or homosexual males accused of assaulting homosexual males. In contrast, New York and North Carolina are two states in which the rape of a male is a lesser charge than rape of a female. An area for further research may be into the analysis of rape criminal codes across the country.

Just as in female rape cases, according to Groth and Burgess (1980) male rape appears to be underreported because of the stigma associated with it. Before reviewing literature on the specifics of male rape, it is important to review the literature on the reasons that males do not report the rape. Smith, Pine, and Hawley (1988) suggested that male subjects viewed the episode in sexual terms and failed to grasp the violence component of the rape. The do report however, that male victims have greater difficulty in dealing with their traumatic experience than do females. Males seldom reveal their experiences to others because they are ashamed of what happened to them and don't expect others to understand the level of trauma they have experienced. They fear being stigmatized if they reveal what happened to them. Groth and Burgess (1980) found that the male victim may be bewildered by his physiological response during the sexual assault and, therefore, may be discouraged from reporting the assault for fear associated with his sexuality; he may have a fear of being viewed as a homosexual.

A study of social cognitions about adult male victims of female sexual assault viewed the male victim more likely to be judged as having initiated or encouraged the sex acts. Laurent (1993) reported that the male masculinity has already been challenged once by the attack, and the male victim, when reporting the incident, may feel that authorities will challenge it again. Similarly, Groth and Burgess (1980) stated three reasons that male victims gave for not reporting rape: 1) feelings that he should have been able to defend himself against sexual assault, 2) fear that his sexuality will become suspect, and 3) distress associated with recalling and describing the incident.

The next component of male rape to look at is the attackers. We will look at both methods used and reasons for the attack. Women are taught to be careful of their behavior, be mindful of their surroundings and always travel in groups at night. However, when it comes to men, our society doesn't seem to require them to take such extreme measures. Groth and Burgess (1980) stated that men are assaulted where they live, work, travel and relax. They appear to be at greater risk in solitary activities, such as hitchhiking. In their study, 38 percent of the victims were hitchhiking and 36 percent were engaged in an out-of-doors activity, such as swimming at a beach or hiking in the woods. Finkelor and Russell (1984) reported that 84 percent of those who rape males are male and a vast majority of them are heterosexual. A study by Frazier (1993) that designed to compare information about male and female rape victims found that male victims were more likely to have been raped by more than one assailant, by a Caucasian assailant and were more likely to have been physically harmed. The style of attack of the offenders seemed to vary. Groth and Burgess (1980) stated that the offenders show three major methods: entrapment, intimidation and/or physical force. In a study conducted of convicted rapists, Groth and Burgess (1980) reported that in some cases, the gender of the victim didn't seem to be of primary importance to the rapist, in other cases the intended targets were males.

There are five possible categories for the victims and their attackers: female attacker/male victim, male heterosexual attacker/male heterosexual victim, male heterosexual attacker/male homosexual victim, male homosexual attacker/male heterosexual victim, and male homosexual attacker/male homosexual victim. As we look at male victims responses to rape and the motives and methods of the attackers, these distinctions often become important. An area for further research would be to examine the extent of these five attacker victim relationships.

Like female rape, male rape is more often about domination than sex. In those cases where the intended targets were in fact males, the rapist's assaults were attempts to deal with unresolved and conflict-ridden aspects of their lives. Similarly, Kaufman, et al. (1980), reported that the male victims of sexual assault seemed in general to be unaffiliated with the homosexual community. In accordance with other studies, they did find that sexual assaults of males appeared to be an expression of anger, power and dominance over another. In a study conducted with 930 gay men, Hickson, Davies, Hunt and Weatherburn (1994), 27.6 percent reported they had been subject to nonconsensual sex at some point in their lives; 3 percent involved female assailants. One-third reported that they had been forced into activity, usually anal intercourse, by men with whom they had previously had or were currently having sexual activity. The results did not support the assertion that male rape is usually committed by men identified as heterosexuals, primarily as an expression of power and control.

In terms of the sexual acts themselves, Groth and Burgess (1980) found that in slightly more than half of the cases (N=12; 55%) only a single type of sexual activity occurred during the offense, and in fewer than half of the cases (N=10; 45%) several types of sexual acts (oral, anal, and masturbatory) took place. In the majority of the assaults (N=14; 64%) the offender sexually penetrated his victim in some fashion, whereas the offender accepted penetration, by performing fellatio on his victim, only in 7 of their cases (32%). The most common sexual act was sodomy, with oral penetration being the next most frequent act. Comparably in Kaufman, et al. (1980), they reported that all of their males victims (N=14) were sodomized and 9 were forced to commit fellatio.

Much of the research literature suggested that males commonly experience many of the reactions that females experience (Manzano 1998; Isley 1991; Brochman 1991; Mezey and King 1989), such as depression, sexual dysfunction, anger, self-blame, suicidal feelings, guilt, flashbacks and increased sense of vulnerability. According to a study by Struckman-Johnson and Struckman-Johnson (1992), 60 percent of male survivors believed they were going to be killed during the assault. They also noted that men suffer from some of the same emotional issues as that of women. In a study conducted by Groth and Burgess (1980), 22 convicted rapists reported the impact of rape on male victims was similar to the effect of rape on female victims, disrupting their biological, psychological and social functioning.

According to Frazier (1993), male victims were rated as more depressed and hostile immediately following the rape than were female victims. Groth and Burgess (1980) reported that male victims make it clear that 1) rape is stressful, 2) reporting the assault is difficult, and 3) one's lifestyle becomes disrupted. Struckman-Johnson and Struckman-Johnson (1994) suggested that most men had no or very mild negative reactions to the unwanted female contact. However, there was evidence of moderate to strong negative reactions to the experience of a male-initiated unwanted contact. Brochman (1991) reported that the experience may affect gay and heterosexual men differently. Most rape counselors pointed out that gay men have difficulties in their sexual and emotional relationships with other men, and think that the assault occurred because they are gay, whereas straight men often begin to question their sexual identity and are more disturbed by the sexual aspect of the assault than the violence involved. Struckman-Johnson and Struckman-Johnson (1994) stated that heterosexuals were the most upset by contact initiated by another man, either acquaintance or stranger, and especially if it occurs in a sudden or unexpected manner or involves any kind of physical restraint. The researchers contributed it to their feelings about their own sexual identity and fear of homosexuality. Romano and DeLuca (2001) reported that the effects of sexual abuse was similar in males to that of females and includes depression, self-blame, low self-esteem, anger, anxiety and sexuality problems. Coxell and King (1996) studied coercion in gay relationships in the UK with a sample of 1,480 males and found that problems reported after sexual assault by males include confusion about sexual orientation, sexual problems, posttraumatic stress disorder, problems facing close relationships, mistrust of adult men, suicide and various mood disorders. They further reported that sexual assault by females may leave men less traumatized than sexual assaults by men because they are less likely to involve physical force and because same-sex sexual contact, which heterosexuals may find traumatic itself, is not involved.

Contradictory to many other research findings, in a longitudinal study conducted by Gil-Rivas, Fiorentine, Anglin and Taylor (1997), of 330 participants from 26 outpatient programs, results suggested that sexual abuse among women was associated with higher levels of depression, anxiety, suicidal ideation, suicide attempts, and post-traumatic stress disorder (PTSD), and for men sexual abuse was only associated with anxiety. They further reported no significant association between sexual and physical abuse for men.

In a study of male rape in the UK, Rogers (1997) stated that even though some evidence is being reported that male rape survivors develop posttraumatic stress disorder (PTSD) following the assault, to date there have been no systematic prevalence studies that have found a relationship between PTSD and assault in male survivors of rape.

Calderwood (1987) suggested that most male rape is by other men, and males often sustain more injuries than females. A study conducted by Kaufman (1980) compared 14 male rape victims treated in a county hospital emergency room over a 39-month period with 100 randomly selected female victims treated over the same period. Their findings showed that the males as a group sustained more traumas, were more likely to have been a victim of multiple assaults from multiple assailants, and were likely to have been held captive longer. The males were also more reluctant to reveal initially the genital component of their assault and were more likely to use denial and control their emotions in reaction to the assault.

A study conducted by Mitchell, Hirschman, and Hall (1999) examined the differences concerning the relationship between the sexual orientation of a male victim and attributions of the victim's degree of responsibility, pleasure, and trauma associated with assault. The results showed that victims attributed more responsibility, more pleasure, and fewer traumas to a homosexual victim than a heterosexual one. Male respondents more than females attributed more responsibility and pleasure. Frazier (1993) suggested that male victims were rated as more depressed and hostile immediately following the rape than were female victims.

Another study conducted by Smith, Pine, and Hawley (1988) suggested that compared to other victims-assailant conditions, the male victims of sexual assault were judged more likely to have encouraged or initiated the episode, to have derived more pleasure from it and to have experienced less stress. In terms of pleasure, 47 percent of male subjects in their particular study rated the sexual episode as pleasurable, compared with only 9 percent of females.

Treating the male victim has proven to be even tougher. Calderwood (1987) suggested that some of the problems in treating the male rape victim include the reluctance of many men to report sexual assault, lack of facilities for helping men, and lack of knowledge about the phenomenon. Frazier (1993) as well as Groth and Burgess (1980) suggested that one reason male survivors of sexual assault may be less likely to report or seek treatment for their assault is partly because they view rape crisis centers and hotlines as serving only women. According to Kaufman (1980) proper diagnosis and treatment of male rape victims requires a high index of suspicion and sensitivity to the likelihood of major, hidden trauma. Leskela, Dieperink and Kok (2001) suggested that group therapy is an effective modality in treating men who have been sexually assaulted. Due to some of the stigmatization of male rape, these victims need their own facilities devoted to their treatment needs.

Most of the studies of male rape victims indicated that they face serious psychological problems due to being raped. However, due to underreporting by male victims, as well as societies view of the male rape victim we don't really know enough about the victim to draw conclusions. Much is left to be said about the male rape victim. From the literature that is available, we are able to conclude that most male victims suffer from some of the same psychological problems as female victims. One major component to look into is the sexual orientation of the victim and the offender and how that affects the victim.

It does seem that male rape victims are now going through some of the same painful processes that female rape victims go through. Females were and some still are embarrassed about the rape, just as the men are, and feel that it was some how their fault. Females also had the stigma of rape attached to them, just as males do. Before the passage of Rape Shield Laws, female victims were even more reluctant to report out of fear of being ridiculed or blamed. The court system may want to reassess their laws regarding rape of males.

References

American Academy of Pediatrics. *Committee on Adolescence: Sexual Assault and the Adolescent.* Washington DC: Author, 1994.

Brochman, S. "Silent Victims: Bringing Male Rape Out of the Closet." *The Advocate* 582, (1991): 38–42.

Calderwood, D. "The Male Rape Victim." *Medical Aspects of Human Sexuality* 21 no. 5, (1987): 53–55.

Coxell, A.W., and M.B. King. "Male Victims of Rape and Sexual Abuse." *Sexual and Marital Therapy* 11 no 3, (1996): 297–308.

Dupre, A.R., H.L. Hampton, H. Morrison, and G.R. Meeks. "Sexual Assault." *Obstetrical and Gynecological Survey* 48, (1993): 640–648.

Finkelhor, D. and D. Russell. "Women as Perpetrators." *Child Sexual Abuse: New Theory and Research.* New York Free Press, 1984: 171–187.

Forman, B. D. "Reported Male Rape." *Victimology International Journal 7,* (1982): 235–236.

Frazier, P.A. "A Comparative Study and Female Victims Seen at a Hospital-Based Rape Crisis Program." *Journal of Interpersonal Violence 8* no. 1, (1993): 64–76.

Gil-Rivas, V., R. Fiorentine, M.D. Anglin, and E. Taylor. "Sexual and Physical Abuse: Do They Compromise Drug Treatment Outcomes?" *Journal of Substance Abuse* Treatment 14 no. 4, (1997): 351–358.

Groth, N., and W. Burgess. "Male Rape: Offenders and Victims." *American* Journal of Psychiatry 137, (1980): 806–810.

Hickson, F.C.I., P.M. Davies, A.J. Hunt, and P. Weatherburn. "Gay Men as Victims of Nonconsensual Sex." *Archives of Sexual Behavior 23* no. 3, (1994): 281–294.

Hill, J.M. "The Effects of Sexual Orientation in the Courtroom: A Double Standard." *Journal of Homosexuality 39* no. 2, (2000): 93–111.

Isley, P. "Adult Male Sexual Assault in the Community. A Literature Review and Group Treatment Model." *Rape and Sexual Assault III: A Research Handbook.* New York: Garland Publishing, Inc, 1991.

Kaufman, A., P. Divasto, R. Jackson, P. Voorhees, and J. Christy. "Male Rape Victims: Noninstitutionalized Assault." *American Journal of Psychiatric Association* 137 no. 2, (1980): 221–223.

Laurent, C. "Male Rape." *Nursing Times 89* no. 6, (1993): 10–16.

Leskela, J., M. Dieperink, and C.J. Kok. "Group Treatment with Sexually Assaulted Male Veterans: A Year in Review." *Group 25* no. 4, (2001): 303–319.

Manzano, L. J. "Men Raped: Supporting the Male Survivor of Sexual Assault on the College Campus." (1998) http://www.uvm.edu/~vtconn/journals/1998/manzano.html (retrieved July 2003).

Mezey, G., and M. King. "The Effects of Sexual Assault on Men: A Survey of 22 Victims." *Psychological Medicine 19* no. 1, (1989): 205–209.

Mitchell, D., R. Hirschman, and G.C.N. Hall. "Attributions of Victim Responsibility, Pleasure and Trauma in Male Rape." *Journal of Sex Research* 36 no. 4, (1999): 369–373.

Rogers, P. "Post Traumatic Stress Disorder Following Male Rape." *Journal of Mental Health-UK 6* no. 1, (1997): 5–9.

Romano, E., and R.V. DeLuca. "Male Sexual Abuse: A Review of Effects, Abuse Characteristics, and Links with Later Psychological Functioning." *Aggression and Violent Behavior* 6 no. 1, (2001): 55–78.

Smith, R., C.J. Pine, and M. Hawley. "Social Cognitions About Adult Male Victims of Female Sexual Assault." *The Journal of Sex Research* 24, (1988): 101–112.

Sorenson, S.B., J.A. Stein, J.M. Siegel, J.M. Golding, and M.A. Burman. "The Prevalence of Adult Sexual Assault: The Los Angeles Epidemicologic Catchment Area Study." *American Journal of Epidemiology* 126, (1987): 1154–1164.

Struckman-Johnson, C., and D. Struckman-Johnson. "Acceptance of Male Rape Myths among College Men and Women." *Sex Roles: A Journal of Research* 27 no. ¾, (1992): 84–100.

Struckman-Johnson, C., and D. Struckman-Johnson. "Men Pressured and Forced Into Sexual Experience." *Archives of Sexual Behavior* 23 no. 1, (1994): 93–114.

U.S. Department of Justice, Bureau of Justice Statistics. *Criminal Victimization in the United States*, 1999. Washington, D. C.: Government Printing Office.

When a friend or family member discloses a sexual assault to you: <u>Guidelines for Helping Sexual Assault Victims</u>

- Listen to her and let her reveal information at her own pace.
- Let her express her emotions in her own way.
- Believe her.
- Reassure her that she is safe now.
- Stay with her if she wants you to stay.
- Encourage her to report the assault to the police. Let her have control of the decision.
- Encourage her to seek medical attention. Let her have control of the decision unless there is a medical emergency.
- Allow her to make her own decisions about who to tell.
- Be supportive by using a sympathetic tone of voice, maintaining natural eye contact, using empathetic facial expressions and body language, and keeping a nonjudgmental attitude.
- Offer to get whatever she needs or to make phone calls for her.
- Let her know that her feelings and responses are normal reactions to a traumatic event.
- Tell her that she did nothing wrong and that her victimization was not her fault.
- Let her talk about the assault as often as she wants to talk about it.
- Be patient. Recovery from a sexual assault takes a long time.
- Support her through the stages of recovery.
- Respect her wishes.
- Offer to help her find resources for support, such as a local rape crisis center.
- Offer to accompany her to the hospital, police, station, rape crisis center, or court.
- Offer to be available when she needs to talk.
- Don't physically touch or hug her without asking if she is comfortable with it.
- Don't vent your own shock, anger, and outrage at the assault to her.
- Don't seek revenge against the perpetrator (s).
- Don't try to keep her busy so she won't think about it.
- Don't dwell on the sexual aspects of the assault.
- Don't overprotect her. Allow her to exercise her independence.

When a friend or family member disclosed a sexual assault to you: Guidelines for Taking Care of Yourself

- Recognize that her assault will have an impact on you, including emotional trauma.
- Accept that the assault was not your fault. The perpetrator is the only one responsible.
- Understand that you will also experience stages of recovery.
- Know that it is normal to experience anger, sadness, self-blame, and feelings of powerlessness.
- Realize that while a desire for revenge is a common response, acts of revenge are detrimental to recovery.
- Allow yourself to express your feelings about the assault, and to seek support from formal or informal sources.

Compiled by Diane Daane, J.D.

PART III

THE OFTEN UNACKNOWLEDGED VICTIMS

Chapter 8

Sexual Abuse of Men in Prisons

Robert D. Hanser, Ph.D. and Chad Trulson

Introduction

There currently exists no national level data on the prevalence of inmate-on-inmate rape in prisons (Human Rights Watch 2001).[1] Of the research on prison sexual violence, what is known has been generally divided into two areas. One area focuses on the narrative accounts from actual victims. The second area of research has attempted to construct a picture of the actual incidence of prison rape among male inmates.

Despite what is known, most all attempts at measuring the incidence of prison sexual violence, both qualitative and quantitative, are plagued with problems of discovery, documentation, and the generalizability of findings (Dumond 2000; Lockwood 1994). Indeed, many sexual incidents are simply not discovered, many fail to get documented, and research, whether qualitative or quantitative, is simply limited to the time, institution, and population studied. In the end, the bottom line is that sexual violence among male inmates is largely a hidden event and what is known is likely a small and distorted portion.

---

1. We use prison "rape" interchangeably for inmate "sexual violence" or "sexual assault." This definition does not include the more ambiguous definition of a solicitation, later accompanied only by a physical assault with no sexual intent or overtone. This does not include other sexual related victimization, most notably sexual harassment, gesturing, or propositions. Though not specifically defined as sexual violence, these behaviors are nonetheless important when understanding how the events build toward the ultimate rape act itself. Thus, these behaviors will also be discussed to provide the reader with a complete understanding of prison sexual violence.

There are other reasons for the conservative numbers on sexual violence in prisons. One of these is the failure to report by the victims themselves (Robertson 1999; Saum, et al. 1995). Fear of retaliation, embarrassment, humiliation, and the lack of an adequate means of redress are frequently given as explanations for the underreporting of sexual violence among male inmates (Bowker 1980; Eigenberg 1989; Nacci and Kane 1983; Propper 1981; Saum, et al. 1995). Other reasons for underreporting, which seem to be more unique to male victims, also relate to differing social mores and norms within the prison and society at large (Robertson 1999; Saum, et al. 1995). These factors will be explored further through an analysis of the social context in which sexual violence occurs among male inmates. Furthermore, the issue of sexual violence is preceded by many behaviors that pave the way toward victimization of many inmates. These behaviors may include, but are not limited to, intimidation, posturing, gesturing, and various forms of sexual harassment (Robertson 1999). We explore these dynamics in framing the issue of prison sexual violence.

The purpose of this chapter is to first explain the misleading nature of "homosexual rape" as it is applied to male sexual violence in prisons. Second, this chapter examines the notion that there is a higher incidence of sexual violence in prisons than is documented in official statistics. Lastly, this chapter demonstrates the complex nature of sexual violence in prisons and frames sexual violence from a power-based class system perspective. That is, the power dynamics between differing social groups, expressed in the form of sexual violence, domination, and exploitation, emerge as common themes within the prison environment and can help situate the issue of sexual violence in prisons.

Sexual Violence as Power and Social Status: The Misnomer of Homosexual Rape

Violence, in many ways, is an expression of power (Riedel and Welsh 2002). For those lacking the means to obtain desired goods and services, violence or the threat of violence becomes a viable and potentially effective option (Riedel and Welsh 2002). In prisons this is even more so the case given the restricted accesses to various commodities that individuals in the free society would otherwise be able to obtain. Indeed, Gresham Sykes observed over 40 years ago that the "pains of imprisonment," including the deprivation of liberty, goods, services, autonomy, security, and heterosexual relationships become important wares in the prison environment (Sykes 1958). Those able to procure these commodities, or a semblance of them, are frequently those who hold the power within correctional institutions.

Much as in the wider society, sex in prisons is a commodity which is open for trade. Sex is often an expression of power and status in prisons (Bowker 1980), and violence is one way of obtaining this commodity. The sexually violent inmate gains an increase in both status and power, while the victimized and assaulted inmate suffers a corresponding loss in status and prestige (Robertson 1999; Scacco 1975; Tucker 1981). Indeed, one's place in the stratified inmate subculture is partly sex-based with sex roles being grounded in aggression (Dumond 1992; Robertson 1999). Aggressive and dominant forms of inmate roles include that of the "wolf," "pitcher," and the "daddy," with submissive roles often being referred to as "punk" or "fag" (Knowles 1999; Robertson 1999; Sykes 1958).

Perpetrators and Victims: Homosexual Conversion, Homosexual Rape, and Sexual Harassment

When considering male prison rape, violence and the threat of violence allow for the domination and control of the victim, even in such relationships that prison officials may term voluntary or consensual (Davis 1982; Eigenberg 1989). This connection between forced and voluntary "homosexuality" has been illustrated in interviews conducted by Davis (1982) where he found that most "consensual" homosexuals were really heterosexuals who had been forced to engage in sex to avoid harm (Robertson 1999).[2] This process, referred to as being "turned out" or "punked out" effectively redefines the victim's role in the prison as that of a "homosexual." Indeed, once the role as a "homosexual" or "punk" is attached, the victim acquires a clearly defined "jacket". This "jacket", which is prison slang for a role label, becomes a new external identity that is ascribed to the inmate via the prison subculture (Nacci 1978; Smith and Batiuk 1989; Tucker, 1981). Again, in this type of situation the victim is not, in actuality, of homosexual orientation by self-choice. The motivation for engaging in these activities is one of fear from the threat of harm (Davis 1982; Tucker 1981). For instance, one inmate described his situation:

---

2. See Lockwood (1994) for a competing view of this dynamic of inmate sexual violence.

> I had no choice but to submit to being Inmate B's prison wife. Out of fear for life, I submitted to…sexual activity [our wording]…and performing other duties as a woman, such as making his bed (HRW, Interview with M.R.).

Openly homosexual males are not immune from sexual violence either, and in many instances, can be targeted for more intense victimization because of their self-professed sexuality, their outward appearance, and importantly, the ambivalence by prison administrators due to the belief that the alleged victimization is "consensual" because of their sexual orientation. One homosexual inmate remarked:

> Since I've been in prison I have endured more misery than most people could handle…All open homosexuals are preyed upon and if they don't choose up they get chosen (HRW, Interview with M.R.).

The perpetrator, on the other hand, is typically heterosexual when in mainstream society, but plays the role of aggressor to avoid the role of victim (Smith and Batiuk 1989; Scacco 1975; Weiss and Friar 1974). Within the prison subculture, rapists are considered masculine conquerors of effeminate "punks" (Weiss and Friar 1974). The aggressor is not considered a homosexual, but is simply assuming a "one up" position within the norms of prison life. In fact, "most sexual aggressors in prison are neither homosexual nor bisexual; they are heterosexuals who define sexual aggression as affirmation of heterosexuality even though their victims are of the same sex" (Robertson 1999, 26).

It cannot be overemphasized that the pursuit of power via sexual violence, coupled with the enslavement of weaker prisoners, is an integral feature of imprisonment in prisons throughout the United States (Knowles 1999; Rideau and Wikberg 1992). However, rape in prison should not be perceived as a solely sexual act, but is an act of violence that reflects both politics and power roles (Knowles 1999; Rideau and Wikberg 1992). According to Knowles (1999), "the act of rape in the ultra masculine world of prison constitutes the ultimate humiliation visited upon a male by forcing him to assume the role of a woman" (p. 8). Rideau and Wikberg (1992) further elaborate by noting that sexual assault in prison is not considered "sexual" and not really regarded as "rape" in the same sense that society regards the term. In fact, one of the perverse mores in the world of the prison subculture is that victims of sexual violence are rarely regarded as victims (Knowles 1999). A key element of the prisoners' belief system is that a 'man' cannot be forced to do anything that he does not want to do (Knowles 1999). Thus, a 'real man' cannot be exploited (Knowles 1999). Those unable to meet these rigid demands are consequently not considered 'men', but rather as being weak and unworthy of respect from those who are 'men' (Knowles 1999). Accordingly, their weakness both invites and justifies exploitation (Knowles 1999; Rideau and Wikberg 1992).

For many inmates who have been socialized into this system, sexual arousal has come to be associated with aggression (Knowles 1999). It is interesting to point out that this is no different for any other type of rapist who finds pain infliction and violence to be associated with sexual arousal and gratification (Holmes and Holmes 2002). For the perpetrators of these acts, the degree of satisfaction derived from the sex act is often directly proportional to the degree of force and humiliation inflicted upon the victim (Bartol 1999; Holmes and Holmes 2002; Knowles 1999; Wooden and Parker 1982). In its most extreme form, this sexualized aggression is manifested in outright acts of violence such as rape. But in prison, less severe cases such as sexual intimidation, domination, and manipulation, can lead to the same eventual victimization (Knowles 1999; Wooden and Parker 1982). For example, although not physically coerced, one inmate explains the events that led to his subsequent victimization:

> One inmate would stake a claim to you by becoming your "friend" hanging out with you all the time. In reality, he was saying "don't touch he's mine." It's a gradually [sic] process that you become dependent on this person whether its financial, physical, or emotional. But sooner or later there comes a time when he wants a return in his investment…you don't want to ruin your "friendship" by saying no…so you do what he wants, I did, and that's how you get hooked (HRW interview with P.E.).

The above discussion shows how behaviors that are not overt attacks can still coerce victims into a sexual relationship. Similarly, other acts such as the sexual harassment of inmates by other fellow inmates and/or prison staff can likewise be very damaging, despite the fact that no overt assault has taken place (Robertson 1999). The emotional humiliation inflicted by sexually harassing behaviors serves to label and intimidate the victim into ultimate compliance. This is especially true in shaping the behaviors of victims who are engaged in 'voluntary' sexual relationships within the prison (Knowles 1999).

Sexual harassment among male inmates, like prison rape, can be attributed to the conditions of confinement as well as the sub-cultural values that inmates bring with them to prison. These two factors share a common theme: that sexual harassment among male inmates is an act of sexual aggression born from a need to dominate others (Robertson 1999). In need of affirming their masculinity, some inmates turn to a strategy that is readily open to them in the prison environment–victimization of their fellow inmates (Robertson 1999). Western males in general and lower class males in particular, who comprise much of the prison population, equate aggression and domination with masculinity (Robertson 1999). As the ultimate act of domination, prison rape is thus transformed into a statement of one's masculinity and strength.

> Rape is not primarily motivated by the frustration of sexual needs. It is more the sexual expression of aggressive expression of sexuality.... The rape of male inmates occurs in correctional settings not because it is a substitute for sex with women, but for the same reasons it occurs in the community: to hurt, to humiliate, to dominate, to control, and to degrade (Cotton and Groth 1982, 50).

Within this context, sexually suggestive behaviors among male inmates perform at least two functions. First, predatory heterosexual inmates employ sexually harassing behaviors as a means of feminizing inmates targeted for sexual exploitation (Robertson 1999). Second, sexually suggestive behaviors among male inmates promote an involuntary identity transformation and role assignment within the inmate social world. By succumbing to the pressure to be a "punk" a victim of such suggestive behavior acquires a clearly defined "jacket" as that of a sex slave who can be traded during the remainder of his incarceration (Robertson 1999). Evidence indicates that sexually suggestive behaviors among male inmates are widespread; much more so than actual prison rape (Hensley 2000; Lockwood 1994).

Though most male inmates define themselves as heterosexual, many are still propositioned for sexual activity (Struckman-Johnson and Struckman-Johnson 2000; Robertson 1999). Unless these propositions are forcefully rebutted, propositions can mark the targeted inmate as a homosexual (Lockwood 1994; Robertson 1999). In addition to propositions, other forms of related behavior, such as touching and rubbing potential victims are frequent and serve to test masculine boundaries (Robertson 1999). These forms of sexual harassment are typically not overt enough to be detected by prison staff, nor serious enough to be reported by inmates. However, this form of sexual harassment sets the foundation for the role that selected male inmates will play during the remainder of their prison sentence. Despite this obvious system of conversion from new inmate to recycled punk, prison staff often fail to appropriately intervene in this process of victimization, even if it is known (Weiss and Friar 1974).

Sex for Trade

For the middle and upper-class in the larger society, power is exerted through various mechanisms such as education, money, politics, and law—for the poor, the most immediate means of achieving power are quite frequently physical (Messerschmidt 1999; Tucker 1981). The upper and middle-class condemn this method of achieving equality as it upsets their comfortable status quo (Messerschmidt 1999; Tucker 1981).

In prisons however, with its deprivations and disproportionate populations of lower-class members, there are no proscriptions against violence. Indeed, violence is the most direct means to obtain power over this commodity, and is the tool most often employed. Thus, it is sex that becomes the medium by which social status is determined in prisons and violence becomes the means to obtain it. "Ready to kill or maim rival inmates, the prison rapist monopolizes his selected victim's services, for punks are a commodity always in short supply" (Weiss and Friar 1974, 138). Therefore, sex is a commodity within the prison economy and being a perpetrator equals status and power (Robertson 1999; Tucker 1981).

The masculine identity within prison for male inmates becomes crucially important, for if one is not masculine, one is by proxy considered feminine. There is little middle ground or room for negotiation. "The end result of victimization in a correctional institution is usually sexual aggression and domination as a political act based on a show of force" (Scacco 1975, 3). Thus, sexual aggression is more than an act of sexual gratification as a result of heterosexual deprivation, it is an outward demonstration of his own masculinity (Scacco 1975). Prior sexual and social styles of masculinity are thus adapted and shaped within prisons so that the male inmate does not lose his position of dominance and control. To fail to do so results in the male inmate accepting a subservient role, or in the prison subculture, the role of the woman. In essence, the mindset is that of 'rape or get raped,' those who rape are the "haves" in the prison economy, and those who get raped are the "have nots."

With this in mind, it becomes easy to see why sexual assault goes unreported. Those who are the "haves" do not wish to loose their hold on their precious resource; the punks who serve them. Those who are the "have nots," on the other hand, cannot possibly report their situation without living in constant fear of retaliation. Further, for those who ultimately report their victimization, the result is absolute isolation from the mainstream of prison life and the few amenities that are offered; amenities not available when placed under close institutional protection.

Prison staff also has little incentive to report or prevent sexual assault since the power-base of the current inmate "pecking order" serves to perpetuate a sense of informal institutional structure and order. For these reasons, a veritable "dark figure" of sexually violent crime exists within many prison systems, leaving most institutional sexual assaults largely undetected, or at the very least, unreported. From this point, we now turn our attention to these issues and their impact on reported rates of prison sexual assault.

The Dark Figure of Sexually Violent Crime in Prison

Similar to the often cited dark figure of crime within society at large, researchers have suggested that there is a significant dark figure of sexual violence that occurs within the prisons of America (Dumond 2000; Saum, et al. 1995). By whatever definition, sexual victimization, ranging from harassment to rape has been said to be "one of the most illusive statistics in the criminal justice field" (Struckman-Johnson and Struckman-Johnson 2000, 379).

The most recent research on inmate sexual violence has estimated that more minor forms of sexual victimization (e.g., fondling or failed attempts at intercourse) are most prevalent and hover around 15–20 percent in samples of prisoners studied, while actual completed rapes are less frequent, about 1–2 percent in samples of inmates (Hensley 2000; HRW 2001; Struckman-Johnson and Struckman-Johnson 2000).[3] Previous research has generally confirmed this finding (Lockwood 1994). Yet despite these most recent figures, identifying, detecting, and documenting sexual victimizations in prisons are difficult at best. Indeed, it is a falsity to talk of prisons and prisoners as if only one kind existed, and research has generally been limited to the study of a few particular institutions within larger prison systems, or several interstate comparisons of the prevalence of sexual violence. At the least, there are significant differences both within and between correctional systems around the country, not to mention conflicting methodologies and definitions utilized in correctional research which serve as further impediments to accurate accounts of sexual violence in prisons (Lockwood 1994; Saum, Surratt, Inciardi, and Bennett 1995). Simply, what we know about sexual violence in prisons is plagued by underreporting, underdiscovery, lack of generalizability, and importantly, inconsistent definitions of what sexual violence actually entails.

There is a great deal of difficulty in determining a distinction between rape and consensual sexual activity. According to Eigenberg (1989), "research has failed to clearly distinguish between consensual homosexual acts and acts of rape" (p. 39). Eigenberg explains that "inmates who participate in homosex-

---

3. See Wooden and Parker for estimates of completed rape which are as high as 14 percent of their samples in a California medium-security prison.

ual acts after threats of rape are bona fide rape victims, yet these acts are frequently perceived as homosexual acts rather than acts of rape" (1989, 40). Again, in the end it seems that many acts of sexual violence fail to be uncovered and/or reported, while what is known suffers from definitional issues in determining what even constitutes prison sexual violence.

Coupled with the previous problem, the discrepancy in official statistics occurs because many male inmates who have been victims of sexual violence are too embarrassed to confide in their experience—and this contributes significantly to sexual violence as an underreported event (Davis 1982; Eigenberg 1989; Saum, Surratt, Inciardi, and Bennett 1995; Weiss and Friar 1974). For many male inmates, there is no shame that can equal this loss for it is a perceived loss of manhood which is real in its consequences (Weiss and Friar 1974). Research on the rape of women in society at large has demonstrated that attitudes which stigmatize the victim or imply that the victim is somehow at fault also contribute to underreporting (Eigenberg 1989). This same stigmatization and trauma may be equally true for male inmates (Cotton and Groth 1982). For instance, one male inmate professed that:

> I was put in a cell with a gang member who made me give him oral sex…I went to see a psychologist who told me that I'd caused that inmate to sexually abuse me…I can see that I was going through a brake down [sic] mentally. Anyway, I'd made up my mind that I was taking my life….it is truly impossible to put into words what goes through one's mind when becoming a victim of rape. Being made into a person of no self worth, being remade into what ever the person or gang doing the raping wants you to be (HRW, interview with R.G.).

Despite the embarrassment of reporting, there is also the fear of retaliation for male inmates who report sexual victimization. There is an understood rule against being a "snitch" and going to prison staff, meaning that problems between inmates are to be handled inmate-to-inmate. Violating this norm can have lethal repercussions if the inmate is not protected by the prison administration (Sykes 1958). Yet to gain protection results in being ostracized by other inmates and retaliation is a looming threat during the following months or even years (Weiss and Friar 1974). In short, there is a skeptical attitude toward institutional protection and most "inmates have little faith in the ability of guards to protect them from retaliation should they complain about sexual assaults" (Scacco 1975, 30). Some inmates are essentially told that they have three options outside of snitching, they can "…submit, fight, or go over the fence" (Weiss and Friar 1974, 3).

Related to the previous point, many male inmates simply see no adequate from of redress in which to air their grievance. In these instances, grievance procedures simply pay 'lip service' to airing complaints, failing to truly investigate or resolve inmate concerns. Further, many inmates find that the institutional system simply does not care, does not believe the inmate allegations, and even encourages sexual violence through deliberate indifference. According to Scacco, "the shocking fact is that there is both overt and covert implication of officers in the attacks that take place in penal institutions" (1975, 30). Likewise, Weiss and Friar (1974) comment that prisoners are convinced that prison rape is an integral part of the prison punishment system—in part the belief that rape is sanctioned by prison authorities. They view it as the ultimate method of control and punishment (Eigenberg 2000; Weiss and Friar 1974, x). In this same way, Tucker (1981) adds that "rape exists and will continue to exist in confinement institutions because it serves the interests of too many powerful elements of jail and prison societies, including the administration" (p.6). Similarly, Knowles (1999) points out that officials use the fear of rape to divert institutional aggression, destroy potential leaders, and to intimidate prisoners into becoming informers (Eigenberg 2000). Knowles observed that these tactics were used by New Mexico prison officials just prior to the New Mexico prison riot (1999). Further, Scacco (1982) states that inmates at the top of the prison power structure benefit sexually, psychologically, and financially, from the punks who are turned out by this male rape process. With both prison administrators and powerful inmates benefiting from this form of violence, incentive to change such a power structure is unlikely to materialize.

Considerations for Sexual Violence Among Male Inmates

The decision of the U.S. Supreme Court in *Farmer v. Brennan* (1994) was a landmark precedent for those concerned with the issue of prison rape (Donaldson 1994). The "deliberate indifference" of state prison systems regarding inmate rape denied inmates the minimal means of safety necessary to serve their sentence. "The Court resolutely pronounced that prison rape 'serves no legitimate penological objective' cannot be squared with 'evolving standards of decency' and is simply no part of the penalty" (Donaldson 1994, 2).

This is important as prison rape and sexual exploitation serve no functional purpose within the Constitutional requirements of the criminal justice system. Yet, prisons and their staff, either through negligence or gross criminal violation of their duties, have experienced great difficulty in achieving environments free of sexual violence. Is prison sexual violence among male inmates an elusive culprit that well meaning prison systems are not equipped to handle? Or is it instead the case that sexual violence is a tool that has served the prison system well, through the intimidation, exploitation, control, and domination of those inmates who are the most difficult to control? In either case, it would appear that prison sexual violence is a concern deserving significant attention, particularly when considering potential long-term social costs for such violence.

In fact, Scacco (1982) argues the most serious cost of prison rape to society is that it takes non-violent offenders and turns them into people with a high potential for violence, full of rage and eager to take vengeance on the society which they hold responsible for their utter humiliation and loss of manhood.[4] The value structure of the lower-class subcultures found in prison, regardless of their racial or ethnic background, places extreme emphasis on maintaining and safeguarding the inmate's manhood and his sense of masculinity (Wooden and Parker 1982).

To be sure, there are other considerations coupled to prison sexual violence. Of the many considerations, some of the most notable relate to the threat of sexually transmitted diseases, medical injuries, and continued victimization, in addition to the profound impact of being labeled and stigmatized (Dumond 2000). Other areas worthy of consideration fall outside of inmate-on-inmate victimization, but rather center on the sexual victimization of inmates by guards, or guards by inmates (see Marquart, Barnhill, and Balshaw-Biddle 2001).

Solutions and Conclusions

Some argue that to deal with the problem of prison rape the inmate social structure itself must be changed (Eigenberg 1989; Knowles 1999; Robertson 1999). Ibrahim (1974) argues there are several ways to decrease prison violence. One method suggested is to institute conjugal visits or home furlough release programs (Knowles 1999; Ibrahim 1974). But Lockwood (1980) contends that conjugal visits would not help most sexual aggressors, because very few inmates are legally married or have common-law wives. Also, Knowles (1999) points out that most offenders would be ineligible for home furlough because they are too violent and would put communities at risk if released.

---

4. Lockwood (1994) does dispute this claim and cites there is little credible evidence that suggest that victims will commit crimes upon release because of their "hate and hostility" towards the public (p. 99).

Alternatives such as conjugal visits also do not appear to be a satisfactory solution because the foundation of prison rapes has been shown to be grounded in power gratification, rather than sexual gratification (Bowker 1980; Knowles 1999; Robertson 1999; Scacco 1975; Tucker 1981).

One possible remedy to prison sexual violence is to improve the inmate classification process (Knowles 1999). Knowles contends that the classification systems should identify potential rapists, or more importantly the potential victims, and separate them (1999). A particularly effective classification system might target what could be called the "irreducible 10%" of our nation's most persistent and chronic violators (Trulson 2002). At the other end, classification systems might also lend more support to those who fit the category of the most "vulnerable 10%" or those inmates with little physical redress to ward off attacks.[5] Indeed, Lockwood's (1994) research suggests that targets of sexual exploitation who revert to "demonstrations of violence," even after being the victim of sexual violence, were almost always only one time victims (p. 99). Thus, their show of violence was a "protective" factor against chronic sexual assaults or other forms of sexual victimization. Further separating the two extremes might produce dividends by isolating the irreducible 10 percent and protecting the vulnerable 10 percent to preempt any need for the show of violence in the first place.

Yet while potential remedies such as those just mentioned seem to possess intuitive appeal, it is likely that such procedures would be costly and overly optimistic. This is especially true when considering the burgeoning prison population within the United States. The manipulative inmate will easily find means by which they can circumvent classification schemes. In fact, identification of prison rapists and prison victims has proven difficult simply because of the natural resistance of the inmate population to disclose such activities. Unlike classification systems that can more readily identify problem inmates such as gang members, trying to tag the potential rapist in prison is fraught with ambiguities. At best, prison policies might only be reactive in nature when dealing with sexually predatory inmates especially when compared to other problem populations in the prison setting.

By focusing on these largely topical remedies, the true problem of sub-cultural beliefs held by both staff and inmates will then simply be overlooked.

---

5. The "irreducible 10%" is a subjective figure that notes those groups falling outside of the "typical" inmate. Indeed, almost 10 percent of our nation's prisoners, across all state prison systems, are considered threatening enough to be placed in administrative or punitive segregation. The vulnerable 10 percent are those in custodies for protection (e.g., protective custody).

This is precisely where problems with prison rape develop and are maintained, for if sub-cultural definitions of power were different, much of the motivation for prison sexual violence would be eliminated. It is then apparent that the deep-seated belief systems held by the culture of both prison inmates and the prison administration is where the true basis for the etiology of sexual victimization in prison can be found. Rather than focusing on programs designed to alleviate sexual outlets, or programs that attempt to 'outsmart' the efforts of determined inmates, a better approach is likely to entail the eradication of the initial motivation to dominate and exploit others—though this may be easier said than done.

Though changes in the inmate subculture may be the most effective process, such changes are difficult given the well established norms held in the prison environment. These norms are based on the crudest and most basic of human motivations for dominance and environmental control. Until these norms are challenged and modified, other attempts at intervention or prevention will provide only band-aid solutions and stop-gap measures to the problem of sexual violence in prisons. It is possible that training programs for staff and inmates, coupled with initiatives that provide positive reinforcement for compliance with new cultural norms, that changes in the subculture might be slowly implemented (Eigenberg 2000). However, change is difficult and this must be recognized as a long term process in which victimizations will undoubtedly be experienced in the short term.

Regardless of the means by which such change is implemented, it is certain that change will be an absolute necessity for any prison system that truly desires to eliminate sexual violence within its confines. Failure to do so will provide continued tacit approval for such sub-cultural norms, regardless of any official form of response. In short, overlooking the needed change in sub-cultural norms will produce nothing but short-sighted and disastrous results. This ironically has the potential of leaving the victim of prison sexual assault worse off than they had been before the intervention had ever been applied.

References

Bartol, C. *Criminal Behavior: A Psychosocial Approach.* New Jersey: Prentice Hall, 1999.

Bowker, L.H. *Prison Victimization.* New York: Elsevier, 1980.

Cotton, D.J. and A.N. Groth. "Inmate Rape: Prevention and Intervention." *Journal of Prison and Jail Health* 47, (1982).

Davis, A.J. "Sexual Assaults in the Philadelphia Prison System and Sheriff's Vans." In *Male Rape. A Casebook of Sexual Aggressions, ed.* A.M. Scacco, Jr. New York: AMS Press, Inc, 1982.

Donaldson, S. "Rape of Incarcerated Americans: A Preliminary Statistical Look" (7th ed.). Available: http://www.igc.org/spr/docs/stats, 1994

Dumond, R.W. "The Sexual Assault of Male Inmates in Incarcerated Settings." *International Journal of Sociology* 20, *(1992).*

Dumond, R.W. "Inmate Sexual Assault: The Plague that Persists." *The Prison Journal 80 no.*4, (2000): 407–414.

Eigenberg, H. "Male Rape: An Empirical Examination of Correctional Officers' Attitudes Toward Rape in Prison." *The Prison Journal* 69, (1989): 39–56.

Eigenberg, H. "Correctional Officers and Their Perceptions of Homosexuality, Rape, and Prostitution in Male Prisons." *The Prison Journal* 80 no. 4, (2000): 415–443.

Farmer v. Brennan, 511 U.S. 825, (1994).

Hensley, C. "Consensual and Forced Sex in Male Oklahoma Prisons." Paper presented at the annual meeting of the Academy of Criminal Justice Sciences, New Orleans, L.A (2000 March).

Holmes, S.T., and R.M. Holmes. *Sex Crimes* (2nd ed.). Thousand Oaks, CA: Sage Publications, 2002.

Human Rights Watch. No Escape: Male Rape in U.S. Prisons. http://www.hrw.org/reports/2001/prison/report.html (2001).

Ibrahim, A.I. "Deviant Sexual Behavior in Men's Prisons." *Journal of Crime and Delinquency,* 20, (1974): 38–44.

Knowles, G.J. "Male Prison Rape: A Search for Causation and Prevention." *Howard Journal of Criminal Justice* 38 no. 3, (1999): 267–283.

Lockwood, D. *Prison Sexual Violence.* New York: Elsevier, 1980.

Lockwood, D. "Issues in Prison Sexual Violence." In *Prison Violence in America (2nd Edition),* eds. M. Braswell, R. Montgomery and L. Lombardo. Cincinnati: Anderson Publishing Co, 1994.

Marquart, J.W., M. Barnhill, and K. Balshaw-Biddle. "Fatal Attraction: An Analysis of Employee Boundary Violations in a Southern Prison System, 1995–1998." *Justice Quarterly* 18 no. 4, (2001): 877–910.

Messerschmidt, J.A. "Masculinities and Crime." In *Criminological Theory: Past to Present, eds.* F. T. Cullen and R. Agnew. Los Angeles, CA: Roxbury Publishing Company, 1999.

Nacci, P. L. "Sexual Assault in Prisons." *American Journal of Corrections* 40, (1978): 30–31.

Nacci, P. L., and T. R. Kane. "The Incidence of Sex and Sexual Aggression in Federal Prisons." *Federal Probation* 7, (1983): 31–36.

Propper, A. M. *Prison Homosexuality: Myth and Reality.* Lexington, MA: D C Heath, 1981.

Rideau, W. and R. Wikberg. *Life Sentences: Rage and Survival Behind Bars.* New York: Time Books, Random House, 1992.

Riedel, M. and W. Welsh. *Criminal Violence: Patterns, Causes, and Prevention.* Los Angeles, CA: Roxbury Publishing Company, 2002.

Robertson, J. E. "Cruel and Unusual Punishment in United States Prisons: Sexual Harassment Among Male Inmates." *American Criminal Law Review* 13 no. 1, (1999).

Saum, C. A., H. L. Surrat, J. A. Inciardi, and R. E. Bennett. "Sex in Prison: Exploring the Myths and Realities." *The Prison Journal* 75 no. 4, (1995): 413–430.

Scacco, A. M., Jr. *Rape in Prison.* Springfield, IL: Charles C. Thomas, 1975.

Smith, N. E., and M. E. Batiuk. "Sexual Victimization and Inmate Social Interaction." *The Prison Journal* 69, (1989): 29–38.

Struckman-Johnson, C., and D. Struckman-Johnson. "Sexual Coercion Rates in Seven Midwestern Prison Facilities for Men." *The Prison Journal* 80 no. 4, (2000): 379–390.

Sykes, G. M. *The Society of Captives.* New Jersey: Princeton University Press, 1958.

Trulson, C. *Judicial Intervention, Desegregation, and Inter-Racial Prisoner Violence: A Case Study of Desegregation in the Texas Prison System.* Unpublished doctoral dissertation, Sam Houston State University, 2002.

Tucker, D. *A Punk's Song: View from the Inside.* Fort Bragg, CA: AMS Press Inc, 1981.

Weiss, C. and D. J. Friar. *Terror in Prisons: Homosexual Rape and Why Society Condones It.* Indianapolis: Bobbs-Merril, Inc., 1974.

Wooden, W. S. and J. Parker. *Men Behind Bars: Sexual Exploitation in Prison.* New York: Plenum Press, 1982.

Chapter 9

Labeling Theory as an Etiological Paradigm for Prison Rape

Robert D. Hanser and Nathan R. Moran

Introduction

According to Labeling Theory, group reactions are imperative when trying to understand the events that lead to antisocial behavior. Labeling theory essentially asks why some acts are labeled deviant when others are not (Akers 2000). This theory asserts that social group reactions serve to make certain behaviors deviant, regardless of the individual context in which they occur (Vold, Bernard, and Snipes 1998). This begs the question as to who it is that creates the label associated with deviant behavior. The answer to this inquiry lies with those who hold the power within a given social structure. Some sociologists have asserted that it is the powerful, not the powerless, who create the standard for labels that are applied to individuals (Schur 1973). It is from this perspective that this chapter will serve to demonstrate the labeling and cognitive dissonance processes involved in homosexual rape within prisons. The inmate power structure and the labeling process are dovetailed against a sub-cultural backdrop of norms held by inmates and prison staff. This power structure and subcultural analysis will be used to demonstrate how both serve to force the victim to assume a deviant role and an undesired label. The assumption of this role leads to the application of a label that holds negative consequences for the individual targeted during this process. Finally, the means by which these labels are applied and the consequences for the male rape victim within a prison setting will be addressed.

Labeling Theory as a Paradigm for Prison Rape Etiology

In order to understand labeling theory, one must also understand the underlying power structures within any given social order in which the labeling process occurs. This is crucial because it is the powerful members of a society that impose labels upon those who are less socially prominent (Schur 1973). The label is determined by the standards of the affluent and upwardly mobile, with those at the lower echelons of the social structure being nearly, though not entirely, powerless to "throw off the yoke" of the labeling process (Becker 1963).

For the upper and middle classes, power can effectively be expressed through economic, vocational, and academic avenues. For the lower classes, however, many of these routes to upward social mobility are denied, leaving only direct physical means for obtaining power or control (Miller 1958). Correspondingly, a standard based on physical prowess and ability can develop (Messerschmidt 1999). Many perform physically oriented jobs, and likewise find the physical realm of achievement to be their best hope in moving upward through the social order (Messerschmidt 1999). Such an example might be the "ghetto kid" turned pro football or basketball star, or the rural small town kid turned Marine Corps hometown hero. These images themselves are stereotypes that serve to maintain the power structure as well as the means of achievement.

With the prison population being drawn disproportionately from the less affluent members of society, it should come as no surprise that prison norms may, in various subtle ways, exemplify power status norms held by the lower classes (Tucker 1981; Miller 1958). The members of the "prison society" are even less socially powerful than their socioeconomic counterparts who are not incarcerated. For these members, physical prowess and coercion becomes the primary method for achieving power in the prison setting. Thus, aside from some rare exceptions, such as successful "writ writers" or inmates who have affluent family members, those who are physically powerful tend to be the most socially powerful within the prison. Within the male inmate subculture, the expression of physical prowess as power is frequently paired with roles of masculinity, which, in turn, reinforces the subculture of physical prowess within the prison setting (Messerschmidt 1999).

The meaning of masculinity is different in prison than in mainstream society. In prison these meanings are reinforced when inmates act to affirm their masculinity in the limited ways that are available (Messerschmidt 1999). This results in a modified form of "hegemonic masculinity," which emphasizes negative attitudes toward authority, control over others, aggressiveness, and social reinforcement for violent acts (Messerschmidt 1999). Previously learned sexual and social styles of masculinity, as exercised in the broader society, are adapted and altered within prison so that the male inmate does not lose his position of dominance and control. To fail to do so results in the male inmate accepting a subservient role, or as it is termed in the prison subculture, the role and label of a "woman" (Tucker 1981). In essence, sexual violence among inmates is a statement of power, status, and control.

It is through both the means and threat of violence that dominance and control is achieved, with the victim ultimately being given the label of "punk." This is true even in cases that prison officials may term "voluntary" or "consensual" sex. This connection between forced and voluntary homosexuality was illustrated in interviews conducted by Davis (1982), during which he found that "consensual" homosexuals tended to be subjugated heterosexuals who had been forced to engage in sex to avoid physical harm. This process, referred to as being "turned out" or "punked out," effectively redefines and labels the victims' role in prison as that of a "punk," or subjugated homosexual (Tucker 1981). Thus, the homosexual orientation and label placed upon the deviant is not one of self-choice or personal preference, but is forced upon him by more powerful members of the inmate subculture.

According to Lemert (1999), the deviant is a product of gradual, unconscious processes that are part of socialization, especially subcultural socialization. Lemert (1999) also asserted that the personality change that occurs from accepting and internalizing a deviant label is not always gradual, but can be sudden. As Lemert (1999) states, "…it must be taken into consideration that traumatic experiences often speed up changes in personality…" (p. 386). This is especially true for inmates who are victims of prison gang rape, in which multiple assailants attack and repeatedly rape an inmate-victim. For the victim of gang rape, entering into a sexual relationship with one man in return for protection can be an adaptive coping mechanism for survival within the prison subculture. Lemert further states that "when a person begins to employ his deviant behavior or role…as a means of defense, attack, or adjustment to the overt and covert problems created by the consequent societal reaction to him, his deviance is secondary" (1999, 388). In this instance, the initial gang rape can be thought of as the source of primary deviance, whereas the deliberate decision to engage in "consensual" homosexuality with a single partner essentially results in a more solidified self-identity. This process from primary to secondary deviance creates a degree of cognitive dissonance within the individual that, when resolved, tends to leave the victim more willing to engage in future homosexual conduct, referred to by Lemert as secondary deviance (Festinger 1958; Lemert 1999).[1] Indeed, this is a logical extension of Lemert's work to include cognitive dissonance between the initial act of primary deviance and future acts of secondary deviance.

Through this process, the sexual values of mainstream society are completely inverted within the prison subculture. The inmate perpetrator who willingly engages in predatory homosexual activity would typically be given the marginalized label of "homosexual" or "bisexual" in the broader society. Ironically, however, within the prison there is exactly the opposite effect with a corresponding increase in social status and "manhood" for the perpetrator of sexual assault. Within the prison subculture, rapists are considered masculine conquerors of effeminate "punks" (Weiss and Friar 1974). The aggressor is not held as homosexual in orientation, but is simply assuming a position of power within the subcultural norms of prison life. The victim of the prison sexual assault, however, suffers an injury greater than the sexual assault alone, as the victim's entire social position within the prison is effectively compromised and redefined.

According to Becker (1999), "being caught and branded as deviant has important consequences for one's further social participation and self-image," adding "the most important consequence is a drastic change in the individual's public identity" (p. 392). This also applies to inmate-victims of prison rape. For many inmates, the role of prison "punk" produces a self-fulfilling prophecy. Over time, many inmates who are forced into the subjugated role of "punk" learn that certain creature comforts can be obtained if they are willing to comply with sexual demands. Thus, many come to identify with and dress the part, act the part, and even to rationalize their role (e.g., the interrelationship between cognitive dissonance and primary and secondary labeling processes). Indeed, this role can frequently go well beyond that of simple sexual services, extending to a relationship of complete and total servitude. Many will submit to cooking, cleaning, mending, and other activities typically held to be "feminine" by the prison subculture as well as mainstream society. Some inmates, upon acceptance of the "punk" label and resolution of the dissonance associated with secondary deviance, will even go so far as to involve themselves in competitive hypergamy, or the practice of achieving upward mobility through "marriage" within the prison subculture (Tucker 1981).

While these inmates will frequently rationalize their activity as one of survival, their participation can lead them to a complete internalization of the

---

1. It is not implied here that homosexual conduct is necessarily "deviant." Rather, Lemert's concept of "secondary deviance" is used to illustrate the relationship between the cognitive dissonance and labeling processes.

role. With the label fully applied, many "homosexual" inmates will thus make the most of their remaining time in prison and will strive to obtain whatever securities their role can bring them. When the inmate begins to see himself as a "punk" and resolves his feelings of dissonance, the label becomes a source of self-identity. While the label of punk denotes lower status within the inmate pecking order, the punk learns to fulfill the role in a manner that allows a relatively trouble-free existence, so long as he continues to live the role. Thus, what was once a forced or coerced label effectively becomes a label with which the victimized inmate identifies with and accepts as a definition of his self.

Structural Issues

Lemert (1999) maintains that role conceptions of the individual must be reinforced by the reactions of others. Many inmates have found that the institutional system simply does not care, lending tacit approval to sexual violence through a form of conscious disregard. According to Scacco, "the shocking fact is that there is both overt and covert implication of officers in the attacks that take place in penal institutions" (1975, 30). Likewise, Weiss and Friar (1974) assert that "prisoners are convinced that prison rape is an integral part of the prison punishment system," adding that inmates frequently contend that "…prison rape is sanctioned by prison authorities. They view it as the ultimate method of control and punishment" (1974, x). It is in this manner that the prison staff essentially serves to perpetuate and exacerbate the labeling process for "homosexuals" within the prison.

Moreover, prison staff, both wittingly and unwittingly, serves to further marginalize the inmate labeled as "punk" when separating them from the general inmate population. These protective measures have a negative side effect since they can further reinforce the label punks are given. Likewise, the inmate punk is hesitant to go to prison authorities for assistance, due to further negative labels of being an informant or "snitch." Such labels can have deadly results for the inmate. Thus, the inmate who seeks to avoid the labeling process finds himself with few avenues of escape. The inmate either must fight off their assaults or be cursed with one adverse label or another, if not both "punk" and "snitch." In either case, the prospects are frequently grim, with the most likely result being that the punk label is assumed by the inmate.

An inmate with the label of punk is cut off and isolated from participating in conventional activities that the dominant inmate enjoys. Once the status of "punk" is given, it is effectively ironclad, and the punk finds himself marginalized within the prison population, leading him to seek out others who share a similar set of circumstances (Tannenbaum 1938). The role of punk is one that allows the "weaker" inmate within the prison power structure to exist, but through that of an exploitative (rather than consensual) relationship. The powerful within the inmate subculture have thus effectively labeled the punk, who "voluntarily" assumes the role. The superior masculine role, desired and maintained by the majority of inmates, has been denied the punk, who is now considered deviant by both inmate subculture and larger social norms.

References

Akers, R. A. *Criminological Theories: Introduction, Evaluation, and Application.* Los Angeles, CA. Roxbury, 2000.

Becker, H. S. *Outsiders: Studies in the Sociology of Deviance.* New York: Free Press, 1963.

Becker, H. S. "Career Deviance." In *Theories of Deviance*, eds. S. H. Traub and C. B. Little. Itasca, IL: Peacock Publications, 1999: 390–397.

Davis, A. J. "Sexual Assaults in the Philadelphia Prison System and Sheriff's Vans." In *Male Rape: A Casebook of Sexual Aggressions*, ed. A. M. Scacco, Jr. New York: AMS Press, Inc, 1982

Festinger, L. "The Motivating Effect of Cognitive Dissonance." In *Assessment of Human Motives*, ed. Gardner Lindzey. New York: Holt, 1958: 69–85.

Lemert, E. M. "Primary and Secondary Deviance." In *Theories of Deviance*, eds. S. H. Traub and C. B. Little. Itasca, IL: Peacock Publications, 1999: 385–390.

Messerschmidt, J. A. "Masculinities and Crime." In *Criminological Theory: Past to Present*, eds. F. T. Cullen and R. Agnew. Los Angeles, CA: Roxbury Publishing Company, 1999.

Miller, W. "Lower Class Culture as a Generating Milieu of Gang Delinquency." *Journal of Social Issues* 14, (1958): 5–19.

Scacco, A. M. Jr. *Rape in Prison.* Springfield, IL: Charles C. Thomas, 1975.

Schur, E. M. *Radical Nonintervention: Rethinking the Delinquency Problem.* Englewood Cliffs, NJ: Prentice Hall, 1973.

Tannenbaum, F. *Crime and the Community.* Boston: Ginn, 1938.

Tucker, D. *A Punk's Song: View From the Inside.* Fort Bragg, CA: AMS Press Inc, 1981.

Vold, G. B., T. J. Bernard, and J. B. Snipes. *Theoretical Criminology*, Fourth Edition. New York: Oxford University Press, 1998.

Weiss, C. and D.J. Friar. *Terror in Prisons: Homosexual Rape and Why Society Condones It*. Indianapolis: Bobbs-Merril, Inc, 1974.

Chapter 10

A Violation of Trust and Professional Ethics: Sexual Abuse of Women Prisoners by Correctional Staff

Zelma Weston Henriques, Ph.D.
and Delores Jones-Brown, Ph.D.

"That was not part of my sentence, to…perform oral sex with the officers."

> —Tanya Ross, prisoner in New York, November, 1998
> as cited by Amnesty International, 1999

"It's not consensual-they have the power, the uniform, the badge"

> —Elizabeth Bouchard, prisoner in Massachusetts, November,
> 1998 as cited by Amnesty International, 1999

Introduction

Dumond (2000) notes that the problem of inmate sexual assault has been known and examined for the past 30 years. And, although inmates are at risk for sexual abuse and assault from both inmates and staff, sexual contact between correctional staff and correctional residents presents special problems of power imbalance, improper personal and professional ethics (for staff members), victimization and trauma (for inmates) and threats to system integrity (for the criminal justice system). While both male and female inmates run the risk of sexual abuse and assault from staff, this chapter focuses on the unique vulnerability of women offenders to sexual advances from those whose job it is to keep them confined.

Background

According to Rafter (1990) the very structure and function of prisons and jails make them conducive to the exploitation of women. She notes:

> The custodial model was a masculine model: derived from men's pris-ons, it adopted their characteristics—retributive purpose, high se-curity architecture, a male-dominated authority structure, programs that stressed earnings, and harsh discipline...(p. 21 as cited in Pol-lock 1997, 42).

Given these characteristics, women became potential sexual victims on sev-eral fronts. In contrast to the Tanya Ross quote noted above, under retribu-tive ideology, sexual assaults by staff could be viewed (by the perpetrators) as part of the deserved punishment being meted out by dutiful employees, since women in custodial units were considered the "dregs of the state prison pop-ulation" (Rafter 1990, 21). Pollock (1997) recounts a 1930's description of women entering a women's prison where fondling by the warden was part of the intake routine. In addition, the orientation speech included a warning that anyone "who do[es] not submit to their superiors will be punished" (p. 43).

Prison literature dating back to 1871 includes references to the sexual ex-ploitation of women by their male overseers (Anonymous 1871). The pre-vention of such abuse had been a main goal of women reformers such as Eliz-abeth Fry, who advocated for separate correctional institutions for women in the early 1800s (Henriques and Gilbert 2000; Freedan 1974).

Even with the advent of separate facilities, women's prisons continued to be controlled by males. Some women who found themselves in these male-dominated high security structures viewed themselves as tainted and unde-serving of decent treatment, hence they became prime targets for sexual ex-ploitation by coercion or "consent" (Henriques 2001; Williams 1996).[1] For these women, sexual contact with staff sometimes involved forcible rape. Or,

---

1. See Williams, 1996 quoting a twenty-two-year-old inmate at Bedford Hills Correc-tional Facility for women in New York: "In their eyes I was the criminal, so why not go with the officer."

in keeping with the masculine model, they learned that they could "earn" various privileges, favors, or necessities in exchange for sex. In an investigation by Sims (1976), women reported trading sexual favors in order to receive "better treatment," a candy bar, or a Coke. In other accounts, women reported having to engage in various forms of sexual contact with staff in order to receive tampons, sanitary napkins, or other items to meet hygienic and other needs (Bomse 2001). In modern prisons (and jails), sex can be traded for desirable work assignments and better living quarters (Bomse 2001; Pollock 1997). A Human Rights Watch (HRW) Report (1996) notes that male officers "have used their near total authority to provide or deny goods and privileges to female prisoners, to compel them to have sex, or in other cases, to reward them for having done so" (quoted in Bomse 2001, 85).

Yet another set of women are vulnerable to sexual exploitation by correctional staff because of the relational nature of women's socialization (Gilligan, Brown, and Rogers 1990) and the isolating nature of the correctional setting. That is, some women inmates may enter into sexual relationships with correctional staff members in order to resolve feelings of loneliness (Rafter 1990) and in order to fulfill their need for intimacy. While both the inmate and the staff member may see the relationship between them as consensual, as noted in the opening quote by Elizabeth Bouchard, the imbalance of power between the two makes such relationships inherently coercive and violates canons of professional ethics and institutional rules (or criminal statutes) prohibiting *any* staff-inmate sexual contact (see Amnesty International 1999).

In addition, while Richie (1996) notes that many women who end up in the criminal justice system have already acquiesced to a lifetime of male influence, domination and control, hence making them more vulnerable to sexual exploitation within male-dominated correctional settings, contemporary reports of sexual misconduct by correctional staff have included incidents where the staff member was female (Reilly 2003).[2]

Defining the Problem

Unlike the common law offense of rape, which could only be perpetrated by a man upon a woman (and only if that man was not her husband), in many

---

2. For example, in 2000, a female corrections officer at the Edna Mahan Correctional Facility for Women, in Hunterdon County, New Jersey was charged with official misconduct and criminal sexual contact for allegedly groping four inmates during the prior three years. She was sentenced to probation following a guilty plea.

jurisdictions, *sexual assault* is the gender-neutral term now used to refer to the sexual violation of both women and men by a perpetrator that is male or female (Henriques and Gilbert 2000). Tuite (1992) defines *criminal sexual assault* as "any genital, anal, or oral penetration, by a part of the accused's body or by an object, using force or without the victim's consent" (quoted in Henriques and Gilbert 2000, 260). While the terms *sexual assault* and *sexual abuse* is sometimes used interchangeably, it has been suggested that the term *assault* more accurately describes a specific incident and *abuse* indicates a pattern of behavior. The term sexual contact, used throughout this chapter, is intended to cover both these types of sex crimes which typically involve physical contact of some sort. But, as used here, the term is also used to address incidents of non-contact *sexual harassment*, considered a pattern of sexual abuse. As such, sexual abuse, in the form of harassment, includes solicitations for sex with the promise of reward, and/or the imposition of punishments for failure to comply with requests for sexual favors.

Williams (2001, 161) identifies demands or requests for sexual exchanges by correctional staff from inmates as "high-level corruption." Similarly, some jurisdictions (New Jersey, for example) by statutory definition, make it a sex crime for persons in prison settings with supervisory positions over inmates to engage in sexual contact with such inmates whether consensual or not. In fact, the way the criminal law is designed, because of the circumstances, legally, the inmate cannot give consent.

Even when not considered a sex crime per se, various forms of sexual behavior between custodial staff and inmates may fall under the rubric of official misconduct. For example, in 2003, a lieutenant and 20-year veteran of the New Jersey Department of Corrections was charged with two counts of second-degree sexual assault and three counts of second-degree official misconduct for allegedly photographing a nude inmate at the women's correctional facility and for having had sexual contact with her, apparently in exchange for money.[3] The lieutenant was also accused of taking nude photographs and having sexual contact with another woman in a community-based corrections program and offering to take nude photos of yet another inmate. If convicted, the defendant could receive up to a 10-year prison sentence (Reilly 2003).

Given the complexity of the situation, the responsibility falls to individual correctional departments (DOCs) to develop standards of conduct that comply with legislative and institutional ethical demands. For example, the Federal Bureau of Prisons (BOP) defines staff-on-inmate sexual abuse/assault as:

---

3. The allegations include the fact that he "sent her money" (Reilly 2003).

Engaging in, or attempting to engage in a sexual act with any inmate or the intentional touching of an inmate's genitalia, anus, groin, breast, inner thigh, or buttocks with the intent to abuse, humiliate, harass, degrade, arouse, or gratify the sexual desire of any person (BOP 1997).

The provision further notes that, "Sexual acts or contacts between an inmate and staff member, even when no objections are raised, are always illegal" (quoted in American Medical Association (AMA) 2000:1).

Magnitude of the Problem

Although as reported by Amnesty International (1999, 38), "[M]any women in prisons and jails in the USA are victims of sexual abuse by staff, including sexually offensive language, male staff touching inmates' breasts and genitals when conducting searches; male staff watching inmates while they are naked; and rape" because there is no national, systematic data collection procedure, the actual extent of custodial assault and sexual misconduct by staff against inmates is unknown (AMA 2000).

Figures from 1993 conservatively estimated the number of male and female inmates sexually assaulted behind bars at more than 290,000 (Donaldson 1993; Henriques and Gilbert 2001). Some sources (see Alarid 2000 citing Donaldson 1995) place the figure for women assaulted behind bars in U.S. prisons significantly lower, at about 5,000.

Despite this significant gap in the estimate of actual victims, growth in the pool of *potential* victims can be confirmed. As of June 30, 2002, there were more than 96,000 women under the authority of a State or Federal prison system (BJS 2002). This figure represents an increase of 1.9% over the figure for June 30, 2001 (BJS 2002). When the figures for local and Federal detention centers and jails are taken into consideration, the number of incarcerated women rises to almost 140,000. And, the total number of women under some form of correctional supervision (including probation and parole) for 1997 was estimated at nearly 900,000 (BJS 2001).

Information from surveys conducted with correctional officials, lawyers, advocacy groups and prisoners incarcerated in prisons in six jurisdictions (California, Georgia, Illinois, Michigan, New York, and The District of Columbia) implies that sexual abuse of women is widespread as is retaliation by the accused officer and his or her colleagues (HRW 1996). Evidence of the problem is also suggested by data showing that approximately half of U.S. State

Departments of Correction (DOCs) report involvement in litigation arising from sexual misconduct (National Institute of Corrections (NIC) 1996; NIC 2000 as cited in AMA 2000).

While as noted previously, there have been some incidents of female staff involvement in sexual misconduct, according to Amnesty International (1999), in the overwhelming majority of complaints for sexual abuse by female inmates against staff, men are reported as the perpetrators. They note that, contrary to international standards, prisons and jails in the US employ men to guard women and place relatively few restrictions on the duties of male staff. As a consequence, much of the touching and viewing of their bodies by staff that women experience as shocking and humiliating is permitted by law.

Regardless of the actual numbers, in 2000 the situation of staff-on-inmate sexual misconduct grew to one of such concern as to cause the American Medical Association to recognize it is a major health concern for incarcerated women. In 2000, the AMA issued a report noting that medical professionals at correctional facilities must take steps to report and prevent its occurrence.

Resolution 404 (1-99) was submitted as part of the Medical Student Section and encouraged its Board of Trustees to:

1. Urge health care professionals working in prisons to be aware of the growing problem of custodial assault and sexual misconduct, and report it to the proper authorities without requiring the inmate to report it him/herself to alleviate guard retaliation; and,
2. Urge all states to create statutes providing legal protection for inmates against custodial molestation and abuse (Report 2 of the Council on Scientific Affairs (1-00).

In 2000, NIC issued a report "Sexual Misconduct in Prisons: Law, Remedies, and Incidence..." which provided information on efforts and changes that prisons have taken since the previous NIC report in 1996 to prevent sexual abuse of inmates by staff. According to the report:

> All but eight states[4] have statutes that prohibit sexual misconduct involving correctional staff and inmates. Statutes define sexual misconduct as either a misdemeanor (8), felony (27), or both (5).

---

4. Alabama, Kentucky, Minnesota, Montana, Oregon, Utah, Vermont and West Virginia.

References

Alarid, L. F. "Sexual Assault and Coercion among Incarcerated Women Prisoners: Excerpts from Prison letters." *The Prison Journal 80* no. 4, (2002): 391–406.

American Medical Association (AMA). *Report of the Council on Scientific Affairs (1-00): Preventing Assault and Rape of Inmates by Custodial Staff.* (2000). Retrieved on line: www.ama-assn.org/ama/pub/article/2036-3592.html.

Amnesty International. *Not Part of My Sentence: Violation of Human Rights of Women in Custody.* Campaign on the United States. New York, 1999.

Anonymous. *An Illustrated History and Description of State Prison Life By One Who has Been There.* Written by a Convict in a Convict's Cell [Prison Life, 1865–1869]. New York: Globe, 1871.

Bomse, A. Prison Abuse: Prisoner-Staff Relations. In *Discretion, Community, and Correctional Ethics,* eds. J. Kleinig and M. Smith. Lanham, MD: Rowman & Littlefield Publishers, Inc, 2001.

Bureau of Justice Statistics. *Summary Findings.* BJS Homepage, 2002. Retrieved from www.ojp.usdoj.gov.

Bureau of Justice Statistics. *Demographic Trends in Correctional Population By Gender, 1986–97.* BJS Homepage, 2001. Retrieved from www.ojp.usdoj.gov.

Bureau of Justice Statistics. *National Crime Victimization Survey.* Washington, DC: U.S. Department of Justice, 1995.

Bureau of Prisons (BOP). *Health Services Manual.* December 31, 1997.

Donaldson, S. Rape of Incarcerated Americans: A Preliminary Statistical Look. 7th ed. Fort Bragg, CA: Stop Prisoner Rape…web cite refer PRISON Journal article Vol. 80 #4 p.413—Dumond—Inmate Sexual Assault article, 1995.

Donaldson, S. *Prisoner Rape Education Program: Overview for Administrators and Staff.* Bandon, VT: The Safer Society Press, 1993.

Dumond, R.W. "Inmate Sexual Assault: The Plague that Persists." *The Prison Journal* 80, 4 (2000): 406–414.

Freedan, E.B. "Their Sisters' Keepers: An Historical Perspective on Female Correctional Institutions in the United States, 1870-1900." *Feminist Studies* 22, (1974): 77–95.

Gilligan, B. L., and A. Rogers. "Psyche Imbedded: A Place for Body, Relationships, and Culture in Personality Theory." In *Studying Persons and*

Lives, eds. A. Rabin, R. Zucker, R. Emmons, and S. Frank. New York: Springer, 1990.

Henriques, Z. W. "The Path of Least Resistance: Sexual Exploitation of Female Offenders as an Unethical Corollary to Retributive Ideology and Correctional Practice." In *Discretion, Community, and Correctional Ethics*, eds. J. Kleinig and M. Smith. Lanham, MD: Rowman & Littlefield Publishers, Inc, 2001.

Henriques, Z. W., and E. Gilbert. "Sexual Abuse and Sexual Assault of Women in Prison." In *It's a Crime: Women and Justice*, 2d ed, ed. R. Muraskin. Saddle River, NJ: Prentice Hall, (2000).

Human Rights Watch Women's Rights Project. *All Too familiar: Sexual Abuse of Women in U.S. State Prisons*. New York: Human Rights Watch, 1996.

National Institute of Corrections (NIC) Information Center. *Sexual Misconduct in Prisons: Law, Remedies, and Incidence*. Longmont, Colorado, 2000.

National Institute of Corrections Information Center. *Sexual Misconduct in prisons: Law, Agency Response, and Prevention*. Longmont, Colorado, 1996.

Pollock, J. M. *Prisons: Today and Tomorrow*. Gaitherburg, MD: Aspen Publishers, 1997.

Pollock-Byrne, J.M. *Women, Prison and Crime*. Pacific Grove, CA: Brooks/Cole, 1990.

Rafter, N. H. *Partial Justice: Women, Prisons and Social Control* (2nd ed.). Boston: Northeastern University Press, 1990.

Richie, B. *Compelled to Crime: The Gender Entrapment of Battered Black Women*. New York: Routledge, 1996.

Reilly, M. "Ex-Corrections Officer at Hunterdon Women's Prison Indicted on Charge," *The Star Ledger*, May 9, (2003): 45, 47.

Sims, P. "Women in Southern Jails." In *The Female Offender*, ed L. Crities. Lexington, MA: D.C. Heath, 1976.

Tuite, P. Ignorance is No Excuse. Chicago: Nelson-Hall, 1992.

Wasserman, J. "Prison Rapes 'Routine'", *Daily News*, January 28, (2003): 72.

Williams, J. "Ideology into Practice/Practice into Ideology: Staff-Offender Relationships in Institutional and Community Corrections in an Era of Retribution." In *Discretion, Community, and Correctional Ethics*, eds. J. Kleinig and M. Smith. Lanham, MD: Rowman & Littlefield Publishers, Inc, 2001.

Williams, M. "Bill Seeks to Protect Inmates from Guards Who Seek Sex." *The New York Times*, April 23, 1996: A1, B1.

Chapter 11

Sexual Abuse of Children

Heidi Moore

Introduction

Sexual abuse of any type is problematic, but the sexual abuse of children is especially troubling. Some feel that the sexual abuse of children is so widespread that it constitutes a "significant public health problem in the United States" (Dominques, Nelke and Perry 2002). Statistics on the prevalence of this problem seem to paint a confusing picture. Some of the statistics seem to be contradictory and there is a definite problem in the validity of child abuse data collection. Do the numbers we see provide an accurate picture of this crime?

Part of the problem with the statistics is that traditionally in the study of sexual assault, we examine, among others, the National Crime Victimization Survey, as it includes unreported crime. The issue with child sexual abuse is that the National Crime Victimization Surveys only requests information from people age 12 and older and misses information on those 11 or younger. Another problem is that the sexual abuse of children often goes unreported; the estimates vary from 77 to 85 percent of the crimes go unreported (RAINN 2002; Stop it Now 2002). For example, even the results of the newer FBI crime reporting system, the National Incident-Based Reporting System (NIBRS) has been limited by sample size, but the results suggest that previous national data collection efforts were missing over a third of sexual assaults (Snyder 2000).

In 2000, there was an estimated 3 million reports made to child protective agencies across the United States. These reports concerned 5 million children and after investigation, abuse and neglect was substantiated in the cases of 879,000 children. Ten percent of these children were the victims of child sexual abuse (U.S. Department of Health and Human Services 2002a). Recent statistics suggest that the number of reported and substantiated child sexual abuse cases in the United States have decreased each year since 1992. This follows a pattern of consistent increase from 1977–1992 (Jones and Finkelhor 2001). However, there are numerous explanations possible for this recent pattern of decline. There may, in fact, be a decrease in child sexual abuse, or perhaps there has been a change in standards, policies, regulations or maybe even an attitude change which generates fewer reports and also fewer substantiated cases of child sexual abuse (Jones and Finkelhor 2001). These explanations present us both ends of a continuum – one end inspires optimism and the other does not. However, the explanations could be a combination of reasons, or there could be other unrecognized reasons for the patterns we see (Jones and Finkelhor 2001).

Finally, we cannot ignore what perhaps is the most cited type of statistics regarding child abuse. Statistics from the Center for the Prevention of Sexual and Domestic Violence state that before the age of 16, 1 in 4 girls and 1 in 6 boys will become victims of sexual abuse (2002). Before age 18, one in three girls and 1 in 5 boys will become the victims of child sexual abuse (Dominquez, Nelke and Perry 2002).

Definitions

One general definition for the sexual abuse of children does not exist (Murry 2000). However, according to the Child Abuse Prevention and Treatment Act, sexual abuse is:

> The employment, use, persuasion, inducement, enticement or coercion of any child to engage in, or assist any other person to engage in, any sexually explicit conduct or simulation of such conduct for the purpose of producing a visual depiction of such conduct; or the rape, and in cases of caretaker or inter-familial relationships, statutory rape, molestation prostitution or other form of sexual exploitation of children, or incest with children (U.S. Department of Health and Human Services 2002b).

Obviously, sexual abuse does not necessarily mean intercourse, in fact, quite the opposite. Intercourse may be the final act in abuse that gradually increases over time, and begins with such actions as fondling the child, voyeurism, exhibitionism, or using the child in pornography. All of these activities in and of themselves are considered sexually abusive (Guidelines for 1999; American Humane Association 2002). None of these forms of abuse is less threatening or harmful to a child than another, they are all forms of sexual abuse and they are all detrimental to the proper development of a child.

Definitions for the sexual abuse and sexual play of children vary depending on if you are in the medical or legal field and then there are various definitions for laypeople. A legal definition was previously provided while a medical definition includes sexual play which is somewhat different than sexual abuse. Sexual play is considered normal in the medical field and occurs when children of the same age and development stage are mutually interested in exploring each other by looking, touching, or both (Guidelines for…1999).

Symptoms and Effects

One should use caution when examining the symptoms of sexual abuse. According to an article in Pediatrics many of the symptoms may be so general that they could be signs of other forms of abuse or no-abuse stressors (Guidelines for…1999). Symptoms might also appear in the siblings of abused children. Some of the general signs may include changing sleep patterns, wetting the bed and/or having nightmares, experiencing stomach pain, verbalizing new words for various body parts and/or acting out inappropriate sexual activity. Other more specific signs may include cutting or burning oneself as an adolescent, experiencing rectal or genital bleeding, having sexually transmitted diseases, pain, itching, bleeding, fluid, and/or rawness on the thighs or genital area (Stop it Now 2002; Guidelines for…1999; National Center for Missing and Exploited Children 2002).

If abuse is suspected, it is very important for the adult to remain calm and listen to the child. Children have often been threatened and told that no one will believe them if they tell of the abuse. It is therefore, important to believe the child. Either a pediatrician or mental health provider should evaluate all sexually abused children; both are also mandated reporters to authorities (Guidelines for…1999).

Before an examination, the process needs to be explained to the child so that any additional emotional damage can be prevented. The examiner must have patience and allow substantial time for the examination. This is essential for the child to feel less anxious. Of paramount importance is that if a parent or guardian is suspected to be the cause of the child abuse, they must not be allowed to be present during the examination. By necessity, physical exams may include the collection of biological evidence if the abuse occurred within 72 hours of the examination or if there is bleeding (Guidelines for…1999).

False claims of sexual abuse do occur, although they are rare. Estimates range from 2 to 8 percent of reports being intentionally false (American Humane Association 2002; Everson and Boat 1996). Research has shown that law enforcement and judges are less likely to believe a child than mental health and child protection service workers (Everson and Boat 1996). When one looks at the number of false reports verses the number of sexually abused children, why take the risk of not believing the child?

Effects of abuse can be devastating to a child. "The most commonly experienced effect of {child} sexual abuse is posttraumatic stress disorder (PTSD). Posttraumatic stress disorder is a clinical syndrome whose symptoms fall into three clusters; reenactment of the traumatic event; avoidance of cues associated with the event or general withdraw and psychological hyperactivity" (Dominquez, Nelke, and Perry 2002, 202). The effects can be long-term and research suggests that they may be worse in children who have been placed in foster care after the abuse (Smith, and Howard 1994). Sexual acting out is often an effect of sexual child abuse. Smith and Howard (1994) discuss the effect of traumatic sexualization, which happens because children have not developed the tools to handle the sexual stimulation from the abuse, thus their sexuality is dysfunctional. Their behavior may vary between sexual attention-seeking to sexual aggression toward other children. In addition they are confused about sexual norms, their own sexuality, and the emotions that they have learned to associate with sexual activities. Other effects often cited include depression, identity confusion, difficulty in trusting adults, low self-esteem, sense of powerlessness, feelings of guilt and self-abusive behavior (Murray 2000; Smith and Howard 1994; American Humane Association 2002). In addition, these effects were most damaging when a father figure was involved, genital contact occurred, and the perpetrator used force (Murray 2000).

Who Commits the Crime?

The perpetrator or offender plays an important role in the study of the sexual abuse of children and statistics suggest that 75 to 95 percent of the children know their offender (Center for the Prevention of Sexual and Domestic Violence 2002). Strangers are rarely the perpetrator of young victims (Snyder 2000). The Office of Juvenile Justice and Delinquency Prevention (2001) notes that 92 percent of sexual assault of children is committed by males. Although, offenders are generally male, females can be offenders as well. In addition, many offenders claim that as children they were sexually abused (Murray 2000).

When we think of the people who molest children, we commonly hear the terms "child molester" and "pedophile" used interchangeably. In reality, not all child molesters are pedophiles. A pedophile prefers children sexually and has recurrent sexual fantasies for at least six months involving sexual activity with a prepubescent child (Lanning 1987; Murray 2000; National Center for Missing and Exploited Children 2002). Child molesters are those who prefer adults sexually but who molest for any number of reasons. These might include "simple availability, curiosity, or a desire to hurt a loved one of the molested child" (Lanning 1987, 2). Some experts suggest that there appears to be a lesser number of true pedophiles than there are child molesters, though the true pedophile will molest a much higher number of children (Lanning 1987). Some children fall victim simply because they are available to the molester. Nonetheless, the effect on the child is still the same.

Sexual Exploitation of Children

The sexual exploitation of children is an international problem and universally defined as the exploitation of children for profit and for sexual purposes. The industry includes sex tourism, trafficking of children, and child pornography. It is a multi-billion dollar industry with over one million children involved worldwide (Embassy of the United States of America Stockholm 1996).

In some African and Middle Eastern countries children employed as servants are expected to include sexual acts. In addition, refugee camps supply local men with sex. In Asia, child prostitutes provide services for men. Sometimes these children are kidnapped; sometimes their families have sold them for money, often not realizing they are bought by the sex industry. High tech child pornography and pedophile organizations are trafficking children throughout Europe, the United States, and Australia. The children who come from all over the world, are getting younger. In some circumstances, babies are being traded (Embassy of the United States of America Stockholm 1996).

The child pornography industry has advanced with the development of technology. Not only over the Internet, but with the availability of home camcorders and other recording equipment, pornography is easier to produce and more difficult to trace (Embassy of the United States of America Stockholm 1996; National Center for Missing and Exploited Children 2002). The Internet has made the exchange of pornography much simpler and has created a new way to seek victims. This venue allows child molesters to pose as whoever they feel will attract a child.

In addition to all the concern of this type of abuse, the health concerns for these abused children are devastating. Some abused children are being infected with HIV/AIDS because of their exploitation and some are being forced to have reconstructive surgery because their customers want virgins. Many others end up as drug addicts, sometimes by self-medicating, and sometimes some are drugged to keep them complacent as slaves; others commit suicide (Embassy of the United States of America Stockholm 1996).

Conclusion

The sexual abuse of children is not a new phenomenon and unfortunately, although the statistics suggest less reported and substantiated cases of child abuse in the United States, the problem is not going to disappear. In fact, we really do not understand the true scope of the problem as there are so many cases of child sexual abuse that go unreported. In addition, child sexual abuse is not something that we like to think happens.

However, child abuse has recently been thrust to the forefront of the media's attention with the many news stories of the clergy having been involved in sexual abuse. Therefore, there is concern that the very communities that ought to be the safest hide abuse. The Center of Prevention of Sexual and Domestic Violence (2002) reports that the norm in most religious communities is silence, honor thy parents, and not to question the actions of elders. There is most probably a connection between the silence of children who are abused and what the Center of Prevention of Sexual Abuse and Domestic Violence cite as the normal expectation of children's behavior in the religious community. However, do not be complacent, this is a pattern reflected in our communities and other institutions as well.

This chapter has briefly introduced the problem of child sexual abuse. Researchers continue to study the prevalence, extent, and reasons for child sexual abuse. The varying definitions of child sex abuse make this research difficult as well as the natural phenomenon of secrecy surrounding the offense. Children are vulnerable prey and adults must be willing to really listen to children, both their verbal and non-verbal communications, to help tackle this problem.

References

American Humane Association. *Fact Sheet: Child Sexual Abuse, 2002.* Retrieved from http://www.amerhumane.org/children/factsheets/sx_abuse.htm (January 2003).

Center for the Prevention of Sexual and Domestic Violence. *Child Abuse,* 2002. Retrieved from http://www.cpsdv.org/CA/child.htm (January 2003).

Dominquez, R.Z., C.F. Nelke, and B.D. Perry. "Child Sexual Abuse". *Encyclopedia of Crime and Punishment* Vol. 1, ed. David Levinson, 202–207. Thousand Oaks, CA: Sage Publications, 2002.

Embassy of the United States of America Stockholm. *World Congress Against the Commercial Exploitation of Children,* 1996. Retrieved from http://www.usemb.se/children/csec/overview.html (January 2003).

Everson, M.D. and B.W. Boat. "Beliefs among Professionals about the Rates of False Allegations of Child Sexual Abuse." *Journal of Interpersonal* Violence 11 no. 4, (1996): 541–554.

"Guidelines for the Evaluation of Sexual Abuse of Children: Subject Review." (1999). *Pediatrics* 103 no. 1, (1999): 186–192.

Jones, L. and Finkelhor, D. *The Decline in Child Sexual Abuse Cases.* U.S. Department of Justice, Office of Juvenile Justice and Delinquency Prevention. Washington, D.C.: Government Printing Office, 2001.

Lanning, K.V. *Child Molesters: A Behavioral Analysis: For Law Enforcement Officers Investigating Cases of Child Sexual Exploitation.* National Center for Missing and Exploited Children, 1987.

Murray, J.B. "Psychological Profile of Pedophiles and Child Molesters." *Journal of Psychology,* 134 no. 2, (2000): 211–225.

National Center for Missing and Exploited Children, (2002). Retrieved from http://ncmec.org/html (January 2003).

Office of Juvenile Justice and Delinquency Prevention. "Child Abuse Reported to the Police." *Juvenile Justice Bulletin.* Washington, D.C.: Government Printing Office, 2001.

RAINN. *RAINN Statistics, 2002* Retrieved from http://www.rainn.org/statistics.html (January 2003)

Smith, S.L. and J.A. Howard. "The Impact of Previous Sexual Abuse on Children's Adjustment in Adoptive Placement." *Social Work,* 39 no. 5, (1994): 491–502.

Snyder, H.N. *Sexual Assault of Young Children as Reported to Law* Enforcement: Victim, Incident, and Offender Characteristics. National Center for Juvenile Justice: Washington D.C.: U.S. Department of Justice, 2000.

STOP IT NOW. (2002). Retrieved from http://www.stopitnow.org/comquest.htm (January 2003).

U.S. Department of Health and Human Services. "Child Maltreatment 2000." Administration for Children and Families, Children's Bureau. Washington D.C.: U.S. Government Printing Office, (2003a).

U.S. Department of Health and Human Services. "Child Abuse Prevention: An Overview." *Administration for Children and Families.* Washington D.C.: U.S. Government Printing Office, (2003b).

Chapter 12

Reading Incest: Interpreting Signs of Victimization and Family Dysfunction in One Survivor's Account

Miriam R. Fuller, Ph.D.

My name is Miriam R. Fuller. I have a doctorate in English literature, and am a university professor. I am married with two children. I enjoy theater, music, gourmet cooking, and travel. I have also survived childhood sexual abuse, occurring between the ages of three and seventeen, the perpetrators of which were two male relatives. I am now at a point where, having been through several years of therapy and done extensive reading on the topics of incest and sexual abuse, I am recovered, not only enough to lead a full and satisfying life, but to inform others about my experience, in the hope that doing so will help people who have been in similar circumstances and help those in the criminal justice and counseling systems assist victims of child sexual abuse. My goals in this particular essay are to help dispel some of the prevalent and harmful myths about incest victims and perpetrators by describing the circumstances of my own abuse and my family of origin; to discuss the elements in our culture that reinforce and even enable sexual abuse of children and adults; and to offer my own perspective on what we can do to aid victims of sexual abuse and to stop that abuse from occurring. Since I am trained as a literary critic, this chapter will be in the form of a narrative and a deconstruction and interpretation of that narrative—a presentation and discussion of the signs, as it were, of the abuse I experienced and the family framework that surrounded and informed it.

My father sexually abused me beginning when I was around three years of age. It developed very insidiously out of cuddling, with my father gradually touching me in increasingly inappropriate places. The abuse occurred mainly at night and in my room. It escalated in severity and frequency in my ninth year, after my father's mother died, again occurring mainly at night in my room, though sometimes at the dinner table as well. When I was seventeen my father raped me while we were out of town at an audition. As well as abusing me physically, my father abused me verbally and psychologically, a very common pattern for incest perpetrators. He would discuss his sexual experiences with my mother and other women with me and describe the sort of women who attracted him. Whenever he took me out to eat when I was a teenager, he would announce loudly that I was his daughter and not his date, and then make me take out my driver's license to prove it to the other diners—he did this to one of my older sisters too. My older brother (I am the youngest of four children and my siblings are all considerably older than I) abused me as well, though the abuse was not as severe. It took the form of grabbing me in inappropriate places and exposing himself to me. I blocked out most of my father's abuse for many years until I began getting disturbing flashbacks at the age of twenty-five, and began therapy.

Since I had blocked out most of the abuse consciously, it manifested in various indirect ways and affected me negatively even after I recovered my memories of it. I had frequent nightmares. At the age of three I developed stress-induced asthma. From the ages of nine—when the abuse started escalating—to eleven I had a recurring ear infection that frequently kept me out of school. As a teenager and young adult my relationships were sometimes unhealthy, and I developed a compulsion about checking and re-checking that all the doors and windows were locked at night. I had reproductive surgery and fertility problems. Though the actual sexual abuse stopped over twenty years ago, I am still dealing with its effects. It is not a situation that I would wish on anybody.

It is imperative to realize that child sexual abuse can occur in any family, regardless of income, race, ethnicity, religion, education, occupation, political affiliation, or social class. My parents were middle-class Jews from the East Coast; my father was in business, my mother attended college, both were well-read and culturally sophisticated, and we lived in a fairly affluent suburb on the West Coast. I have met survivors from very diverse backgrounds: one woman was abused by her father, a bank president; another came from a family that ran a crime syndicate; one upper-middle-class woman was abused by her baby-sitter; another, abused by her uncles, grew up in a poor rural community; one woman, molested by her father, was raised in the inner city by social activists. Child sexual abuse, like cancer, can be found in all walks of life. *There is no "typical" kind of family where sexual abuse occurs.*

Thus, child sexual abuse, like other kinds of domestic violence, can occur in families that look fine to outsiders, and in fact, sexual abuse can occur in families that may be successful and emotionally healthy in other aspects. In fact, abuse is harder to spot in families whose members are very intelligent or well-educated, because the family members often develop very complex and effective mechanisms to disguise, rationalize, or cope with the abuse. Often they will intellectualize the problem to keep their emotional turmoil at bay. When I was 17, shortly after I was raped, I wrote a term paper for a psychology class on the effects of father-daughter incest on the daughter—I had decided that I was going to become a psychologist and treat rape and incest victims. I had blocked out the severest episodes of incest from my memory, and the less severe incidents I had rationalized as "not being abuse." Writing that term paper and deciding to "help" other victims was an extremely complicated coping mechanism that enabled me to deal with my own situation at a safe distance, and also to implicitly "announce" to my family that there was a problem. I would, for example, leave the research books I had checked out lying around the kitchen table for days, all the while thinking that I really ought to put those books in my bedroom, and that I hoped no one thought that I was implying that my father was molesting me. My family thought there was nothing strange about my research topic, but my high school teacher, after having read the paper, kept me after class, and asked me very gently if there was anything going on in my family that I wanted to discuss. I was rather frightened—I remember thinking that I didn't want to get my father in trouble—and replied that everything was fine at home. At that time, since the incest was still occurring, I was not able emotionally to face this trauma on anything but an academic level. However, I was also able to help myself in a way by finding out about the effects of incest and by understanding, at some level, that I was not to blame for what was happening to me. I still feel that researching and writing that paper helped to avoid, unconsciously, some of the most severe aftereffects of the abuse.

As the above incident shows, sexual abuse had not injured my intellectual ability. In fact, many abuse victims do very well in academics, athletics, performing arts, etc. I was actively involved in theatre and music while in high school and college, and I know several survivors who are artists of various kinds. Being a "high achiever" often helps the victim to avoid the trauma of dealing with the reality of the abuse, especially when the abuse is still occurring. It is very important, therefore, to realize that sexual abuse doesn't always render a child incapable, incompetent, or totally miserable. I did not have the happiest childhood, but I did manage to enjoy my friends and activities. I even occasionally, at the times when the abuse was not occurring, enjoyed being with my family. My parents were generous in many ways and very affectionate, and told me frequently that they loved me. We went out to dinner together and attended plays, movies, and ball games. My parents encouraged all of us to excel in school and helped fund our college educations. Families where sexual abuse is happening are not necessarily totally dysfunctional or devoid of love. This doesn't mean that sexual abuse isn't harmful—it is extremely harmful and needs to be stopped. But what it does mean for law enforcement officials is that it can be very hard to spot abuse when it is occurring within a family that is successful and stable in other ways and to a child who in other respects is being loved and well cared for. It is also imperative that the whole family get psychological counseling, even if some members are not victims or perpetrators, because incest is only one manifestation of a dysfunctional family. A family is not unhealthy because there is incest occurring; incest occurs because a family is unhealthy in certain ways.

Even though there are no "typical" families where incest occurs, there are typical elements which characterize these families, and which can manifest themselves in different ways. One element is a lack of healthy boundaries, especially physical boundaries and invasions of privacy. Members of my family, especially my parents, rarely knocked when entering my room. My mother sometimes would enter my room when I was dressing, and walked around the house for brief periods in her underclothes. My brother would burst into the bathroom, often undressed, without knocking, when I was already there. I would lock the door, but the lock wasn't very strong and he would force it open. When I complained to my mother and asked her to speak to my brother or get a latch for the inside of the door, she told me to use another bathroom. Since I was the one who was in the bathroom first, it should have been my brother who used another bathroom, but this did not occur to her. The door to my bedroom was warped and wouldn't close properly, and my parents refused to have it fixed, claiming that it would cost too much. When I wanted to get a latch for my door, my mother replied that she wouldn't feel comfortable if there was a fire or other emergency and she couldn't get into my room. My mother was also always reaching out to tug and adjust my and my sisters' clothes even after we were well past our teens.

This latter behavior reflected my mother's extreme concern with appearance. Often in families where sexual or other types of abuse is occurring there is an obsession with physical appearance, so that things will look good on the outside. In the case of my family, my mother was not consciously aware that the abuse was occurring and my father was in denial, but it was fairly obvious that their marriage was deteriorating, so they may have trying to compensate by making sure that their children performed well in school and the outside world. My parents not only wanted their children to do well, they wanted us to look well, and both, in their own way, were obsessive about our appearance and weight. When my mother took me shopping, especially as I got older, she would spend hours trying to determine which clothes made me look thinnest—something she did with herself as well—and was always fussing with my and my sisters' hair. Once, when one of my sisters came home from college for the weekend, my mother told her to fix her hair before she even said hello to her. My father, as well as my older brother, were constantly admonishing me to lose weight and frost my hair—they were both fond of blondes—and my parents frequently pointed out attractive young women as examples for me to improve my own appearance. My mother was also very concerned with the appearance of our house, especially the public rooms, like the living room and dining room. Significantly, the more private rooms, like the bedroom and sewing room, were usually very messy, reflecting my family's reality that however neat things looked on the outside, there was a lot of mess on the inside.

This mess was not entirely of my parents' creation, as their childhoods had not been ideal, especially my father's. If children are raised in families with dysfunctional elements, they will often as adults create similar dysfunctional elements without their own families. Usually perpetrators of child sexual abuse have themselves been abused as children— though not always sexually—and when child sexual abuse occurs within a family, the non-abusive parent frequently was either abused or somehow treated in a severe, or extreme fashion. My parents were no exception. My father's father was very strict with him; his mother was selfish and immature, and may have had an extramarital affair. His family was rich, but his grandfather died of cancer when my father was twelve and my grandmother spent most of the money within a few years. She made my father sign over the money that his father had put away for his college education, and spent it on his older sister's wedding. She would also wake my father up in the middle of the night and tell him that she had seen his father's ghost. She made my father buy her and his sister sanitary supplies, which would have been very embarrassing for him, especially as a young boy. My mother's parents were loving and intelligent but very strict, especially her mother, who expected the best out of her children and very rarely complimented them, especially my mother, who had to help keep the house immaculate and who was never allowed to "talk back." After the Depression hit, my grandparents had to sell their home and move in with my grandmother's parents, and my great-grandmother was even stricter than my grandmother, and obsessed with cleanliness and decorum. She once made my mother's cousin spend an entire day cleaning the bathroom.

Both my parents' families of origin had very different standards of behavior for girls than for boys. My father was disciplined strictly while his sister was indulged. In my mother's family, girls were expected to behave much more responsibly and decorously than boys. My mother's younger brother and several of her uncles were often very boisterous, teasing and playing practical jokes, and nobody tried to discipline them much, sometimes taking a sort of exasperated pride in their "escapades" (my uncles, for example, when visiting someone in the hospital, would steal gurneys and trays with medical instruments and wheel each other down the hall on them). My uncle frequently teased my mother, and my grandmother always told my mother to ignore her brother and the teasing would stop, which it didn't.

These differences had a harmful effect on the way my siblings and I were disciplined. My sisters and I were expected to behave politely at all times and to help with household chores. My brother did not have as many chores to do, and the ones he had he shirked frequently. My mother did not want to turn my brother into a "mama's boy," so she did not correct his behavior the way she did mine and my sisters'. He frequently teased, hit, and punched me. If I complained, my mother would either tell me to ignore him, or to keep out of his way since he was older and bigger than I was, which made me feel very unsafe. He would frequently eat food with the serving spoon straight from the serving dish at the table and steal food from my plate without a serious reprimand. My sisters and I were scolded if we left hairs in the bathtub or dirty dishes in the sink; I was expected to clean up after my brother's mess in the bathtub because I was a girl. On the other hand, my mother confided in my sisters and me much more than she did my brother, and my father indulged my sisters and I much more than he did my brother, and pushed my brother very hard to do well in school and choose an appropriate profession. This discrepancy between acceptable behavior for boys and for girls is certainly prevalent to a certain degree in Western society, but when it exists to the extent that it did in my family, it sets up very harmful patterns for both genders; encouraging boys to be overly aggressive and use violence and strength to take what they want, and encouraging girls to be submissive and afraid to protect themselves.

This double standard of behavior for boys and girls is just one example of the hypocrisy that usually goes on in families where sexual abuse occurs. The perpetrator of the abuse, and sometimes other family members as well, will be very hypocritical about the abuse that is committed, as well as about sexual morals in general. My father, for example, had extramarital affairs frequently and told one of my older sisters about them when she was a teenager. However, when this same sister moved in with her boyfriend in her late 20's, my father sent her a very harsh letter accusing her of being promiscuous and ruining her life. When my mother once saw my father putting his hand into the back of my pants at the dinner table, she told him that I was too old for him to do that anymore (overlooking the fact that such behavior is never appropriate, no matter the age of the child), and he replied that I was his daughter and he could do whatever he wanted with me. My mother was not as hypocritical about sexual matters, but she did try to rationalize certain issues. When I confronted my mother years later about her allowing my brother to sexually abuse and physically mistreat me, she maintained that she thought it was just part of how siblings interacted with each other. When I pointed out that he was almost nine years older than I so she ought to have intervened, she said that she had never really considered it that way. Ironically, it was my father who got enraged when he heard about my brother exposing himself to me in the bathroom. This hypocrisy and rationalizing were part of my parents' way of denying the reality of what was going—my father was denying that his actions were abusive and my mother was denying that she was letting my brother abuse me.

Blame is another type of denial. Often, if family members do acknowledge the abuse or any other significant problem some way, they will blame it on the victim or on some other family member, and deny responsibility for it. My parents—whose marriage eventually ended in divorce when I was nineteen—blamed each other for the deterioration of their relationship; my mother was convinced that my father was the culprit because he didn't spend enough time with the family and wasted money, while my father blamed my mother because she nagged him and spent too much time cleaning house. Neither could see that both of them were responsible for the breakdown of their marriage and family. Each thought that if only the other person would listen and follow his or her advice, then things would be fine. Each of them firmly believed that he or she was the only injured party and the only one who really knew how to solve the problem.

This is typical behavior that exists in almost all dysfunctional relationships. There is a strong tendency for family members in a family where abuse is happening to pride themselves on their own wisdom, knowledge, and ability to help and advise other people with their problems, usually the same problems that the family members are denying about themselves. My blocking out the abuse and wanting to help others who were abused is an example of this phenomenon. My mother frequently tried to nurture other children in our neighborhood whose parents were not, in her opinion, rearing them properly, but she often spoke sharply to us. When a friend of mine fell out of our swing, she rocked and cuddled him, though he wasn't hurt by the fall. When I fell out of the same swing a few days later she looked at me briefly and said I was fine and that she was too busy to hold me. She once was concerned about a teenage friend of mine, suspecting this friend's father of abusing her, and wondering if she should go to the police or offer to help my friend. She would often discuss the psychological problems of people she knew, including my father, and recommend therapy for them, though she didn't feel she was in need of therapy herself. And my father, who was quite fat, with very poor exercise and eating habits, frequently pointed out and criticized people that he thought needed to lose weight.

My family's strong tendency to criticize "helped" others with the problems we ourselves had is a classic example of the denial that is so prevalent in families with abuse. Along with the compulsion to help others who are perceived as less fortunate, there is often a pervasive feeling in dysfunctional families, at least with some members, that the family is somehow superior to and different from other families. This is another manifestation of the family's denial to face their own problems and can be a very effective defense mechanism. I certainly sensed from both my parents that they felt themselves to be superior intellectually to most of our neighbors, and we were expected to live up to that image. Whenever I brought home a good report card or did very well on a test, my mother would say, "Well, that doesn't surprise me; I expect the best from my children." My father bragged excessively about our various achievements and would always try to make me speak French to people. I think that they were trying to convince themselves that our family had so many "important" things going for it that there couldn't be anything seriously wrong. But clearly there were a lot of problems going on in the family, problems that my parents were trying to cover up. And it seemed that as the problems got worse, my parents were more determined that things looked good on the outside.

I have written this description of my family in the hopes that it will shed some light on some basic characteristics of families where sexual victimization is occurring and enable you to read between the lines, as it were, when observing or interviewing alleged perpetrators and victims of sexual abuse and their families. It is crucial not to be fooled by respectability, friendliness, community involvement and financial success—sexual abuse can and does exist within families that possess many positive traits. My own family of origin seemed very far, at least on the outside, from a family in which incest would occur. It probably would have been very difficult for an outsider to figure out that sexual abuse was occurring in my family, because on the outside we looked fairly good, but anyone who knew us well or had psychological training would have spotted underlying problems. My parents were both very friendly and outgoing, but both of them tended to offer too much information to people too soon. My mother would go into too many details about her life or try to offer advice when people hadn't asked for it. My father would make inappropriate sexual comments to attractive women. Law enforcement officials, psychologists, and social workers need to be able to correctly recognize and interpret the telltale but often subtle behavioral signs that sexual abuse is occurring in a seemingly healthy family.

I myself would not have recognized these signs for what they were until I started the recovery process, which involved a lot of therapy, both individual and group counseling, and reading about sexual abuse and dysfunctional families. Because of my training as a literary critic and feminist scholar, I also read a number of works about the objectification of women and children in literature and society, and was able to connect them with the psychological texts I had read and with my own experiences. Due to my therapy and my reading, I was able to read the inappropriate elements of my family's behavior as signs of our inner problems. I understood how my father's own childhood experiences directly contributed to his becoming a perpetrator of sexual abuse, how my mother's upbringing got in the way of her protecting her daughters from abuse, and how my family's dynamics allowed that abuse to go on for so long undetected. I realized, as a result of my therapy and reading, that sexual abuse is only one symptom of a dysfunctional family, that my abuse was not an isolated incident but grew out of my family's overall problems with personal boundaries, appearance, and control. Understanding why and how the abuse happened, knowing that the abuse was not in any way my fault, and realizing what did and didn't work in my family were my greatest aids in recovery, along with the love and support of my boyfriend, my mother, who did go into therapy after my disclosure of the abuse, and a few close friends.

My recovery process, as well as my training in analyzing and critiquing literature, has helped me to understand many aspects about childhood sexual abuse in general, and to realize how, in many ways, our society unknowingly enables and even encourages child and other forms of sexual abuse to occur. Understanding how our culture unwittingly promotes sexual abuse will help us, I hope, to change our culture and ideas, and thus, ultimately, to eradicate child sexual abuse. Some of the thoughts I am about to present may seem strange, extreme, or even ridiculous to you, but I hope you will read and consider them with an open mind.

Child sexual abuse will continue to be a very big problem until our society stops sexualizing children, and stops glorifying sexual violence and coercion. Little girls are sexualized to an obscenely large extent in this society, and I am not even talking about blatant child pornography. Clothing for young girls is often form-fitting, with short skirts, low-cut tops, and other adult styles. Little girls are encouraged to wear make-up, stylish clothes, worry about their figures, and have "boyfriends" at a very young age. Children in ads are often posed very provocatively, wearing very little clothing. When my daughter, aged six at the time, was in a jazz and tap dance class, the costumes chosen for the class recital were "flapper" outfits, with short fringed skirts, low-cut bodices, and feathers in the hair. My husband and I were upset, but none of the other parents minded; they thought it was cute. (We moved our daughter to a ballet class, where the costumes were more demure and age appropriate). I once saw bibs for sale that said "World's Sexiest Baby." People ask a colleague of mine if her three-year-old son has "a little girlfriend" yet. People routinely refer to babies and toddlers being friendly as "flirting." I do not think that most people really mean to sexualize children, but it has become so prevalent in our country—mostly due to the advertising industry—that we do it innocently and unconsciously without any harmful intentions. But we need to become aware of what we are doing and why it can be dangerous in the long run. Stopping childhood sexual abuse involves stopping sexualizing children, ceasing to dress children in revealing clothing, and letting them BE children without forcing inappropriate and potentially harmful adult interpretations on their behavior.

Just as importantly, we need to let children own their bodies and learn how to protect themselves. Babies and children are very cute and cuddly, and it is natural to want to pick them up and snuggle and kiss them. But it is vital to let the child choose whether she wants to be hugged or touched. I have seen so many parents order their children to hug or kiss adults that the children don't want to hug, or adults hug or kiss children when the children obviously don't want to be touched. My brother and sister-in-law are always telling their children to hug relatives goodbye; I always ask children if I may hug them and tell them that it's okay if they don't want to. If a child is told that he "has to" kiss Aunt Sue or hug Uncle Jim or sit on Santa's lap, he will find it harder to defend himself against potential abusers. And the majority of child sexual abuse is very insidious. Perpetrators often start with "appropriate" physical contact, such as hugging or sitting on laps, then gradually begin touching the child in progressively more "borderline" areas like the thighs, lower back, and lower abdomen, and move on to the genital region. This type of insidious sexual abuse is very difficult for children to defend themselves against because it begins with behavior that they are "supposed to" accept from adults. It is especially difficult when children have been made to feel that they cannot refuse adult attention. Children and adults need to learn that physical contact is appropriate only when both people want it. They also need to be allowed to protect themselves physically against anyone who is behaving in a physically inappropriate manner towards them, whether it is a pervert on the street exposing himself or—the more likely and often more dangerous scenario—a family member touching or grabbing them.

Our society, along with discouraging our children from protecting themselves against unwanted physical contact, still tends to blame victims of sexual assault. This blame can take various forms. There is the classic example of blaming a rape victim because she was revealingly or attractively dressed, or drinking, or in a secluded area. The rationale is that the victim was making herself "irresistible" to the perpetrator, who then was powerless to resist because of overwhelming sexual urges. In the case of child sexual abuse, perpetrators often claim that the child was "asking for it" by "flirting" or somehow behaving sexually. This kind of reasoning is seriously flawed on several accounts. First of all, sexual assault is not a crime of passion; it is a crime of power. Perpetrators need to feel completely powerful and in control and so they pick victims whom they think they can control easily. Sex offenders do not choose their victims on the basis of physical attractiveness; they choose their victims on the basis of physical and emotional powerlessness. Secondly, people often interpret others' behavior in a way that benefits their own perceptions and desires. Students, for example, might misinterpret a professor's friendly demeanor as an indication that she is an easy grader. A child's playful, friendly behavior does not have the same impulse or intent as an adult's flirting at a party. (Flirting at a party, for that matter, is not an indication of an immediate desire for a sexual encounter). Children may be inherently sexual, as some people claim, but if they are it is in an extremely different way from adults, and they are not conscious of being sexual. Children do not desire sex. And finally, the idea of the "irresistible temptation" is a false one, constructed to give people an excuse for committing selfish or irresponsible actions. Adults should be capable of controlling themselves and refraining from infringing on or violating other people's personal and physical rights; if they are not, they should be physically restrained. The victim of child sexual abuse is in no way responsible for the crime occurring; the perpetrator is. The sex offenders, not the victims, are to blame, and the offenders need to face the consequences—physical, legal, and social—of their heinous and reprehensible actions.

Unfortunately, we live in a culture where criminal behavior and irresponsible actions are often seen as symptoms of illness and where criminals and irresponsible people receive pity and sympathy—often more than their victims receive. I feel that this attitude has been taken to harmful extremes. It is certainly necessary to understand why people commit crimes, in order to help them and to prevent potential criminals. But when a victim of abuse commits abuse, he ceases to be a victim and becomes a perpetrator. An act of sexual abuse does not lessen in severity because it was committed by someone who was abused; most sexual abuse is in fact committed by people who were abused sexually or otherwise. But there are many abuse victims who do not go on to commit abuse; *they* are the ones who should receive society's compassion and support. It is also completely outrageous and wrong to expect victims of sex abuse to participate in their perpetrators' psychological treatment or to help them in any way. People have asked me why I haven't tried to help my father and get him past his denial of the abuse he committed and into psychological treatment. My response is that it is not my responsibility; if anything, it was my father's responsibility to help me heal from the abuse. My responsibility is to heal myself only. My father committed the abuse, and the responsibility for his treatment and recovery rests squarely on his own shoulders. Making an abuse victim part of the perpetrator's treatment process is like making her relive the trauma of the abuse. Certainly perpetrators of sexual abuse need to get psychological treatment, both for their own sakes and to prevent them from committing more crimes. But they also need to take responsibility for their crimes and make some kind of meaningful restitution to their victims, restitution above and beyond any incarceration time they might serve.

I myself have not had any experience with the legal aspects of child sexual abuse. By the time I realized that I had been a victim of sexual abuse and started the recovery process, the incest had been over for some time, so it was not necessary for me to deal with law enforcement officials. However, I have given much thought to how law enforcement and other officials can most effectively approach and treat victims of alleged child sexual crime. (Though I will be speaking about children here, this advice can certainly be applied to dealing with adult victims of sexual abuse as well.) The most important thing is to respect the victim and the victim's feelings. Trust what the victim is telling you. Don't ask things like: "Are you sure that really happened?"; "You're not making that up, are you?"; "I can't believe a nice person like your mom/dad/uncle/teacher would do a thing that"; "Are you sure you're not just trying to get back at him because you're angry about something else?" Don't belittle the child's feelings if she gets upset or angry; don't tell her she's lucky that nothing worse happened. The first step in recovery is realizing that the abuse WAS terrible and that it shouldn't have happened. Let the victim express her feelings for as long as she needs to. On the other hand, don't feel the victim's feelings for him. Sometimes the victim will seem very emotionless about the abuse because she is still trying to block it out, or he is still in shock. When I was first in therapy and describing what had happened to me, people told me

I sounded like I was reading from a laundry list. Some children need to feel very safe before they show emotion about the abuse, especially if the perpetrator was a close relative or has a lot of power in their life. Don't put words in the victim's mouth or tell him what a monster the perpetrator was or assume that he's feeling a certain way. Instead, concentrate on what the victim is saying, her tone of voice, what she is doing, and use that information to validate her experience. Say things like, "You sound very calm, about this" or "You keep twisting your hands when I mention your dad touching you. You seem very uncomfortable about discussing what happened," or "You sound very scared, and I completely understand, but I promise you are safe here." When questioning a child, keep the questions as neutral as possible: "What happened after that?" instead of, "What else did your cousin do to you?" If you appear calm, sympathetic but not pitying, and open to whatever the child has to say, the child will open up to you and give you more information. Sometimes the victim will give information in a roundabout or indirect way, especially a young or badly frightened child; if that happens you'll need to be patient and help the child by repeating what she said: "So your dad said he was tired?" "Your aunt took you for a walk in the garden?" Never in any way state or imply that the abuse is the child's fault. It isn't. And never, never question or interview a victim of sexual abuse in the presence of the alleged perpetrator.

When giving presentations on my experience as an incest victim, I have often been asked why I did not choose to prosecute my father or brother in civil court. I did contemplate doing so briefly—and I uphold the right of all victims of sex crimes to prosecute the perpetrators no matter how much time has elapsed after the crime—but I chose not to for several reasons. First of all, what I wanted from them was not so much financial compensation as emotional compensation—acknowledgement from them that they had abused me and apologies for having done so. I confronted them both by letter. My brother made me a very vague, general apology; my father denied ever having abused me and even took a lie detector test to "prove" he had not done so. A legal court would not have been any more successful than I had been in extracting an apology. Further, even if I had wanted to obtain financial compensation from them, it would have been very difficult to prove their guilt in a court of law, as it would have been my testimony against theirs, and the evidence was mostly circumstantial. There were witnesses for some of the more minor offenses, but these witnesses either did not see these offenses as sexual abuse or did not see what precisely was going on; my mother, for example, remembers that my father used to put his hand inside the waistband of my pants at dinner but didn't realize that he was doing anything further. There were certainly people who could attest to my father and brother's inappropriate behavior—a cousin, who is now a psychologist, remembers when my father groped a friend of hers at a holiday dinner, and told me she was not surprised to learn that my father had abused me sexually.

This, of course, in an ongoing problem for victims and law enforcement officials alike when detecting and prosecuting childhood sexual abuse—the perpetrator usually commits the abuse in private and whatever abuse he might commit in the presence of others is what might be termed borderline or inappropriate rather than molestation. For example, grabbing or patting someone's buttocks could be considered as sexual molestation by some people, but as affectionate or teasing by others. Inappropriate behavior or conversation can also indicate that there is sexual abuse going on, but I don't know how much it can be used in conviction or prosecution of sexual behavior. For instance, when I was seventeen, my father offered to pay my way through college if I would promise to remain a virgin until I was twenty-one. I refused and told him that my private life was none of his business. Later, at a family dinner, he announced to everyone that I had agreed to accept his offer. Could these events be considered as strong circumstantial evidence in an abuse case or simply as very unsuitable behavior? I feel that these sorts of events and behavior ought to be able to be used as part of the evidence to convict an accused perpetrator because they are strong public indications of his private behavior.

I also feel very strongly that convicted sex offenders—whether they were tried in a civil or criminal court—ought to be registered with national, state, and local law enforcement agencies, as well as any local schools, and in their place of employment, and that the neighbors within a certain radius ought to be informed of the nature of the offender's crime. This may seem harsh, especially if the offender has "reformed," but the government needs to protect its citizens against sex crimes, and even if offenders have been through therapy they may still repeat their crimes. I do not see these registration measures as punishment for the offender but as protection for potential victims. The offenders chose to abuse; they need to live with the consequences not only for the incarceration period but for the rest of their lives. It is their responsibility to reestablish creditable reputations in society, and they must do this through their own good behavior. Registration of sex offenders is not victimizing the offender; it is protecting the rest of society.

Child sexual abuse is a hard thing to know about and to read about. It has been a hard thing for me to write about, and excruciating to experience. But knowledge is the only way to stop this terrible crime and help victims on the road to healing and recovery—to turn them from victims into survivors. I hope this information will help.

Incest victim caught in justice-system trap

DEAR ABBY: Recently my husband and I heard Norman Early, the district attorney from Denver, speak on the criminal justice system—from the victim's point of view. He read the enclosed account of a victim of incest. I thought it worthy of your column. I hope you agree.

Mary Dean Armstrong

DEAR MARY: I do. And here it is:

I asked you for help and you told me you would if I told you the things my dad did to me. It was really hard for me to say all those things, but you told me to trust you—then you made me repeat them to 14 strangers.

I asked you to believe me, and you said you did, then you connected me to a lie detector, and took me to court, where lawyers put me on trial. I can't help it if I can't remember times or explain why I couldn't tell my mom. You confused me, which made you suspicious.

I asked you for help and you gave me a doctor with cold metal gadgets and cold hands (just like my father), who said it wouldn't hurt (just like my father), who said not to cry. He said I look fine—good news for you. You said, bad news for my "case".

I asked you for privacy and you let the newspaper get my story. Does it matter that they left out my name when they put in my father's and our address? My best friend's mother won't let her talk to me.

I asked for protection and you gave me a social worker who patted my head and called me "Honey" (because she couldn't remember my name). She sent me to live with strangers in a different school district.

Do you know what it feels like to be the one everyone blames for all the trouble? Do you know what it's like when your sisters hate you, and your brother calls you a liar? It's my word against my father's. You say you believe me—who cares, if nobody else does?

I asked you for help and you forced my mom to choose between us—she chose him, of course. She was scared and had a lot to lose. I had a lot to lose, too—the difference was you never told me how much.

I asked you to put an end to the abuse—you put an end to my family. You've exchanged my private nightmare for a very public one.

Feelings by Cindy, age 12

Put into words by Kee MacFarlane

Communicating as a GAL/CASA volunteer (2001).

Workbook Chapter 7, p. 16

Retrieved from

http://www.nccourts.org/Citizens/GAL/Documents/Workbook/chapter7.doc

PART IV

THE OFFENDERS

Chapter 13

Rapists

Deborah L. Laufersweiler-Dwyer, Ph.D.
and Gregg Dwyer, M.D., Ed.D.

Introduction

A major thesis of this book is that sexual crimes are an acquired behavior, an act of normal deviance, found in many societies and cultural groups. Rape is a behavioral act. When examining the motivation of rapists, there are several avenues by which to explore the concept. Often attributed to the psychological perspective, the first view identifies sex acts as those which are motivated by sexual needs or reasons. This particular definition is very difficult to justify objectively. Opinion differs (Dietz 1983; Groth 1979; and Knight and Prentky 1990) as to whether the motivation for rape should be limited to the conscious motivation or the unconscious motivations of the offender. It should be noted before examining the motivations of rapists that human behavior is a result of many factors. Actions reflect multiple drives, social forces, and situational variables. As this chapter begins, the reader will be struck with motives such as expression of anger, desire to control, the desire to inflict pain, and the desire for sexual gratification. Many researchers feel that "motivation" is the wrong term to use when describing why offenders commit a particular act (Dietz 1983; Groth 1979; and Knight and Prentky 1990). Instead, the crime of rape should be defined by the emotional determinants rather than the motivational determinants (Dietz 1983; Groth, 1979).

Many studies focus on the offenders' reasons for committing offenses, and from these studies typologies of offenders are derived. These typologies classify offenders into basic categories based upon characteristics of the offenders and their offenses. The difficulty of categorizing the behavior of rapists in a scientifically meaningful manner reflects a more general problem in the fields of victimology and criminology. A universal science must be founded on universal characteristics of human behavior. Many have moved in their research to try and overcome this flaw. Victimology and criminology have shifted the view to include the biological determinants as well as the psychological determinants to construct a more concise method of exploring the universal human characteristics that underlie rape.

In addition, rape cannot be understood apart from the sociocultural perspective. In this chapter we will also examine the numerous sociocultural perspectives in an attempt to create a complete picture concentrating on the dynamics of the offense, the characteristics of the offender and the characteristics of the victim.

While some offenders might have similar characteristics, there is no single typology that can account for all offenders. We must uncover the principles that bring about the most valuable separation of a group into subgroups that have theoretically important similarities (Prentky and Burgess 2000). Through such a process we can make sense of the phenomena. Classification systems that have the greatest opportunity for use start out with the simple question "What is the intended mission or purpose of the system?" In criminology and victimology the purpose has been to increase the accuracy of predictions of dangerousness or reoffense risk for sex offenders.

Sex Offender

There are a number of competing ideas surrounding sex offenders. The first is derived from the popular stereotypes. In the examination of motivations and typologies, the reader must understand that rapists seldom fit the "movie stereotype". Rapists are seldom the stranger jumping from behind the bushes. Rape is still often mistaken as a crime prompted solely by sexual desire. This misunderstanding has caused two familiar stereotypes to permeate American culture. The first is the offender, who, through circumstances beyond his control, misunderstandings or defective communication, becomes involved in the allegation of coerced sexual relations. The second stereotype is of the offender whose insatiable sexual needs drove him to commit acts that could satisfy his sexual gratification.

Many erroneous images have been formed as a result of emotional responses to ongoing crimes, past media hype and films depicting offenders as sex fiends, sex maniacs, or sex psychopaths (Dietz 1983). These images result in considerable pointlessness in societal reactions to offenders. In many instances societal responses have been severe to the least dangerous offenders while maintaining policies of little or no punishment for those offenders who attack the most helpless.

Many of the theories that have been used to explore the motivation behind an individual's behavior rely on normative conceptions or the dominant sociological view of deviance to explain the behaviors of sex offenders. These views are problematic in that they rely on community norms which are likely to vary from the slight to the extreme. In addition, many sexual behaviors are not criminal. Consensual sexual activities that involve paraphilias are often not defined within the legal arena.

As was stated above, the majority of offender classifications are developed based on the motivational concepts. Many with this view see sex offenses as being motivated by a need. This need is most often defined in sexual terms. A specific problem with this approach to classifying sex offenders is that many offenders have multiple reasons for their actions. In addition, if the motivation was sexual gratification, the requirement of orgasm would be present. In many rapes or attempted rapes the offenders may not, for various reasons, achieve orgasm, eliminating them from these categories.

Motivational Typologies

Knowing the limitations placed on this "science" by the numerous competing factors, it is necessary to examine the number of different typologies, recognizing the limitations that each presents. Several different classifications schemes have been proposed throughout the years. As early as 1952, Guttmacher and Weinhofen attempted to classify offenders as either true sex offenders, aggressive offenders or sadistic offenders. True sex offenders used rape as an explosive expression of a pent-up sexual desire. The second offender committed rape as a general pattern of criminal behavior. The third offender was, as stated, sadistic.

Though rape is a sexual crime, many researchers have pointed to the non-sexual needs that motivate the offender. Kopp (1962) developed a dichotomy based on whether the rapists could be characterized as "ego-syntonic or "ego-dystonic". In this motivational scheme the rapists was either an antisocial psychopath or a an individual with "feelings" who is later likely to feel remorse or guilt. Gebhard, Gagnon, Pomeroy, and Christenson (1965) set down four categories of offenders within which the seven subtypes of offenders were identified. Within these were the amoral delinquent, the double standard, the explosive rapist and the assaultive-sadistic rapist.

Table One—Cohen and Seghorn's Typology

Compensatory type	Motive is more sexual than aggressive. Force is simply used to gain compliance. The rape fantasy is foremost in the offenders mind. The rape often compensates for feelings of inadequacy.
Displaced Aggressive type	The sexual assault is an expression of anger. The rapist's intent is to physically harm, degrad, defile and humiliate the victim. The offender experiences an uncontrollable impulse often precipitated by an event involving a significant woman in the offenders life. The offense is the displacement of the anger towards this other woman.
Sex-aggression-diffusion type	This offender displays clinical sadism, feeling arousal and anger during the assault. The two feelings are synergistically related.
Impulse type	For this offender neither sexual nor aggressive motives are central to the assault. The offenses predatory and part of the key pattern of impulse antisocial behavior.

In 1969, Cohen, Seghorn and Calmas identified four types of rapists based on the relative amounts of aggression and sex present in the offense. This research produced four types that subsequently led to further research and the more popular "motivational models" or typologies. In their research, Cohen et al., identified the compensatory type, the displaced aggressive type, the sex-aggression-diffusion type and the impulse type. Table One illustrates the characteristics attributed to each category.

Amir (1971), in his early research on victim precipitation and rape, identified several types of rapists. In his categorization of rapists, Amir identified offenders based on aberrations of their personality, or those who commit rape as a "demand of the youth culture". Rada (1978) in his research closely following Amir described five types of rapists. The first was identified as the sociopathic offender, whose behavior was impulsive and antisocial. The second type of rapist was the masculine identify conflict offender. This offender was characterized by feeling of inadequacy and hypermasculine attitudes. The third type of offender was identified as the situational stress offender. His behaviors were characterized by depression and feelings of guilt. The fourth type of offender characterized by Rada was the sadistic offender. This offender is aroused by and gains pleasure from the degradation, pain and humiliation of the victim. The last type of rapist described by Rada was the psychotic offender. This offender is set apart by his bizarre and violent behavior.

Berlin et al., (1997) believed that the offender's actions and their consequences were not enough to illuminate motivation. Sexual offenses can be enacted out of a variety of motivations. In some cases, the behaviors in question may be a manifestation of a psychiatric disorder accompanied by severe impairment. In their typologies, Berlin et al. (1997), attempted to explore and identify six motivational factors. In this examination, Berlin et al. (1997), identified typologies of the opportunistic rapist. Type one is an offender who has prominent narcissistic personality traits. He may have an inflated sense of his own worth, masking insecurities, or an exploitative personality style that does not otherwise adequately consider the perspectives of others. He believes he is not accountable to social norms or the law. Type two has dependent personality traits, and may be may be generally unassertive and submissive. He has low self-esteem, little initiative, and a positive and helpful attitude towards others. However, he experiences uncharacteristic outbursts of irrational behavior which in some cases takes the form of sexual aggression.

The second category of rapists identified by Berlin et al. (1997), was the angry rapist. This type commits rape out of anger or frustration. The anger is often identified with one person or incident and then redirected within the rape. The third category of rapists is the developmentally-impaired rapist. These individuals suffer from either mental retardation or are developmentally impaired. They often experience difficulties leading to an inability to learn and control their sexual urges in socially acceptable ways.

The fourth category of rapist is the psychotic rapist. These are individuals who have an independent confirmatory history of major mental illness. The fifth category is identified as a paraphilic or sexually-driven rapist. Often identified as a paraphiliac coercive disorder these offenders have recurrent cravings for coercive sex. The final category is the rare case of the sexual assault associated with voyeurism. The authors note that voyeurism is almost always a non-violent offense. It is in rare instances that this offense may turn to violence.

Groth, Burgess, and Holmstrom (1977) developed a classification scheme based on the concepts of power, control, and sexuality. This classification system has conceptual distinctions very similar to Cohen and Seghorn's typologies. Within their model, Groth et al., identified four types of rapists, to include power reassurance, power assertive, anger-retaliatory, and anger excitation. This model has been used extensively in practical rather than theoretical applications (Turvey 1999). Most students of victimology and criminology are familiar with these dimensions. This model has been modified for use by law enforcement as a mechanism for identifying possible offenders and targeting investigatory efforts. Additionally, this model was revised by the National Center for the Analysis of Violent Crime (NCAVC). In part, this model was modified to describe the offenders' behaviors during the act as a method of aiding in criminal profiling. The NCAVC motivational typologies describe offenders' behaviors as follows:

- **Power Reassurance:** offender behaviors suggest an underlying lack of confidence and inadequacy, or belief that the offense is consensual, expressed through minimum force and low confidence.
- **Power Assertive:** offender behaviors suggest an underlying lack of confidence and inadequacy, expressed through a need for control, mastery and humiliation of the victim, while demonstrating authority.
- **Anger Retaliatory:** offender behavior suggests a great deal of rage, either towards a specific person, group, institution or symbol of either.
- **Anger-Excitement/Sadistic:** offender behavior suggests the offender gets sexual gratification from the victim's pain and suffering.
- **Opportunistic:** offender behavior suggests an offender who is out to satisfy his immediate sexual impulses.

Although extensive in considering both the psychological needs and purposes of the offender, it is however limiting, in that it does not consider the cultural components of human behavior. In addition it does not provide for a dynamic, developmental model that identifies possible transformation in the offender.

Prentky, Knight, and Rosenberg (1988) developed a typology that can be considered, perhaps, as the most comprehensive of classification models. This model included three categories, which identified eight types of offenders. This model assesses a) the aggression of the offense (instrumental or expressive), b) the meaning of sexuality in the offense (compensatory, exploitive, displaced-anger, sadistic), and c) the impulsivity reflected in the history and life-style of the offender. This model, unlike earlier models, includes both the biological, psychological and cultural components necessary to define human behavior.

This model was later modified to include a ninth subtype. It is a motivation-driven system that consists of four primary presumptive motivating factors: opportunity, pervasive anger, sexual gratification, and vindictiveness. This classification model (Table Two) includes the following major dimensions: expressive aggression, juvenile and adult antisocial behavior, social competence, global or pervasive anger, sadism, sexualization, and offense planning.

Profiles of Specific Rapists

Although other chapters have addressed the occurrence of rape, it is necessary to again look at the sources of data and some of the numbers produced by this data. Data from this section came from official statistics gathered by police, self-report surveys done by the Bureau of Justice Statistics and inde-

Table Two—Prentky, Knight, and Rosenberg Motivational Typologies

Primary Motivation	Types and brief identifiers	
Oppor-tunistic	*Type one—High Social Competence*	*Type Two—Low Social Competence*
	Aggression is likely to be instrumental; no gratuitous violence and no evidence of pervasive anger. Moderate impulse, antisocial behavior in adulthood, relatively high level of social and interpersonal competence	Aggression is likely to be instrumental; no gratuitous violence and no evidence of pervasive anger. Moderate impulse, antisocial behavior in adulthood, relatively low level of social and interpersonal competence
	Offenses are not typically to be sexualized; no history of paraphilias and no evidence of sadism. Offenses do not appear to be compulsive, offense planning is minimal, and there is little evidence of premeditation	Offenses do not typically appear to be sexualized; no history of paraphilias and no evidence of sadism. Offenses do not appear to be compulsive, offense planning is minimal, and there is little evidence of premeditation
Pervasively Angry	*Pervasively Angry—Type Three*	
	Characterized by a high level of aggression and gratuitous violence in most aspects of the offenders life. A history of aggression directed at men and women. Moderate impulse, antisocial behavior in adolescence and adulthood. Offenses do not typically appear to be sexualized; history of paraphilias is unlikely, and no evidence of sadism. Offenses do not appear compulsive, offense planning is minimal, and there is little evidence of premeditation	

...continued on next page

pendent research. Relying strictly on official statistics would give the reader a skewed view of the profile for both the rapists and their victims.

Two sources of statistical data are maintained by the Department of Justice as a tool to learn more about the prevalence and characteristics of sexual crimes. The Uniform Crime Report provides significant data on those crimes reported to police. NCVS gathers information about crimes from a nationally representative sample of U.S. residents age 12 and older. In the late 1980's an effort was put forth to enhance the surveys to better obtain information on rape and sexual assaults. This restructuring included incidents of sexual assault and unwanted sexual contact.

General Picture

In order to create a profile we will start with the general characteristics for all arrested rapists. Then we will identify these characteristics by the type of rape committed by the offender. To understand fully the different categories of rape it is necessary to understand how these rapists are similar in nature as well as diverse.

Sexual	Sadistic		Non-sadistic	
	Overt—Type Four	*Muted—Type Five*	*High Social Competence—Type Six*	*Low Social Competence—Type Seven*
	Characterized by a high level of aggression and gratuitous violence, mostly notably in sexual offenders. A history of pervasive or generalized anger is present. Sexual offenders are marked by sadism (fusion of aggression with sexual arousal); there must be clear evidence of a connection between sexual acts and the pain, suffering, or humiliation of the victim. Moderate amount of impulse, antisocial behavior in adolescence and adulthood. History of other paraphilias often is present. Offense planning and premeditation are evident.	Aggression is likely to be instrumental; no gratuitous violence is evident. Although impulsive, antisocial behavior may be present, it is not a critical feature. Sexual offenders are marked by sadism with a low level of violence and limited physical injury to victims; sexual acts tend to by symbolic and noninjurious. Key difference between Overt and Muted is the relative absence of aggression in the muted type. History of other paraphilias often is present. Offense planning and premeditation are evident	Aggression is likely to be instrumental. No gratuitous violence and evidence of pervasive anger. Minimal impulsive, antisocial behavior in adolescence. Moderate impulse, antisocial behavior may be present in adulthood. Relatively high level of social and interpersonal competence. Sexual offenses marked by high degree of sexualization, rape fantasy, and expressed interest in the victim as a sex object. Although a history of other paraphilias often is present, there is no evidence of sadism. Offense planning and premeditation is evident.	Aggression is likely to be instrumental. No gratuitous violence and evidence of pervasive anger. Minimal impulsive, antisocial behavior in adolescence. Moderate impulse, antisocial behavior may be present in adulthood. Relatively low level of social and interpersonal competence. Sexual offenses marked by high degree of sexualization, rape fantasy, and expressed interest in the victim as a sex object. Although a history of other paraphilias often is present, there is no evidence of sadism. Offense planning and premeditation is evident.
Vindictive	*Low Social Competence—Type 8*		*Moderate Social Competence—Type 9*	
	Characterized by a high level of aggression and gratuitous violence that is directed specifically at women, both in sexual offenses and otherwise. Anger is misogynistic and there is no history of pervasive anger. Minimal impulse and antisocial behavior in adolescence. Moderate impulsive and antisocial behavior in adulthood. Relatively low level of social and interpersonal competence. Offenses do not typically appear to be sexualized. There is no history of paraphilias and no evidence of sadism. Offenses do not appear to be compulsive, planning is minimal and there is little evidence of premeditation.		Characterized by a high level of aggression and gratuitous violence that is directed specifically at women, both in sexual offenses and otherwise. Anger is misogynistic and there is no history of pervasive anger. Minimal impulse and antisocial behavior in adolescence. Although some impulsive and antisocial behavior may be present in adulthood, it is not extensive. Relatively high level of social and interpersonal competence. Offenses do not typically appear to be sexualized. There is no history of paraphilias and no evidence of sadism. Offenses do not appear to be compulsive, planning is minimal and there is little evidence of premeditation.	

Note: Abstracted from Pretenky and Burgess 2000

In 2000, an estimated 90,186 forcible rapes were reported to police (UCR 2000). This represents an increase from the previous year, but a rate still lower than that reported in the mid 1990's (UCR 2000). Regionally, the greatest percentage of reported rapes occurred in the South. As described in the previous section, cultural factors help explain this phenomena. Many of the theories surrounding rape are strongly supported by the "subculture of violence" theory and the hypermasculinity theories.

Of the rapes reported, 89.5 percent were completed while only 10.5 percent accounted for attempts. Again it must be noted that these are those rapes or attempted rapes reported police. In addition, the profile created is of those offenders arrested.

The consequences of low reporting of sexual assault are that it places severe restrictions on creating a profile of the offender, victim attributes and the situational dynamics of the crime (Miethe and McCorkle 2001). In 1994 and 1995, 32 percent of rapes identified by NCVS were reported to law enforcement (Greenfield 1997). Under these conditions, offender profiles should be interpreted with caution.

In 1994 (Greenfield 1997), of those crimes reported as sexual assault/rape, 35.8 percent were strangers and 64.2 percent were included in the nonstranger category. When asked to describe the relationship to the offender, the majority (33.1%) said the offender was well known to them. This was closely followed by strangers at 30.9 percent. Most instances of sexual assault/rape involved only one offender, whether the offender was known or not.

There are some characteristics that are similar to all rapists. These include gender. Of all rapes reported during 2000 to both the UCR and NCVS 99.4 percent were males. The majority of those arrested were under 25 years of age. In addition, the racial breakdown has remained stable, with whites being approximately 60 percent of those arrested.

NCVS and UCR provide limited data on the characteristics of the victim. What has been discovered in a review of this data is that the majority of rape victims are young, unmarried and economically disadvantaged. In 1994, the NCVS reported little statistical difference in martial status and rape. The numbers were evenly distributed across all categories.

Offender Specialization and Escalation

In creating a profile of rapists the question is often asked "Where did they start?" The majority of rapists did not start out as minor sex offenders. As opposed to the popular belief that voyeurs and exhibitionist will soon escalate to rape, the majority of offenders in prison had no previous record for a nonviolent sex crime. There are some exceptions as different types of rapist are pro-filed. Those who commit marital rape and acquaintance rape may escalate from aggressive or battering nonsexual behaviors to sexual behaviors.

Planning and Spontaneity

Although popular culture has characterized rapists as calculating individ-uals who have well thought out plans for their actions, the majority of rapists do not fall within this category. For most rapists, the level of planning is low, if any. This is particularly true when a prior relationship exists between the parties involved (Miethe and McCorkle 2001).

Situational Elements and Circumstances

Transient factors associated with sex offenses include: offender motivation, the victim-offender relationship, and the situational dynamics of the crime. Offender motivation has been addressed in great depth earlier in this chapter. It must be noted however, that the majority of typologies or motivational clas-sification schemes have been limited to forcible-stranger rape. Typologies for acquaintance rape, date rape and marital rape will be discussed later in this chapter.

Victim offender relationships are extremely important in creating profiles for both the offenders and their targets. These relationships often dictate mo-tivation on the part of the offender. There is an extreme degree of debate over the frequency of stranger versus non-stranger rape. Some of the explanations given for this are that many of the rapes that occur between non-strangers are not likely to be reported to the police.

Situational dynamics are primary factors such as time and place aspects, types of weapons used, victim resistance, financial, marital and other stressor, nonpsychosexual mental disorders and alcohol and drug use. Many studies show that sex offenders were reasonably well adjusted men who committed their first offenses while drinking heavily, experiencing extreme emotional stressor, in groups, or during a depressive, manic, or schizophrenic episode. The sexual na-ture of the crime often requires additional explanation. These often go to the emotional feelings of the offender at the time of the offense (Dietz 1983).

Stranger Rape

In forcible rapes, sex offenders are disproportionately young and African-American (UCR 1998). This distribution has remained fairly stable over time. As with many other violent offenses, rape is most often intraracial. The socioeconomic status of forcible/stranger rapes has also remained consistent over time. In early research, Amir (1971) found that most rapists arrested were unemployed and of low-socioeconomic status. Research done in 1994 by Miethe and Meier supported this by identifying the majority of rapes occurring in neighborhoods with high unemployment and low family income.

In terms of situational factors, sexual assaults occur in a social context defined primarily by time and physical location. According to data, summer months (especially July and August) are the peak season for rapes known to the police, and rapes are most infrequent during the winter months (UCR 1998). More than one-third of sexual assaults occur between 6:00 p.m. and midnight (NCVS 1998). A higher proportion of rapes occur on the weekend than on other days the week, and nearly half take place at or near the victim's home. A smaller proportion (about 20 percent) occur on school property or in commercial buildings, and less than 10 percent happen in parking lots, parks, or alleys (NCVS 1998). Stranger assaults, however, are more likely to occur in open public areas than sexual assaults among nonstrangers. Weapon use is estimated in 18 percent of sexual assaults but only about 10 percent of those assaults involving acquaintances as offenders (NCVS 1998).

Acquaintance Rape

There are several different definitions attached to this form of rape. Most have been developed by law enforcement and researchers for aid in categorizing offenders. Many individuals believe that the phenomenon of acquaintance rape is new. However, references to this form of rape can be found in the Old Testament (Allison and Wrightsman 1993). It has been only recently, that public attention has been brought to a strikingly frequent event. In describing the profiles of these rapists it is necessary to divide acquaintance rape into three separate categories. The will be acquaintance rape, date rape and marital rape.

Acquaintance rape is any rape in which the parties know each other. This definition is often seen as nonconsensual sex between adults who know each other. This includes neighbors, coworkers, friends, etc. Often this is a person with who the victim knows, but not a close friend (Parrot and Bechhofer 1991). Acquaintance rape compared to the characteristics of stranger rape is unique. In comparison there are two areas where distinct differences can be found. These are the force used, and the time at which the act occurs. In acquaintance rape, as opposed to stranger rape, the force used by the offender reflects more subtle types of coercion (Muehlenhard and Schrag 1991).

The majority of research on the subject of acquaintance rape has been done with college students. The reasons for this are the risk of victimization, their willingness to participate in research, and the organizations found on college campuses that have been associated with acquaintance rape.

Date Rape

Date rape is commonly viewed as a less serious and less traumatic offense than stranger or acquaintance rape (Van Wormer and Bartollas 2000). Five types of date rape have been proposed to capture the diversity of these sexual assaults. Shotland (1992) identified beginning date rape, early date rape, relational date rape, rape between sexually active couples and rape between sexually active couples who previously dated. Each of these arose at a different point in the relationship, both in terms of the length of the relationship and previous sexual activity (Byers and O'Sullivan 1996).

Beginning rape has been defined as those occurring during the first few dates. Associated with these rapes, Kanin (1967) stated that the rapist may have a need for more varied sexual experience. In addition, it was identified that women who date extensively or engage in having sex with a number of different males are more likely to expose themselves to an aggressive male. This is not to say that they brought on the rape. The variety in experiences increases their chances of encountering an aggressive male.

The second instance in which rapes are likely to occur in the dating relationship is the "early date rape". A number of different explanations have been given for rapes that occur during this period of courtship. A significant explanation has been the poor skills in coping with sexual frustration and poor impulse control on the part of the male. Foreplay leads to mixed feelings. Kanin (1967, 1985) identified that college men who were dissatisfied with the frequency of their sexual activity were more likely to rape. Kanin (1985) also identified that these behavior may be a last resort when all other forms non-coercive behaviors have failed.

The third and fourth types of date rape are referred to as relational date rape. The first type occurs in an ongoing relation where the couple has not engaged in sexual activity. In these instances, many of the men see this as a step toward marriage or believe that others couples are already engaged in sexual relations. This leads the male to encourage and in many instance coerce the female into participating in sexual activities.

The last type of rape occurs after the relationship has ended. In many instances as a mechanism for revenge on the part of the male, but also as a way to "win" back the victim's love. Offenders often feel that this is what the victim wants or what they, as a spurned lover, deserve.

Situational elements and circumstances are most often identified in this type of rape. Several studies have examined the situational elements and found that the definition of rape becomes extremely muddied when research participants are asked to include these elements. Giarrussi, Johnson Goodchilds, and Zeller (1979), Fischer (1986), Muehlenhard, Friedman, and Thomas (1985), and Korman and Leslie (1982) found several factors that participants identified as changing the definition of the act from rape to sexual activity. These included money spent by the male, heavy petting, going to the man's apartment, women initiating the date, and alcohol use on the part of one or both parties.

The men who commit these offenses have a number of characteristics in common. They are more aggressive, more likely to view pornographic material, more likely to use alcohol, hold hostile attitudes toward women, and seek out peer groups that reinforce stereotypical views of women (Johnson and Sigler 1997). In addition, several other studies have found these men are more likely to condone rape and violence, hold traditional roles and more likely to be sexually experienced (Kanin 1967; Koss, Leonard, Beezley and Oros 1985; and Rapaport and Burkhart 1984).

The description above fits into many of the typologies presented earlier in this chapter. Groth's power-assertive and Knight and Pretensky's sexual rapist are most likely to be identified with the date rapists.

Marital Rape

In order to understand the offenders of marital rape it is necessary to understand the definition this offense takes on. Much variety exists in state laws defining exactly what elements must be satisfied for marital rape to have occurred. All states currently have some statue defining marital rape. These are, however, far from clear. In many states exemptions still exist keeping prosecutors from charging husbands.

In its simplest form, marital rape is defined as any intercourse or penetration obtained by force, threat of force or where the individual was unable to give consent. Finkelhor and Yllo (1985) developed a typology of marital rapists. They divided these offenders into three groups: force only, battering, and sadistic/obsessive.

Force only rape has been describe as coerced sex. These are instances where the husband will use only the amount of coercion necessary to obtain submission (Johnson and Siegler 1997; Bergen 1996; Finkelhor and Yllo 1985).

Table Three—Overview of the Proposed Four-Type Integrated Batterer Typology

Type	Type of Violence	Generality of Violence	Percentage in General Batterer Population
Family-only	Nonsexual Only	Only/predominately marital	45%
Dysphoric/borderline	Sexual/nonsexual	Predominately marital	25%
Generally violent/antisocial	Sexual/nonsexual	Marital/extramarital	25%
Sexually Sadistic	Sexual Only	Marital/extramarital	5%

Many victims in these instances do not define the action as rape causing significant problems in identifying the extent to which this crime occurs. The second category within marital rape is battering rape. This is seen as the extension of the battering, either occurring during the physical violence or after the violence. In the cases where the rape occurs after the violence, it often takes on the form of "making-up". The abuser in an attempt to show his "love" for his spouse coerces her into having sex against her will (Johnson and Siegler 1997; Bergen 1996; Finkelhor and Yllo 1985). The final category within marital rape is the sadistic/obsessive rape. These offenses involve torture, physical violence, and/or perverse sexual acts (Johnson and Siegler 1997; Bergen 1996; Finkelhor and Yllo 1985).

Russell (1990) identified three different types of husband rapists: husbands who prefer raping their wives over having consensual sex with them, husbands who are able to enjoy both rape and consensual sex, but are indifferent to which it is, and husbands who prefer consensual sex, but who are willing to rape their wives when sex is denied. Russell contends that the motivations are different for each group. She reverts back to the common elements of power and anger in identifying motivations.

A fourth type of sexual batterer was added to Finkelhor and Yllo's (1985) typology by Monson and Langhinrichsen-Rohling (1998), who identified the "sexually-obsessive" batterer. In their typology, battering only and sexual battering have been combined to create an integrated typology of marital violence. Table Three represents the marital violence typology developed by Monson and Langhinrichsen-Rohling (1998).

Marital rape typologies are not well developed. Some researchers argue that marital rape is just one extension of domestic violence (Johnson and Sigler 1997). The research is often anecdotal and relies upon survey research whose reliability is questionable. In addition, the sample sizes have been limited by the victim's willingness to come forward, as well as the victim's own conception of what constitutes a rape (Monson and Langhinrichsen-Rohling 1998).

Attempting to create a profile of marital rapists is difficult. All the information gathered on those who commit this offense has come from the victims. In addition, the majority of information has been collected in conjunction with domestic violence. This has limited the sample to only those men who are violent—sexual or nonsexual. Little or no information has been gleaned from the perpetrators. Characteristics that are common to these offenders are a history of family-of-origin violence, substance abuse, extreme jealousy, domination/control and diminished marital satisfaction In addition, marital dysfunction, a need for sadomasochistic sex, and greater jealousy toward their wives has been associated with sexually aggressive men compared to nonsexually aggressive men (Bowker 1983). There is some evidence that premarital pregnancy is associated with marital rape (Davidson 1978; Walker 1979).

It is important for the reader to understand that marital rape is not limited to those in lower socioeconomic levels. It is not limited to those who marry young, nor is it limited to relationships that are violent from the beginning. In one of the largest studies of marital rape, martial rape was found to occur at all levels of society. African American women were slightly more likely than Caucasian women to be the victims of marital rape (Russell 1990).

Russell (1990) also determined that women who are raped within the marital relationship have often entered into the relationship at a very young age. In addition, Russell also found that these women had been victims of other types of sexual violence prior to their marriage.

Child Molesters

At this point in the chapter will we specifically look at two types of child sexual abusers—Child Molesters and Pedophiles. You may be thinking—"Aren't they the same thing?" The answer is no. No single molester profile exists. Child molesters arrive at deviancy via multiple pathways and engage in different sexual and nonsexual acting-out behaviors (Pretenky, Knight and Lee 1997). Remember this as you read through this material, that not all child molesters are pedophiles and not all pedophiles are child molesters.

Commonly used by the media and law enforcement "child molesters" can mean anyone who engages in any type of sexual activity with individuals legally defined as children. When using this term, there are no distinctions between single or repeat offenders or violent and nonviolent offenders. Many of us still adhere to the image of the dirty old man at the playground offering children candy as a means of seducing them away and molesting them. It is necessary that we understand the difference between a child molester and a pedophile. As stated before, not all child molesters are pedophiles, and not all pedophiles are child molesters.

Classification of Child Molesters

There are a number of different types of classification models for child molesters. The first types are the clinically derived classification systems. The earliest of these classification systems was developed by Finch (1962). Finch identified the immature offender, the frustrated offender, the sociopathic offender, the pathological offender and the miscellaneous offender. Finch did use in his typology the characteristic of whether the offenses were seen as a preferred and long standing form of sexual behavior, an immature offender or as a reaction to some sexual or emotional frustration at the adult level, the frustrated type.

Kopp (1962) in his examination of child molesters identified only two categories within his typology. These included the Type I offender, an individual who is drawn to children as a result of passive and somewhat withdrawn relationship to peers. Type I offenders do not see these relationships as abnormal or inappropriate. The Type II offender is described as maintaining adult relationships in a relatively normal framework. The lack of dimension has lead to little use of this typology.

Swanson (1971) identified four types of child molesters. These included first, the classic pedophiliac, whose sexual preference is only children. And secondly, the situational violator, who is most likely to have long term peer relationships, but, due to environmental circumstances or situational factors, offends. The third type described was the inadequate sociopathic violator who does not show a specific attraction to children, but exploits a child for convenience or self-gratification. The last type was the brain damaged. This offender molests as a result of some clinical condition such as mental retardation.

Classification systems stemmed from these early efforts resulted in extensive research done at the Massachusetts Treatment Center in Bridgewater and the development of several profiles (Cohen, Garofalo, Boucher, and Seghorn 1971; Cohen, Seghorn and Calmas 1969; Groth and Birnbaum 1979). The initial classification system developed out of this research was produced by Cohen, Seghorn and Calmas in 1969. Within this research, three types of pedophilia were identified. These included the pedophile-fixated type, the pedophile-regressed type and the pedophile-aggressive type. A fourth type was later added, the exploitative type.

Dr. Nicholas Groth (1978) developed a similar classification model. As with other research efforts, Groth distinguished between offenders who manifest fixation on children and those whose molestation represents a regression. In his book, Groth et al. (1978), identified two patterns, fixed and regressed (Common Types 1 and 2, respectively) and three distinct motivations sex-pressure, sex-force, and incest.

Yet another classification scheme was proposed in 1992. In the Crime Classification Manual, Douglas et al. (1992), attempted to provide a comprehensive DSM-like list of primary categories with subtypes. This system was designed to aid law enforcement rather than define clinically the behavioral, motivational and emotional aspects of other classification systems. Within this system, child molesters were identified as belonging to one of twelve categories. These included the nuisance offender (with four subtypes), the domestic sexual assault, entitlement rape, subordinate rape, power-reassurance rape, exploitative rape, anger rape, sadistic rape, child/adolescent pornography, historical child/adolescent sex rings, multidimensional sex rings and abduction rape.

Dr. Park Dietz (1983) developed a classification system dividing individuals who sexually molest children into two broad categories: situational and preferential. These typologies again had been developed in an effort to aid law enforcement in the identification, arrest, and conviction of offenders. In this model, the difference between the two types of child molesters was that situational child molesters do not have a true sexual preference for children, but engage in sex with children for varied and sometimes complex reasons. The preferential child molester is a pedophile. These individuals have a definite sexual preference for children. Their sexual fantasies and erotic imagery focus on children. The preferential type doesn't experience stress as does the situational child molester.

Within the situational type, four subtypes have been identified, which include, regressed, morally indiscriminate, inadequate, and the sexually indiscriminate. The first type is the regressed child molester. This individual often leads the most stable life of the situational child molesters. They are however plagued by low self-esteem and poor coping skills. When they molest, they often turn to the victim as a substitute for the preferred adult sexual companion. They are most likely to obtain a victim based on availability. This is why many of these offenders molest their own children. They may use force, promises or some other type of coercion to get the child to have sex. Among incest offenders, this type is the most prevalent.

The second subtype of situational child molester is the morally indiscriminate child molester. This subtype is simply continuing a pattern of behavior. He is a user and abuser of all he encounters. Children are simply part of that chain. He often chooses his victims based on their vulnerability and opportunity. Unlike the regressed situational child molester, the majority of his victims are strangers. This is not to say that his own children could not be his victims.

The third subtype of situational is the inadequate child molester. These individuals are often suffering from psychoses, a personality disorder or mental retardation (Lanning 1986). The offenders seem to become sexually involved with children out of insecurity or curiosity. Children are viewed as nonthreatening, allowing these individuals to explore sexual fantasies. These individuals can, however, due to their lack of impulse control, become angry and hurt the child.

The last subtype in the situational category is the sexually indiscriminate child molester. This individual differs in that he appears to be discriminating in his behavior except when it comes to sex. His is a often referred to in law-enforcement circles as a "try-sexual". This simply means that he is willing to try anything. He is most often confused with a preferential child molester. Although he has numerous defined paraphilias or sexual preferences, he has no clear preference for children. Of all the situational child molesters, he is far more likely to have multiple victims, and be from a higher socioeconomic background.

Within the preferential category, there are three subtypes: seductive, introverted, and sadistic. The first subtype, also know as the fixated type, will seduce or court his victims, often buying them gifts, toys, or loaning them money. As this person slowly becomes more intimate with the child, he begins to introduce sexual innuendo and eventually sexual pornography and paraphernalia. He is the master manipulator and often has numerous individuals at different stages of seduction. This individual frequently identifies children who have some emotional need.

The second type of preferential offender identified by Dietz was the sadistic pedophile. This subtype, also called a mysoped, often stalks, uses force to obtain compliance and must inflict pain, suffering and humiliation to become sexually gratified. These offenders have been identified as most likely to kill their victims.

The final type identified by Dietz was the introverted pedophile. This offender has a preference for children, but lacks the social and interpersonal skills necessary to seduce them. He engages in little or nonverbal communication with his victims. He is the old stereotype of the dirty old man or the guy hanging around the playground. He is similar to the inadequate Situational Child molester, except for his sexual preference for children alone.

Table Four—Situational Child Molester

	Regressed	Morally Indiscriminate	Sexually Indiscriminate	Inadequate
Basic Characteristics	Poor coping skills	User of people	Sexual Experimentation	Social misfit
Motivation	Substitution	Why not?	Boredom	Insecurity and curiosity
Victim Criteria	Availability	Vulnerability and opportunity	New and Different	Nonthreatening
Method of operation	Coercion	Lure, force, or manipulation	Involve in existing activity	Exploits size, advantage
Pornography Collection	Possible	Sadomasochistic detective magazines	Highly Likely: varied	Likely

Table Five—Preferential Child Molester

	Seduction	Introverted	Sadistic
Common Characteristics	1. Sexual preference for children 2. Collects child pornography or erotica		
Motivation	Identification	Fear of Communication	Need to inflict pain
Victim Criteria	Age and Gender preferences	Strangers or very young	Age and Gender preferences
Method of Operation	Seduction Process	Non-verbal sexual contact	Lure or force

Tables adapted from: Deviant and Criminal Sexuality (1993),
2nd edition, NCAVC, FBI Academy.

The MTC:CM3 (Massachusetts Treatment Center: Child Molester 3) model was developed by researchers at the Massachusetts Treatment Center. This model is described as a two axis typology. In Table 6 on Axis I fixation and social competence are completely independent dimensions. The concept of regression was dropped and a newly defined fixation dimension, intensity of pedophilic interest, was crossed with a dimension of social competence. This new model yielded four independent types. Axis II was added to describe the behavioral dimension of an offender. Also included within this Axis was the degree of violence employed by the offender. This combination yielded six distinct types within Axis 2 (Knight, Prentky, and Lee 1997).

The last type of child molester identified by clinicians and police is the incest offender. It is clear that, as a group, these offenders are as heterogeneous as nonincest offenders (Rist 1979; Summit and Kryso 1978; Prentky and

Table Six—MTC:CM3 Typology of Child Molesters

Axis I		Axis II	
Type 0—High Fixated—Low social competence In order to be considered high fixation the offender must have sexual thoughts dominated by children, had three or more sexual contacts with children, evidence of enduring relationships with children, offender initiates contact with children in numerous situations.	*Type 1—High Fixated/ Low Social Competence* Offenders with high social competence have lasting employment, adult sexual relationship lasting one year or longer, offender has assumed significant responsibility in parenting for 3 years or longer, offender is active in adult activities, and offender has a friendship with an adult lasting one or more years. Offenders do not have to meet all criteria only two. Offenders with low social competence do not meet the criteria.	*Type 1 Interpersonal*: high contact with children, nongenital, nonorgasmic sexual acts. Offender known prior to sexual relationship, long term relationship or multiple contacts with same victim, high degree of planning.	*Type 2 Narcissistic*; high contact with children, interests are in sexual gratification, primary aim is orgasm, victims are often strangers, single encounters, numerous victims, offenses are often spontaneous with little planning.
Type 2—*Low Fixated/ Low Social Competence*	*Type 3—Low Fixated/ High Social Competence*	Type 3 Exploitative: low contact with children, no more force than necessary to gain compliance, no evidence that aggression is eroticized or sexualized, sexual gratification is the primary aim, victims are typically strangers and offenses so a moderate degree of planning.	*Type 4 Muted Sadistic*: Low contact with children, no more force than necessary to gain compliance, aggression was eroticized—sadistic fantasies, victims are strangers, moderate planning.
Axis II			
Type 5 Aggressive Low contact with children, high degree of physical injury (take many forms from repressed aggression to accidental injury), primary aim is orgasm, no evidence of sadism, little evidence of offense planning.		*Type 6 Sadistic* Low Contact with children, high degree of physical injury, Injuries are indicative of sadism on the part of offender, victims are strangers, high degree of planning.	

Note: Abstracted from Prentky and Burgess (2000)

Burgess 2000). Incest is a sexual relationship with a near relative (including parent-child, grandparent-grandchild, brother-sister, uncles, and aunts).

Parent and child relationships are the most frequently reported, although brother and sister relationships are not uncommon. There has been little effort made to develop any classification system, either clinical or empirical (Prentky and Burgess 2000). In one of the earliest attempt to classify these offenders, Weinberg (1955) identified two types: the ingrown family and the promiscuous family. Summit and Kryso (1978) in a clinical examination of offenders, identified ten categories of offenders. Significant to their classification was the diverseness of this group. Researchers believe that the heterogeneous nature allows for the application of nonincest models to incest offenders. Table Seven outlines the categories identified by Summit and Kyrso (1978).

Table Seven—Typology of Incest Offenders—Summit and Kyrso (1978)

Type	Description
Incidental Sexual Contact	Isolated incidents of interest or dependency. The often take the form of sexual games that are not considered abusive.
Ideological Sexual Contact	The parent believes that the child will benefit from the expression of sexual instincts and feelings.
Psychotic Intrusion	Psychotic thinking is a driving factor in the abuse.
Rustic Environment	This is where families living in rural areas have traditionally participated and accept incest.
Perverse or Pornographic Incest	This category represents what many lay persons may characterized as sick, lechery, perverted. This is bizarre and many times ritualistic.
Child Rape	This refers to men who exhibit antisocial behaviors—one of which is to sexually abuse their children.
Pedophilic Incest	These are individuals who have fantasies about children and act out these sexual needs with their own children.
True Endogamous	This is where stressors associated with the father's life and a "dysfunctional" family where the daughter has taken on many of the "wifely" duties. Lines become blurred and the daughter is abused.
Misogynous	This individuals hatred for women is often taken out on his daughter as a form of punishment.
Imperious Incest	This offender believes and acts as the king. He believes that those around him are subject to his wishes—including sexual favors. As a means of showing loyalty the daughters often become the victims of abuse.

Adapted from Prentky and Burgess, 2000

Several other researchers have identified general traits and behavioral patterns common to incest offenders. According to the booklet published by Life Skills Education (1991), a number of characteristics can be found common to incest incidents. These include multiple sexual encounters, lack of social skills within the family, isolation of the family, and victims often experience the first incident at around age eight with the average age of victims at eleven years old.

Unlike media portrayals of child abduction and sexual assault by strangers, most child molesters and pedophiles, with estimates ranging from 70 to 95 percent, are acquaintances, family friends, or relatives of the victims. As with the preferential child molester described by Dietz (1982) or the high-social competence identified by Prentky and Burgess (2000) the members of the family know the abuser. Many of these individuals choose to target families in need or with children who require "special" attention. In addition, a great number of these offenders have placed themselves in positions of trust within the community. This is evident by the incidents recorded within the Catholic church, the boy scouts and other youth oriented activities. These offenses are often disguised as expressions of affection (Howell 1982).

Many child molesters display similar characteristics to rapists: they tend to be socially inept in adult relationships, have low self-esteem, have feelings of inadequacy, and a sense of worthlessness and vulnerability. These characteristics depart from rapists when analyzing characteristics such as aggressiveness, acting on impulse, insensitivity to victims feelings (West 1987). Finkelhor (1984) identified four preconditions that must exist for child abuse to occur. His conditions take into consideration both the psychological and the sociological variables of the offender. Offenders must have some motivation to abuse; must overcome internal inhibitions; most overcome external inhibitions; and must overcome the child's resistance to the abuse.

Conclusion

Sexual crimes are acquired behavior, an act of normal deviance, found in our society as well as many others around the world. When examining the motivation of rapists, we have explored a number of different concepts associated with defining behavior. We have examined the psychological perspective which identifies sex acts as those which are motivated by sexual needs or reasons. As we have seen, there is much debate resulting in a number of different motivational models. We have identified, through the analysis of these models, how actions reflect multiple drives, social forces, and situational variables. Many of the models do have similarities such as, the expression of anger, desire to control, the desire to inflict pain, and the desire for sexual gratification. As the reader has moved through this chapter, it is hoped that instead of defining rape based solely on the emotional determinants, readers have considered the integration of both motivational and emotional determinants.

Classification systems are temporary and artificial, often serving a time-limited purpose. As the reader has seen, few systems endure, and those that do are constantly undergoing modification. The application of reliable and valid classification systems to legal and clinical settings implies a new and growing notion that cooperation is needed for planning and decision-making where sex-offenders are considered.

The types of rape committed and the profiles of the offender and victim provide the reader with just a start. There is much more to be done in the examination of rapists, especially in the areas of acquaintance rape, date rape and marital rape. Differences exist between and within the categories of sex offenders. The information available to researchers has been limited due to the societal reactions to these types of rape and the victim's assumed responsibility. Researchers must gain access to diverse research populations in order for the profiles to be applicable to the general population.

References

Allison, J.A., and L.S. Wrightsman. *Rape: The Misunderstood Crime*. California: Sage Publications, 1993.

Amir, M. *Patterns of Forcible Rape*. Chicago: University of Chicago Press, 1971.

Berger, R.K. *Wife Rape: Understanding the Response of Survivors and Service Providers*. Thousand Oaks, CA: Sage, 1996.

Berlin, F.S., G.K. Lehne, H.M. Malin, W.P. Hunt, K. Thomas, and J. Fuhrmaneck. "The Eroticized Violent Crime: A Psychiatric Perspective with Six Clinical Examples." *Sexual Addiction and Compulsivity* 4 no. 1, (1997): 9–31.

Bowker, L. *Beating Wife Beating*. Lexington, MA: Lexington Books, 1983.

Byers, E.S. and L.F. O'Sullivan L.F. *Sexual Coercion in Dating Relationships*. Haworth Press. New York, 1996.

Cohen, M.L., T.K. Seghorn, and W. Calmas. "Sociometric Study of Sex Offenders." *Journal of Abnormal Psychology* 74, (1969): 249–255.

Cohen, M.L., R.F. Garofalo, R. Boucher, and T. Seghorn. "The Psychology of Rapists." *Seminars in Psychiatry 3*, (1971): 307–327.

Davidson, T. *Conjugal Crime: Understanding and Changing the Wife-Beating Problem*. New York: Hawthorn Books, 1978.

Davis, M.H. "Measuring Individual Differences in Empathy: Evidence for Multidimensional Approach." *Journal of Personality and Social Psychology* 44, (1983): 113–125.

Dietz, P.E. (1983). "Sex Offenses: Behavioral Aspects." In *Encyclopedia of Crime and Justice*, ed. S.H. Kadish, 1485–1493. New York: Free Press, 1983.

Douglas, J.E., A.W. Burgess, and C.R. Hartman. *Crime Classification Manual.* New York: Lexington Books, 1992.

Federal Bureau of Investigation. *Crime in the United States-1998.* Washington, DC: U.S. Government Printing Office, 1998.

Federal Bureau of Investigation. *Crime in the United States-2000.* Washington, DC: U.S. Government Printing Office, 2000.

Finch, J. H. "Men Convicted of Sexual Offenses Against Children: A Descriptive Follow-Up Study." *British Journal of Criminology* 3, (1962): 18–37.

Finkelhor, D. *Child Sexual Abuse: New Theory and Research.* New York: Free Press, 1984.

Finkelhor, D. and K. Yllo. *License to Rape: Sexual Abuse of Wives.* New York: Holt, Rinehart, and Winston, 1985.

Gebhard, P.H., J.H. Gagnon, W. B. Pomeroy, and C.V. Christenson. *Sex Offenders: An Analysis of Types.* New York: Harper and Row, 1965.

Giarrusso, R., P. Johnson, J. Goodchilds, and G. Zellerman. "Adolescent Cues and Signals: Sex and Sexual Assault," a paper presented to a symposium of the Western Psychological Association Meeting. San Diego: 1979.

Greenfield, L.A. *Sex Offenses and Offenders: An Analysis of Data on Rape and Sexual Assault.* U.S. Department of Justice, 1997.

Groth, A.N. "Sexual Trauma in the Life Histories of Rapists and Child Molesters." *Victimology: An International Journal* 4, (1979): 10–16.

Groth, A.N. and A.W. Burgess. "Motivational Intent in the Sexual Assault of Children." *Criminal Justice and Behavior* 4, (1977): 253–264.

Groth, A.N., A.N. Burgess and L.L. Holmstrom. "Rape: Power, Anger, and Sexuality." *American Journal of Psychiatry* 134, (1977): 1239–1243.

Groth, A.N. and J. Birnbaum. *Men Who Rape: The Psychology of the Offender.* New York: Plenum Press, 1979.

Guttermacher, M.S. and H. Weihofen. *Psychiatry and the Law.* New York: Norton, 1952.

Howell, S. "Twisted Love: Pedophilia." In *Victimization* of the Weak: Contemporary Social Reactions, eds. J. Scherer and G. Sheperd. Charles C. Thomas: Springfield, Il, 1982.

Johnson, I.M., and R.T. Sigler. *Forced Sexual Intercourse in Intimate Relationships.* Brookfield VT: Dartmouth/Ashgate, 1997.

Kanin, E.J. "Reference Groups and Sex Conduct Norm Violations." *Sociological Quarterly* 8, (1967): 495–504.

Kanin, E.J. "Date Rapists: Differential Sexual Socialization and Relative Description." *Archives of Sexual Behavior* 14, (1985): 219–231.

Knight, R.A., and R.A. Prentky. "Classifying Sex Offenders: The Development and Corroboration of Taxonomic Models." In *The Handbook of Sexual Assault: Issues, Theories, and Treatment of the Offender,* eds. W.L. Marshall, D.R. Laws and H.E. Barbaree, 23–52. New York: Plenum Press, 1990.

Knight, R.A., R.A. Prentky, and A.F. Lee. "Risk Factors Associated with Recidivism among Extrafamilial Child Molesters." *Journal of Consulting and Clinical Psychology* 65, (1997): 145–149.

Kopp, S.B. "The Character Structure of Sex Offenders." *American Journal of Psychotheraphy* 16, (1962): 64–70.

Koss, M.P., K.D. Leonard, D.A. Beezley, and C.J. Oros. "Nonstranger Sexual Aggression: A Discriminant Analysis of the Psychological Characteristics of Undetected Offenders." *Sex Roles* 12 (1985): 981–992

Lanning, K. *Child Molesters: A Behavioral Analysis for Law Enforcement Officers Investigating Cases of Sexual Exploitation.* Washington DC: National Center for Missing and Exploited Children, 1986.

Life Skills Education. *Incest: A family Secret.* Northfield, MN: Life Skills Education, 1991.

Miethe, T.D. and R.C. McCorkle. *Crime Profiles: The Anatomy of Dangerous Persons, Places, and Situations.* California: Roxbury Publishing Company, 2001.

Miethe, T.D. and R.F. Meier. *Crime and Its Social Context: Toward Integrating Theory of Offenders, Victims and Situations.* Albany; State University of New York Press, 1994.

Monson, C.M. and J. Langhinrichsen-Rohling. "Sex, sex-Role Beliefs, and a History of Co-Occurring Nonsexual Violence: How do these Factors Influence Attributes about Marital Rape?" *Journal of Interpersonal Violence* 11, (1996): 410–424.

Muehlenhard, C.L., D.E. Friedman, and C.M. Thomas. "Is Date Rape Justifiable? The Effects of Dating Activity, Who Initiated, Who Paid, and Men's Attitudes Toward Women." *Psychology of Women Quarterly 9,* (1985): 2987–309.

Muehlenhard, C.L. and J. Schrag. "Nonviolent Sexual Coercion." In *Acquaintace Rape: The Hidden Crime*, eds. A. Parrot and L. Bechhofer, 115–128. New York: Joghn Wiley and Sons, 1991.

National Crime Victimization Survey (NCVS). *Criminal Victimization in the United States, 1998. Statistical Tables, May 2000.* Washington, D.C: National Institute of Justice, 1998.

Parrot, A. and Bechhofer, L. *Acquaintance Rape: The Hidden Crime.* New York: John Wiley and Sons, 1991.

Prentky, R.A., R.A. Knight, and R. Rosenberg. "Validation Analysis on the MTC Taxonony for Rapists: Disconfirmation and Reconceptualization. In *Human Sexual Aggression: Current Perspectives*, eds. R.A. Prentky and V. Quinsey, 21–40. New York: New York Academy of Sciences, 1988.

Prentky, R.A. and A.W. Burgess. *Forensic Management of Sexual Offenders.* New York: Kluwer Academic/Plenum Publishers, 2000.

Rada, R.T. "Classification of Rapists." In *Clinical Aspects of the Rapists*, ed. R.T. Rada, 117–132. New York: Grune and Stratton, 1978.

Rappaport, K. and B.R. Burkhart. "Personality and Attitudinal Characteristics of Sexually Coercive College Males." *Journal of Abnormal Psychology* 93, (1984): 216–224.

Rist, K. "Incest: Theoretical and Clinical Views." *American Journal of Orthopsychiatry* 49, (1979): 680–691.

Russell, D.E. *Rape in Marriage.* Indianapolis: Indiana University Press, 1982, 1990.

Shotland, R.L. (1992). "The Theory of the Causes of Courtship Rape: Part 2." *Journal of Social Issues* 48 no. 1, (1992): 127–143.

Summit, R.C. and J. Kryso. "Sexual Abuse of Children: A Clinical Spectrum." *American Journal of Orthopsychiatry* 48, (1978): 237–251.

Swanson, D.W. "Who Violates Children Sexually?" *Medical Aspects of Human Sexuality* 5, (1971): 184–197.

Teten, H. and B. Turvey. "A Brief History of Criminal Profiling." *Knowledge Solutions Library.* Electronic Publication, (1998). URL: http://www.corpus-delicti.com/demo/

Turvey, B. *Criminal Profiling: An Introduction to Behavior Evidence Analysis.* London: Academic Press, 1999.

Van Wormer, K.S. and C. Bartollas. *Women and the Criminal Justice System.* Pearson Allyn and Bacon: Boston, MA, 2000.

Walker, L.E. *The Battered Woman.* New York: Harper and Row, 1979.

Weinberg, S. *Incest Behavior.* New York: Citadel Press, 1955.

West, D.J. "Sexual Crimes and Confrontations: A Study of Victims and Offenders." In *Cambridge Studies in Criminology*, ed. A.E. Bottoms. Aldershot: Gower, 1987.

PART V

THE CRIMINAL JUSTICE SYSTEM

Chapter 14

A Brief History of Rape Law and Rape Law Reform in the United States

Frances P. Reddington, Ph.D.

Introduction

The first rape laws in the United States were based on English Common Law and specifically can be tracked back to the laws of medieval England (Allison and Wrightsman 1993). In English Common Law rape was defined as "carnal knowledge of a woman by force and against her will" (Largen 1988, 271). Under English common law, the rape statute was designed to protect a man's property and rape was not considered a personal crime against the woman (Bohmer 1991). This common law was adopted into the early Colonies and became law. The first rape statute in the new colonies in America was passed in Massachusetts in 1642 and rape was defined as a crime if a man had "carnal copulation" with "any woman child under ten years of age, forcibly and without consent ravished any maid or woman that is lawfully married or contracted, or ravished any maid or single woman with her by force or against her will, that is above the age of ten" (quoted in Allison and Wrightsman 1993). The English Common Law influence on American rape laws is obvious, especially if the later, revised statutes are examined. They stated that rape was defined as "illicit carnal knowledge of a female by force and against her will" (quoted in Allison and Wrightsman, 1993).

Under English common law, rape had five elements that needed to be proven in a court of law. One would be that the act was defined as criminal (illicit), the second that carnal knowledge, which is usually defined as penile-vaginal sexual intercourse, (Russell and Bolen 2000) took place in the course of the attack, third that the victim was a woman, fourth that force was used during the attack and finally, that the force used was against the will of the victim. Obviously this definition and the legal elements left much interpretation up to the individual court and jurors (Allison and Wrightsman 1993).

This definition of rape remained a standard in the United States into the 1970s, when attention was given to rape law and movements for reform were started. The impetus behind this movement was multifaceted. The literature cites many reasons for the birth of the reform movement including the following: the questioning of the concept that women were property (Spohn 1999), reported rapes increased dramatically in the 1960s, and in fact increased faster than all other types of crime (Largen 1988; Spohn, 1999; Burgess 1985), challenges to long held misconceptions about rape (Largen 1988), the rights for women movement (Largen 1988; Burgess 1985), the emergence of women into the legal arena and criminal justice professions (Largen 1988), and a growing concern about female victims of crime, in particular by the criminal justice community who wanted to see reporting and successful prosecution of rape increase (Spohn 1999; Burgess 1985). According to Csida and Csida, "the feminists have been the primary motivating force in focusing national attention on the growing problem of rape and probably the greatest single force in activating sectors of society…towards seeking solutions" (in Burgess 1985, 1). Several areas of rape law and its legal practices were examined and changed during this time.

Beginning in the state of Michigan, where the first comprehensive law on sexual assault was enacted in 1974, some form of reform in the rape laws eventually touched all fifty states (Bachman and Paternoster 1993). Whatever the impetus, and whichever group or issue was the driving force behind the rape reform movement, the goal of reform remained consistent: to change laws that stopped victims from reporting rape and to remove the numerous roadblocks that made a successful prosecution of a rape case almost impossible (Spohn and Horney 1996). In addition to the law reform movement going on during this time frame, other areas concerning sexual assault were coming of age as well. Both the creation of rape crisis centers and the availability of federal funds for research about sexual assault were first reported during this same time frame (Burgess 1985; Largen 1985).

This section will examine eight separate areas of reform. These include non-consent and force; the act of rape and the gender of the victim; the rape statutes; corroboration; cautionary instructions; the marital exception; rape shield statutes; and rape as a hate crime. There will follow a brief discussion of the effectiveness of the reforms, and a look at present areas of concern for reformers. The chapter will end with some concluding remarks.

Non-Consent and the Use of Force

Force and non-consent are really two separate issues. Force focuses on the offender and non-consent focuses on the victim. However, it appears as though the early courts could not really distinguish the two in terms of how to examine them legally in court. Under English common law, it appears that both were determined by the amount of resistance that the victim offered during the attack. Resistance was the way that the courts could examine the elements of "by force" and "against her will" (non consent) during the trial. Before we examine that closer, it is important to note that during this time, the courts were designed to protect the virtuous, and thus believed that a woman of virtue would rather submit to serious bodily injury, maybe even death, than to have sexual intercourse with anyone who was not her husband (Gordan and Riger 1989). Therefore, in English Common Law, the courts determined that the level of resistance displayed by the victim had to be the very highest level of resistance; it had to be the "utmost resistance" or "resistance to the utmost". This is defined as "that the victim did everything possible, exercised every physical means within her power, to prevent the assailant from completing the assault" (Gordon and Roger 1985, 59). The more physically bruised and battered the victim was, the greater her chance of demonstrating resistance to the utmost in court.

It is interesting to note that this legal interpretation also placed the emphasis of the rape trial on the actions of the victim and not the accused. The victim's behavior was the heart of a rape trial (Estrich 1987). Not to mention that the whole resistance standard was designed by males and in reality defined how males might respond in such a situation, but fighting to the utmost was most likely not the typical response of most women in a rape situation (Bohmer 1991). Nonetheless, this element of the English Common Law definition was adopted into U.S. laws. Sometimes, a state's higher courts had to interpret the actions of a rape victim and try to determine if her resistance was "to the utmost" as demonstrated in the following case heard by the Wisconsin State Supreme Court.

In 1904, a sixteen year old girl was walking across the field to her grandmother's house when she passed a neighbor boy she had known all her life. According to the girl, she spoke to the accused.

> "He at once seized her, tripped her to the ground, placed himself in
> front and over her, unbuttoned her underclothing, then his own

clothing, and had intercourse with her. That the only thing she said was to request him to let her go, and, throughout the description of the event, her only statement with reference to her own conduct was, repeatedly, "*I tried as hard as I could to get away. I was trying all the time to get away just as hard as I could, I was trying to get up; I pulled at the grass; I screamed as hard as I could, and he told me to shut up, and I didn't, and then he held his hand on my mouth until I was almost strangled*" (Brown v. State, 106 N.W. 536 (1906). (Italics added for emphasis.)

The conviction was overturned, because, among other reasons,

"subject to the exception where the power of resistance is overcome by unconsciousness, threats, or exhaustion, in order to constitute the crime of rape, *not only must there be entire absence of mental consent or assent, but there must be the most vehement exercise of every physical means and faculty within the woman's power to resist the penetration of her person, and this must be shown to persist until the offense is consummated*" (Brown v. State, 106 N.W. 536 (1906). (Italics added for emphasis.)

According to Susan Estrich (1987), U.S. courts did not always rely on the strict "to the utmost" standard in rape cases, and sometimes lowered that standard to what seemed reasonable under the circumstances, though the court's discretion seemed to be based on something other than legal factors, including race and social class of the accused and the victim. As early as the 1950s, there were some statutory changes in the U.S. laws regarding force and consent. By the 1960s, the "reasonable resistance standard" had replaced the "to the utmost standard" for the most part (Estrich 1987). The reasonable resistance standard stated that the victim resisted as was reasonable under the circumstances. Though still vague and open to interpretation, it did allow the courts to examine the individual circumstances of the rape and the victim. It seems that courts began to understand that every woman might not react the same when confronted with the violent crime of rape (Allison and Wrightsman 1993) and that in some cases resistance might actually escalate the violence of the attack and place the victim in greater danger (Spohn 1999).

Today, what do the various states' criminal codes say about force, consent and non-consent in their sex crime laws? And more importantly, how do the courts interpret these laws? The way that most states responded in this area was to examine and change their resistance by the victim requirements. The different states enacted a wide array of new requirements regarding their resistance standards in sex crimes' law (Spohn 1999). The overall result is, according to Allison and Wrightsman that "Perhaps the greatest discrepancy in laws in different jurisdictions is in the resistance standard; some states have eliminated it but most have not (as of 1988, 38 states still imposed it)" (1993, 214). However, many states did not stop with just changing the resistance requirements but also looked at what constituted force as well. Generally, speaking, force was defined as physical force. However, during the reform movement many states "expanded their definition of *force* to include coercion or intimidation by the alleged rapist" (Allison and Wrightsman 1993, 214) These changes added additional components, such as fear of death or injury, to the definition of force. It could be more than just physical force that a rapist used, such as threats to the victim, and those threats in and of themselves, would meet the legal definition of force. For example, in Missouri forcible rape is defined as when a "person has sexual intercourse with another person by the use of forcible compulsion. Forcible compulsion includes the use of a substance administered without a victim's knowledge or consent which renders the victim physically or mentally impaired so as to be incapable of making an informed consent to sexual intercourse" (Missouri Revised Statutes, 2002). In Missouri, forcible compulsion is defined as either:

> "(a) Physical force that overcomes reasonable resistance; or
> (b) A threat, express or implied, that places a person in reasonable fear of death, serious physical injury or kidnapping of such person or another person" (§56.061 R.S.Mo. 2003).

Thus, in Missouri, the traditional definition of force which suggests a physical element is expanded to include a threat that places someone in fear for their life, physical injury or kidnapping of self and others. The interpretation of threat, fear and reasonable resistance in an individual rape case is left to the courts and its workers.

The Act of Rape and the Gender of the Victim

Rape was defined as carnal knowledge (sexual intercourse) that was perpetrated on a woman victim by a male offender. It did not include any oral or anal forced sexual activity or the use of objects in a sexual assault. It did not include male victims (Allison and Wrightsman 1993). Reformers of the 1970s addressed these issues for two reasons, one to include male victims and also to expand the definition of rape to include other types of sexual assault.

How states addressed this issue varies. Most states made their statutes gender neutral. Some replaced the word rape with words such as sexual assault, sexual battery, or some other similar term (Spohn 1999). This was done to eliminate the negative connotations the word rape carried with it, to foster a new awareness of male victims, and to have the criminal justice system refocus on the violent nature of the crime rather than the misunderstood sexual aspect that was historically linked with the word rape (Allison and Wrightsman 1993). Generally speaking, in addition, the new legal terms broadened the definition of rape to include anything done to the victim orally, anally, or with objects or other body parts. Other states left rape in their statutes but created twin crimes to include any activity outside of penile-vaginal penetration and named that crime, for example, sodomy.

Rape Statutes—Providing Options and Looking at the Punishment

Concern about the low number of convictions in rape cases led to the examination of the definition of rape and the punishment for rape. In most states rape was defined as it was in English Common Law and individual circumstances of the rape did not impact the charging of the crime or the punishment. For example, did the attacker use a weapon, or seriously injure the victim beyond the rape itself? How much force was used and what was the age of the victim? Was the rape committed in the commission of another felony? In response to these queries and the growing sense that different circumstances were present in different rapes, many states examined their rape laws and expanded the options for charging and prosecuting rape cases. Most commonly seen were the creation of rape laws in the first, second and third degree or aggravated vs. simple rape based on the level of coercion used on the victim, injury to the victim and age of the victim (Allison and Wrightsman 1993; Spohn 1999).

Once states graded the crime, the punishment would have to be graded as well. Under English Common Law rape was punishable by death. Reformers were concerned that this penalty might seem unduly harsh to juries and prevent some convictions. By 1971, 16 states and the federal government defined rape as a capital crime punishable by death. In 1972, *Furman vs. Georgia* put a hiatus on sentencing anyone to death, and when states had to rewrite their death statutes to be in line with *Gregg v Georgia* in 1976, only three states came back with rape listed as a capital offense (Allison and Wrightsman 1993). This reform effort was very controversial and the main question came down to a debate between two camps. Did this trivialize the crime of rape or would the new lesser punishment actually put rape victims in less danger as their rapists would not face capital punishment for rape, unless they killed the victim?

The Supreme Court ended the argument in 1977 when *Coker v Georgia* held that the death penalty for rape was "grossly disproportionate and excessive" and in violation of the 8th and 14th Amendments (Allison and Wrightsman 1993). The Supreme Court said that they had considered public attitudes about rape and the death penalty in their ruling. Looking back fifty years, they found that of the states with the death penalty, only a small number considered rape a capital crime. Therefore, the Supreme Court reasoned, public opinion would indicate that the death penalty was too harsh a punishment for the crime of rape (Allison and Writghtsman 1993). Thus, as of 1977, rape could not be viewed as a capital crime in any state, and the present punishments for rape and sexual assault vary among the states.

Corroboration

According to Largen (1988, 271), Edwardian—era scholar, John Henry Wigmore theorized about "sexually precocious minors and unchaste women who fantasize about rape" as a cause for concern in the prosecution of rape cases. How to tell who was lying about being raped? Such concerns set the stage for the corroboration doctrine. This doctrine required additional evidence to accompany the victim's testimony about the rape. The additional evidence would indicate that the person was not lying about being raped. In fact, "a conviction for rape could not rest on the unsupported testimony of the complainant alone, and corroborating evidence provided an objective standard by which to measure complainant credibility" (Largen 1988, 272). Obviously requiring this additional corroborating evidence to prosecute would cut down on the number of prosecutions. In essence, it was as if the rape victim had to prove she was a victim before the case could be prosecuted. As with other reform issues, trying to remove the corroboration requirement was met with resistance.

"Some who defended the corroboration requirement argued that a woman would deliberately lie about being sexually assaulted to explain away premarital intercourse, infidelity, pregnancy, or disease, or to retaliate against an ex-lover or some other man" (Spohn 1999, 125). However, eventually, the reform movement of the 1970s was successful in having the corroboration requirement in rape cases repealed in all states that still required it (Largen 1988).

Cautionary Instructions

It is suggested that because other sexual acts historically defined as sex crimes (adultery, statutory rape) and rape were distinguishable only because of the use of force element (Largen 1988), and because there was a real fear of false accusations of rape (Spohn 1999), the legal arena handled rape differently than other crimes. For example, Lord Chief Justice Matthew Hale added this quote into his cautionary instructions to juries about the crime of rape: "It is true, rape is a most detestable crime, and therefore ought severely and impartially be punished with death; *but it must be remembered that it is an accusation easily to be made, and hard to be proved, and harder to be defended by the party accused, though ever so innocent*" (Italics added for emphasis) (quoted in Bohmer 1991, 317). Hale's statement or some derivative was not uncommon to be given to a jury before they went into deliberation in a rape case (Estrich, 1987).

Obviously, this concerned the reformers who suggested that cautionary instructions of that nature given to the jury would, in all likelihood, be prejudicial against the victim. The success of the reformers to have these cautionary instructions removed from the judicial process was not as quickly successful as some of the other reforms. However "in later years, the majority of states applying such instructions would eliminate them either through law or through practice" (Largen 1988, 276).

The Marital Exception

Under English Common Law, a man could not be accused of raping his wife as she was considered his property and the marriage contract implied that she was sexually available at her husbands' request and thus did not have the right to say no (Gordon and Roger 1988). Obviously, the courts did not delve into issues of the marital bedroom. In the 1970s, this issue was addressed by reformers and changes were made in the laws stating that a man could be charged with raping his wife, or more legally correct, a spouse could be charged with raping a spouse. In fact, though changes were made, these changes were not easily made nor were they made without controversy (Kirkwood and Cecil 2001). An article by Kirkwood and Cecil includes the 1979 quote from California State Senator Bob Wilson who, while addressing a group of lobbyists for women's rights said, "But if you can't rape your own wife, who can you rape?" and a quote from Senator Jeremiah Denton from Alabama who, while addressing congress, stated "Dammit, when you get married, you've got to expect a little sex" (2001, 1234).

Yllo (1999) offers some insight into the controversial issue that still continues to elicit strong debate.

"I have come to the conclusion that there is something about the very concept of marital rape that impedes our work. It contains a cultural contradiction inherent in no other form of violence and it goes to the very heart of the institution of marriage. In our contemporary romantic image of marriage, love and sex are inextricably linked and form the very foundation of the relationship. The wedding both legitimizes and celebrates this sexual bond. The very idea of this bond turning into sexual bondage falls outside of this frame of reference" (p, 1060).

In addition to the above stated concern, there was fear that making spousal rape legal would hinder reconciliation (Bohmer 1988) as well as initiate an onslaught of false allegations of rape made by angry housewives (Gordon and Riger 1989).

Eventually, all states made raping your spouse a crime, though the statutes vary considerably (Kirkwood and Cecil 2001). In some states, the marital rape laws include some modifications from the existing rape law, such as there is a shorter time limit for reporting the rape, or there needs to be proof of physical injuries or evidence that the couple is no longer living together (Gorden and Riger 1989). This was best publicly exemplified by the 1993 John Bobbitt case. John Bobbitt's wife Lorena cut off her husband's penis with a kitchen knife. She said she did this as the result of repeated marital rapes. The couple was living together, though they were planning to divorce. In Virginia, the laws stated that for marital rape charges to be filed, the couple must be living apart and that the victim must demonstrate serious physical injury as a result of the rape. Because of these requirements, Virginia prosecutors could only charge John Bobbitt with marital sexual assault, which carried a lesser penalty (USA Today, Final Edition, November 9, 1993).

Rape Shield Statutes

Under English Common Law, there was no protection for the victim once she took the stand. She could be asked any question about her sexual behavior, personal habits, emotional history and life. Many victims were hesitant to take the stand as to some it seemed as though their lifestyle was more on trial than were the actions of the accused. Reformers began to question this open door access to the victim of rape if she took the stand to testify. What relevance did her personal habits, particularly her sexual habits, have on whether she was raped during the incident in question? This was controversial, as many people felt that her life choices did in fact need to be known. Would a sexually active woman be more likely to lie about being raped, or be more likely to not say no (Allison and Wrightsman 1993)?

"The notion that the victim's prior sexual conduct was pertinent to whether or not she consented was based on the assumption that an unchaste woman would be more likely to consent to intercourse than a woman without pre-marital or extramarital sexual experiences" (Spohn 1999, 126). The reform-ers pushed to create some kind of law which would protect the victim while on the stand, and to limit the information she could be asked about while on the stand. In response, most states have enacted some form of rape shield statutes. Though these are laws designed to protect the victim from inappro-priate questions while on the stand, in the bigger picture, these laws are de-signed to stop unnecessary questions about the victims' past sexual history, encourage the reporting, filing and successful prosecution of rape cases, and to put the focus of the trial back on the behavior of the accused (Spohn 1999).

According to Largen (1988, 275), "rape shield laws restricting the scope of cross-examination about the complainant's prior sexual conduct were the most vigorously opposed" of the reform efforts. Some states, such as Hawaii, Iowa, North Carolina and Florida have actually reversed some of their rape shield statutes (Allison and Wrightsman 1993). Generally speaking, rape shield statutes usually limit the discussion of the victim's sexual past to: consensual sexual acts between the accused and the accuser, or to demonstrate that the accused was not the cause of semen, impregnation nor responsible for giving the victim a sexu-ally transmitted disease, or to attack the credibility of the victim (Allison and Wrightsman 1993). Though less common, some statutes also allow discussion of evidence to suggest that the victim is prejudice or has a reason to make a false allegation, may have made a false allegation previously, or that the accused rea-sonably thought the victim consented (Spohn 1999). All in all, what can be asked of the victim about her sexual history while on the stand will be decided by the rape shield statutes of the state, case law and the opinion of the trial judge (Al-lison and Wrightsman 1993).

Hate Crimes

There have been hate crimes for hundreds of years, yet it has only been about twenty years that hate crimes were legally recognized in the American criminal justice system (Jenness and Grattet 2002). Most states have added some form of hate crime definition into their criminal statues, though there is much debate about the need for and the reasoning behind hate crime leg-islation (Lawrence 2003).

According to the Community Relations Service of the U.S. Department of Justice a "hate crime is the violence of intolerance and bigotry, intended to hurt and intimidate someone because of their race, ethnicity, national origin, religious, sexual orientation or disability". If you notice, this definition does not include the word gender, and thus sets the stage for another reform debate. Is rape a crime that can be motivated based on the gender of the victim? Some recent developments seem to suggest that some think that gender should be included into the protected classes.

The Violence Against Women Act (VAWA) of 1994 gave women the civil right to be protected from crimes of violence that are based on the sole fact of gender. The VAWA may give the victim of a violent crime access to the federal courts for litigation against their attacker. "VAWA creates a civil cause of action under federal law that may be used to remedy abuse by an intimate against either a female or male partner, as well as to remedy rape and sexual assault, sexual harassment at work, child sex abuse, and gay-bashing attacks" (Pincus and Rosen 1997, 20). Some authors contend that many of the violent crimes which have primarily female victims are based on the fact that the victim is a female (Pincus and Rosen 1997). With this kind of protection at the federal level, should state hate crime statutes include the word gender and should sexual assault crimes be prosecuted under this statute?

There is much controversy about the need for hate crime statutes, and about whether state statutes should include gender in their protected classes. The addition of gender into the protected classes is seen "less commonly" than other biases (The National Center for Victims of Crime). As of January, 2003, there were seven states whose hate crime laws specifically included gender. They are California, Hawaii, Minnesota, Missouri, New Mexico, Pennsylvania and Vermont, as well as the District of Columbia (Human Rights Campaign 2003).

There are questions being raised as to the overall sentiment to include gender in the protected classes and to prosecute sex crimes as hate crimes.

"In May 2000, the Court struck down part of the Violence Against Women Act that allowed victims of sexual assaults to sue their attackers in federal court. Rehnquist and Congress' power to protect civil rights does not extend to "purely private" acts of violence that do not cross state lines, a decision that probably dooms prospects for a national Hate Crimes Act. The plaintiff in this case, Virginia Tech freshman Christy Brzonkala sued after the university took no disciplinary action against a football star accused of raping her" (Savage 2001, 34).

In 2002, the senate republicans blocked efforts to add gender, sexual orientation and disabilities to the 30 year old federal hate crime statue (AFL-CIO 2002).

The Effectiveness of Rape Law Reform

According to Bryden and Lengnick (1997), many of the reforms that were made regarding rape laws were designed to encourage victims to report their rape victimization and to give prosecutors the tools necessary to convict offenders. They conclude that "There is growing evidence that, while performance of the justice system in rape cases may have improved, the legal reforms have generally had little or no effect on the outcome of rape cases, or the proportions of rapists who are prosecuted and convicted" (1997, 1199). Likewise, Spohn suggests that although "reformers clearly had high hopes for the rape law reforms, their expectations may have been unrealistic. Although the results of studies examining rape law reform's efforts are somewhat mixed, most find very limited effects on case outcomes" (1999, 129).

In a comprehensive study of the Michigan law, often cited as the most comprehensive sex crime bills package passed, Marsh et al. conclude that the effectiveness of the Michigan law is "mixed" (1982, ix). "The enactment and implementation of the Michigan law were expected to affect victims, actors in the legal system, and perhaps perpetrators of future rapes. The experience in that state indicates that the reform bought about changes in procedure but not in basic attitudes or definitions of the crime" (1982, ix).

Changing Times, New Reforms

As time advances, new issues regarding rape law and its practice emerge and rape law reform remains an important topic. Issues such as the counselor-privilege, medical exam costs, AIDS testing and results disclosure, the use of polygraphs on rape victims, and the statute of limitations to report sex crimes are but a few of the topics being addressed in various political and reform arenas (Institute for Law and Justice 1997). In addition to that, there has been an active legislative agenda regarding sex offender laws, including registration, notification, sexual predator laws and chemical castration laws. These will be discussed in a later chapter of this book.

Conclusion

Starting in the 1970s rape law reform touched every state. However, based on the fact that there were numerous groups pushing reform—sometimes with different agendas, each state reformed their laws as they saw fit, and there is still widespread disparity in rape laws. However, according to Horney and Spohn (1993), there are four common themes that ran through the heart of the rape law reform of the 1970s and 1980s. One is that the crime of rape was replaced by a series of offenses that graded the crime and the punishment and that included all the elements that might happen during a sexual assault (oral and anal penetration, use of objects, etc.) and that included gender equality. Two, is that most states addressed their resistance requirements, by either changing or eliminating that requirement. Three, was that the corroboration requirement was eliminated and four, most states enacted a rape shield statute designed to protect the victims from unnecessary testimony regarding their previous sexual histories (in Bachman and Paternoster 1993). We have certainly examined those reforms and others in this chapter. It is evident that the reform movement's efforts changed the laws.

The bigger question, however, remains the question of effectiveness of the reform movements. To determine effectiveness, you would have to look at the stated goals of the reform movement. Cited evidence in this chapter suggests that research results are "mixed" when researching whether reforms were successful at increasing reporting, prosecution and conviction of sex crimes.

However, does that mean the reforms were not successful in other ways? According to Spohn,

> "passage of the reforms sent an important symbolic message regarding the seriousness of rape cases and the treatment of rape victims. In the long run, this symbolic message may be more important than the instrumental change that was anticipated. Those who lobbied for rape law reform sought to shift the focus of a rape case from the character, reputation, and behavior of the victim to the unlawful acts of the offender. The rape law reforms may have started a process of long-term attitude change that is difficult to measure in a legal impact study but may ultimately lead to instrumental change" (1999, 129–130.)

We can only hope this is true, and continue to push for positive changes. It is disheartening sometimes to realize that despite thirty-something years of rape law reform, some things have not changed very much at all. However, if we examine the reforms made in the last 30 years in the law, we can hope that these changes will continue to influence practice, and that changed practice will promote attitudinal changes. Attitudinal changes will impact reporting, prosecution and conviction of sex crimes. We owe that to all rape survivors, past and future.

References

AFL-CIO, December 4, 2002. aflcio.org/issuespolitics/civilrights/ns06242002. cfm?

Allison, J., and Wrightsman, L. *Rape: The Misunderstood Crime.* Sage Publications, 1993.

Bachman, R., and Poternaster, R. "A Contemporary Look at the Effects of Rape Law Reform: How Far Have We Really Come?" *The Journal of Criminal Law and Criminology* 84 no. 3, (1993): 554–574.

Bohmer, C. "Acquaintance Rape and the Law, Chapter 20." In *Acquaintance Rape: The Hidden Crime*, eds. A. Parrot and L. Bechhofer. New York: John Wiley & Sons, Inc., 1991.

Brown v. State, 106 N.W. 536, 1906.

Bryden, D. and S. Lengnick. (1997). "Rape in the Criminal Justice System." *The Journal of Criminal Law & Criminology 87*, no. 4, (1997): 1195–1384.

Burgess, A. *Rape and Sexual Assault: A Research Handbook.* Garland Publishing, Inc, 1985.

Coker v. Georgia, 433 U.S. 584 (1977)

Estrich, S. *Real Rape.* Harvard University Press, 1987.

Furman v. Georgia, 408 U.S. 238 (1972)

Gordon, M., and S. Riger. *The Female Fear.* The Free Press, Macmillion, Inc, 1989.

Gregg v. Georgia, 428 U.S. 153 (1976)

Human Rights Campaign. http://www.hrc.org/issues/hate_crimes/background/statelaws.asp

Institute for Law and Justice. *Review of Sexual Assault Laws, 1997.* http://www.ilj.org/sa/sexassault.html

Jenness, V., and R. Grattet. "Making Hate a Crime: From Social Movement to Law Enforcement." *Journal of Criminal Law & Criminology* 93 no. 1, (2002): 306–307.

Kirkwood, M.K., and D. Cecil. "Marital Rape: A Student Assessment of Rape Laws and The Marital Exception." *Violence Against Women* 7 no. 11, (2001): 1234–1253.

Largen, M.A. "Rape Law Reform: An Analysis, Chapter 15." In *Rape and Sexual Assault*, ed. A. Burgess. Garland Publishing, Inc, 1988.

Largen, M.A. "The Anti-Rape Movement: Past and Present, Chapter 1." In *Rape and Sexual Assault*, ed. A. Burgess. Garland Publishing, Inc, 1985.

Lawrence, F. "Contextualizing Bias Crimes: A Social and Theoretical Perspective." *Law & Social Inquiry* 28 no. 1, (2003): 315–339.

Marsh, J., A. Geist, and N. Caplan. *Rape and the Limits of Law Reform.* Boston: Aubrun House publishing Company. 1982.

Missouri Revised Statutes, 2002

Pincus, S., and D. Rosen. "Fighting Back: Filing Suit Under the Violence Against Women Act." *Trial 33* no. 12, (1997): 20–27.

Russell, D., and R. Bolen. *The Epidemic of Rape and Child Sexual Abuse in the United States.* Thousand Oaks, CA: Sage Publications, 2000.

Savage, D. "United They Sit." *ABA Journal 87,* (2001): 34–35.

§56.061 R.S.Mo. 2003

Spohn, C. "The Rape Reform Movement: The Traditional Common Law And Rape Law Reforms." *Jurimetrics* 39 no. 2, (1999): 119–130.

Spohn, C., and J. Horney. "The Impact of Rape Law Reform on the Processing of Simple and Aggravated Rape Cases." *Journal of Law & Criminology* 86 no. 3, (1996): 861.

The National Center for Victims of Crime. Ncvc.org.gethepl/hatecrimelegislation/

USA Today. "Marital Rape Laws Examined." November 9, 1993, Final Edition, 1993.

US Department of Justice. *Community Relations Service.* http://www.usdoj.gov/crs/pubs/htecrm.htm

Yllo, K. "Wife Rape: A Social Problem for the 21st Century." *Violence Against Women 5* no. 9, (1999): 1059

Acquittal of husband spurs anger; Wife accused him of raping her

COLUMBIA, S.C—A jury's decision to acquit a man shown on videotape having sex with his wife, who was tied up with her mouth and eyes taped shut, has left women's rights advocates angry.

"It's going to take a while to change the attitudes in South Carolina," Candy Kern, state president of the National Organization for Women, said after Thursday's verdict.

The 33-year-old man was brought to trial under the marital rape law signed by Gov. Carroll Campbell last June. So far, only one person has been convicted, and prosecutor Knox McMahon said he feared that Thursday's verdict would make victims reluctant to come forward.

"I don't know what we're going to tell these women when they come here with a whole lot less evidence than this and want a conviction," McMahon said.

"If this isn't marital rape, it doesn't exist." The woman, who is separated from her husband and seeking a divorce, sobbed and buried her face in her hands when the verdict was read. Her husband smiled and hugged supporters.

One of the jurors, Danny Taylor, said he believed in the law,but he maintained that the prosecution hadn't proved its case.

"I had to vote on what my conscience told me to do," he said.

The eight-woman, four-man Lexington County jury took less than an hour to reach its verdict.

Jurors saw a videotape of the man having intercourse with his wife while her hands and legs were tied with rope and her mouth and eyes were covered with duct tape.

"No, I didn't rape my wife. How can you rape your own wife?" the 33-year-old husband testified. He was not identified to protect his wife's identity.

The husband's attorney, Wayne Floyd, argued that the woman enjoyed watching pornographic movies and engaging in unconventional sex acts involving sex toys.

"Was that a cry of pain and torture? Or was that a cry of pleasure?" Floyd asked as the tape was played Wednesday.

Donna Jordan of the Rape Crisis Network in the Midlands said Friday that her office's phone lines were jammed with angry calls after the verdict.

A domestic violence group, Sistercare, said it would hold a protest next week at the Statehouse.

Women's groups lobbied for five years for the marital rape law. It requires that a victim report the crime within 30 days and show physical proof of abuse.

Alabama is now the last state in the country without any marital rape law, said Beth Stafford-Vaughan, a research librarian at the Women's Studies Center at the University of Illinois.

So far, one person has been convicted under South Carolina's law and is serving the maximum 10-year prison sentence.

In the latest case, the woman testified that her husband dragged her by the throat into a bedroom, tied her hands and legs, put duct tape on her eyes and mouth and put stockings and a garter belt on her legs. He then turned on the videotape and assaulted her, she said.

The judge blocked the prosecution's attempt to call the husband's former wife to testify that she also had been tied up and raped by the man.

Kern said sometimes it is harder to convince female jurors than men in such a case.

"Some of it is denial," she said. "If we can say, 'She did something wrong and that's why she was raped,' then somehow, this won't happen to us."

Prosecutors said the woman broke free about midnight and ran to the home of a neighbor, who called police.

Her husband was found an hour later with the videotape, video camera and other items used in the encounter in his van.

The Houston Chronicle (1992, April 18). Section A; pg. 3

Chapter 15

Police and Victims of Sexual Assault

Betsy Wright Kreisel, Ph.D.

Introduction

The crime of sexual assault has circumstances that make it different from other crimes with respect to the law enforcement perspective. "The crime of forcible rape is a relatively infrequent event confronting police agencies and yet it can be one of the most serious forms of criminal victimization that can befall any of their constituents" (Battelle Law and Justice Study Center 1978; 7). Sexual assault is a traumatic victimization for two reasons. Victims are traumatized first, by the humiliation of their physical violation, and secondly, by the fear of being severely injured or killed (Woods 2001). The victim can be greatly and further impacted by the police officer's response to their victimization.

As law enforcement handle these sensitive cases, they have three primary responsibilities in sexual assault cases. First, police officers need to protect, interview, and support the victim. This police officer role sometimes conflicts as police investigate the offense, which is a task that can conflict with offering the victim emotional support (Holmstrom and Burgess 1978). Second, they have to investigate the crime and possibly apprehend the perpetrator. And third, police officers must collect and preserve evidence of the assault to assist in the assailant's prosecution. Collection of evidence in sexual assault cases is unlike many other crimes, as it may include a physical examination at the hospital, and more likely, primary evidence collection may be through interviewing, as physical evidence is often not available. Regarding these three responsibilities, law enforcement has not historically performed them well.

However, there is evidence that police officers have recently improved in the processing of sexual assault cases.

Regarding the law enforcement process in rape cases, it is important to note that rape is the most underreported violent crime. When law enforcement does get the call it is critically important to handle it properly from the start (Albrecht 2000; Wood 2001). Law enforcement generally becomes involved with a sexual assault case when a crime is reported, normally by a victim. A police officer will respond, assess the victim's physical and emotional condition and take an initial report if possible. If it is necessary, the officer will transport the victim to the hospital for treatment and for gathering forensic evidence. It is usually law enforcement's responsibility to submit the hospital examination materials ("rape kit") to the crime laboratory for analysis. Other evidence may be collected at the crime scene. If and when law enforcement decides whether an investigation is forthcoming, it will include an interview with the victim, usually in police department surroundings that probably will be neither private nor comfortable (Battelle Law and Justice Study Center 1978). The law enforcement phase, for the most part, ends with the arrest of a suspect and turning the case over to the prosecutor (Doerner and Lab 1998). The following discussion is of empirical works surrounding the law enforcement process of initial response and investigation of sexual assault cases.

This is followed by consideration of law enforcement decision-making in sexual assault cases. This chapter concludes with a discussion of the innovative approaches to handling sexual assault cases, as well as police guidelines on approaching victims of sexual assault.

For purposes of clarifying terminology in this chapter's discussions, the terms of sexual assault and rape are generally used interchangeably. In addition, while both men and women are victims of rape, women are disproportionately affected by this crime. According the National Violence Against Women survey (Tjaden and Thoennes 1998), 1 in 6 women compared with 1 in 33 men report having experienced an attempted or completed rape in their lifetimes. Therefore, for the purposes of this paper, females are generally referred to as the victim and males are generally referred to as the offender.

Police Process and Response to Sexual Assault Victims

Research indicates that the first police officer to respond to a report of rape is the most readily available patrol officer (Battelle Law and Justice Study Center 1978). This was reported by 82 percent (230 agencies) of the police departments surveyed, while specifically designated individuals or units were first to respond in the remaining few agencies. This indicates that there is a need for all patrol officers to be informed of the sensitivity necessary in handling sexual assault victims, in addition to the processing of evidence. However, only 84 percent (175) of the agencies in the Battelle Law and Justice Study Center (1978) study reported that the compulsory preservice law enforcement training provides specific information on handling sexual assault cases. That leaves some officers responding to sexual assault cases with no victimology-specific training. For those that receive preservice training regarding how to handle sexual assault victims, the length of training is likely to be less than a day and the quality of that training is an issue yet to be determined (Battelle Law and Justice Study Center 1978). Also, in preservice training police officers are receiving vast amounts of training in almost all areas of policing, making it difficult for police officers to retain specifics on how to treat different types of crime victims when encountered. In addition, because the rape event is infrequent, the officer may approach this investigation like that of any other crime and fail to note details that later will be important to the case (Battelle Law and Justice Study Center 1978).

Many police agencies tend to have specialized units or officers who ultimately handle the investigation of sexual assault cases (Battelle Law and Justice Study Center 1978). However, because rape reports are not a common police call (Albrecht 2000), a majority of the sexual assault investigation officers also handle other types of investigation such as homicides and felonious assaults (Battelle Law and Justice Study Center 1978). Nonetheless, there are techniques of interviewing the victim that investigators have developed.

One of the most common interview techniques with sexual assault victims is the behavioral-oriented interview. This includes interview questions that focus toward establishing the type of rapist in addition to collecting evidence for prosecution (Merrill 1995). Typologies of rapists are discussed in a previous chapter. By establishing the type of rapist this may assist in the identification of the rapist, if not already known. Interview questions may focus upon how the offender maintained control of the victim; whether by intimidation, threats or force. Other questions focus upon the amount of physical force employed by the attacker as well as whether the victim resisted the attacker. This latter question is *not* intended to be victim-blaming, and will be followed by questions of how the rapist responded to the resistance to help assess rapist typology. Other law enforcement questions may appear intrusive and irrelevant. For example, there will be questions about any sexual dysfunctions of the rapist and the type and sequence of sexual acts that occurred during the assault. Questions about verbal activity between the rapist and victim will be asked, as will whether the rapist had any sudden change in attitude during the attack, or whether there may have been some precautionary actions taken by the offender, such as wearing a mask or having the victim shower after the attack (Hazelwood and Burgess 1987).

No matter what the interviewing technique, it is easy to perceive the police line of questioning as insensitive and suspicious, but they must collect all the facts. Despite the intrusive questions, if the police report is thorough and complete, the chance of a successful prosecution increases (Wiseman as cited in Bryden and Lengnick 1997).

Police Officer Discretionary Decisions: Legal and Extra-legal Factors

The police officer has a number of decisions that will need to be made in the processing of a sexual assault case. Police officers will first make the decision as to whether to found this sexual assault as a crime. Police officers will decide if and how to proceed in the investigation, as well as whether to make an arrest. Some police discretion in these decisions is limited by departmental policies or state regulations. Nonetheless, police officers can impact the outcome of a sexual assault case at many stages of the process. The following discusses the stages of police officer discretionary decisions in sexual assault cases and the legal factors that affect those decisions. Extra-legal factors affecting police officers decisions will be subsequently discussed.

Founding of a Rape

Policing founding decisions tend to relate to the evidentiary issues of the case. Police officers, usually patrol officers, will look for two main factors in the report in order to classify the event as rape. First, is the proof of penetration, which the hospital will provide and secondly is the use of force by the offender, as evidenced by injury to the victim or by her statement. If either or both of these elements is/are missing, research indicates that the agency is likely to unfound the report (Battelle Law and Justice Study Center 1978). Kerstetter (1990) suggests that whether police found a rape complaint ultimately depends upon whether they believe that the government can prove the elements of the crime.

According to a nationwide estimate by the Federal Bureau of Investigation, the percentage of unfounded rape reports is eight percent (FBI 2002). Several studies have been conducted looking at the reasons associated with the unfounding of the rape decision by police officers. Research findings indicate that rape cases may be unfounded because the purported victim's contributory negligence, and by her perceived immorality (Bryden and Lengnick 1997; Ledoux and Hazelwood 1985). The following are among some of the reasons that law enforcement may use as a means of rationalizing the unfounding of sexual assaults:

1. The female is unmarried but sexually experienced, promiscuous, or even a prostitute
2. The female was drinking or taking drugs or is a drug addict.
3. The female's story has inconsistencies or she keeps changing it or it does not all "add-up."
4. Police are unable to corroborate her story, for example by injuries to her sex organs.
5. She exposed herself to risk of rape by voluntarily accompanying him to the site of the alleged rape or by inviting him into her home.
6. She has, apart from the rape, severe mental or emotional problems, perhaps evidenced by a history of psychiatric treatment or an attempted suicide or running away from home.
7. She does not appear to be upset by the alleged rape.
8. She is unattractive.
9. She knew the alleged rapist, or had been voluntarily sexually intimate on other occasions.
10. There is no large discrepancy between her age and his.
11. She is a least 12 years old.
12. The alleged offender does not have a previous criminal record.
13. She has prior trouble with the police.
14. The offense was not promptly reported.
15. The putative victim failed a polygraph test.
16. She is uncooperative (Lonsway 2002; Bryden and Lengnick 1997; Kerstetter 1990; Holmstrom and Burgess 1978).

Other research indicates that unfounding decisions may be based upon improving the perception of the agency or community. By routinely unfounding certain sexual assault cases, departmental statistics can be used to make the community's incidence of rape appear relatively low and the rate of police clearance relatively high. Another motivation for unfounding sexual assault cases is for the benefit of police officers themselves. Unfounding of sexual assault cases serves as a means of closing cases that would otherwise remain active and this provides a reduced caseload for the department or unit (Lonsway 2002). In addition, Lonsway (2002) contends that some officers are motivated to unfound in order to avoid thoroughly investigating what are perceived to be "difficult cases." Other common factors used as a basis for improperly unfounding rape cases include the police are unable to locate the victim, the victim decides not follow through with the prosecution, and/or that no assailant can be identified (Lonsway 2002).

Overall, founding or unfounding decisions of sexual assault cases by law enforcement are highly subjective. The reasons for improperly unfounding sexual assault cases are numerous, not always mutually exclusive and may be based upon judgments made about the victim or may be due to self-centered departmental, community statistics or officer motivations.

Decision to Investigate

Once the decision to found the report by the responding police officer is made, the investigation phase of the rape case is usually passed to a police officer who specializes in sexual assault investigations, but who also investigates homicide and felonious assault cases. The investigator will look at such elements as proof of penetration, use of force, promptness of victim reporting, victim injuries, relationship between victim and suspect, use of weapon, and identification of a suspect in deciding whether to go forward with an investigation (Battelle Law and Justice Study Center 1978; Bryden and Lengnick 1997). Research suggests that a majority of rape cases receive peripheral or shallow investigations at best. Most criminal cases receive a day or less investigation and sexual assault cases tend to be no different than other violent crimes (Greenwood 1975).

Decision to Arrest

Once the decision to investigate is made, the investigator will pursue fairly routine investigative strategies looking into, among other things, whether an arrest is possible. The investigator will take particular interest in issues that directly relate to the evidentiary needs of the prosecutor. A number of studies have found that in making the decision to arrest a suspect and file formal charges, the investigator will consider first, the ability of the victim to identify the suspect, and second, the victim's willingness to prosecute (Bryden and Lengnick 1997; LaFree 1981). And third, it was discovered that proof of penetration, relationship between victim and suspect, use of physical force by suspect, and the availability of witnesses all impacts the police officer's decision to arrest in a sexual assault case (Battelle Law and Justice Study Center 1978). One exception to the above factors is the victim's ability to identify a suspect, which is nearly always present in acquaintance rapes, and therefore is unhelpful in analyzing police decisions in these cases (Bryden and Lengnick 1997; LaFree 1981).

Extra-Legal Factors Affecting Police Decisions: Rape Myths & Secondary Victimization

Despite the legal factors affecting police officers' discretion during sexual assault cases, there is empirical evidence that extra-legal variables may impact officers' decisions. These extra-legal variables are associated with the rape myths that so many of the general population believe. These myths lead law enforcement to hold negative attitudes toward sexual assault victims and frequently subject victims to the phenomena known as "secondary victimization" (Carrington and Watson 1996). Secondary victimization has been defined as the victim-blaming attitudes, behaviors and practices of community service providers including the police (Campbell, et al. 2001; Campbell and Johnson 1997).

Extra-legal factors that have been found to impact law enforcement's decision, particularly with whether or not to found the crime of rape, may include the behavior and lifestyle of the victim prior to the assault, as well as at the time of the assault (Chandler and Torney 1981). One national survey of police officers uncovered a prevailing attitude of suspicion and lack of concern for rape victims (LeDoux and Hazelwood 1985). Other studies suggest that police officers ascribe to victim-blaming attitudes, such as believing women provoke rape and often lie about the occurrence of rape (Campbell, et al. 2001; Campbell and Johnson 1997). In addition, other studies have reported that victims have been outright told by law enforcement that they are not believable or credible. Even in the absence of such verbal communication, many women still felt doubted in their interactions with law enforcement (Campbell, et al. 2001).

The secondary victimization may occur not only because of what law enforcement decide to do, but also because of what they decide not to do. As previously stated, not founding a case as rape and not following up with an investigation are law enforcement options (Campbell, et al. 2001). Recently, in Philadelphia it was discovered that thousands of sexual assault cases were shelved with little or no investigation. And unfortunately, "there is little reason to believe that the problem is unique to Philadelphia" (Lonsway 2002, 3). In the Phoenix Police Department approximately one-third of the sexual assault reports are typically filed as "information only," which means they are not treated as an active criminal case, nor counted in crime statistics. As another example, in 1990, the Oakland Police Department "routinely unfound cases without sufficient investigation. They subsequently re-opened hundreds of cases for investigation" (Lonsway 2002, 4). As a result of these atrocities, victims are denied access to the criminal justice system and perpetrators of sexual assault go undetected and unpunished.

The above obviously leads to the view of police as being indifferent and insensitive toward rape victim cases. This is somewhat of a historically widespread view and as evidenced, not without some empirical support.

False Allegations of Rape

Police officers decisions in rape cases go beyond the decision to found or unfound, or to use legal or extra-legal factors in deciding founding, investigation, or arrest. Police officers also bear the burden of attempting to determine when someone is making a false allegation of rape. Determining a false allegation of rape avoids an injustice to a wrongly accused individual. At the same time, for reasons of professional pride, the police officer does his/her best to avoid looking naïve by falling for a story that turns out false (Holmstrom and Burgess 1978).

Extent of False Allegations

"Prior to the rise of modern feminism in the 1970s, male judges and scholars often indicated that false allegations of acquaintance rape were common. Rape, Sir Mathew Hale instructed an 18th century jury, 'is an accusation easily to be made and once made, hard to be proved, and harder to be defended by the party to be accused tho never so innocent'" (Bryden and Lengnick 1997, 1296).

Definitively calculating the ratio of true to false reports of rape is generally extremely difficult and a highly subjective enterprise (Bryden and Lengnick 1997). A number of scholars have attempted to estimate how often rape reports are false. These studies' conclusions vary radically, with the estimated percentages of false reports ranging from 2 percent (Katz & Mazur as cited in Bryden and Lengnick 1997) to 41 percent (Kanin 1994).

Feldman-Summers and Palmer (1980) found that the police officers who participated in their study would expect that three of every five rape complaints are either untruthful or mistaken. They contend that this belief is likely communicated to the rape victims, even if officers attempt to treat the victims with respect. However, their study, though widely cited, only surveyed approximately fifteen officers.

A two year study of all rape allegations by the New York City Sex Crimes Analysis Squad found that the rate of false allegations for rape and sexual offenses was around two percent. This makes it comparable to false allegations for other crimes (Polly Pattullo cited in Bryden and Lengnick 1997, 1308). In separate research Hursh (1977) examined the Denver police records of 1973. She designated rape reports as false "only if the victim finally admitted that she had originally lied about being attacked or if the police concluded from other evidence that she had lied." Her findings were similar to New York City's findings, as they found that only two to three percent of rape reports were false.

On the other side of the extent of false allegation spectrum, Kanin (1994) examined 109 consecutive rape reports during a nine-year period in a "small metropolitan community." He labeled a complaint false only if the complainant later recanted to the police. Of the 109 forcible rapes, 45 (41%) were false allegations by his definition. Kanin (1994) reasons that the high rates of his study, relative to other studies, are due to departmental policy. The chief of police in the city of study insisted that every rape report be thoroughly investigated, because of the relatively low crime rate of the city. "In other cities, busy police sometimes do not even record the most obviously false rape reports" (Kanin as cited in Bryden and Lengnick 1997). Others contend that maybe the recantations were false, rather than the accusations (Bryden and Lengnick 1997).

Kennedy and Witkowski (2000) claim to have replicated Kanin's study in a suburb of Detroit and found similar results as Kanin. Of the 68 reports of forcible rape 32.3 percent were classified as false by the complainants' own admissions.

Despite the fear of false complaints and despite the conflicting research on rates of false rape allegations, the National Institute of Law Enforcement and Criminal Justice (NILECJ)(1978) justice contends that there is not a disproportionate number of false rape complaints. In addition, those few that are false are readily screened out prior to trial. The NILECJ states that "it is doubtful that a woman would proceed very far with such complaints in the face of the unpleasantness she must endure to pursue....By crying rape, she faces personal harassment and embarrassment and yet is less likely to succeed in securing a conviction than if, for example, she brought any other charge" (p. 29).

Reasons for Making False Allegations of Rape

Despite the enormous disadvantages outlined above of falsely reporting rape, it may not always be as pathological or stupid as it may sound. False rape allegations appear to serve three major functions for the complainants: providing an alibi, seeking revenge, and obtaining sympathy and attention (Bryden and Lengnick 1997; Kanin 1994). In the replication study of Kanin's the most frequently cited reason for false allegations was alibi, followed by attention/sympathy-getting and only in one instance did the complainant admit to revenge as the primary reason for the false allegation.

Falsely reporting rape provides an alibi in cases where a teenage girl becomes pregnant and instead of confessing to her parents she is sexually active, she claims rape. Seeking revenge may seem logical when, for example, a prostitute whose customer fails to pay for sex may retaliate by falsely accusing him of rape.

Identifying False Allegations of Rape

The National Institute of Law Enforcement and Criminal Justice (1978) suggests that law enforcement is proficient at screening out the occasional false charge. In fact and unfortunately, police officers probably screen out far more than fabricated complaints. However, no one knows which demographic groups, if any, are disproportionately likely to lie to the police about rape, or at least to tell stories that sound less credible than most rape reports (Bryden and Lengnick 1997).

Nonetheless, if means of detecting false allegations of rape arise, it will only serve to better all of the criminal justice system. First, fabrications waste the time and resources of an already overtaxed justice system. Second, for each false report that results in an arrest, a man is imprisoned when he has committed no offense. And third, these falsehoods degrade and trivialize the experience of every legitimate rape survivor who will ever tell her story to the police officer or jury (Fairstein 1993). For the benefit of the victim's emotional state and the betterment of case processing, law enforcement should be advised to approach every allegation of sexual assault as truthful until there is solid evidence to prove otherwise.

Victims' Perceptions of Police in their Response to Sexual Assault Victims

With respect to the above discussion of documented law enforcement indifference and insensitivity, one may wonder how victims perceive law enforcement services and ultimately how this may impact victim reporting to law enforcement.

Victims' Perceptions of Police Response

While a majority of historical rape literature touts the negative experiences of rape victims with law enforcement, other literature finds the opposite. Holmstrom and Burgess (1978) found that most victims spoke favorably about the police who had questioned them. Only about 10 percent of their sample expressed a negative reaction. Those negative reactions were due to such explanations as police behavior that was perceived as overbearing, harsh or moralistic. Frazier and Haney (as cited in Campbell, et al. 2001) found that victims of sexual assault "held positive attitudes toward investigating officers but were frustrated by the overall response of the criminal justice system" (p. 1241).

On the other hand, coinciding with the historical literature, many women recounted their experiences of police investigations to other researchers disclosing negative encounters and reported feeling disbelieved and unsupported by the police (Brownmiller 1975; Chambers and Millar 1986; Hall 1985; Holmstrom and Burgess 1978; Wright 1984).

Jordan (2001) has conducted the most current study on victims' experiences with law enforcement. Jordon interviewed 48 women with a total of 50 experiences of sexual assault. Jordon found that only 50 percent of the victims expressed overall satisfaction with the police. However, three-quarters of the victims responded that they would encourage other victims to report to the police. The women that were dissatisfied complained of "not feeling believed by the police and of not having their experience understood by law enforcement. Others felt that the police focus on information gathering prevented them from recognizing the needs of victims. The women who were satisfied with law enforcement referred to having their impressions of the police changed for the better as a result of reporting this incident" (p. 694).

Holmstrom and Burgess (1978) stated that "the nature of the material that is discussed—the details of an extremely frightening and humiliating sexual experience—mean that the encounter (with the police) may be unsettling for many victims even under the best of circumstances" (p. 35). Jordan (2001) somewhat echoes those sentiments.

> That the victim is trying to manage the effects of trauma and regain a sense of personal equilibrium at the same time as the police are making excessive demands on her stamina and seeking to establish her veracity as a complainant. Attempts to resolve this inherent conflict can begin only with an acknowledgement of its existence. The police focus is likely to be on the identification and apprehension of the offender, which may or may not be something that the victim can assist with, and may or may not be a goal she shares. What she is likely to need most is to have a sense of safety restored and to be able to heal and re-establish control of her life, something that police are not trained to provide and which some of their procedures may even work against. The police role is not designed to assist in healing—this role rightly belongs to support workers and therapists, whose involvement can assist both police and victims alike (p. 703).

Reporting Sexual Assault Victimizations to Police

One factor that may reflect victims' perceptions of law enforcement is the level of reporting by victims. Sexual assault is the most underreported crime in American and it has been that way for decades. According to the National Crime Victimization Survey (U.S. Department of Justice 2003) only 38.6 percent of all sexual assaults were reported to law enforcement in 2001.

The most often cited reason of the victim for *not* reporting the crime to law enforcement was "other reasons," followed by "it was considered a personal matter". "Fear of reprisal" was also a concern for many, as well as victims "reported it to another official" (See Table 1) (Greenfeld 1997). The victim-offender relationship appears to impact the decision to report as the closer the relationship between the female victim and the offender, the greater the likelihood that she would not report. When the offender was a current or former husband or boyfriend, about three-fourths of all victims were *not* reported to police. When the offender was a friend or acquaintance, 61 percent of completed rapes were *not* reported to the police. When the offender was a stranger, 54 percent of completed rapes were not reported to the police (Rennison 2002).

Table 1—Percent of Reasons for Not Reporting Sexual Assault
to the Police—2001

Reasoning	Percent
Other reasons	31.2
It was a personal or private matter	29.4
Fear of reprisal	8.1
Reported to another official	6.7
It was not important enough to report	5.9
Too inconvenient or time consuming	5.7
Offender unsuccessful	5.3
Lack of proof	4.7
Police inefficient, ineffective or biased	2.9

*Source: U.S. Department of Justice, Criminal Victimization
in the United States, 2001 Statistical Tables*

The most common reason given by victims of sexual assault for reporting the crime to the police was to stop the incident or prevent it from happening (23.8%), followed by preventing further crimes by the offender against them (14.6%) (See Table 2) (Greenfeld 1997).

Table 2—Percent of Reasons for Reporting Sexual Assault to the Police—2001

Reasoning	Percent
To stop the incident or prevent it from happening	23.8
To prevent further crimes by offender against victim	14.6
Needed help due to injury	4.5
To recover property	2.1

Source: U.S. Department of Justice, Criminal Victimization in the United States, 2001 Statistical Tables

Police Innovations in the Investigation of Sexual Assault

In order to improve police response to victims and improve reporting of sexual assault, new police approaches or innovations in handling sexual assault cases have emerged. These new innovations have also been encouraged by the feminist movement, new sexual assault laws in many states, and successful lawsuits against police departments who failed to adequately respond to sexual assault victims (The Associated Press 1994). The approaches to sexual assault cases range from unique forms of training to the involvement of oversight boards.

Training

Almost unheard of 20 years ago, many of today's police officers receive sensitivity training in responding to victims of sexual assault. The research evaluating the value of this training finds that it is having a positive impact for police officers. Lonsway (as cited in Campbell, et al. 2001) evaluated a training intervention with police academy recruits. Her findings suggested that additional instruction on sexual assault and victim interviewing techniques improved recruits' skills, which was positively received by the interviewees. Other research indicates that participation in a rape-awareness program reduces adherence to rape myths (Foubert and Marriott 1997; Proto-Campise, et al. 1998).

Training is now being made available for specific types of sexual assaults as well as types of interviewing techniques. The National Center for Women and Policing recently developed training curriculum targeted for law enforcement in their specific investigation of Acquaintance Sexual Assaults. This curriculum emphasizes investigative tools and techniques for those cases in which a consent defense—rather than identity—is raised (Lonsway 2002).

No matter what the training, Jordan (2001) contends that "stressing victim sensitivity in training programs is wasted effort unless police officers, in their day-to-day policing, are monitored, evaluated and able to be rewarded for displaying competencies in this area. The message needs to be conveyed within the police occupation culture that displaying sensitivity to the needs of victims does not detract from sound law enforcement practice—it *is* sound law enforcement practice" (p. 704).

Specialized Sexual Assault Policing Units

Rather than train all officers with respect to responding to sexual assault victims, some departments have created specialized sex crime units. These units consist of police officers with intense training on responding to sexual assault victims. Police officers are trained to prioritize their response to sexual assault cases and to treat victims with sensitivity while thoroughly investigating cases (Wilson 2002). The purpose of these specialized units is to enhance the agency's efficiency and/or to send a message to the community that the department is deeply committed to solving sex crime (Kilpatrick 2000).

Other departments have developed in-house victim/witness assistance units. These units are usually directed by non-sworn trained individuals that review all reports, sort out the felonies, and contact each victim of a felony crime, usually by phone. "Law enforcement-based victim assistance professionals make referrals to rape crisis centers, contact victims who have delayed reporting, and provide community education in rape awareness and prevention" (Kilpatrick 2000, 21). The purposes of these units are similar to the specialized police officer units as they are looking to make a solid effort in police community relations, as well as provide an improved method of assisting victims in our criminally focused system.

Coordinated Care Teams

Selected communities throughout the United States have developed coordinated care programs which attempt to bring together police, prosecutors, doctors, nurses, social workers, and rape victim advocates to work as an integrated team in assisting rape survivors. The sexual assault response team concept was developed in California. This model involves a "coordinated response among various professionals to meet the needs of the assault victim and to collect physical evidence associated with the complaint" (Wilson 2002, 15). Team members work together to ensure a sensitive, thorough investigation. The benefits of the team approach is that members attend professional training, stay abreast of current research and developments, and thoroughly network among other entities in the community and criminal justice system (Wilson 2002). Police departments have found that these teams benefit them in that they receive re-liable, consistent medical examinations, which yield more accurate and rele-vant information than previously available (Wilson 2002).

Overall, these coordinated care teams have yet to be evaluated as to their effectiveness in assisting the rape survivor. Nonetheless, the U. S. Department of Justice (1994) contends that the coordinated programs "helped maintain a successful stance against rape" (as cited in Campbell, et al. 2001).

Blind Reporting System

One innovative approach to encouraging the reporting of sexual assault vic-timizations is by offering an anonymous telephone reporting system. Blind reporting of sexual assault benefits victims, law enforcement and the com-munity as well. First, it allows victims to share critical information with law enforcement without requiring that victim to sacrifice confidentiality. It also allows victims an opportunity to gather procedural information about the criminal justice system without having to immediately commit to an investi-gation. If handled appropriately, this may ultimately encourage an otherwise unwilling victim to report (Garcia and Henderson 1999).

Blind reporting enables law enforcement to gain information about crimes of sexual violence that likely otherwise will go unreported. The current statis-tics of sexual assault reflect only a fraction of the violations that occur. Via the blind reporting, law enforcement may be able to gather information about local offenders' patterns of behaviors or the characteristics of emerging high risk sit-uations or locations. This, in theory, allows investigators a clearer picture of sex-ual violence in their communities. In addition, some blind reports become full reports and lead to investigations and subsequent prosecutions. Others provide useful information for investigation of other cases (Garcia and Henderson 1999).

The community benefits by blind reporting because they are getting more complete information about sexual violence in their community. When law enforcement can determine dangerous scenarios based upon past offending behaviors, they can better educate the public. This in turn may improve com-munity relations and possibly garner information on other neighborhood crime problems (Garcia and Henderson 1999).

Citizen Oversight of Sexual Assault Investigations

In the last couple of decades there have been many law enforcement agen-cies across the country that have established citizen oversight mechanisms of police misconduct. These are mechanisms which involve non-sworn individuals at some point in the evaluation process of citizen complaints (Walker and Kreisel 1996). This concept has been developed as a means of evaluating and classifying sexual assault complaints in the Philadelphia Police Department. Members of women's organizations from the community are selected to serve on the oversight mechanism. The oversight mechanism was prompted by the disclosure that the department for years mislabeled rapes as lesser offenses or shelved cases altogether. The group will oversee the process as police evaluate complaints and will be "the final say" on the classification of sexual assaults (Anonymous 2000b).

Evaluation of Innovative Approaches

Evaluations of many of these new initiatives are yet to be conducted. However, initial discussions of such initiatives indicate that officers are more sympathetic toward, and hold more positive attitudes about, victims of sexual assault (Campbell 1995; Campbell and Johnson 1997; Temkin 1996). Nonetheless, in order for the improvements and innovations to be effective at improving police responses and investigations to sexual assault victims, they must be touted starting with the administration, for they are individuals that set the tone of expected behavior for an entire department. Recently in Philadelphia the Police Commissioner, John F. Timoney, announced that he was going to improve the response of his Special Victims Unit by instigating a "major overhaul" of the unit. Reforms included retiring and reassigning some officers and adopting a policy that requires investigators to be more sympathetic to victims who come to police for assistance (Anonymous 2000a).

Administration needs to be committed to changing the occupational subculture of policing that exacerbates the rape myths and insensitive responses or little substantive improvement in the police response to rape complaints can realistically be expected (Jordan 2001). Jordan and others may be getting the message out there as many departments across the country currently, appear to be expressing verbal and attitudinal commitment to victims' needs by the top levels of administration (The Associated Press 1994).

Police Guidelines on Approaching Victims of Sexual Assault

Whether or not a police agency has an improved or innovative approach to sexual assault victims, there are guidelines and materials that law enforcement agencies can provide for their officers. Police of all aspects can assimilate the following information to be utilized with many victims of crime, but especially victims of sexual assault.

There are three major needs of victims of crime that can apply to victims of sexual assault. First is the need of victims to feel some sense of safety again. Second, victims need to express their emotions whether or not law enforcement feels it is valuable for the clearance of the case. And third, victims need to know what comes next after their victimization. Therefore, it is essential law enforcement inform victims of the process ahead of them and the resources that are available to victims (Woods 2001).

More specific to victims of sexual assault, Woods (2001) writing for the Office for the Victims of Crime, offers the following tips.

- Be prepared for virtually any type of emotional reaction by victims. Be unconditionally supportive and permit victims to express their emotions, which may include, crying, angry outbursts and screaming.
- Avoid interpreting the victims' calmness or composure as evidence that a sexual assault did or did not occur. The victim could be in shock.
- Approach victims calmly. Showing your outrage at the crime may cause victims even more trauma.
- Ask victims whether they would like to contact a family member or friend.
- Offer to contact a sexual assault crisis counselor. Ask victims whether they prefer a male or female counselor. In addition, ask the victims whether they would prefer talking with your or a law enforcement officer of the opposite sex.
- Be careful not to appear overprotective or patronizing.
- Remember that it is normal for victims to want to forget, or to actually forget, details of the crime that are difficult for them to accept.
- Encourage victims to get medical attention, especially to check for possible internal injuries. In addition, a medical examination can provide evidence for the apprehension and prosecution of the victim's assailant. Keep in mind, however, that victims may feel humiliated and embarrassed that their bodies were exposed during the sexual assault and must be exposed again during the medical examination. Explain what will take place forensically during the examination and why these procedures are important.
- Notify the hospital of the incoming victim/patient and request a private waiting room. Escort victim to the hospital. If no crisis intervention counselor is available, wait at the hospital until the victim is released and escort her to her destination.

- Be mindful of the personal, interpersonal, and privacy concerns of the victims. They may have a number of concerns, including the possibility of having been impregnated or contracting sexually transmitted diseases such as the AIDS virus; the reactions of their spouse, mate, or parents; media publicity that may reveal their experience to the public; and the reactions and criticism of neighbors and coworkers if they learn about the sexual assault.
- Interview victims with extreme sensitivity. Minimize the number of times victims must recount details of the crime to strangers. If possible, only one law enforcement officer should be assigned to the initial interview and subsequent investigation.
- Offer to answer any further questions victims may have and provide any further assistance they may need.
- Encourage victims to get counseling. Explain that your recommendation for counseling is based on having seen other victims benefit from it in the past. Explain that they may experience posttraumatic stress symptoms in the next few months. Identify and refer them to support services for assistance

(Woods 2001, 8–10; Kilpatrick 2000).

Conclusion

Sexual assault cases can prove to be challenging for many law enforcement officers. How those police officers respond and make discretionary decisions in these cases can make a tremendous impact on the victims' emotional well-being, as well as determining if and how the case will be processed through the criminal justice system. Because of the unique nature of sexual assault cases, there appears to sincerely be a need for all law enforcement to be specifically trained on the sensitivity and delicateness of approaching and investigating sexual assault cases. Law enforcement officers' responses to victims appear to be on the appropriate path of improvement, but there is still room for additional advancement by many police officers.

"It's not enough to just have good police skills; you must be able to interact professionally with the victim, or she is likely to withdraw her cooperation and drop out of the investigative effort. When this occurs, a sex offender escapes justice. He is free to continue his acts, reinforced in the belief that law enforcement is powerless to stand in his way" (Albrecht 2000, 57).

References

Albrecht, S. "Crime Scenes and Rape Investigations." *Law and Order* 48 no. 11, (2000): 55–57.

Anonymous. "Women's Groups Oversee Sex Cases." *Law and Order* 48 no. 4, (2000a): 6.

Anonymous. "Philadelphia Changes Rules for Rape Unit." *Crime Control Digest* 34 no. 50, (2000b): 2–3.

Associated Press, The. "Crime Victims' Rights: Sensitizing Police to Victims' Needs." *The New York Times*, June 12, 1994.

Battelle Law and Justice Study Center. *Forcible Rape: Police Volume.* Washington D.C.: U.S. Government Printing Office, 1978

Brownmiller, S. *Against Our Will: Men, Women and Rape.* Harmondsworth: Penguin, 1975.

Bryden, D.P. and S. Lengnick. "Rape in the Criminal Justice System." *The Journal of Criminal* Law and Criminology 87 no. 4, (1997): 1195–1384.

Campbell, R. "The Role of Work Experience and Individual Beliefs in Police officers' Perceptions of Date Rape: An Integration of Quantitative and Qualitative Methods." *American Journal of Community Psychology* 23, (1995): 249–277.

Campbell, R., and C.R. Johnson. "Police Officers' Perceptions of Rape." *Journal of Interpersonal Violence* 12, (1997): 255–274.

Campbell, R., S.M. Wasco, C.E. Ahrens, T. Sefi, and H.E. Barnes. "Preventing the 'Second Rape': Rape Survivors' Experiences with Community Service Providers." *Journal of Interpersonal Violence* 16 no 12, (2001): 1239–1260.

Carrington, K., and P. Watson. "Policing Sexual Violence: Feminism, Criminal Justice, and Governmentality." *International Journal of the Sociology of Law* 24, (1996): 253–272.

Chambers, G. and A. Millar. *Prosecuting Sexual Assault.* Edinburgh: Scottish Office Central Research Unit, 1986.

Chandler, S.M., and M. Torney. "The Decisions and Processing of Rape Victims Throughout the Criminal Justice System." *Sociologist* 4 no. 155, (1981).

Doerner, W.G., and S.P. Lab. *Victimology* 2nd ed. Cincinnati, OH: Anderson Publishing Co., 1998.

Fairstein, L.A. *Sexual Violence: Our War Against Rape.* New York: William Morrow and Co., 1993.

Federal Bureau of Investigation. *Crime in the United States—2001*. Washington D.C.: U.S. Government Printing Office, 2002.

Feldman–Summers, S., and G. C. Palmer. "Rape as Viewed by Judges, Prosecutors and Police Officers." *Criminal Justice and Behavior* 7 no. 19, (1980): 36.

Foubert, J.D., and K.A. Marriott. "Effects of a Sexual Assault Peer Program on Men's Belief in Rape Myths." *Sex Roles* 36, (1997): 259–268

Garcia, S., and M. Henderson. "Blind Reporting of Sexual Violence." *FBI Law Enforcement* Bulletin 68 no. 6, (1999): 12–16.

Greenfeld, L.A. Sex *Offenses and Offenders: An Analysis of Data on Rape and Sexual Assault*. Washington, D. C.: U.S. Department of Justice, 1997.

Greenwood, P. *The Criminal Investigation Process*. Santa Monica, CA: Rand, 1975.

Hall, R. *Ask Any Women: A London Inquiry into Rape and Sexual Assault*. Brison: Falling Wall Press, 1985.

Hazelwood, R.R. and A.W. Burgess. "The Behavioral–Oriented Interview of Rape Victims: The Key to Profiling." In *Practical Aspects of Rape Investigation: A Multidisciplinary Approach*, eds. R. R. Hazelwood and A. W. Burgess, 151–168. New York: Elsevier, 1987.

Holmstrom, L.L., and A.W. Burgess. *The Victim of Rape: Institutional Reactions*. New York: Jon Wiley, 1978.

Hursch, C.J. *The Trouble with Rape*. Chicago: Nelson Hall, 1977.

Jordan, J. "Worlds Apart? Women, Rape and the Police Reporting Process." *British Journal of* Criminology 41, (2001): 679–706.

Kanin, E.J. "False Rape Allegations." *Archives of Sexual Behavior* 23 no. 1 (1994): 84–85.

Kennedy, D.B. and M.J. Witkowski. "False Allegations of Rape Revisited: A Replication of the Kanin Study." *Journal of Security Administration* 23 no. 1, (2000): 41–48.

Kerstetter, W.A. "Gateway to Justice: Police and Prosecutorial Response to Sexual Assault against Women." *Journal of Criminal Law and Criminology* 81, (1990).

Kilpatrick, D. "Chapter 9: Sexual Assault." In *1999 National Victim Assistance Academy*, eds. G. Coleman, M. Gaboury, M. Murray and A. Seymour. Washington D. C: Office for Victims of Crime, 2000.

LeDoux, J.C. and R.R. Hazelwood. "Police Attitudes and Beliefs Toward Rape." *Journal of Police Science and Administration* 13, (1985): 211–220.

LaFree, G. D. "Official Reactions to Social Problems: Police Decisions in Sexual Assault Cases." *Social Problems* 82 no. 582, (1981).

Lonsway, K. A. "Sexual Assault Cases." *Women Police 36* no. 1, (2002): 3–7.

Merrill, W. F. "The Art of Interrogating Rapists." *FBI Law Enforcement Bulletin* 64 no. 1, (1995): 8–12.

National Institute of Law Enforcement and Criminal Justice (NILECJ). *Forcible Rape: An Analysis of Legal Issues*. Washington D.C.: US Government Printing Office, 1978.

Proto-Campise, L., J. Belknap, and J. Wooldredge. "High School Students' Adherence to Rape Myths and the Effectiveness of High School Rape-Awareness Programs." *Violence Against Women* 4, (1998): 308–328.

Rennison, C. M. *Rape and Sexual Assault: Reporting to Police and Medical Attention, 1992–2000*. Washington D.C.: U.S. Department of Justice, 2002

Temkin, J. "Doctors, Rape and Criminal Justice." *The Howard Journal 35*, (1996): 1–20.

Tjaden, P., and N. Thoennes. *Prevalence, Incidence, and Consequences of Violence Against*

Women: Findings from the National Violence Against Women Survey. Atlanta, GA: Center for Disease Control and Prevention, Center for Injury Prevention and Control, 1998.

U.S. Department of Justice. *Criminal* Victimization in the United States, 2001 Statistical Tables. Washington D.C.: Bureau of Justice Statistics, 2003.

Walker, S. and B. W. Kreisel. "Varieties of Citizen Review: The Implications of Organizational Features of Complaint Review Procedures for Accountability of the Police." *American Journal of Police 15* no. 3, (1996): 65–88.

Wilson, C. R. "Police and the Sexual Assault Examination." *FBI Law Enforcement Bulletin* 71 no. 1, (2002): 14–17.

Woods, T. O. *First Response to Victims of Crime: A Handbook for Law Enforcement Officers* on How to Approach and Help Elderly Victims, Victims of Sexual Assault, Child Victims, Victims of Domestic Violence, Survivors of Homicide Victims, 2001. Available online: http://www.ojp.usdoj.gove/ovc/publications/infores/firstrep/2001/NCJ189631.pdf (retrieved June 2003).

Wright, R. "A Note on Attrition of Rape Cases." *British Journal of Criminology* 24 no. 4, (1984): 399–400.

In the Words of a Police Officer

The most challenging aspects of my work are:

- Making the criminal justice system non-intimidating and non-victimizing for the victim
- Convincing a prosecutor that the victim did not "ask" or "deserve" to be raped
- Educating first responding officers in appropriate methods of interviewing victims

When I attended the police academy in 1985, there was little, if any training about investigating sex crimes. My training came from various conferences and training sessions throughout the years, and much of it was self-initiated due to my interest.

To get more sex crime victims to report their victimization, there would need to be a societal attitude change regarding sex crime victims. Since the majority of sex crimes are committed by non-strangers, the tendency is to focus on what the victim did or did not do to put themselves in a risky situation, therefore minimizing the crime and blaming the victim. If all sex crime victims were treated as victims, and sex crime offenders were treated and punished as criminals, it is more likely that victims would report these crimes.

I also believe that victim advocacy plays a very important role in encouraging a victim to report the incident and continue to assist in the investigation. Well-trained, well-funded victim advocacy programs are essential to an effective sexual assault intervention. Victim advocates can help recognize and minimize some of the re-victimization that might occur, if the advocate accompanies the victim throughout the process.

Although I work in the prevention and education field, and I encourage all victims to report crimes to the police and provide many reasons for reporting it, I wonder if I would follow that advice myself. I have a 15 year old daughter, and I often wonder if she were sexually assaulted by an acquaintance if I would encourage her to report the incident to the police, knowing what she would likely be put through. More often than not, the report results in little or no consequences for the offender, and a high likelihood that she would be re-victimized by the system.

Suggestion to improve the CJS with respect to sex crime victims and offenders: The thing that seems to be working in the domestic violence and sexual assault areas are specialized units and coordinated responses that consist of specially trained law enforcement, victim advocacy, social services, prosecution, and courts that focus specifically on domestic violence or sexual assault.

Improving the system would require changing attitudes and beliefs. I think a jurisdiction could spend a lot of time spinning wheels trying to change attitudes and beliefs of those within the system with authority to make the improvements. Even the best written policies, protocols and laws are useless if those in positions of implementing them choose not to do so. Sometimes it takes a specialized, coordinated unit made up of those who already have a demonstrated understanding of sex crimes, the victims and the offenders to really make an improvement.

The other suggestion is to continue, expand and coordinate efforts to involve males in becoming part of the solution to prevent violence against women and to ensure the offenses are treated in the system as serious crimes. Since females are most often the victims, it is important for male role models to join the efforts to end violence against women, and realize that by allowing the system to continue in this manner, they become part of the problem. The system could benefit from the majority of males who are not sex offenders taking a leading role in reducing the incidents and holding offenders accountable.

I have investigated 5-10 sex crimes per calendar year.
18 years in police work.

Kim Drake
Police/Community Services Sergeant
Department of Public Safety.
Central Missouri State University

Report exposes lie detector tests that await some Ohio rape victims

While it was never a secret, neither did dozens of Ohio police departments make it widely known that they administered polygraphs and other truth-verification tests to victims in sexual assault cases—that is, until a draft report by the state Department of Health brought the practice to light in February.

The study, conducted by a task force created in 2002 to examine how rape cases are prosecuted, found the practice to be widespread.

"We've let an awful lot of victims down," said W. Duncan Whitney, a Delaware County Common Pleas judge. "I have heard a lot of counties say they are doing well, but they are taking only the easy cases."

Among the 10 key recommendations made by the task force was that all counties adopt "quality local protocols" that would establish an appropriate response to victims and support the pursuit of justice.Whitney, a former prosecutor who served on the task force, blamed lazy police officials for not aggressively pursuing rape cases. He told The Columbus Dispatch that he was appalled to learn that polygraphs were used to gauge a victim's credibility.

Not true, police insist.

Lie-detectors and computerized voice-stress analyzers (CVSA), officials says, are used strictly as an investigative tool, on a voluntary basis, and only in those cases where it would help uncover the guilt or identity of an offender. Investigators will use them, however, when a victim's allegations raise red flags, particularly in cases of acquaintance rape, or when the accused is a family member.

"Obviously, you do this with sensitivity," said Chief Walter Ugrinic of the Shaker Heights Police Department, in an interview with Law Enforcement News. "The operator also has to have a talent to sometimes help the person remember issues. In some cases it brings up deception, but in most cases it brings up evidence to help in the identity of a suspect—that's why we use it."

The Shaker Heights department is one of 40 in the state that engages in the lie-detection practice, according to the Ohio Coalition on Sexual Assault.

Ed Roberts, a probation officer who retired in 1999 from the Fairfield Police Department, where he had headed the agency's detective bureau, said truth-verification tests were never administered arbitrarily, nor were they routine in sexual assault investigations.

When a case involved a forcible rape where there was perhaps a break-in, a test was given if the information provided by the victim did not match the physical evidence found at the scene. More often, however, the tests were administered when the victim and the offender knew each other.

"Let's just say it was a forcible rape and your victim didn't know the person, broke into the house, maybe caught them outside—that would be probably be the last person you would give a truth-verification test to," he told LEN.

Investigators would be more apt to use a CVSA when the victim's version of the situation is completely different from the story police are getting from the alleged offender, said Roberts.

In those cases—although CVSA tests are not admissible in court—having the victim pass a polygraph gives police leverage against the accused, said Detective Sgt. Steven Truitt of the Miami University of Ohio Police Department.

"We talk to him and say, 'Hey, it's your word against the young lady's. She has come in and shown us she believes what she's saying by taking a truth-verification test, you up for the task?' It encourages him, so we get a nice one-on-one, prolonged conversation with the individual," he told LEN.

The point of the tests is not to embarrass a victim, or question anyone's integrity, said Ugrinic. "We don't put them on the polygraph to find out if it's true," he said, adding that if a victim does not want to take the test, police will still pursue the investigation.

But victims' advocates content that since the tests cannot be used in court, using them only serves to inflict further trauma.

Stacy Kitchen, executive director of the Ohio Coalition on Sexual Assault, contends that the stress victims are under could appear on a polygraph or CVSA as lying. Moreover, she told LEN, just because a victim might not be forthcoming with police, or her story does not add up to investigators, does not mean she is not telling the truth.

Yet unless legislation prohibits police from using truth-verification tests, it is unlikely that the practice would stop, Kitchen said, given that agencies find the tests very effective.

"What we would like is to see is some very strict guidelines in place, and if we could work together with law enforcement on that, we would be happy to do that," she said. "But we do not support the use of these devices at all."

While it is natural that victims' advocates would oppose what appears to be an unsupportive stance by police, Truitt noted that it is law enforcement's job to remain open-minded.

"Anything you say to the victim that makes it seem you may have doubts about what she's told you is naturally going to be met with a certain amount of resentment because that's not seen as the proper thing to do," he said. "Unfortunately, in our line of work, we've got to maintain a certain open-minded approach to the thing, and we can't go into it with preset attitude of this guy is guilty, we're just going to hang him out to dry. We have to look at it from a practical standpoint, provide as much support for the cases as we can."

Law Enforcement News, John Jay College of Criminal Justice/ CUNY. April 15, 2003, page 1,10.

Chapter 16

Prosecution of Sex Crimes

Jeffrey W. Spears

Introduction

Someone walked over and asked what we were talking about. About
rape, I replied; no, actually about cases that aren't really rape. The D.A.
looked puzzled. That was rape, he said. Technically. She was forced to
have sex without consent. It just wasn't a case you prosecute.

—Susan Estrich, *Real Rape*

In general, after a sexual assault suspect has been arrested, the next step in
the criminal justice process is to notify the prosecutor that a crime has been
committed and that a suspect has been arrested. Prosecutors then review the
facts and evidence presented to them, evaluate the case, and decide if charges
should be filed or rejected (Jacoby 1980). The importance of this initial screening decision is indicated by the fact that from one-third to one-half of all
felony arrests do not result in the filing of felony charges (Boland 1983; Brosi
1979). As you can see, very few cases make it past this initial screening decision and even fewer actually make it to trial. For example, a recent survey by
the Bureau of Justice Statistics indicated that 96 percent of felony convictions
were the result of a guilty plea, not a trial (Reaves 2001). Clearly, the prosecutor plays an important gatekeeping function that determines the character
of the American criminal justice system (Jacoby 1980; Kerrstetter 1990).

The extensive exercise of discretion by decision makers is a defining feature
of the American criminal justice system. The prosecutor is a key figure and
decides who will be charged, what charge will be filed, who will be offered a

plea bargain, and the type of bargain to be offered. The prosecutor also may recommend the sentence the offender should receive. As Supreme Court Justice Jackson observed in 1940, "the prosecutor has more control over life, liberty, and reputation than any other person in America" (Davis 1969, 190). The most crucial discretionary decision made by the prosecutor is the initial decision to prosecute or not. Prosecutors have nearly unfettered discretion in making this decision; there are no legislative or judicial guidelines on charging and a decision not to file charges is immune from review. In fact, the United States Supreme Court, in *Bordenkircher v. Hayes* [434 U.S. 357, 364 (1978)], examined this prosecutorial decision. The Court ruled that, "so long as the prosecutor has probable cause to believe that the accused committed an offense defined by statute, the decision whether or not to prosecute, and what charge to file or bring before a grand jury, generally rests entirely in his discretion" [*Bordenkircher v. Hayes*, 434 U.S. 357, 364 (1978)].

Although a prosecutor's discretion is significant, there have been some limits placed on it. Specifically, the Supreme Court has found that a prosecutor's decision to charge a suspect may not be "deliberately based upon an unjustifiable standard such as race, religion, or other arbitrary classification" [*Bordenkircher v. Hayes*, 434 U.S. 357, at 364 (1978)]. In general, this finding compels the prosecutor to use only legally relevant information when deciding whether or not to prosecute a suspect.

Research on the charging decision has generally concluded that prosecutors attempt to "avoid uncertainty" (Albonetti 1987). What this means is that, if, after the initial screening, prosecutors believe that they can obtain a conviction, they will file charges. On the other hand, if they believe the likelihood of a conviction is low, they will reject the case. In making this determination, several factors come into play.

Legal factors are the primary determinants of the charging decision. For example, the seriousness of the offense (Albonetti 1987; Jacoby, et al. 1982; Mather 1979; Miller 1969; Myers 1982; Rauma 1984; Schmidt and Steury 1989), the strength of evidence in the case (Albonetti 1987; Feeney, et al. 1983; Jacoby, et al. 1982; Miller 1969; Nagel and Hagan 1983), and the culpability of the defendant (Albonetti 1987; Mather 1979; Miller 1969; Schmidt and Steury 1989; Swiggert and Farrell 1976) have been found to influence prosecutors' charging decisions.

In addition to legal factors, many studies have highlighted the importance of victim characteristics (Albonetti 1987; Amir 1971; Hepperle 1985; Kerstetter 1990; Miller 1969; Stanko 1988; Williams 1978). These studies suggest that prosecutors use stereotypes about genuine victims and appropriate behavior (Estrich 1987; Frohmann 1991; LaFree 1989) to predict how judges and juries will react to victims. Prosecutors attribute credibility to victims "who fit society's stereotypes of who is credible: older, white, male, employed victims" (Stanko 1988, 172). Victims who do not fit this image or who engage in "precipatory behavior" (Amir 1971) are deemed less credible. As Stanko (1988, 170) concludes, "the character and credibility of the victim is a key factor in determining prosecutorial strategies, one at least as important as 'objective' evidence about the crime or characteristics of the defendant."

In this chapter, I summarize a number of studies that have examined prosecutorial decision making in sexual assault cases. In addition, I also will briefly discuss rape law reform.

Prosecutorial Decision Making in Sexual Assault Cases

In a widely cited study, LaFree (1989) examines the decisions made by police, prosecutors, judges, and jurors in Indianapolis. He found that the strongest predictors of these decisions were legal factors such as the ability of the victim to identify the suspect, the offense type, and the use of a weapon. Several extralegal variables, however, also were important. Evidence of victim misconduct, the victim's age, the promptness of the victim's report, and the racial composition of the offender-victim dyad influenced decision making. For example, victim misconduct or nonconformity was defined as women who had illegitimate children, who were out alone late at night, were at a bar alone, or were hitchhiking. Cases with victims that fell into one of these categories were less likely to have charges filed, and, if charged, more likely to end in an acquittal. The importance of this is illustrated by a comment made by a prosecutor that LaFree interviewed (1989, 100): "It's tough to try the case if the victim comes across as being loose, or if the victim has frequented bars. Also important is where she was when she was picked up and what time of the night it occurred." He concluded (p. 241) that while decisions in rape cases were affected by the "typifications of rape held by processing agents," they also were "influenced strongly by considerations that most observers would interpret as justified."

Another study examined the processing of sexual assault cases in Chicago. Kerstetter (1990) looked at the prosecutor's decision to file charges against sexual suspects. This decision and the police officer's decision to treat the incident as a crime forms what Kerstetter (1990, 268) refers to as the "gateway to the criminal justice system." As he notes, "these decisions determine which incidents will be taken seriously and which victims will be afforded the full redress of criminal law" (1990, 268). Generally, what happens in Chicago after the police have arrested a suspect, an assistant prosecutor meets with police officers to discuss the case and review the evidence (Kerstetter 1990). They also may interview the victim and offender. Once this is finished, the prosecutor decides whether or not to charge the suspect.

Kerstetter (1990) found that prosecutors were more likely to reject charges in cases where the victims and suspects knew each other. In cases where the victim did not know the suspect, the decision to file charges was positively associated with the victim's willingness to prosecute, and negatively associated with the victim being unable to identify the suspect, the suspects use of a disguise, and a delay in reporting the incident by the victim (Kerstetter 1990). He suggests that, in the prosecutor 's eyes, the reporting delay may be an indicator of the victim's credibility. In other words, the prosecutor knows from previous experience with sexual assault cases that this may cause problems with the case later down the road.

Frohmann (1991) examined case rejection decisions by prosecutors in sexual assault cases. During a 17 month period, she sat in on conversations between detectives and prosecutors regarding the decision about going forward with the case. In addition to this, she also conducted interviews with prosecutors and police detectives to determine how and why they decided not to go forward with the case. Frohmann (1990) made the point that these decisions are made within the organizational context of the prosecutor's office. For example, when a prosecutor makes the decision to charge or not, they always have in the back of their mind that they must maintain a high conviction rate. In addition to the conviction rate for the office, they also need to keep their individual conviction rate high because this indicates that they are proficient at their job and, thus, deserving of promotion. This is not unique to the jurisdiction in her study; most, if not all, prosecutors' offices make decisions about cases with this in mind.

Frohmann indicates that "a central feature of prosecutorial accounts of case rejection is the discrediting of victims' allegations of sexual assault" (1990, 215). Several techniques are used to accomplish this. One is what she refers to as "discrepant accounts." If the victim's accounts of the incident are consistent throughout the criminal justice process, the prosecutor tends to view the victim as credible. On the other hand, if her accounts have "discrepancies," the credibility of the victim is questioned by the prosecutor. In cases such as the latter, the prosecutor may be unwilling to file because, for example, they don't believe the victim's story.

Another method of determining the truthfulness of an allegation of sexual assault is using what Frohmann (1990, 217) refers to as "typifications of rape-relevant behavior." Essentially, what this is referring to is knowledge that has been gained based on their experience as a prosecutor. Put simply, rape victims are expected to act a certain way, and, if they don't, their credibility is called into question. She has several categories of these typifications, all of which have a negative effect on the prosecutor's decision to charge a suspect. The first one she discussed was "typifications of rape scenarios" (Frohmann 1990, 217). What she is referring to here is that prosecutors tend to ascribe certain characteristics to different types of sexual assaults and that they compare these with the victim's version of the rape. If they don't fit a prosecutor's typification, the prosecutor then questions the credibility of the victim's accusation. Another category is "typifications of post-incident interaction." The prosecutors in her study pointed out that the typical behavior after a rape is for the victim and suspect not to see one another. Consequently, when they get a case where the victim voluntarily sees the suspect after the rape has occurred, they immediately question the woman's truthfulness.

The third category is "typifications of rape reporting." The focus here is on the timeliness of the report. The belief here is that if the woman was raped, she will report this to the police very soon after the assault. If the "woman reports 'late,' her motives for reporting and the sincerity of her allegation are questioned if they fall outside the typification of officially recognizable/explainable reasons for late reporting" (Frohmann 1990, 219). A justifiable reason is, for example, getting family support first. The importance of reporting soon after the assault is that, if there are injuries, they will still be visible and corroborate her story. The final category is "typifications of victim's demeanor." The focus here is the ability to "distinguish between behavior that signifies 'lying' versus 'discomfort'" (Frohmann 199, 220). People who are lying, according to the prosecutors interviewed in this study, act a certain way. Yawning a lot or acting nervous during an interview is an indicator of lying. Prosecutors are unwilling to file charges in cases with a victim like this either because they think she is lying or she will make a poor witness at the trial. Frohmann (1990, 224) concludes "that prosecutors are orienting to a 'downstream' concern with convictability."

Another study by Spears and Spohn (1996) focused on the prosecutors' initial decision of whether to file charges. Using a sample of arrests for sexual assault made by the Detroit Police Department in 1989, they tested the hypothesis that charging decisions are affected by prosecutors' stereotypes concerning real rapes and genuine victims. The authors, were particularly interested in the concept of the "genuine victim." Estrich (1987), LaFree (1989) and others suggest that criminal justice decision makers, including prosecutors, use a set of victim characteristics to create an image, not of a *typical* rape victim, but of a *genuine* rape victim. They argue that complainants whose backgrounds and behavior conform to this image will be taken more seriously, and their allegations treated more seriously, than complainants whose backgrounds and behavior are at odds with this image.

They used six factors to create a scale designed to measure the degree to which the victim conforms to the stereotype of a genuine victim. The authors believe that prosecutors ascribe certain characteristics to the genuine victim of a sexual assault. According to Spears and Spohn (1996), prosecutors define the genuine victim as a woman whose moral character is not in question, who did not engage in any type of risk-taking behavior at the time of the incident, who was raped by a stranger, who demonstrated her nonconsent by both screaming and physically resisting her attacker, and who reported the crime to the police immediately. The more closely the victim conforms to this image of the genuine victim, the more likely it is that the prosecutor will decide to file charges.

Their results suggest that victim characteristics, but not evidence factors, affect prosecutors' charging decisions. In fact, the only significant predictors of charging in these types of cases were the age of the victim and the genuine victim scale (Spears and Spohn 1996). Prosecutors in Detroit are much less likely to file charges if the victim is under age 13. They are more likely to file charges if the victim conforms more closely to the image of the genuine victim. In other words, prosecutors believe that the genuine victim of a sexual assault is a woman whose background and behavior conform to traditional gender-role expectations. The more closely the victim conforms to this stereotypical image, the more likely it is she will be viewed as a genuine victim, her assault as a real rape. It's important to note that the *only* factors that influenced the decision to charge were victim characteristics. None of the evidence variables influenced the prosecutor's decision to charge or not. This conflicts with the United States Supreme Court's decision in *Bordenkircher v. Hayes*.

Spohn and Horney (1996) examined the impact of rape law reform on several case processing decisions. The decision to dismiss all charges against the defendant will be discussed here. Once charges are filed, the prosecutor or the defense attorney can motion to have the charges dismissed. The judge then decides whether or not to grant the motion and dismiss the charges. The authors found that charges were less likely to be dismissed when the victim screamed during the attack. They also found that the length of time between the rape and reporting had an influence on the dismissal decision. Spohn and Horney (1996) found that when the victim reported the rape to the police within one hour, charges were less likely to be dismissed. The number of charges also had an influence. The likelihood of charge dismissal was less when the defendant was charged with more than one offense.

A study by Spears and Spohn (1997), looked at the effect of evidence factors and victim characteristics on prosecutors' charging decisions in sexual assault cases. None of the evidence factors had a significant influence on this decision. However, three of the victim characteristics were statistically significant. For example, the victim's moral character influenced the charging decision. Specifically, if the police file contained information about the victim's prior sexual activity with someone other than the suspect, pattern of alcohol and/or drug abuse, prior criminal record, information about alleged prostitution, or history of working as an exotic dancer and/or in a massage parlor, prosecutors were less likely to file charges.

Another variable in the study measured the victim's risk-taking behavior at the time of the incident. Prosecutors were less likely to file charges against the defendant when the police file indicated that the victim was walking alone late at night, was hitch-hiking, was in a bar alone, was using alcohol or drugs, or invited the suspect to her residence (Spears and Spohn 1997). The age of the victim also had a statistically significant effect of the prosecutor's charging decision. When the victim was younger than 13, prosecutors were less likely to file charges against the defendant. Previous research has demonstrated that sexual assault cases involving children are more difficult to prosecute. This reflects the fact that children may be unable to articulate what happened to them. It also reflects the fact that children who allege that they have been sexually assaulted are regarded as more impressionable and thus as less credible than older victims. The authors suggest that these factors, coupled with concerns about the psychological impact of testifying at trial, apparently affect prosecutors' assessments of convictability and produce a higher rejection rate for cases with child victims (Spears and Spohn 1997).

In a continuation of her research discussed above, Frohmann (1997) discovered another method used by prosecutors to justify case rejection in sexual assault cases. She refers to this as the "construction of discordant locales." Essentially, she argues that "discordant locales are prosecutors' categorizations of places and people associated with them that they encounter in the work of case prosecution" (1997). In other words, certain places have a certain type of person that resides there and from this, the prosecutor makes an assessment about the person's moral character. For example, victims and potential jurors often come from different areas of the city. This causes a problem for prosecutors because it "may lead to misinterpretations by jurors of victims that would result in 'not guilty' verdicts if cases were forwarded." Consequently, prosecutors use this as a reason to reject the case.

A final study, (Spohn, Beichner, and Davis-Frenzel 2001), replicated and extended the works of Frohmann discussed above. Using data from Miami, they examined the prosecutor's decision to reject sexual assault cases. The authors point out that, in Miami, the prosecutor provides a summary of the disposition of each case. This "closeout memorandum" was reviewed to determine the reasons given by the prosecutor for rejecting the case (2001). In addition to this, Spohn also interviewed several prosecutors that were assigned to the Dade County State's Attorney's Office. This is important because it provided the authors with an additional source of information to supplement the information obtained in the closeout memorandum.

They found that approximately 41 percent of the sexual assault cases were rejected by the State's Attorney. They found that prosecutors rejected charges for the following reasons: the victim did not come to the pre-file interview or they could not locate them, the victim did not cooperate or she asked that the case not be prosecuted, the victim recanted her testimony, there were inconsistencies in the victim's story, or the prosecutor believed that the victim was lying (Spohn, Beichner, and Davis-Frenzel 2001). The authors concluded that, similar to Frohmann's (1990) study, Miami prosecutors look at the case closely to determine if there are problems that will affect their ability to obtain a conviction. With the exception of two cases, every case that was prosecuted ended in a conviction. Clearly, they are proficient at predicting which cases will result in a conviction.

Prosecutorial Decision Making in Sexual Assault Cases: A Summary and Discussion

From the information presented above one can see that American prosecutors have extraordinary discretionary powers. In general, prior research indicates that, at the initial screening stage, prosecutors attempt to avoid uncertainty. If a prosecutor believes that he/she will be able to obtain a conviction, he/she is more likely to file charges against the suspect in question. As noted above, the likelihood of filing a charge is determined primarily legal factors. Extralegal factors, however, also play a role. Moreover, in sexual assault cases, victim characteristics seem to play a pivotal role. Prosecutors sometimes consider victim misconduct, the relationship between the victim and the suspect, the credibility of the victim, age of the victim, promptness of her report, and her behavior at the time of the incident.

These findings suggest that criminal justice officials do not treat all rapes the same (Bohmer 1974; Estrich 1987; Griffin 1977; Ireland 1978; Williams 1984). They suggest that case outcomes are affected by stereotypes about rape and rape victims and that only "real rapes" with "genuine victims" will be taken seriously. Estrich (1987, 28), for example, suggests that criminal justice officials differentiate between the "aggravated, jump-from-the-bushes stranger rapes and the simple cases of unarmed rape by friends, neighbors, and acquaintances." There are several reasons that might explain why this happens.

For example, prosecutors are part of an organization—the office of the prosecutor. Every prosecutor's office wants a record that reflects a high conviction rate. First of all, the chief prosecutor needs this to demonstrate to the public that he/she is doing a good job. If they can do this, their likelihood of being reelected is increased. Another reason, is that each prosecutor also wants a high conviction rate. As mentioned above, this demonstrates to their supervisor that they are proficient at their job, which, in turn, influences their likelihood of getting a raise or getting promoted. If there is so much of a focus on conviction rates, it's not surprising that prosecutors are reluctant to go forward with a case that, in their mind, won't result in a conviction. In addition, they also realize that the office has limited resources available to prosecute cases, and, thus, are reluctant to use these resources on a case that can't be won.

As Frohmann (1990, 224) notes, "prosecutors are orienting to a 'downstream' concern with convictability." They are making a prediction about how judges and juries will react to victims. Research provides support for this. For example, research has found that some prosecutors' offices use a trial sufficiency policy in determining whether or not to go forward with the case. According to Jacoby (1980), prosecutors using this policy regard the screening and charging decisions as the most critical decisions in the office. Here, the prosecutor will only file charges if he/she believes that the case could be won before a jury. The prosecutor will refuse to file charges if he/she feels that the case will not result in a conviction if it were to go to trial. As previously discussed, prosecutors who do not file because a jury conviction is unlikely are "avoiding uncertainty." If, after the initial screening, a prosecutor is not certain that he/she can obtain a conviction at a jury trial, the case is likely to be rejected for prosecution (Albonetti 1987).

One source of uncertainty that seems to be consistently mentioned in the research is the credibility of the victim. According to many prosecutors, a "stand-up" victim is an essential element of a strong case (Stanko 1988). Stanko defines this as a person whom a judge and/or jury would consider credible and undeserving of victimization. One of the district attorneys interviewed by Stanko, discussing a case involving an elderly female robbery victim, stated, "Any case that has a stand-up complainant should be indicted. You put her on the stand—the judge loves her, the jury loves her—dynamite complainant!" (Stanko 1988, 174).

In attempting to assess a victim's credibility, prosecutors tend to rely on stereotypes about the behavior of certain types of people (Myers 1991). For example, most prosecutors feel that students are law-abiding citizens, and thus will be considered credible by judges and/or jurors (Stanko 1988). LaFree (1989) asserts that nontraditional women, or women who engage in some type of "risk-taking" behavior are less likely to be viewed as genuine victims who are deserving of protection under the law. Estrich (1987) similarly argues that only certain types of sexual assaults will be regarded as "real rapes" with "genuine victims."

A study by Reskin and Visher (1986) provides support for practice of prosecutors making predictions about how juries may react to victims focused on jury decision making. Reskin and Visher (1986) interviewed the jurors from sexual assault trials in Indianapolis. They asked these jurors if they believed that the defendant was guilty or innocent. They also asked them if their decisions were affected by the evidence in the case and by their perceptions of the victim's and defendant's personal characteristics. The results of the study indicated that extralegal variables had a significant effect on jurors' verdicts. For example, the jurors' verdicts were affected by their personal evaluation of the victim's moral character and by their beliefs that the victim exercised poor judgment at the time of the assault.

Reskin and Visher (1986) also determined, however, that the influence of these extralegal factors varied by the strength of the evidence in the case. They found that all five of the extralegal variables they examined influenced jurors' verdicts in cases with weak evidence, but only one influenced the verdicts in cases with strong evidence. They concluded that their results provided support for Kalven and Zeisel's (1966) "liberation hypothesis"—that is, that jury nullification is most likely to occur when evidence is weak.

The fact that prosecutors' assessments of convictability accurately reflect jurors' perceptions and beliefs does not, of course, justify consideration of extralegal victim characteristics at screening. Prosecutors have an ethical obligation to file charges if they believe that the suspect committed the crime in question. The fact that the victim of a sexual assault engaged in "risk-taking behavior," does not act like the typical rape victim, or goes to bars by herself should be irrelevant. The fact that they are not irrelevant, but play an important role in the decision to charge or not, suggests that Estrich (1986) was correct when she asserted that only "real rapes" with "genuine victims" will be taken seriously by criminal justice officials.

Rape Law Reform

As you can see from the above discussion, the victim is often the focus when the case involves a sexual assault. More to the point, many have argued that the victim is the one on trial, not the perpetrator of the assault. As Spohn and Horney (1992, 17–18) note:

> Feminists, social scientists, and legal scholars questioned the laws focus on the character and behavior of the victim rather than on the offender. They criticized rules of evidence that required corroboration of the victim's testimony, and that allowed evidence of the victim's past sexual conduct to be admitted at trial. They also criticized common-law definitions of rape that excluded male and spouses as victims and that excluded acts other than sexual intercourse.

As a result, all 50 states have enacted some type of rape law reform (Kennedy and Sacco 1998). In this section, I will discuss these reforms and examine their impact on the criminal justice system.

The definition of rape has changed significantly. Most states used the common law definition of rape which defined it as the carnal knowledge of a female, not one's wife, forcibly and against her will (Doerner and Lab 2002; Spohn and Horney 1992). Immediately, one can see the problems with this definition. Firstly, it only includes women as victims. Wives are excluded as potential victims. It also requires that the offender use force. In addition, carnal knowledge means penile-vaginal penetration, which means it excludes all other sexual acts (Spohn and Horney 1992). States have made several changes to this traditional definition.

For example, many states have changed the terminology. Many states have replaced "rape" with, for example, "criminal sexual conduct," "sexual assault," "deviate sexual intercourse," and "sexual battery" (Doerner and Lab 2002; Reidel and Welsh 2002; Spohn and Horney 1992). In addition to changes in terminology, many states eliminated the spousal exemption. The basis of the exemption lies in the assumption "that the marriage vows provide an irretractable contractual arrangement to deliver exclusive sexual services upon demand" (Doerner and Lab 2002, 111). Put simply, the wife is seen as the husbands sexual property to do with as he sees fit. Several states continue to include this exemption. For instance, some grant the husband "absolute exemption," which means husbands can't be charged with raping their wives under any circumstances. Others only allow a "partial exemption." In this case, charging is allowed if, for example, they are in the process of getting a divorce or they are separated.

Another definitional change included expanding the types of behavior that would be defined as sexual assault. Some states now define penetration, in addition to sexual intercourse, as "cunnilingus, fellatio, anal intercourse, or any other intrusion, however slight, of any part of a persons body or of any object into the genital or anal opening of another person's body" (Spohn and Horney 1992, 22). In addition the above, most states also made their sexual assault statutes gender-neutral. This meant that males could now be victims and females could be offenders.

Under common law, it was rape only if the woman did not consent. In other words, she was required to prove that she resisted the perpetrator. Moreover, to prove nonconsent, some statutes specifically stated the woman must "resist to her utmost" (Horney and Spohn 1991). If she didn't, it wasn't legally rape. Now, many states have either eliminated or modified the resistance requirement. For instance, Pennsylvania law specifically states that the victim does not have to resist at all (Spohn and Horney 1992). Others, identified specific circumstances (e.g., use of a weapon) that would constitute nonconsent.

Related to the requirement of nonconsent, was the corroboration requirement. Most laws did not allow a sexual assault defendant to be convicted without corroborative evidence (Horney and Spohn 1991). One rational for this requirement was the argument that some women make false allegations of rape to retaliate against an ex-boyfriend or some other man. In short, states were reluctant to prosecute a man for rape, when the *only* evidence against him was the woman's word.

A final reform was the enactment of rape shield laws. As Doerner and Lab (2002, 134) note:

> A common tactic that many aggressive defense attorneys invoked was to attack the victim's credibility by making an issue of her sexual past. A typical strategy was to imply promiscuity from prior sexual activity with men other than the defendant. Presumably, this information suggested a lack of chastity and, therefore, amply proved the victim's willingness to engage in sexual activity without any reliance on force.

Consequently, many victims of sexual assault were reluctant to report their assault for fear that they would be victimized a second time by the criminal justice system. Now, in the more than 45 states with rape shield laws (Riedel and Welsh 2002), there have been restrictions placed on this type of evidence. Some are very strict and prohibit evidence of this nature, while others are more lenient and allow it under some circumstances.

Impact of Rape Law Reform

At the most basic level, the overall purpose of rape law reform was to "encourage" the criminal justice system to treat rape like any other crime (i.e., focusing on the offender's behavior and not the victim's) (Horney and Spohn

1991). In addition, reformers had several instrumental goals in mind. For example, criminal justice officials would reduce their reliance on victim characteristics when making decisions. This, in turn, would lead to increased reporting by victims. There also was the hope that the reforms would increase the likelihood of arrest, prosecution, and conviction of sex offenders (Spohn and Horney 1992). The studies that have examined the impact of these reforms have yielded mixed results.

An early study of Washington state found that prosecutors did not change the way they evaluated the likelihood of conviction (Loh 1980). Marsh and her colleagues (1982), examined the 1974 Michigan law. This law is considered to be the most comprehensive reform of rape law in the country (Spohn and Horney 1992). They found that arrests for rape increased as did the number of convictions. However, it did not affect the number of reported rapes. Research in California did find some changes. For example, Polk (1985) found an increase in the number a felony complaints that prosecutors filed, but there was no change in the number of convictions.

All of the previous studies examined only one jurisdiction, which limits the generalizability of the results. Spohn and Horney's (1992) study addressed this problem. Their multijurisdictional study examined the impact of rape law reform in six jurisdictions. Overall, in most of the jurisdictions they studied, the reforms did not have an impact. They did find an increase in reporting in two of the jurisdictions and an increase in indictments in one of the jurisdictions.

Interviews with criminal justice officials in each of the jurisdictions did provide some additional insight into the effect of reforms. For instance, they did find that officials in each of the jurisdictions studied supported the reforms. The officials also believed that the reforms had a positive influence on how the criminal justice system treats rape victims. On the other hand, decision makers in every jurisdiction "still believe that resistance by the victim and corroboration of her testimony are important determinants of whether a rape case will result in a conviction" (Spohn and Horney 1992, 159). They also found that criminal justice officials believe prior sexual contact with the offender, despite rape shield laws, will be allowed. Spohn and Horney pointed out that they were not surprised with their findings. Research has consistently demonstrated the effectiveness of the criminal court system's ability to work around reforms.

Conclusion

Within the criminal justice system, the crime of rape is unique. It's the one crime that forces victims to convince criminal justice officials that they were assaulted and did nothing to contribute to it. No other crime requires the victim to do this. It's argued the system is, in effect, victimizing them a second time.

Feminists contend that legally irrelevant victim characteristics influence decision making in sexual assault cases. They argue that criminal justice officials, using stereotypes of real rapes and genuine victims, base their decisions on the victim's background and reputation, the victim's relationship to the accused, and the victim's behavior at the time of the incident. They argue, in other words, that in a rape case the focus shifts from the offender to the victim. The research on prosecutorial decision making discussed in this chapter confirms this.

At least in sexual assault cases, victim characteristics are an important source of uncertainty. Prosecutorial decision making in these types of cases is influenced by stereotypes of rape and rape victims—only real rapes with genuine victims will be taken seriously. This is a cause for concern. As LaFree (1989, 239) noted, "if women who violate traditional gender roles and are raped are unable to obtain justice through the legal system, then the law is serving as an institutional arrangement that reinforces women's gender-role conformity."

References

Albonetti, C. "Prosecutorial Discretion: The Effects of Uncertainty." *Law and Society Review* 21, (1987) :291–313.

Amir, M. *Patterns in Forcible Rape.* Chicago: University of Chicago Press, 1971.

Bohmer, C. "Judicial Attitudes Toward Rape Victims." *Judicature* 57, (1974): 303–307.

Boland, B. *The Prosecution of Felony Arrests.* Washington, D.C.: Bureau of Justice Statistics, 1983.

Bordenkircher v. Hayes 434 U.S. 357, 364 (1978)

Brosi, K. *A Cross-City Comparison of Felony Case Processing.* Washington, D.C.: Institute for Law and Social Research, 1979.

Davis, K. *Discretionary Justice.* Baton Rouge, LA: Louisiana State University Press, 1969.

Doerner, W. and S. Lab. *Victimology.* Cincinnati, OH: Anderson Publishing, 2002.

Estrich, S. *Real Rape.* Cambridge, MA: Harvard University Press, 1987.

Feeney, F., F. Dill, and A. Weir. *Arrests Without Conviction: How Often They Occur and Why*. Washington, DC: Department of Justice, National Institute of Justice, 1983.

Frohmann, L. "Discrediting Victims' Allegations of Sexual Assault: Prosecutorial Accounts of Case Rejections." *Social Problems* 38, (1991): 213–226.

Frohmann, L. "Convictability and Discordant Locales: Reproducing Race, Class, and Gender Ideologies in Prosecutorial Decisionmaking." *Law & Society Review* 31, (1997): 531–556.

Griffin, S. "Rape: The All-American Crime." In *Forcible Rape: The Crime, the Victim and the Offender*, eds. D. Chappell, R. Geis and G. Geis. New York: Columbia University Press, 1977.

Hepperle, W. "Women Victims in The Criminal Justice System." In *The changing Role of Women in the Criminal Justice System*, ed. I. Moyer. Prospect Heights, IL: Waveland Press Inc, 1985.

Horney, J. and C. Spohn. "Rape Law Reform and Instrumental Change in Six Urban Jurisdictions." *Law & Society Review* 25, (1991): 117–153.

Ireland, M. "Rape Reform Legislation: A New Standard of Sexual Responsibility." *University of Colorado Law Review* 49 (1978): 185–204.

Jacoby, J. *The American Prosecutor: A Search for Identity*. Toronto: D.C. Heath and Company, 1980.

Jacoby, J., L. Mellon, E. Ratledge, and S. Turner. *Prosecutorial Decision Making: A National* Study. Washington, DC: U.S. Department of Justice, National Institute of Justice, 1982.

Kalven, H. and H. Zeisel. *The American Jury*. Boston: Little, Brown and Company, 1966.

Kennedy, L. and V. Sacco. *Crime Victims in Context*. Los Angeles: Roxbury Publishing Company, 1998.

Kerstetter, W. "Gateway to Justice: Police and Prosecutorial Response to Sexual Assaults Against Women." *Criminology* 81, (1990): 267–313.

LaFree, G. *Rape and Criminal Justice: The Social Construction of Sexual Assault*. Belmont, CA: Wadsworth, 1989.

Loh, W. "The Impact of Common Law and Reform Rape Statues on Prosecution: An Empirical Study." *Washington Law Review* 55 (1980): 543–625.

Marsh, J.C., A. Geist, and N. Caplan. *Rape and the Limits of Law Reform*. Boston: Auburn House, 1982.

Mather, L. *Plea Bargaining or Trial?* Lexington, MA: Heath, 1979.

Miller, F. *Prosecution: The Decision to Charge a Suspect with a Crime.* Boston: Little, Brown and Company, 1969.

Myers, M. "Common Law in Action: The Prosecution of Felonies and Misdemeanors." *Sociological Inquiry* 52, (1982): 1–15.

Myers, M. "The Courts: Prosecution and Sentencing." In *Criminology*, ed. J. Sheley. Belmont, CA: Wadsworth Inc, 1991.

Nagel, H. and J. Hagan. "Gender and Crime: Offense Patterns and Criminal Court Sanctions." In *Crime and Justice: An Annual Review of Research, Vol. 4*, eds M. Tonry and N. Morris. Chicago: University of Chicago Press, 1983.

Polk, K. "Rape Law Reform and Criminal Justice Processing." *Crime & Delinquency* 31, (1985): 191–205.

Rauma, D. "Going for the Gold: Prosecutorial Decision Making in Cases of Wife Assault." *Social Science Research* 13, (1984): 321–351.

Reaves, B. *Felony Defendants in Large Urban Counties, 1998.* Washington, D.C.: U.S. Department of Justice, 2001.

Reskin, B. and C. Visher. "The Impacts of Evidence and Extralegal Factors in Jurors' Decisions." *Law and Society Review* 20, (1986): 423–438.

Riedel, M. and W. Welsh. *Criminal Violence: Patterns, Causes, and Prevention.* Los Angeles: Roxbury Publishing Company, 2002.

Schmidt, J. and E. Steury. "Prosecutorial Discretion in Filing Charges in Domestic Violence Cases." *Criminology* 27, 1989: 487–510.

Spears, J. and C. Spohn. "The Genuine Victim and Prosecutors' Charging Decisions in Sexual Assault Cases." *American Journal of Criminal Justice* 20, (1996): 183–205.

Spears, J. and C. Spohn. "The Effect of Evidence Factors and Victim Characteristics on Prosecutors' Charging Decisions in Sexual Assault Cases." *Justice Quarterly* 14, (1997): 501–524.

Spohn, C., D. Beichner, and E. Davis-Frenzel. "Prosecutorial Justifications for Sexual Assault Case Rejection: Guarding the 'Gateway to Justice.'" *Social Problems* 48, (2001): 206

Spohn, C., and J. Horney. *Rape Law Reform: A Grassroots Revolution and Its Impact.* New York: Plenum Press, 1992.

Spohn, C., and J. Horney. "The Influence of Blame and Believability Factors on the Processing of Simple Versus Aggravated Rape Cases." *Criminology* 34, (1996): 135–161.

Stanko, E. "The Impact of Victim Assessment on Prosecutors' Screening Decisions: The Case of the New York County District Attorney's Office." In *Criminal Justice: Law and Politics*, ed G. Cole. Pacific Grove, CA: Brooks/Cole, 1988.

Swiggert, V. and R. Farrell. *Murder, Inequality, and the Law*. Lexington, MA: D.C. Heath.

Williams, K. *The Role of the Victim in the Prosecution of Violent Offenses*. Institute for Law and Social Research. Washington, D.C.: U.S. Government Printing Office, 1978.

Williams, S. "Rape Reform Legislation and Evidentiary Concerns: The Law in Pennsylvania." *University of Pittsburgh Law Review* 44, (1984): 955–975.

In the Words of a Prosecutor

As a sex crimes prosecutor, I spent 100% of my time prosecuting cases involving sexual abuse, child abuse and neglect; and kidnapping, harassment and stalking cases. For about 18 months, the victims in my cases were under the age of 14. For the remaining 2½ years, I handled cases involving "adults"—victims 14 and over.

The most challenging aspects of my work as a sex crimes prosecutor…

As a practical matter, it's a challenge to talk to strangers about the intimate details of sexual assault(s). When I started in the unit, I didn't have children and wasn't often around children so it was especially difficult to initially talk to the first several child victims. You have to be able to use the proper anatomical terms as comfortably as if you were discussing any other subject when you speak to colleagues about filing decisions or plea offer suggestions. On the other hand, you have to be able to go with the flow and use the terms your victim is comfortable with (some silly and some vulgar).

On a different level, sex crimes is challenging because of the way it can insidiously creep into your personal life. Before I worked in sex crimes, I would see kids getting off the school bus and imagine those kids running into the house greeted by a hug and anxious to talk about their day. After sex crimes, I worried that every single one of those kids dreaded going in that house because they knew they were going to be molested by someone in their house before mom got home from work. Before this assignment, I knew logically that all children obviously lose their innocence at some point, but I never thought about it happening when they were as young as 3 or 4 or 5 years old and in such horrifically creative ways.

It takes a certain personality to have longevity as a sex crimes prosecutor. Some of my colleagues say they can do it because they don't get sad when they hear about cases—they get angry primarily. Others have said that they don't picture the case happening when they read about them—it's just words to them and that helps avoid being as empathetic and affected. I didn't have the luxury of either of these characteristics. In fact, I do picture things when I read about them. The thing that finally drove me from the unit was once I had children. I substituted their faces for the kids I was reading about because that's what I know, it's my personal experience, and I think there's a natural tendency to do that psychologically when you're reading something you've never experienced. So in my mind, trying to understand what happened so that I could charge cases and plead cases, my two kids had been abused and neglected over and over and over again.

I think registration laws for sexual offenders are a benefit to the community in terms of being perceived by the offenders as a serious punishment. Practically speaking, however, I don't think that most people would have any idea if 10 sex offenders were living next door (until it was too late), despite the registry.It's impossible to draft the registration law without at times including people that you may not feel need to be included while at the same time making sure you've covered everyone you're certain needs to register.

It seems like it wouldn't be a crazy idea to allow certain classes of sex offenders (youthful probationers for first-time low-grade offenses) to petition to be relieved of the registration requirement after a lengthy period given no probation violations. The lifetime requirement seems very burdensome for some cases.

I think the system does about as much as it can with available resources to accommodate the needs of sex crimes victims. We have victim advocates available, we attempt to keep victims apprised of the status of the case (court dates, plea offers, etc) and we try to coordinate with other agencies. With more funding, we could certainly do more.

The greatest hope for improving the CJS with respect to offenders would be to deal directly with the legislature. Sex crimes statutes change often and sometimes the result is inconsistencies that hinder the prosecutor's ability to adequately deal with certain cases. For example, in Missouri there are several offenses which aren't eligible for 120 day program—shock time in the Department of Corrections prior to possible probation. As a result, the only options in those cases are straight probation or 5-10 year minimum sentences. Those aren't fair choices for the prosecutor of the Court so a lot of cases get amended or end up with probation when they should have something more. I don't think it's a good idea to take away prosecutorial discretion in an area of crime in which cases are so unique and truly need to be dealt with on a case-by-case basis.

A.D.
Prosecutor for 5 years
Over 4 years in a Sex Crimes Unit

Chapter 17

Sex Offender Treatment: An Overview

Gregg Dwyer, M.D., Ed. D., and
Deborah Laufersweiler-Dwyer, Ph.D.

Introduction

This chapter provides a cross section of recent literature about sex offender treatment. Goals, actual approaches, and analysis of results are presented. As an overview, the content of this chapter was selected to provide readers with both an introduction to the field of sex offender treatment and to identify a variety of resources for more in-depth exploration of specific topics. The articles reviewed were chosen to offer a wide view of the relevant literature from approximately the last twenty-years with particular focus on the last ten years, while at least mentioning points of historical interest. The twenty-year limit was not strictly enforced given that there were older studies that provide valuable insight into how we have arrived at the present state of offender treatment. Additionally, some forms of treatment are no longer routinely used, if at all, so more dated works had to be included in order to adequately address the field.

Definitions

Review and comparison of the literature regarding sex offender treatment can be problematic due to the disparity in definitions of terms. What defines a "sex offender"? Must the person so labeled be arrested and/or convicted or can a self-admission without legal system involvement be included? Should such a label be used for persons who were under the influence of a substance, psychotic or demented at the time of the offense? It appears that the answers to these questions vary with the authors presenting the data. For example, Burdon and Gallagher (2002) made a distinction between "legal sex offenders", defined as persons convicted of illegal sexual activity, and "clinical sex offenders", defined as persons who had a paraphilic disorder that could be clinically diagnosed, regardless of their legal status relative to commission of a criminal act. Debating the merits of how best to define what constitutes a sex offense and a sex offender is beyond the scope of this chapter. Consequently, for the purposes of this chapter, the following definitions are used. "Sexual behavior" is that behavior which causes or is intended to cause sexual arousal and/or gratification by one or more of the parties involved and/or involves genitalia and/or other erogenous zones of the body regardless of the physiologic or emotion goal or result. "Criminal sexual behavior" is used to refer to sexual activities that can result in criminal charges based on local, state or federal criminal statute(s). When particular authors are cited, their definition of offenders and offenses are used to maintain the integrity of their findings and suggestions.

Treatment Goals

Ultimately, the obvious goal would be to prevent an offender from re-offending. You could even take that ideal a step further and prevent the first sex offense, but this overview is focused on the treatment of those who have already offended at least once. The goals of treatment have varied over time from simply terminating unwanted behavior to encouraging what is considered normal behavior (Crolley, et al. 1998). Hall (1995) listed the ideal goal of psychological treatments as elimination of recidivism because of the tremendous gravity of the impact of even just one sexually aggressive act. If possible, the goal of treatment would be to eliminate the criminal sexual fantasies, desires and actions, while leaving acceptable sexual activity intact (APA 1999; Bradford 1999; Berlin 1983). Other approaches have as their premise that criminal sexual behavior is experienced by the perpetrator as incongruent with his/her desires in much the same way obsessive-compulsive behavior is viewed (APA 1999; Stein, et al. 1992). In this case, the target treatment effect would be to eliminate the incongruent thoughts and behavior while leaving the acceptable ones. A goal of treating paraphilias has been to eliminate the unwanted sexual desires and to create acceptable ones (Bradford 1998).

Unfortunately, such selective methods are not always readily available or practical. According to Berlin and Krout (1986), "sexual desires" are not easily changed after they are established.

As Berlin et al. (1997) stated, the first step in treatment is determining the cause of the offending behavior. As an example, they reported multiple potential psychiatric diagnoses that could contribute to the crime of rape, to include a personality disorder or disorder traits, mental retardation, substance abuse, psychosis, and paraphilic disorder (Berlin, et al. 1997). Berlin and Krout (1986) also illustrated this point by listing the following as potential causes for pedophilic behavior: psychosis, "poor judgment", lack of conscious, low intelligence, intoxication, pedophilic orientation and a combination of any of the aforementioned. Berlin and Schaerf (1985) stated that sex offences can be the result of schizophrenia, mania or dementia, all of which would require very different treatments, despite an apparently similar behavior. Clearly, different treatment modalities would be warranted depending on which one or several diagnoses applied for any given offender. Obviously, offenders can have multiple diagnoses, which may or may not be causative or mediating factors in their sexual offending.

Raymond, et al. (1999) reported that given the intensity of treatment programs, such as cognitive behavioral, comorbid psychiatric diagnosis should be identified and addressed to facilitate offenders' success in treatment. In their study of pedophiles, Raymond et al. (1999) found multiple other disorders, with mood and anxiety categories predominating, which they speculated might explain reports of poor attention, low motivation and denial. Certainly, offenders should receive a comprehensive evaluation to identify not only offending related factors, but other factors which might impact on treatment success.

Approaches

Although possibly an artificial dichotomy, treatment is often divided into two broad categories when addressed in the literature: biological and psychological. This division is artificial in that there is no clear division between the biological and psychological workings of the brain. In this context, biological is used merely to refer to the use of some chemical or physical intervention that changes the chemistry or anatomy of the offender in a measurable way. Psychological refers then to methods that don't physically invade the person being treated.

There can be, and is overlap of the two in actual treatment settings, but the primary focus of each approach can generally be labeled as one or the other.

In addition, programs can use a combination of both in their treatment of offenders. For ease of explanation and review, these two categories will be used for the remainder of this chapter.

Biological

Some biological approaches are based on the notion of reducing the sex drive, a biological function, and subsequently, in theory, criminal sexual behavior. Such an approach can decrease or eliminate all sexual drive. A long standing approach to reducing sexual offending has been to reduce the sex drive (Bradford 1999).

Biological approaches can be further divided into pharmacological and surgical approaches. The use of pharmacology (medications) is certainly the most prevalent of the two currently. For completeness sake, both are addressed herein. Specific dosing of pharmacological agents and details of surgical techniques are beyond the scope of this chapter and therefore not included, but such information is readily available in the literature for those seeking more specific detail.

Pharmacological

The use of pharmacology is currently the primary biological approach to treatment. It includes the use of antiandrogens, hormonal agents and other medications aimed at reducing sexual behavior. Androgens are naturally occurring substances, to include testosterone, associated with male sexual characteristics and sex organ activity (Dirckx 1997). Berlin and Schaerf (1985) stated that abnormalities in the androgen hormone system could result in abnormal sexual desires or problems with controlling sexual behavior. Reduction in levels of testosterone has been associated with reduced libido (Berlin and Krout 1986).

Antiandrogens. Antiandrogens are used to reduce the amount of natural androgens available at their target sites in the body (APA 1999; Freund 1980) or to block their action (Freund 1980). Antiandrogens that have been used for sex offender treatment include cyproterone (APA 1999; Berlin 1983; Freund 1980; Bancroft, et al. 1974), cyproterone acetate (APA 1999; Bradford 1998; Freund 1980; Bancroft, et al. 1974) and flutamide (APA 1999). Cyproterone acetate (CPA) is actually more than just an antiandrogen; it also has antigonadotropic (complete effect only in females) and progestational effects (APA 1999). Antigonadotropic means that the substance blocks the action of a gonadatropin, which is a hormone that can facilitate the growth and activity of gonads, the testes and ovaries (Dirckx 1997). The end results of antiandrogen actions include reductions of sperm synthesis, ejaculation, and erections and a reduction, to complete cessation, of sexual fantasies (APA 1999). CPA can cause major side effects, but these are generally not found at the dosage levels typical for treatment of sexual behavior (APA 1999). Side effects have included gynecomastia (enlarged breast tissue), fatigue, transient depression, weight gain, body hair reduction, increased scalp hair, hypersomnia, and decreased sebaceous (oil) gland secretions (APA 1999). The APA (1999) cites studies to support the idea that CPA use can be stopped after a period from three to twelve months without recidivism, but not for all offenders.

Flutamide, a non-steroid antiandrogen, is primarily used to treat prostate cancer (APA 1999). It has been noted that it can be used to reduce testosterone levels in treatment of persons with paraphilias (Bradford 1998).

Hormones. Hormonal agents, to include medroxyprogesterone acetate (APA 1999; Bradford 1998; Freund 1980), gonadotropin-releasing hormone agonists (APA 1999; Bradford 1998), leuteinizing hormone-releasing hormones (LH-RHs) and butyrophenone cause reduction of sexual drive (APA 1999). Estrogens were also used in the past to decrease male sex drive (Freund 1980; Bancroft, et al. 1974), but have been replaced by progesterone based medications (Freund 1980).

Medroxyprogesterone acetate (MPA), trade name Depo-Provera, has been cited as an appropriate medication to reduce sexual desire/arousal (Burdon and Gallagher 2002; Holmes 2002; Miethe 2001; Bradford 1998; Allison and Wrightsman 1993). MPA is a synthetic progestin (Berlin and Schaerf 1985). It increases the activity of testosterone-A-reductase, which breaks down testosterone (APA 1999), thus reducing testosterone levels in the blood (Holmes 2002; Miethe 2001; APA 1999; Berlin 1989; Berlin and Krout 1986; Berlin and Schaerf 1985) and, in theory, sexual aggression (Holmes 2002; Miethe 2001). MPA is also an antigonadotropic and it interferes with testosterone's ability to bind to testosterone-binding globulin in the blood (APA 1999). Side effects beyond the desired reduction of sex drive, sexual fantasies and sexual activity, can include lethargy, hypertension, (Berlin and Krout 1986; Berlin and Shaerf 1985), weight gain (APA 1999; Berlin and Krout 1986; Berlin and Shaerf 1985; Gagné 1981), headaches (APA 1999; Berlin and Krout 1986; Gagné 1981) decreased sperm synthesis, interference with gallbladder and gastrointestinal functioning, and increased insulin reaction to glucose (APA 1999).

As Berlin and Krout (1986) stated with regards to pedophiles, the use of MPA is to aid the offender in controlling acting on sexual desire for children and has no effect on the actual desire itself. It was been stated that sexual desire, regardless of the focus, is not exclusively a psychological decision that can not be changed merely through choosing to do so (Berlin 1989; Berlin and

Schaerf 1985). In this way it is viewed as a natural drive that requires biological intervention to control (Berlin 1989). Berlin (1989) compared MPA's ability to reduce the desires for, and repeated thoughts of, inappropriate sexual activity of some persons with paraphilias to the ability of food to reduce the desire for and thoughts of eating. Such a comparison certainly illustrates the difficulty in reducing recidivism for that population. Based on recidivism data, it doesn't work for everyone (Berlin and Schaerf 1985) and tends to be helpful only for voluntary users (Berlin 1997). Consider the implication of this observation for the idea of mandatory treatment programs. Additionally, it has been recommended for offenders whose sexual desires are not normal (Berlin and Krout 1986; Berlin 1997). It also shouldn't be viewed as a cure, but rather as one tool to help control behavior and then only while being taken by the offender (Berlin and Schaerf 1985). It is considered a component of a treatment plan, which should also include ongoing group therapy on a regular basis to be successful (Berlin and Shaerf 1985). Gagné (1981) also recommended that it be used in conjunction with counseling. As with any medication, the chance of discontinuation is always present and like other chronic conditions, the return of symptoms must be considered.

Butyrophenone, medication trade name Benperidol, a phenothiazine, has been found to reduce sexual drive (APA 1999; Bancroft, et al. 1974; Tennent 1974). The Tennent (1974), study indicated that although benperidol appeared to reduce the frequency of a subject's sexual thinking, it would be less beneficial in reducing sexual behavior. Noted side effects include drowsiness, dyskinesia, blurred vision, photosensitivity, dry mouth, and reduced exercise tolerance (Tennent, et al. 1974).

It has been reported that LH-RH medications, such as LH-RH ethylamide, warrant the label of "pharmacological castration" (APA 1999), a term Berlin (1997) considers inappropriate for medications used to reduce sex drive. They work by interfering with the hypothalamic-pituitary axis, thus blocking the secretion of gonadotropins (APA 1999). Use of LH-RH ethylamide has resulted in reduced sexual desire, sexual intercourse, fully rigid erections, and morning erections with minimal side effects (APA 1999).

The medication Triptorelin, a gonadotropin-releasing hormone agonist (GnRHa), has also been used in conjunction with CPA to reduce criminal sexual behavior (APA 1999). Rosler and Witztum (1998) reported a decrease in "deviant sexual fantasies and desires" and abnormal sexual behavior with use of triptorelin. They suggested that a combination of continuous triptorelin and supportive psychotherapy might successfully treat male paraphilias (Rosler and Witztum 1998). Again, we note the combination of a medication and some form of psychotherapy.

Other. Most antipsychotic medications, neuroleptics, have a dampening effect on sex drive by some, however it is not yet a fully understood mechanism (APA 1999). They are not used as a first line treatment for sex offenders, unless they are being used to treat a psychotic disorder or psychosis symptoms (APA 1999). Sexual offending by persons with psychotic symptoms is more likely to be the result of the psychotic process causing reduced inhibitions rather than a primary sexual behavior, unless present before the psychosis (APA 1999). This speaks to the point of treating the actual diagnosis rather than just trying to address the symptoms, despite the natural draw to do so because of their horrific affect on innocent others.

Although not currently as well studied as the antiandrogens and hormone medications, the use of psychiatric medications marketed for depression has been used to treat sex offenders. There has been a proposed connection between increasing levels of prolactin and decreasing sex drive and serotonin's role in sexual behavior (APA 1999). Prolactin is a hormone associated with milk production and serotonin is a neurotransmitter present in the central nervous system, to include the brain, among other places (Dirckx 1997). Limited case reports and non-controlled studies have indicated a role in treating sexual behavior with medications that affect serotonin (Kafka 1991; Stein, et al. 1992; APA 1999). Bradford (1999) also stated that there is evidence that implicates serotonin in human sexual behavior.

The similarities between obsessive-compulsive disorders and the paraphilias have also been made both from the perspective of symptoms and the benefit of serotonin reuptake inhibitor medications for both diagnoses (Bradford 1999). Stein et al. (1992) reported, albeit with caveats of a small sample size, rating instruments without validation, and a non-blinded and loosely controlled study, that serotonin reuptake inhibitors may have a differential effect on compulsive sexual behavior and impulsive sexual behavior.

Kafka's study (1991) also reported reduction of sexual behaviors with use of fluoxetine (trade name Prozac), imipramine (trade name Tofranil) and lithium. This study was limited by sample size, self-reported data, a single researcher/data collector, and potential for a confounding variable of concurrent supportive psychotherapy (Kafka 1991). Kafka's (1991) limited number of study subjects reported not only reduced inappropriate sexual thoughts and behaviors but also an increase in acceptable ones.

A better response for persons with sexual obsessions and compulsions than persons with paraphilias and sexual addictions has been reported with the serotonergic medications (Stein, et al. 1992). The effects of serotonergic medications with these populations have been attributed to their side effect of decreased libido, but study subjects (again in both the Kafka and Stein et al.

studies' with their admitted methodology limitations) with sexual addictions voiced no such loss (Kafka 1991; Stein, et al. 1992). Despite limited rigorous study results, the serotonin reuptake inhibitor class of medications appears promising for controlling repeat sexual offenders.

Although infrequently mentioned in the reviewed literature, a few other medications used to treat mood disorders have been used to treat sex offenders. Busprione and clomipramine, which have effects on serotonin, among other effects, have and lithium, a mood stabilizing medication, have also been reported to decrease sexual desire in offenders (APA 1999).

Bradford (1998) pointed out that medication treatment choices are limited in part due to limited pharmacologic research. He speculates that such is the result of the lack of both private and government efforts to conduct or fund research in this field (Bradford 1998). The APA (1999) also noted that this area of pharmacology has inadequate funding. What will it take for increased efforts to be directed to this field, that has the potential to impact everyone directly or indirectly at some point in their lives?

Surgical

Surgical approaches include castration and neurosurgery. Neither is routinely used at this time for the following reasons. Despite their limited use now and in the past, they have been a part of sex offender treatment and as such are addressed, although only briefly.

Castration. Castration is based on the premise that sex drive will be reduced if testosterone is decreased and the testes are the primary production site for testosterone in the male (Holmes 2002; Berlin and Krout 1986; Berlin and Schaerf 1985; Freund 1980). In a review of European studies of castration as treatment for sex offenders, success in reducing recidivism was reported, but research methods were questioned (Heim and Hursch 1979). Freund (1980) reported that the amount and speed of reduction of sex drive through castration is not definitively known. Berlin and Krout (1986) stated that decreasing testosterone through surgery does increase the ability to control sexual behavior. Freund (1980) documented side effects of castration to include depressive symptoms with possible long term presence and full depression in the short term, hot flashes for months post operation, decreased concentration, female pubic hair pattern, osteoporosis, female fat pattern, gynecomastia, and impotence.

As Freund (1980) stated it is a permanent method, unless of course the castrated person takes testosterone replacement. According to Burdon and Gallagher (2002), surgical castration, because of its permanence, is not a choice for modern corrections and as Berlin and Krout (1986) advised, it is not necessary when pharmacologic methods can be employed to accomplish the same goal. Heim and Hursch (1979) were also against the use of castration, citing inadequate scientific support for its efficacy and also ethical concerns. It has been noted to be employed on a voluntary basis in some U.S. states (Burdon and Gallagher 2002).

Neurosurgery. Surgical intervention in the form of stereotaxic neurosurgery isbased on the notion that certain regions of the brain are responsible/involved in sex drive (Freund 1980). Berlin and Schaerf (1985) also stated that it appears that certain parts of the brain have a disproportionate involvement in sexual arousal. A review of the pertinent neuroanatomy is beyond the scope of this chapter, but a brief anatomical reference is made. According to Freund (1980), limited study reports involving humans, in whom the ventromedial nucleus was coagulated, had positive results with decreased sex drive. Side effects included elevated appetite leading to obesity, temporary hostility, and delayed ejaculatory reflex and, for a few, anorgasm and elimination of dreams (Freund 1980).

When documenting his findings, Freund (1980), stated that the evidence was insufficient to warrant neurosurgery as a method for decreasing sex drive. This method is still not currently routinely utilized (APA 1999). When noted in the reviewed literature, it was typically mentioned for its historical significance and as an experimental intervention.

Psychological

The other major category of treatment includes those approaches that attempt to change offenders without introducing chemicals or performing an invasive procedure. They also include the use of medications. As already mentioned, there are experts in the field of sex offender treatment who suggest combination treatment. The primary methods found included behavioral, cognitive and psychodynamic approaches.

Behavioral. The premise of behavior therapy is that people continue behaviors, because they have been conditioned, that is they have learned, to act in a given manner (Kaplan and Sadock 1998). As a result, the behavior can be unlearned and new behaviors learned to replace the unwanted ones (Kaplan and Sadock 1998). Methods include systematic desensitization, relaxation training, graded exposure, flooding, modeling, assertiveness training, aversion therapy, social skills training and positive reinforcement (Kaplan and Sadock 1998). In the case of sex offenders, offending behavior has been changed by administering rewards or punishment (Holmes 2002).

In regards to pedophilic offenders, the goal of behavior therapy is to eliminate sexual desire for children and redirect their desire to adults (Berlin 1983; Berlin and Krout 1986). This is accomplished with group therapy, where methods of controlling "temptations" are addressed, to include someone to call, indicators of impending offending behavior and identifying settings with high risk for offending in order to avoid them (Berlin and Krout 1986). The group method is viewed as a means to provide both peer pressure and support (Berlin and Krout 1986). They also mentioned use of incarceration as a form of punishment, but pointed out that it has no characteristics that will result in a change in sexual desire or improve self-control (Berlin and Krout 1986).

Cognitive. In the cognitive approach, persons are taught how to properly interact with others in society and how to recognize their own dysfunctional methods with the goal of effecting change (Holmes 2002). Offenders are counseled on more appropriate methods of handling their problems (Miethe 2001). Methods include learning empathy by reading books and watching films depicting the victims' perspectives, writing to their victims and meeting with their victims and with victims' counselors, and re-enacting their crimes on video to be viewed by the treatment group and others (Holmes 2002).

Cognitive-Behavioral. The literature reveals a variety of programs utilizing a combination of the aforementioned in cognitive-behavioral models. It has been labeled the "designer treatment of the 1990s" (Prentky and Burgess 2000). Crolley, et al. (1998) studied one such program, the Highland Institute for Behavioral Change (HIBC) in Atlanta, Georgia, to assess its effectiveness. Although the sample size precludes generalizing their positive findings, the design of the program illustrates a cognitive-behavioral model. The HIBC program utilized a combination of individual, group, family and aftercare components designed to encourage nonviolent, consensual, adult sexual activity (Crolley, et al. 1998).

The behavioral piece included activities to control inappropriate sexual arousal by redirecting it to appropriate content, through use of masturbation to approved fantasies, use of desensitization audiotapes of inappropriate content followed by severe consequences, and learning to identify indicators to becoming involved in activities with a strong potential for offending, such as alcohol use (Crolley, et al. 1998). The group component was designed to force the offenders to face erroneous thoughts and beliefs about their sexual offenses, to accept responsibility for inappropriate sexual behavior, acquire empathy for victims, identify and learn to stop the cycle of offending and explore the roles of anger and manipulation through written assignments, sharing with other group members and confronting their beliefs, while in the group setting (Crolley, et al. 1998). Family therapy was designed to inform the offenders' family about the offender's behavior, help with boundary issues, when relevant, and to aid in communication for the benefit of the family (Crolley, et al. 1998). The aftercare element included continued individual and group sessions (Crolley, et al. 1998).

Cognitive behavioral programs are intended to enhance self-control by developing identification of thoughts that put the offender at risk for offending, increased decision making ability and provide social skills (Burdon and Gallagher 2002). A key component of cognitive-behavioral programs is to change the cognitive distortions (Terry and Mitchell 2001). Their study of incarcerated offenders in a sex offender treatment program in England revealed that even for those offenders who didn't want to participate, a reduction in cognitive distortions was observed (Terry and Mitchell 2001). Of interest requiring further research by the author's own admission, the findings were only applicable to offenders with adult victims and not those with child victims.

Treatment Components. Treatment typically includes a component to improve interpersonal relationships through developing social skills. Methods have included assertiveness training, relaxation training, systematic desensitization, self-esteem improvement (Prentky and Burgess 2000) and sex education (Allison and Wrightsman 1993; Prentky and Burgess 2000).

Development of victim empathy is also a common element of treatment as it is seen as a means of blocking aggressive action (Prentky and Burgess 2000). Allison and Wrightsman (1993) supported the need for rapists to see the personal impact their behavior has had on their victims. They also stressed the value of teaching rapists interpersonal relationship and parenting skills (Allison and Wrightsman 1993).

Anger is generally addressed through a cognitive behavioral approach such as anger management training to enhance self-control and techniques to facilitate the learning of acceptable outlets for expressing anger (Prentky and Burgess 2000).

Sexual fantasies are targeted in treatment to effect a change to their content, making it more acceptable (Prentky and Burgess 2000). Techniques include reducing response to unacceptable content through covert sensitization, aversion, masturbation to satiation, biofeedback and shame therapy and increasing acceptable content through systematic desensitization, modifying the fantasy and aversion (Prentky and Burgess 2000).

Common methods of treatment include group therapy targeting cognitive distortions, denial and rationalizing, confrontation to address offenders' blaming of victims, reconditioning of masturbation fantasies, masturbation to satiation to "atypical sexual imagery", sex education and socialization training (Berlin, et al. 1997). Cognitive distortions are also targeted in order to change foundation attitudes that encourage or at least permit offending (Prentky and Burgess 2000). According to Berlin and colleagues, treatment should be customized to each person with specific goals and means of achieving them (Berlin, et al. 1997).

Relapse prevention includes teaching offenders to recognize and break the cycle of offending by avoiding such situations and employing methods to avoid escalation to an offense, if they are encountered (Prentky and Burgess 2000). McGuire (2000) reported that the sex offender literature supports the need for relapse prevention as a component of treatment. He stated that such a model is needed because offending is not spontaneous but rather the conclusion of a series of thoughts and behaviors, which can be interrupted. He conducted research to identify what he termed "lapse" behavior defined as precursors to relapsing into sexual offending. McGuire (2000) described the relapse offending as following a sequence as: affective change, abuse fantasy, passive planning, cognitive distortions, disinhibition, and sexually abusive act. He proposed that the cycle of offending varies depending on the type of sexual offending (McGuire 2000). Allison and Wrightsman (1993) wrote of the importance of relapse prevention as a component of rapists' treatment.

Based on their study of incarcerated sex offenders in a western United States correctional institution, Geer et al. (2001) found potential predictors of successful completion of treatment. Their results indicated that offenders who completed treatment had more education than those who did not and persons claiming they were past sexual abuse victims were less likely to finish (Geer et al. 2001). They caveated their findings by stating that study subjects were incarcerated, voluntarily in treatment, and received participation incentives. Despite these qualifiers, their results should be given further scrutiny, especially given their recommendations for offenders obtaining further education before participation in treatment and adding a component of treatment to focus on the offenders' past sexual victimization (Geer et al. 2001).

Treatment Programs. Although he didn't focus on sexual offending, Mahorney (2002) wrote of sexual addictions and suggested pharmacology for anxiety and depressive symptoms, cognitive behavioral therapy for "distorted thinking" and to change behavior, and the use of 12-step programs.

In 1991, Berlin et al. described the outpatient treatment program of the Johns Hopkins Sexual Disorders Clinic. The program combined individual psychotherapy, group therapy, family therapy and medication to lower testosterone on a case by case basis (Berlin, et al. 1991). Treatment included sessions to target offender rationalizations and denial, identification of causes of inappropriate sexual desires and relapse prevention techniques (Berlin et al. 1991).

Hall (1995) reported that cognitive-behavioral and hormone based programs were more effective than behavioral treatment alone. His research also supported outpatient programs as being the most effective and the use of treatment with the common forms of sexual offending regardless of the offenders' legal status. He did caveat his findings by stating that analyzed studies only used official recidivism results thus had the potential of falling short of actual offending totals.

Psychodynamic. Psychotherapy is used based on the notion that deviant sexual behavior is the result of negative experiences early in life that cause psychological discord of which the offender is not consciously aware (Berlin 1983). Berlin and Krout (1986) stated that psychotherapy has been used to provide insight into negative experiences during childhood which hampered normal maturing.

The goal of such therapy is to correct such errors through providing insight, but understanding the reason for behavior alone is insufficient to effect a change (Berlin and Krout 1986). There is question as to whether this approach could change the sexual desires of paraphilic sex offenders and little evidence to support it as a reliable viable method (Berlin, 1983).

Analysis — Success and Failure

Holmes and Holmes (2002) state that different types of sex offenders do not respond in the same ways to treatment. Through a review of studies of treatment programs, they found that recidivism can be decreased for some offenders with treatment. Dunsieth (2002) agrees that a single treatment modality may not be effective for all offenders. Dunsieth (2002) recommends a multidisciplinary approach to include a cognitive component for relapse prevention, substance abuse treatment, a psychological assessment and evaluation for major mental illness and paraphilias.

In Dunsieth's (2002) opinion, self-help, psychodynamic and 12-step programs are ineffective. The only treatment Dunsieth (2002) credits as effective are the biological models using hormones and the cognitive behavioral systems with a relapse prevention feature. Dunsieth also recommends the use of a polygraph to ensure honesty given that offenders can work the program while lying about their continued fantasies for a variety of reasons which include shame, embarrassment and denial.

Accurate assessment of sex offender treatment programs is difficult. Studies are not readily comparable. Furby, et al. (1989) conducted an extensive examination of sex offender recidivism reporting that as a result of frequent inadequacies of research methods and vast differences in the methods employed, traditional comparisons could not be made. They advised making "tentative conclusions" based on the studies' results (Furby, et al. 1989). Their review is relatively dated given cited articles were from 1953 to 1986, but more recent comments on available studies have been similar (Furby, et al. 1989). Berlin et al. (1991) stated that judging success of a program is complicated by confusion regarding what is being treated, difficulty identifying a result that is representative to study and finding a group of persons not given treatment to use as a study control group. As Prentky and Burgess (2000) reported, there is considerable variety in legal standards, categories of offenders, study follow-up length, participant attrition, treatment content, and post-treatment monitoring. Without a strict randomly assigned treatment versus non-treated group experimental design, proof of treatment can not be definitively made (Berlin, et al. 1991).

Nevertheless, reports of success are made and some conclusions are offered. Berlin et al.'s (1991) survey of the John Hopkins Clinic in 1991 revealed that the majority of their clients, to include exhibitionists, pedophiles and sexually aggressive offenders, who were compliant with treatment, did not repeat sexual offenses. According to Burdon and Gallagher (2002), treatment won't necessarily cure offenders, which is not a reasonable goal, but it can decrease the chance of future sex offending. Burdon and Gallagher (2002) suggested a combination of cognitive-behavioral therapy and biological treatment and they endorse the idea of coercing offenders to start and remain in treatment. Terry and Mitchell (2001) also reported that assessment of treatment success has varied considerably in large part because of the variability of research methods employed.

Hall (1995) conducted a meta-analysis of sex offender treatment research studies and reported results that suggest cognitive-behavioral and hormonal treatment programs are more effective than behavioral treatment. There were no significant differences between the cognitive-behavioral and hormonal treatment approaches (Hall 1995). Hall also noted that in the majority of studies he reviewed, some form of screening of participants was conducted with criteria that imply the offenders with the most serious psychopathology were not admitted. This obviously raises the question of whether the treatments used would have been as effective with the excluded population (Hall 1995). It must be noted, that as with other reviews of treatment results, this meta-analysis had a small sampling with only twelve studies in the final analysis.

For the sake of completeness, surgical intervention should be mentioned as well. According to Freund (1980), castration can reduce repeat sexual offending to almost zero when used with persons who are voluntary, not psychotic, kept confined for a long enough time period for adequate reduction of sex drive post operation, and don't have a history of offending in general coupled with other indicators of trying to control their unacceptable sexual behavior. Heim and Hursch's (1979) review of European studies also indicated reduced recidivism in sex offenders, but there were methodology questions with some of the data presented.

Although the success of various interventions is often questioned, it is clear that simply punishing offenders does nothing to assist them in controlling inappropriate sexual desires (Berlin 1983). It has been suggested that the majority of sex offenses are committed by a "relatively" small number of sex offenders, which given the impact and cost of their offenses, warrants both "prevention and intervention" (Crolley 1998).

Conclusion

This chapter has provided a broad overview of sex offender treatment. Goals, approaches and results have been addressed. Given the limited goal of an overview, specific details were often omitted, but hopefully the reader has a better understanding of what has and is being tried to curb, and ideally eliminate, sexual offending.

As is evident by the contents of this chapter, the field of sex offender treatment is still evolving. Unfortunately, a cure has not been found and control of behavior is far from guaranteed. This is in part of course because sex offenders are a heterogeneous population. As a result, different treatment modalities are likely necessary depending on the etiologies of the offending behavior.

The biological approaches have included medications and surgery to reduce sexual desire and control sexual behavior. Research into pharmacological treatment appears to be the most promising. Psychological approaches have included techniques to target cognitive distortions, modify inappropriate behavior, improve social skills, teach anger management and address methods of relapse prevention. A combination of pharmacology and psychological techniques seems to be the treatment model most widely accepted as effective.

An accurate measure of success has also not readily been defined due to the disparity in assessment methodology and lack of well constructed research designs. In fairness to those attempting to examine efficacy it should be noted that the nature of the treatment does not lend itself well to the ideal double blinded control study so frequently expected before definite conclusions are accepted.

Despite these shortcomings, there are treatment options available with research noting at least some degree of success.

The treatment of sex offenders is a dynamic field. Given the tremendous effect of even one treatment failure, the importance of treatment demands that efforts continue to find ways to reduce sexual offending recidivism and ultimately a means of preventing the initial offense.

References

Allison, J., and L. Wrightsman. *Rape the Misunderstood Crime.* Sage Publications, Inc: Newbury Park, CA, 1993.

American Psychiatric Association (APA). *Dangerous Sex Offenders A Task Force Report of the American Psychiatric Association.* Author: Washington, D.C., 1999.

Bancroft, J., G. Tennent, K. Loucas, and J. Cass. "The Control of Deviant Sexual Behaviour by Drugs: I. Behavioral Changes Following Oestrogens and Anti-Androgens." *British Journal of Psychiatry* 125, (1974): 310–315.

Berlin, F. "Sex Offenders: A Biomedical Perspective and a Status Report on Biomedical Treatment." In *The Sexual Aggressor: Current Perspectives on Treatment,* eds. J. Greer and I. Stuart. VanNostrand Reinhold, Co: N.Y, 1983.

Berlin, F. "The Paraphilias and Depo-Provera: Some Medical, Ethical and Legal Considerations." *Bulletin of the American Academy of Psychiatry and the Law* 17 no. 3, (1989): 233–239.

Berlin, F. "Chemical Castration for Sex Offenders." *The New England Journal of Medicine* 336 no. 14, (1997): 1030.

Berlin, F., W. Hunt, M. Malin, A. Dyer, G. Lehne, and S. Dean. "A Five-Year Plus Follow-Up Survey of Criminal Recidivism Within a Treated Cohort of 406 Pedophiles, 111 Exhibitionists and 109 Sexual Aggressives: Issues and Outcome." *American Journal of Forensic Psychiatry* 12 no. 3, (1991): 5–28.

Berlin, F. and E. Krout. "Pedophilia: Diagnostic Concepts Treatment, and Ethical Considerations." *American Journal of Forensic Psychiatry* 7 no. 1, (1986): 13–30.

Berlin, F., G. Lehne, H. Malin, W. Hunt, K. Thomas, and J. Fuhmaneck. "The Eroticized Violent Crime: A Psychiatric Perspective with Six Clinical Examples." *Sexual Addiction and Compulsivity* 4 no. 1, (1997): 9–31.

Berlin, F. and F. Schaerf. "Laboratory Assessment of the Paraphilias and Their Treatment with Antiandrogenic Medication." In *Handbook of Psychiatric Diagnostic Procedures, Vol. 2,* eds. R. Hall and T. Beresford. Spectrum Publications, Inc, 1985.

Bradford, J. "Treatment of Men with Paraphilia." *The New England Journal of Medicine* 338 no. 7, (1998): 464–465.

Bradford, J. "The Paraphilias, Obsessive Compulsive Spectrum Disorder, and the Treatment of Sexually Deviant Behavior." *Psychiatric Quarterly* 70 no. 3, (1999): 209–219.

Burdon, W. and C. Gallagher. "Coercion and Sex Offenders Controlling Sex-Offending Behavior Through Incapacitation and Treatment." *Criminal Justice and Behavior* 29 no. 1, (2002): 878–109.

Crolley, J., D. Roys, B. Thyler, and P. Bordnick. "Evaluating Outpatient Behavior Therapy of Sex Offenders." *Behavior Modification* 22 no. 4, (1998): 484–501.

Dirckx, J. (ed). *Stedman's Concise Medical Dictionary for the Health Professions, 3rd ed.* Williams and Wilkins: Baltimore, MD, 1997.

Dunsieth, N. "Flaws in the Sexual Addiction Model." *Current Psychiatry* 1 no. 7, (2002): 37–39.

Freund, K. "Therapeutic Sex Drive Reduction." *Acta Psychiat Scandinavica (supplement)* 287 no. 62, (1980): 1–39.

Furby, L., M. Weinrott, and L. Blackshaw. "Sex Offender Recidivism: A Review." *Psychological Bulletin* 105 no. 1, (1989): 3–30.

Gagné, P. "Treatment of Sex Offenders with Medroxyprogesterone Acetate." *American Journal of Psychiatry* 138 no. 5, (1981): 644–646.

Geer, T., J. Becker, S. Gray, and D. Krauss. "Predictors of Treatment Completion in a Correctional Sex Offender Treatment Program." *International Journal of Offender Therapy and Comparative Criminology* 45 no. 3, (2001): 302–313.

Hall, G. "Sexual Offender Recidivism Revisited: A Meta-Analysis of Recent Treatment Studies." *Journal of Consulting and Clinical Psychology* 63 no. 5, (1995): 802–809.

Heim, N. and C. Hursch. "Castration for Sex Offenders: Treatment or Punishment? A Review and Critique of Recent European Literature." *Archives of Sexual Behavior* 8 no. 3, (1979): 281–305.

Holmes, S. and R. Holmes. *Sex Crimes Patterns and Behavior, 2nd ed.* Sage Publications, Inc: Thousand Oaks, CA, 2002.

Kafka, M. "Successful Antidepressant Treatment of Nonparaphilic Sexual Addictions and Paraphilias in Men." *Journal of Clinical Psychiatry* 52 no. 2, (1991): 60–65.

Kaplan, H. and B. Sadock. *Synopsis of Psychiatry Behavioral Sciences/Clinical Psychiatry, 8th* ed. William and Wilkins: Baltimore, MD, 1998.

Mahorney, S. "Sexual Addiction a Diagnosis Whose Time Has Come." *Current Psychiatry* 1 no. 7, (2002): 29–36.

McGuire, T. "Correctional Institution Based Sex Offender Treatment: A Lapse Behavior Study." *Behavioral Sciences and the Law* 18, (2000): 57–71.

Miethe, T. and R. McCorkle. *Crime Profiles, 2nd ed.* Roxbury Publishing Co: Los Angeles, CA, 2001.

Prentky, R. and A. Burgess. *Forensic Management of Sexual Offenders.* Kluwer Academic/Plenum Publishers: New York, 2000.

Raymond, N., E. Coleman, F. Ohlerking, G. Christenson, and M. Miner. "Psychiatric Comorbidity in Pedophilic Sex Offenders." *American Journal of Psychiatry* 156, (1999): 786–788.

Rosler, A. and E. Witztum. "Treatment of Men with Paraphilia with a Long-Acting Analogue of Gonadotropin-Releasing Hormone." *The New England Journal of Medicine* 338 no. 7, (1998): 416–422.

Stein, D., E. Hollander, D. Anthony, F. Schneier, B. Fallon, M. Liebowitz, and D. Klein. "Serotonergic Medications for Sexual Obsessions, Sexual Addictions, and Paraphilias." *Journal of Clinical Psychiatry* 53 no. 8, (1992): 267–271.

Tennent, G., J. Bancroft, and J. Cass. "The Control of Deviant Sexual Behavior by Drugs: A Double-Blind Controlled Study of Benperidol, Chlorpromazine, and Placebo." *Archives of Sexual Behavior* 3 no. 3, (1974): 261–271.

Terry, K. and E. Mitchell. "Motivation and Sex Offender Treatment Efficacy: Leading a Horse to Water and Making It Drink?" *International Journal of Offender Therapy and Comparative Criminology* 45 no. 6, (2001): 663–672.

PART VI

Public Fear and the Legislative Response

Chapter 18

Sex Offender Laws: Some Legislative Responses

Winter Denning

Introduction

While we have examined the response of the criminal justice system to sex crimes offenders, we have not mentioned much regarding the influence that both the American people and the legislators have on criminal justice issues, policies and direction. It appears that for the last couple of decades, criminal justice intervention with sex offenders was not deemed successful by the public, and they pushed legislators to create laws to make things different. This chapter will discuss four public driven, legislatively created or mandated laws designed to deal specifically with sex offenders. They are registration laws, notification laws, sexual predator laws and chemical castration laws. Before we discuss those, let's examine some evidence of the public sentiment that influenced the legislators to act.

We have always been concerned about sexual offenders and the havoc they create, thus laws designed to protect society from them are not new. In as early as 1938 "sexual psychopath" laws were enacted stating that sex offenders should be cured before being released back into society (Matson and Lieb 1997). However, by the 1980s most of those laws were gone because of a concern for offenders' constitutional rights, the question of whether treatment worked, and the changing focus from treatment to punishment for those who committed crimes (Matson and Lieb 1997). There seemed to be an interesting paradox here—a growing sentiment that the current treatment of sex offenders did not work; i.e.—that they would commit more crimes upon release, and thus, the public was not safe from them. Yet, this was coupled with the concern that some of the statutes in the past regarding sex offenders and what the criminal justice system should and could do with them, may have violated the offenders' constitutional rights.

For purposes of our discussion, we will now focus our attention on Washington State. A group of concerned citizens created the Tennis Shoe Brigade in the 1980s in response to a series of sex crimes that captured the headlines. Their concern was that people could no longer "walk free" because of their high risk of victimization. In 1990, the Brigade sent thousands of pairs of shoes to the legislature in a show of concern (Logan 1998; Turning Point: The Revolving Door: When Sex Offenders Go Free—ABC Television Broadcast, Sept 21, 1994).

However, there may have been one crime in Washington that catapulted the Tennis Shoe Brigade and the subsequent legislative response into national attention. The perpetrator was Earl Kenneth Shiner and the year was 1989. Shriner was a "career sexual predator with a 24-year record of attacking children" (Leo 1993). He had been in and out of the criminal justice system despite the fact that "psychologists said he was too dangerous to be at large" (Leo 1993). In 1987, he had been released from prison in Washington, even though the state "considered Shriner extremely dangerous" and despite "his unusual sexually sadistic fantasies with plans to carry them out" (Vanginderen 1998). There was no legal reason to hold him. He could not be committed civilly because he was not mentally ill, and he "hadn't performed recent and overt acts that might put the community in danger" (Leo 1993). Even though he had been in prison for the previous ten years (Leo 1993), the criminal justice system had no legal recourse; they could not hold Shriner for crimes that he might commit in the future.

In 1989, Shriner attacked a seven-year old Tacoma, Washington boy. He stabbed, raped, strangled and then sexually mutilated the boy by cutting off his penis. The boy, who survived, was the victim of a time bomb who was released from prison because there were no other options. Perhaps the worst thing of all, he had made it known that he "had hatched elaborate plans to maim or kill youngsters" if he was released (Leo 1993). Shriner was given 131 years in prison, and the grass roots movement to make legislators do *something* about sex offenders resulted in the creation of a task force by the governor (Leo 1993; Vanginderen 1998). The task force made some recommendations, and the results were the Sexually Violent Predator Act of 1990 (Vandginderen 1998). This act allowed for the civil commitment of sexual offenders who would most likely re-offend if released. The civil commitment would take place after the criminal sentence was served. Obviously, there were immediate concerns raised about this type of law; many of them had to do with the constitutional rights of the offender. We will discuss sexual predator laws later in this chapter.

Each of the concepts to be discussed in this chapter—to make sex offenders register, to notify people that sex offenders live in the neighborhood, to hold sexual predators after they have served their sentence, and to suggest that we should 'castrate' sex offenders chemically, has a reason for their creation and implementation. There are crimes, outcries by the public, action, reaction, laws and then the judgment of those laws. There are two issues to ponder here. One issue is why do we direct these laws primarily at sexual offenders? Are they perceived as the most dangerous offenders? And the second issue is why were laws created that, in some instances, circumvented the criminal justice system?

This chapter will define and discuss offender registry laws, notifications laws, sexual predator laws and chemical castration laws. Arguments for and against the laws will be presented. Any legal challenges that these laws have faced or will face will be discussed, as will any court responses to these challenges. Each section will be completed with a discussion of any amendments or changes that the laws have undergone due to the response of society and/or the courts.

Registration Laws

Sex offender registration laws require a person convicted of a sex offense to register with the proper authorities after their release from prison. How long the offender must register is mandated by specific state laws. The amount and type of information the offender must provide varies from state to state. The time period the offender has to register before or after their release is also mandated by state law.

The Jacob Wetterling Crimes Against Children and Sexually Violent Offender Registration Act, passed in 1994, was the an initial federal law requiring all states to maintain a sex offender registry program (Matson and Lieb 1996). The impetus to create an offender registry was financial—states that did not comply faced a cut in their federal crime control grant (Matson and Leib 1996). It is interesting to note that this Act did not prompt the first registration act in the United States. California was the first state to pass an offender registry act in 1944. The registry included all felony offenders and some serious misdemeanor offenders, and the information collected was made available only to law enforcement personnel (Matson & Lieb 1996).

The creation and use of registration laws has seen three distinct periods of development. The first was from 1944 to 1967. During this time six states passed registration laws. The second period was from 1985 to 1990. There was not much activity during this time. The third period began in 1991 and continues to the present. Between 1991 and 1996, 38 states passed laws and 15 amendments were made to existing acts. Twenty-six states passed legislation between 1994 and 1996. Today all fifty states have registration laws, however, Massachusetts' registration law is experiencing legal challenges that, for now, has prevented collecting registry information (Bureau of Justice Statistics 2002).

As of February 2001, there were 386,000 registered sex offenders in 49 states and the District of Columbia. California has the largest state registry with over 88,000 registered sex offenders. The second largest state registry is in Texas with nearly 33,000 registered sex offenders. As of February 2001, there were 11,575 registered sex offenders in New York state, 20,000 in Florida, 7,500 in Missouri, 8,804 in Colorado, 15,304 in Washington State, and in the District of Columbia, there were 303 registered sex offenders. Maine had the smallest state registry with 473 registered offenders (Bureau of Justice Statistics 2002).

Sex offender registries are generally overseen by a state agency but local law enforcement collects the majority of the information in the registries. This is not the case for six states. In Delaware, Maine, Utah, Virginia, West Virginia, and Oregon state agencies collect and maintain the information for the state registry. As of February 2001, 36 states had published web-site links to the state registry. At the time another four states had plans to publish the registry on the state web-site or make the registry available through other online means (Bureau of Justice Statistics 2002).

Offenders must provide information to the registry. This information usually includes, but is not limited to, name, address, fingerprints, photo, date of birth, social security number, and criminal history. Other required information can include place of employment, vehicle registration, and a blood sample. Michigan is currently the only state that includes a complete DNA profile (Matson & Lieb 1996). Some states require offenders to register both in the county where they live and the county where they work (The Associated Press 2002).

Offenders usually face a time frame for registration. The time frame varies from prior to the offender's release to up to one year after release. The most common time frame is thirty days or less from release of the offender. The type of offense and its seriousness can affect the time frame for the offender in some states as well (Matson & Lieb 1996).

How long an offender must stay registered also varies by state. Most states have a duration period of ten years or more for offenders to register. Life time registration is the standard in fifteen states. Again, the type and seriousness of the offense can affect the duration of the registration for some offenders in some states (Matson & Lieb 1996).

In the majority of states, the sex offender registry information is updated only when offenders notify authorities of a change in information. Most state registry laws have provisions for the verification of information written into the regulations of the laws. However, state funding has made this verification difficult if not impossible. Thus, a number of registries are out dated or have false information in the records (Matson & Lieb 1996).

There are a number of arguments for registration of known sex offenders. These arguments include: assisting law enforcement in investigation of future sex offenses, establishing legal grounds to hold offenders, deterring sex offenders from re-offending, deterring other from initial offense, and offering information to citizens. All of these arguments are justified as necessary for public safety. These arguments fall under scrutiny because of the lack of consideration for the offender, the victim, and the secondary victims in society. No studies have been published that can enlighten on the validity of the arguments for registration of known sex offenders (Matson and Lieb 1996).

There are also a number of arguments against having sex offenders register. These arguments include, but are not limited to the following: denial of civil liberties, the unforgiving message sent to offenders, the laws cause offenders to evade the law, the false sense of public security, the laws implication on offenders, citizen vigilantism, the identification of victims, and the efficiency and accuracy of the data bases. These arguments are based more on the effect the registry has had on society and offenders. A number of the arguments against the registration of know sex offenders are questions regarding punishment or ineffective administration of the laws (Matson and Lieb 1996).

There have been a number of legal challenges to sex offender registration laws. The most popular include ex post facto, due process, and cruel and unusual punishment. Although the above arguments are not the only challenges, they are the challenges entertained by the Supreme Court. The Supreme Court has given some very pertinent opinions regarding these challenges (Mears 2002, 2003).

In *Smith v. Doe*, an Alaska man challenged sex offender registries based on the principle of ex post facto. The man was convicted of abusing his daughter and was released before the registry laws were enacted. Thus, he felt that his requirement to register was, in affect, a punishment after the fact. A federal court ruled that the laws could only be applied to crimes committed after the laws were passed, and the state appealed (Mears 2002). "The court decided the state legislature intended the law to be regulatory, not punitive in nature" (Mears 2003, 2).

"Justice Anthony Kennedy said: 'Our System does not treat dissemination of truthful information in furtherance of legitimate governmental objection as punishment'" (Mears 2003, 2). Thus, registration is not considered a punishment for sex offenders. However, Justice Ruth Bader Ginsburg disagreed as she stated, "However plain it may be that a former sex offender currently poses no threat of recidivism, he will remain subject to long-term monitoring and inescapable humiliation" (cited in Mears 2003, 2). This leaves room for other types of challenges.

Connecticut Department of Public Safety v. Doe involves due process rights. Doe was convicted of abusing a 14-year-old girl. Doe felt that he should have the right to a hearing to determine if he is dangerous before being subjected to the registry requirements. The bases for this challenge also stems from the fact the many registries do not differentiate between the seriousness of sex offender crimes. The courts ruled that the state did not have to determine the dangerousness of an offender to include them on the registry (Mears 2003).

The final most common challenge is cruel and unusual punishment. The majority of courts are not entertaining this challenge due to the ruling in *Smith v. Doe* which found that registry of sex offenders is not a punishment. Though this has not stopped the perception that the registry requirement is a punishment by offenders and their family members, claims of cruel and unusual punishment is not a remedy through the courts (Mears 2003).

Public opinion and court rulings have lead to some changes in the registration laws. Currently, some sex offenses are starting to be excluded from the registries, most notably are those charged with crimes that are in essence consensual gay sex acts, and consensual public sex acts (ACLU 1997). Some cases of statutory rape are being excluded especially if the parties are close in age and both participated willingly, even though one party has not reached the age of consent. Most registries have started to categorize offenses, and some registries have even started to place offenders in tiers by seriousness of offense, amount of violence in the attack, and the age of the victim (Ratchford 2003).

This section has explored sex offender registration laws. The laws were defined, and some general information was given. Statistics were given regarding offenders registered in state registries. The type of information collected, and the arguments for and against were presented, as well as, some of the legal challenges and changes to the registries were described.

Notification Laws

Notification laws "allow the state's discretion to establish criteria for disclosure, but compels them to make private and personal information on registered sex offenders available to the public" (KlaasKids 2003, 1). In other words, notification laws allow for the public disclosure of information regarding specific, individual sex offenders. The type of information made public and the way it is made public is mandated by the individual state's law. The legislation intended for notification laws to be used to inform the public when convicted sex offenders moved into a neighborhood. This was designed to protect the safety of the neighborhood and its individual residents. Notification laws have created many unintended consequences.

Notification laws, also known as Megan's Laws, are connected to and are considered a part of the 1994 Jacob Wetterling Crimes Against Children and Sexually Violent Offender Registration Act. Megan's Laws are named after Megan Kanka, a 7-year-old girl from New Jersey. Megan was kidnapped, raped, and murdered by a twice-convicted sex offender who lived across the street. After this incident, the public cried out to know exactly where sex offenders were in their communities (Finn 1997). As previously stated, notification laws were created to accomplish just that–to tell the public where sex offenders lived as well as possible additional information about their crimes.

Most notification laws are written and passed with registration laws. Many of the goals of notification laws are the same as the goals of registration laws. Most of the arguments for and against notification laws are the same as those for and against registration laws. Do not be fooled, however, because notification laws are very different from registration laws in how they are implemented (Matson and Lieb 1996).

Offenders are categorized into levels or tiers for determining the level of notification the public will receive. Usually, there are three tiers. Tier One (1) is the lowest level, offenders in this tier are classified as the least likely to re-offend. Tier Three (3) is the highest level and offenders in this tier are classified as the most likely to re-offend (Finn 1997).

The level or tier of the offender determines who gets notified of their presence in the community. In Tier One usually the police are the only ones notified of the sex offenders presence. Tier Two can include the notification of parents, school officials, and other child-rich environment personnel. Tier Three can include a door-to-door notification, the posting of flyers in the area, and even media releases (Finn 1997). Obviously Tier Three would be the most intrusive into a sex offender's life.

There are a number of ways a person can be notified of the information about sex offenders. A large number of states maintain web-sites or other internet sources to notify people. The police can be called upon to do door-to-door notifications or to leave written notification with people. The information can be published in newspapers or on local news programs. The information can be passed on by word of mouth or a person can go to the police station and get the information. The tier or level or the offender usually affects the way the public gets the information (Ratchford 2003).

There are a number of arguments for notification laws. These arguments include but are not limited to: they assist law enforcement in the investigation of crimes, they establish grounds for holding offenders, they deter offenders, and they inform citizens. The majority of these arguments are considered a part of public safety. There are also a number of arguments against notification laws, which include but are not limited to: ex post facto punishment, equal protection clause problems, cruel and unusual punishment, citizen vigilantism, and affects on the offender's re-integration into society (Matson and Lieb 1996).

Of the above arguments, equal protection clause problems and the affects on the offender's re-integration into society are the only ones not discussed in the previous section on registration laws. Some offenders feel that their equal protection rights are violated by the tier system of notification laws. Thus, the laws are not equal for everyone. The issue of notification affects the offender's re-integration into society and there have been many instances of the public harassing sex offenders in the community (Ratchford 2003).

At this time, there are not a lot of challenges of notification laws in the courts (Johnson 2001). In *Otte v. Doe,* the courts ruled that the photos and information of known sex offenders can be posted on the Internet. The courts have also ruled that like registration laws, notification laws are a regulatory measure, not a punitive measure. Regardless, the courts have still left a number of issues related to notification laws as challengeable (Finn 1997).

This section has investigated sex offender notification laws. A definition of the laws was provided, as well as, some general information about notification laws. An overview of who is notified and how they are notified was presented. This section ended with a discussion of the arguments for and against notification laws, and the courts response to the challenges presented.

Sexual Predator Laws

Sexual predator laws allow the state to civilly commit a sex offender. This civil commitment of sex offenders deemed to be sexually violent predators after the offender's criminal sentence to prison is served is the involuntary commitment to a mental health agency or other institution (Lieb, Quinsey, and Berliner 1998). According to most laws, the civil commitment requires a civil commitment hearing. During that hearing, the state usually has to prove that the offender has some kind of "mental abnormality" and not just a predisposition to re-offend for the offender to be civilly committed (Suess 2003).

Kansas v. Hendricks is the most widely known case regarding sexual predator laws. It was the Kansas Sexual Predator Law that the Supreme Court examined and held as constitutional in this case. The state used their newly written law to commit Leroy Hendricks after he had served his prison sentence for molesting a child (Vanginderen 1998). Hendricks challenged his commitment and the Supreme Court upheld the Kansas sexual predator law as constitutional.

In most civil commitment cases the state must prove that the person being committed is mentally ill by clear and convincing evidence (Dripps 1997). The sexual predator laws usually require the state to prove that the person they are trying to label a sexual predator has a mental abnormality and not a mental illness. Having a mental abnormality suggests that the person is most likely to be a danger if released, in that he would most likely sexually offend again. Legally speaking, it is the definition of mental abnormality that comes into question (Vanginderen 1998).

A number of criticisms have been leveled at the sexual predator laws. One is that the use of the civil commitment law denies offenders their protections against double jeopardy or ex post facto (Anonymous 2003a; Anonymous 2003b). Remember that the civil commitment takes place after the offender has "served their time' in the criminal justice system. The crimes they have been legally held responsible for and served sentences for, are examined to determine if they are too dangerous to be released and should be committed civilly. Thus, they argue double jeopardy. Another criticism is that once committed the offenders are not receiving treatment for the mental abnormality they are found to have. This argument questions whether it is legal to label someone as a sexual predator and house them in a facility because the state demonstrates that they have a mental abnormality and not offer any treatment towards correcting or changing that mental abnormality. The use of sexual predator laws is widely controversial, although they have held up as constitutional to all challenges made thus far to the Supreme Court (Anonymous 2000).

This section has presented and defined sexual predator laws. The most important case, *Hendricks v. Kansas*, involving sexual predator laws was discussed. Some criticisms of the laws were described. The use of these laws has been minimal, and not much information about them exists because they are relatively new concepts that have not been widely studied. However, the purpose of this section has been to provide some information regarding the definition and use of sexual predator laws.

Chemical Castration

Chemical Castration is the process of reducing or removing the sex drive of a male sex offender by means of chemical injection or some other form of ingestion designed to reduce or eliminate the offender's ability or desire to reoffend. The concept of chemical castration carries a few mistaken beliefs with it. The process of chemical castration does not, in most cases, prevent the male from getting or maintaining an erection. In the majority of cases sexual dysfunction is not a result. In reality, the main result of chemical castration is the reduction to, or removal of, the sex drive which affects the offender's "need" or "want" to engage in sexual activity (Is Chemical Castration…2003).

Offenders are administered doses, usually by injection, of Depo-Provera with the active ingredient of Medroxyprogesteronr or MPA for short (Meisenkothen 1999). The drug is a simple birth control pill for women, but reduces the amount of testosterone in males. The reduction in testosterone usually leads to a reduction in sex drive. There is also a semi-permanent surgical alternative to chemical castration, which might be a reliable option depending on how long someone would have to take the drug (Meisenkothen 1999; Medical 1997).

As of March 2000, California, Florida, Georgia, Iowa, Louisiana, Montana, Oregon, and Wisconsin all have passed laws that deal with the use of chemical castration (Associated Press 2000). Since 1996, there has been a push in Alabama to make the chemical castration treatment mandatory for all sex offenders with the conviction of their second offense. Generally speaking, the use of chemical castration is a condition of parole (Brienza 1997). As with the other laws discussed in this chapter, issues regarding chemical castration laws inspire skepticism and concern.

The main question is does the therapy work? Few studies have been conducted in the United States, however, the ones that have been done show promising results. One thing the studies suggest is that the reduction in male sexual fantasies has been demonstrated. In one study, after Depro-Prevera was used, the recidivism rate fell to 5 percent (Is Chemical Castration…2003). Some scientists disagree with the results of this study, and they suggest that the therapy only works when offenders are willing and seek out help in addition to the chemical therapy (Hansen 1997). Studies in Germany and the Netherlands have also suggested positive results (Hannah 2002).

Another concern about chemical castration is the cost. To administer the program correctly, the drug therapy alone would cost $2,400.00 per offender. "Sex offenders would pay the tab if they could afford it. If not, the state parole board would cover the cost" (The Associated Press 2000, pg.1). Obviously this would create quite a financial burden on a system steel reeling from current massive budget costs and deep financial challenges. Regardless of the positive results that some research suggests, public skepticism persists with respect to the use of chemical castration with sex offenders.

This section has discussed chemical castration. A definition of chemical castration was provided. Information regarding how chemical castration was achieved, how it worked, and who was offered or required to take the treatment was presented. The states that already had laws were presented; some criticisms of the treatment were identified and discussed.

Conclusion

This chapter has presented the topics of sex offender registration laws, sex offender notification laws, sexual predator laws, and chemical castration. Each topic was defined and discussed with regard to the criminal justice system. Each topic was presented with respect to the reaction of society to sex offenders and the arguments for and against each topic. Each section concluded with a brief summary of the topic.

References

ACLU. *States Ease Registration Laws that Swept Up Gays* (November 26, 1997). Available: http://archive.aclu.org/news/w112697c.html

Anonymous. "High Court Debates Sex Predator's Rights." *Corrections Digest* 31, (November 3, 2000).

Anonymous. "Justice Upholds Curb on Sexual Predators." *Juvenile Justice Digest 31*, (May 19, 2003a).

Anonymous. "States Lose Track of 77,000 Sex Predators." *Juvenile Justice Digest* 31, (February 17, 2003b).

Associated Press, The. "Alabama Mulls Chemical Castration Bill," (March 20, 2000). Available: http://www.channel1.com/users/matsa/2ap3-20-00.htm

Associated Press, The. "Sparks Toughens Registration Laws for Sex Offenders," (December 2, 2002). Available: http://www.msnbc.com/local/krnv/M250919.asp?cp1=1

Brienza, Julie. "California Castration Law Greeted with Skepticism," (January 1997). Available: http://proquest.umi.com/pqdweb?TS=1055962075&RQT=309&CC=2&Dtp=1&Did=000

Bureau of Justice Statistics. *Fact Sheet: Summary of State Sex Offender Registries, 2001* (NCJ 192265). Washington, DC: Devon Adams, 2002.

Dripps, Donald A. "Civil Commitment for Convicted Criminals," (August 1997). Available: http://proquest.umi.com/pqdweb?TS=1055961863&RQT=309&CC=2&Dtp=1&Did=0000

Finn, P. *Sex Offender Community Notification.* National Institute of Justice: Research in Action. Washington, DC: Government Printing Office, 1997.

Hannah, Jim. *Chemical Castration Becomes Issue: Drugs Reduce Sex Drive,* (February 18, 2002). Available: http://www.enquirer.com/editions/2002/02/18/loc_chemical _castration.html

Hansen, Mark. *Cruel and Unusual?* (April 1997). Available: http://proquest.umi.com/pqdweb?TS=1055962002&RQT=309&CC=2&Dtp=1&Did=0000

Is Chemical Castration an Acceptable Punishment for Male Sex Offenders? (June 5, 2003). Available: http://www,csun.edu/~psy453/crime_y.htm

Johnson, Charles W. *Worries Over Notification Laws,* (December 12, 2001).Available: http://www.eskimo.com/~cwj2/geekery/archive/000004.html

KlaasKids Foundation. *Megan's Law By State, Victim's Rights By State,* (June 5, 2003). Available: http://www.klaaskids.org/pg-legmeg.htm

Leo, J. "A Need for Sexual Predator Laws." *The Times.* New Orleans, LA.: Picayune Publishing Co, 1993.

Lieb, R., Quinsey, and Berliner. "Sexual Predators and Social Policy." *Crime and Justice: A Review of Research* 23, (1998): 43–114.

Logan, W. "The Ex Post Facto Clause and the Jurisprudence of Punishment." *The American Criminal Law Review* 35 no. 4, (1998): 1261–1319.

Matson, S. and R. Lieb. *Sex offender Registration: A Review of State Laws.* Washington State Institute for Public Policy (July 1996). Available: http://www.wsipp.wa.gov/reports/regsrtn.html

Matson, S. and R. Lieb. *Sexual Predator Commitment Laws.* Washington State Institute for Public Policy, (1997). Available: http://www.wa.gov/wsipp/reports/predlaws.html

Mears, William. *Fairness of Sex Offender Registration Laws*, (November 13, 2002). Available: http://www.prisontalk.com/forums/archive/topic/8204.html

Mears, William. *Supreme Court Upholds Sex Offender Registration Laws*, (March 5, 2003). Available: http://www.cnn.com/2003/LAW/03/05/scotus.sex.offenders/

Medical, Legal Experts Debate Merits of Castration Bill. (May 8, 1997). Available: http://www.sexcriminals.com/news/11869/

Meisenkothen, C. "Chemical Castration—Breaking the Cycle of Paraphiliac Recidivism." *Social Justice* 26, (Spring 1999).

Ratchford, M. M. *Community Notification Of Sex Offenders*, (June 5, 2003). Available: http://www.angelfire.con/ky/Criminal Justice/MeganLaw.html

Suess, E. (February 1, 2003). "2002 Top Ten Most Important Cases on Sexual Predator Law." *St. Louis Daily Record/ St. Louis Countian*, (February 1, 2003).

Turning Point. *The Revolving Door Where Sex Offenders Go Free.* ABC Television Broadcast, September 21, 1994.

United States Supreme Court: Homosexual Issues. (June 5, 2003). Available: http://www.actwin.com/eatonohio/gay/ussupct.htm

Vanginderen, K. G. "Kansas v. Hendricks: Throwing Away the Key." *Thomas Jefferson Law Review* 20, (Summer 1998).

Kansas Statute Excerpt

59-29a01

Chapter 59.—PROBATE CODE

Article 29a.—COMMITMENT OF SEXUALLY VIOLENT PREDATORS

59-29a01. Commitment of sexually violent predators; legislative findings. The legislature finds that there exists an extremely dangerous group of sexually violent predators who have a mental abnormality or personality disorder and who are likely to engage in repeat acts of sexual violence if not treated for their mental abnormality or personality disorder. Because the existing civil commitment procedures under K.S.A. 59-2901 et seq. and amendments thereto are inadequate to address the special needs of sexually violent predators and the risks they present to society, the legislature determines that a separate involuntary civil commitment process for the potentially long-term control, care and treatment of sexually violent predators is necessary. The legislature also determines that because of the nature of the mental abnormalities or personality disorders from which sexually violent predators suffer, and the dangers they present, it is necessary to house involuntarily committed sexually violent predators in an environment separate from persons involuntarily committed under K.S.A. 59-2901 et seq and amendments thereto.

History: L. 1994, ch. 316, § 1; L. 1999, ch. 140, § 1; July 1.

Available: http://www.kslegislature.org/cgi-bin/statutes/index.cgi/59-29a01.html

Contributors

Mark Blumberg, PhD, is Professor of Criminal Justice at Central Missouri State University in Warrensburg, Missouri. He received his bachelor's and master's degrees from the University of Kansas, Lawrence, and an additional master's and doctoral degree from the State University of New York at Albany. He has authored numerous book chapters and journal articles on police use of deadly force, the impact of AIDS on the criminal justice system, and other issues. His work has appeared in such publications as the *Criminal Law Bulletin, American Journal of Police, Justice Professional, Crime and Delinquency, Criminal Justice Policy Review,* and *Prison Journal.* He is also the editor of *AIDS: The Impact on the Criminal Justice System* and the coauthor of the *Mythology of Crime and Criminal Justice.*

Diane M. Daane, J.D. is an associate professor of criminal justice at the University of South Carolina Spartanburg, where she teaches courses in victimology, sexual assault, family violence, women and crime, and corrections. Sexual assault and domestic violence have headed her research agenda for many years. She has authored articles, presented papers, and made numerous professional presentations about sexual assault. She has been awarded grants to study marital rape among battered women in Indiana, and adolescent's attitudes about domestic and peer violence. She is currently conducting research on marital rape prosecutions in South Carolina. She has worked with several community groups on sexual assault and domestic violence issues, and actively works for social change in the attitudes toward sexual assault and family violence.

Elycia S. Daniel is a third year Ph.D. student in Criminal Justice at Sam Houston State University in Huntsville, Texas. Originally from Buffalo, New York, she received her B.A. in Criminal Justice with a concentration in Offender Rehabilitation from Auburn University in Auburn, Alabama in 1996. She then obtained her M.A. in Criminal Justice Administration from Clark-Atlanta University in Atlanta, Georgia in 1998. She has practioner experience as both a Probation and Pre-Trial Release Officer. Ms. Daniel also has experience as a full-time criminal justice instructor and unit head for three years at Denmark Technical College in Denmark, South Carolina. She has also worked as an adjunct instructor at Claflin University in Orangeburg, South Carolina. Her current and past research interests are in the areas of crime mapping, lethal violence, and corrections. Ms. Daniel has intentions of completing her doctoral degree December of 2004.

Winter Denning, grew up in Odessa, MO and graduated from the high school there in May of 1998. Winter received her Bachelor of Science Degree in Criminal Justice from Central Missouri State University in May of 2003. Winter is currently a criminal justice graduate student at Central Missouri State University. Winter would like to thank her mother and husband for all their support.

Elizabeth Quinn DeValve is a doctoral student at Sam Houston State University. Her interests include violent crime, victimology and coping strategies, and women and crime. Her publications can be found in *Women in Criminal Justice, ACJS Today, Proceedings from the Homicide Research Working Group Meetings, TELEMASP Bulletin* and forthcoming in *The Prison Journal.*

Zelma Weston Henriques, Ph.D., is a Professor in the Department of Law, Police Science and Criminal Justice Administration at John Jay College, City University of New York. Her major research interests are imprisoned mothers and their children; women in prison; race, class and gender issues; and cross-cultural studies of crime. She is the author of *Imprisoned Mothers and Their Children.*

Delores Jones-Brown, Ph.D. is an Associate Professor in the Department of Law, Police Science and Criminal Justice Administration at John Jay College, City University of New York. Her research interests and publications address issues related to race, crime and criminal justice administration, sociology of law, juvenile justice and delinquency, and legal socialization. She is the author of *Race, Crime and Punishment* and co-editor of *The System in Black and White: Exploring the Connections between Race, Crime and Justice* and *Policing and Minority Communities: Bridging the Gap.*

Deborah L. Laufersweiler-Dwyer, PhD, received her Bachelor of Science degree in Criminal Justice and her Master of Arts degree in Applied Sociology from Old Dominion University and her Doctor of Philosophy in Public Policy and Administration with a concentration in Administration of Justice from Virginia Commonwealth University. She was a police officer for six years with the Norfolk Virginia Police Department serving in the patrol, vice, crime prevention and detective divisions. Currently, she is a tenured Associate Professor in the Criminal Justice Department, University of Arkansas at Little Rock. Dr. Laufersweiler-Dwyer has authored/co-authored papers/presentations on homicide, serial crimes, juvenile justice issues, police stress, sex offender typologies and treatment, and distance learning.

R. Gregg Dwyer, PhD, received his Bachelor of Science degree in Sociology from the University of the State of New York, his Master of Arts degree in Management from Webster University, his Doctor of Education in Adult and Continuing Education with a cognate in Criminal Justice from Virginia Polytechnic Institute and State University (Virginia Tech) and his Doctor of Medicine from the University of Arkansas for Medical Sciences. He was a special agent (federal criminal investigator) for over ten years with the Naval Criminal Investigative Service, serving in both field and headquarters operational and staff positions. His experience includes criminal investigations and operations, foreign counterintelligence, dignitary protection, training, research and development, and emergency service personnel peer counseling. Currently, he is a Resident Physician in the General Psychiatry Program at the University of South Carolina. Dr. Dwyer has authored/co-authored papers/presentations on educational approaches to law enforcement training, employment and critical incident stress and intervention in emergency service professions, informal learning in police organizations, medical education methods and forensic psychiatry, to include non-guilty by reason of insanity issues and sex offender typologies and treatment.

Miriam R. Fuller, Ph.D., is an Associate Professor of English at Central Missouri State University, specializing in Medieval Studies and Women's Studies. She has published articles in Fifteenth-Century Studies, Tristania, and the Greenwood Dictionary of History. She is the Editor of Publications of the Missouri Philological Association.

Tammy S. Garland, holds a Ph.D. in Criminal Justice from Sam Houston State University. She received a M.S. in criminal justice at Eastern Kentucky University and a B.A. in history at the University of Kentucky. Her research interests include women and popular culture, the victimization of women, and juvenile recidivism. She is an Assistant Professor at the University of Arkansas at Monticello.

Robert D. Hanser, PhD, is an Assistant Professor of Criminal Justice at the University of Louisiana at Monroe. He has worked in corrections as a correctional officer and has extensive experience with highly assaultive and gang-related inmates. He has dealt with both inmate perpetrators and inmate victims of prison sexual assault. Dr. Hanser's current research interests include corrections, domestic violence issues, multiculturalism, and treatment interventions for victims and perpetrators.

Betsy Wright Kreisel, Ph.D., is an Associate Professor of Criminal Justice at Central Missouri State University in Warrensburg, Missouri. She obtained her doctorate from the University of Nebraska at Omaha in 1998. Practical experience includes interning with the Missouri Department of Probation and Parole as well as working as a juvenile probation officer in the Missouri Bodyguard Program. She has conducted research and published in the area of Guardian ad Litems for abused children, juvenile probation and parole officer training, police evaluation, police accountability, police use of force, police stress, and juvenile justice education. Dr. Kreisel serves as a volunteer victim advocate for Johnson County Missouri, is a board member of the Johnson County Domestic Violence Task Force, and serves as a consultant for the Missouri Department of Corrections Board of Probation and Parole, 5th District. Another focus of Dr. Kreisel's is to maintain an active status among professional organizations such as the Academy of Criminal Justice Sciences and the Midwest Criminal Justice Association. In 1997, Kreisel was co-recipient of the Outstanding Paper Award for Excellence by the *American Journal of Police.*

Heidi Moore, is currently working on her Master's Thesis in Criminal Justice at Central Missouri State University in Warrensburg, Missouri. She has presented research on the death penalty, wrongful convictions, and the International Criminal Court. Her research interests include international human rights issues and violent and sexual crimes. Ms. Moore is currently working as an Institutional Parole Officer in Potosi, Missouri.

Nathan R. Moran, PhD, is Assistant Professor of Criminal Justice at Midwestern State University. Dr. Moran's primary research interest is in international crime, specifically organized crime and terrorism. He currently teaches courses in comparative criminal justice and statistics. Dr. Moran completed his Ph.D. in criminal justice at Sam Houston State University.

Frances P. Reddington, Ph.D., is a Professor of Criminal Justice at Central Missouri State University in Warrensburg, Missouri. She earned her Ph.D. in Criminal Justice from Sam Houston State University. Her main areas of research interest include all aspects of juvenile justice. She has published in the areas of: juvenile law, juvenile law in Texas, juveniles in adult jails, transfer of juveniles to the adult court, juveniles and the age of criminal responsibility, training of juvenile probation officers, the use of charter schools, and the role of Guardian ad Litems in abuse and neglect cases in juvenile court. She was the co-recipient of a 1999 Challenge Grant from the Missouri Department of Public Safety and the Office of Juvenile Justice and Delinquency Prevention. She has served as a consultant for the National Institute of Corrections and the Office of Juvenile Justice and Delinquency Prevention in the area of juvenile justice staff training. Dr. Reddington is chair of the Academy of Criminal Justice Sciences Juvenile Justice Section and chair of the Student Affairs Committee of the American Correctional Association. She is an editor for Youth Violence and Juvenile Justice: An Interdisciplinary Journal. She has been on the Board of Directors for both the Missouri Juvenile Justice Association and the Missouri State CASA (Court Appointed Special Advocate) Association. She is currently researching in the area of juvenile justice policy.

Jeffrey W. Spears, Ph.D., is an Assistant Professor of Criminal Justice in the Department of Sociology and Criminal Justice at the University of North Carolina at Wilmington. His research has appeared in *Justice Quarterly*, *Journal of Crime and Justice*, *American Journal of Criminal Justice*, and *Women and Criminal Justice*. His current research interests include sentencing and prosecutorial decision making.

Chad Trulson is a visiting Assistant Professor of Criminal Justice at the University of North Texas. He has published articles in such journals as Law & Society, Crime and Delinquency, Prison Journal, and Criminal Justice Review. His research interests include juvenile and adult corrections and he is currently involved in a project evaluating recidivism among delinquent youth.

Index

Subjects

Names